Learn German with Every Man Dies Alone: Part II

HypLern Interlinear Project
www.hyplern.com

First edition: 2023, August

Author: Hans Fallada
Translation: Kees van den End
Foreword: Camilo Andrés Bonilla Carvajal PhD

ISBN: 978-1-989643-61-7

kees@hyplern.com
www.hyplern.com

Learn German with Every Man Dies Alone: Part II

Interlinear German to English

Author
Hans Fallada

Translation
Kees van den End

HypLern Interlinear Project
www.hyplern.com

The HypLern Method

Learning a foreign language should not mean leafing through page after page in a bilingual dictionary until one's fingertips begin to hurt. Quite the contrary, through everyday language use, friendly reading, and direct exposure to the language we can get well on our way towards mastery of the vocabulary and grammar needed to read native texts. In this manner, learners can be successful in the foreign language without too much study of grammar paradigms or rules. Indeed, Seneca expresses in his sixth epistle that "Longum iter est per praecepta, breve et efficax per exempla[1]."

The HypLern series constitutes an effort to provide a highly effective tool for experiential foreign language learning. Those who are genuinely interested in utilizing original literary works to learn a foreign language do not have to use conventional graded texts or adapted versions for novice readers. The former only distort the actual essence of literary works, while the latter are highly reduced in vocabulary and relevant content. This collection aims to bring the lively experience of reading stories as directly told by their very authors to foreign language learners.

Most excited adult language learners will at some point seek their teachers' guidance on the process of learning to read in the foreign language rather than seeking out external opinions. However, both teachers and learners lack a general reading technique or strategy. Oftentimes, students undertake the reading task equipped with nothing more than a bilingual dictionary, a grammar book, and lots of courage. These efforts often end in frustration as the student builds mis-constructed nonsensical sentences after many hours spent on an aimless translation drill.

Consequently, we have decided to develop this series of interlinear translations intended to afford a comprehensive edition of unabridged texts. These texts are presented as they were originally written with no changes in word choice or order. As a result, we have a translated piece conveying the true meaning under every word from the original work. Our readers receive then two books in just one volume: the original version and its translation.

The reading task is no longer a laborious exercise of patiently decoding unclear and seemingly complex paragraphs. What's more, reading becomes an enjoyable and meaningful process of cultural, philosophical and linguistic learning. Independent learners can then acquire expressions and vocabulary while understanding pragmatic and socio-cultural dimensions of the target language by reading in it rather than reading about it.

Our proposal, however, does not claim to be a novelty. Interlinear translation is as old as the Spanish tongue, e.g. "glosses of [Saint] Emilianus", interlinear bibles in Old German, and of course James Hamilton's work in the 1800s. About the latter, we remind the readers, that as a revolutionary freethinker he promoted the publication of Greco-Roman classic works and further pieces in diverse languages. His effort, such as ours, sought to lighten the exhausting task of looking words up in large glossaries as an educational practice: "if there is any thing which fills reflecting men with melancholy and regret, it is the waste of mortal time, parental money, and puerile happiness, in the present method of pursuing Latin and Greek[2]".

Additionally, another influential figure in the same line of thought as Hamilton was John Locke. Locke was also the philosopher and translator of the Fabulae AEsopi in an interlinear plan. In 1600, he was already suggesting that interlinear texts, everyday communication, and use of the target language could be the most appropriate ways to achieve language learning:

> ...the true and genuine Way, and that which I would propose, not only as the easiest and best, wherein a Child might, without pains or Chiding, get a Language which others are wont to be whipt for at School six or seven Years together...[3]

---

1 "The journey is long through precepts, but brief and effective through examples". Seneca, Lucius Annaeus. (1961) Ad Lucilium Epistulae Morales, vol. I. London: W. Heinemann.

2 In: Hamilton, James (1829?) History, principles, practice and results of the Hamiltonian system, with answers to the Edinburgh and Westminster reviews; A lecture delivered at Liverpool; and instructions for the use of the books published on the system. Londres: W. Aylott and Co., 8, Pater Noster Row. p. 29.

3 In: Locke, John. (1693) Some thoughts concerning education. Londres: A. and J. Churchill. pp. 196-7.

Who can benefit from this edition?

We identify three kinds of readers, namely, those who take this work as a search tool, those who want to learn a language by reading authentic materials, and those attempting to read writers in their original language. The HypLern collection constitutes a very effective instrument for all of them.

1. For the first target audience, this edition represents a search tool to connect their mother tongue with that of the writer's. Therefore, they have the opportunity to read over an original literary work in an enriching and certain manner.
2. For the second group, reading every word or idiomatic expression in its actual context of use will yield a strong association between the form, the collocation, and the context. This will have a direct impact on long term learning of passive vocabulary, gradually building genuine reading ability in the original language. This book is an ideal companion not only to independent learners but also to those who take lessons with a teacher. At the same time, the continuous feeling of achievement produced during the process of reading original authors both stimulates and empowers the learner to study[1].
3. Finally, the third kind of reader will notice the same benefits as the previous ones. The proximity of a word and its translation in our interlinear texts is a step further from other collections, such as the Loeb Classical Library. Although their works might be considered the most famous in this genre, the presentation of texts on opposite pages hinders the immediate link between words and their semantic equivalence in our native tongue (or one we have a strong mastery of).

---

1 Some further ways of using the present work include:

1. As you progress through the stories, focus less on the lower line (the English translation). Instead, try to read through the upper line, staying in the foreign language as long as possible.
2. Even if you find glosses or explanatory footnotes about the mechanics of the language, you should make your own hypotheses on word formation and syntactical functions in a sentence. Feel confident about inferring your own language rules and test them progressively. You can also take notes concerning those idiomatic expressions or special language usage that calls your attention for later study.
3. As soon as you finish each text, check the reading in the original version (with no interlinear or parallel translation). This will fulfil the main goal of this collection: bridging the gap between readers and original literary works, training them to read directly and independently.

Why interlinear?

Conventionally speaking, tiresome reading in tricky and exhausting circumstances has been the common definition of learning by texts. This collection offers a friendly reading format where the language is not a stumbling block anymore. Contrastively, our collection presents a language as a vehicle through which readers can attain and understand their authors' written ideas.

While learning to read, most people are urged to use the dictionary and distinguish words from multiple entries. We help readers skip this step by providing the proper translation based on the surrounding context. In so doing, readers have the chance to invest energy and time in understanding the text and learning vocabulary; they read quickly and easily like a skilled horseman cantering through a book.

Thereby we stress the fact that our proposal is not new at all. Others have tried the same before, coming up with evident and substantial outcomes. Certainly, we are not pioneers in designing interlinear texts. Nonetheless, we are nowadays the only, and doubtless, the best, in providing you with interlinear foreign language texts.

Handling instructions

Using this book is very easy. Each text should be read at least three times in order to explore the whole potential of the method. The first phase is devoted to comparing words in the foreign language to those in the mother tongue. This is to say, the upper line is contrasted to the lower line as the following example shows:

»Wir	sind	ja	hier	unter	uns,	Max«,	fuhr	der	Anwalt	fort,
We	are	yes	here	under	us	Max	drove	the	lawyer	away
				between friends			continued the lawyer			

»diese	Tür	ist	gut	gepolstert,	wir	können	also	offen
this	door	is	well	padded	we	can	thus	open

miteinander	sprechen.	Du	wußtest	doch	auch,	wenigstens	ein
with each other	speak	You	knew	indeed	also	at least	a

ganz	klein	bißchen,	wieviel	schreiendes,	blutiges,
completely	small	bit	how much	screaming	bloody

herzzerreißendes Unrecht heute in Deutschland geschieht –
heartbreaking injustice today in Germany happens

und kein Hahn kräht danach. Im Gegenteil, sie rühmen
and no rooster crows there-after In the contrary they boast
nobody cares about it On the

sich noch laut ihrer Schande. Aber weil der
themselves still loud their shame But because the

Schauspieler Harteisen ein ganz kleines Wehwehchen hat,
actor Harteisen a completely little boo-boo has

entdeckt er plötzlich, daß Unrecht in der Welt geschieht,
discovers he suddenly that injustice in the world happens

und schreit nach Gerechtigkeit, Max!«
and cries after justice Max

The second phase of reading focuses on capturing the meaning and sense of the original text. As readers gain practice with the method, they should be able to focus on the target language without getting distracted by the translation. New users of the method, however, may find it helpful to cover the translated lines with a piece of paper as illustrated in the image below. Subsequently, they try to understand the meaning of every word, phrase, and entire sentences in the target language itself, drawing on the translation only when necessary. In this phase, the reader should resist the temptation to look at the translation for every word. In doing so, they will find that they are able to understand a good portion of the text by reading directly in the target language, without the crutch of the translation. This is the skill we are looking to train: the ability to read and understand native materials and enjoy them as native speakers do, that being, directly in the original language.

»Wir sind ja hier unter uns, Max«, fuhr der Anwalt fort,
We are yes her … way

»diese Tür ist … fen
this door is … en

miteinander sprechen. Du wußtest doch auch, wenigstens ein
with each other speak You knew indeed also at least a

ganz klein bißchen, wieviel schreiendes, blutiges,
completely small bit how much screaming bloody

herzzerreißendes Unrecht heute in Deutschland geschieht –
heartbreaking injustice today in Germany happens

und kein Hahn kräht danach. Im Gegenteil, sie rühmen
and no rooster crows there-after In the contrary they boast
nobody cares about it On the

sich noch laut ihrer Schande. Aber weil der
themselves still loud their shame But because the

Schauspieler Harteisen ein ganz kleines Wehwehchen hat,
actor Harteisen a completely little boo-boo has

entdeckt er plötzlich, daß Unrecht in der Welt geschieht,
discovers he suddenly that injustice in the world happens

und schreit nach Gerechtigkeit, Max!«
and cries after justice Max

In the final phase, readers will be able to understand the meaning of the text when reading it without additional help. There may be some less common words and phrases which have not cemented themselves yet in the reader's brain, but the majority of the story should not pose any problems. If desired, the reader can use an SRS or some other memorization method to learning these straggling words.

»Wir sind ja hier unter uns, Max«, fuhr der Anwalt fort, »diese Tür ist gut gepolstert, wir können also offen miteinander sprechen. Du wußtest doch auch, wenigstens ein ganz klein bißchen, wieviel schreiendes, blutiges, herzzerreißendes Unrecht heute in Deutschland geschieht – und kein Hahn kräht danach. Im Gegenteil, sie rühmen sich

noch laut ihrer Schande. Aber weil der Schauspieler Harteisen ein ganz kleines Wehwehchen hat, entdeckt er plötzlich, daß Unrecht in der Welt geschieht, und schreit nach Gerechtigkeit, Max!«

Above all, readers will not have to look every word up in a dictionary to read a text in the foreign language. This otherwise wasted time will be spent concentrating on their principal interest. These new readers will tackle authentic texts while learning their vocabulary and expressions to use in further communicative (written or oral) situations. This book is just one work from an overall series with the same purpose. It really helps those who are afraid of having "poor vocabulary" to feel confident about reading directly in the language. To all of them and to all of you, welcome to the amazing experience of living a foreign language!

Additional tools

Check out shop.hyplern.com or contact us at info@hyplern.com for free mp3s (if available) and free empty (untranslated) versions of the eBooks that we have on offer.

For some of the older eBooks and paperbacks we have Windows, iOS and Android apps available that, next to the interlinear format, allow for a pop-up format, where hovering over a word or clicking on it gives you its meaning. The apps also have any mp3s, if available, and integrated vocabulary practice.

Visit the site hyplern.com for the same functionality online. This is where we will be working non-stop to make all our material available in multiple formats, including audio where available, and vocabulary practice.

Table of Contents

Der Weg der Karten

The Road of the Card

Der Schauspieler Max Harteisen hatte, wie sein Freund
The actor Max Harteisen had as his friend

und Anwalt Toll sich auszudrücken beliebte, aus
and lawyer Toll himself to express liked from
used to

vornazistischen Zeiten noch reichlich viel Butter auf dem
pre-nazi times still richly much butter on the

Kopf. Er hatte in Filmen mitgespielt, die von jüdischen
head He had in films played along which from Jewish
acted by

Regisseuren geleitet waren, er hatte in pazifistischen
directors led were he had in pacifist
directed

Filmen mitgespielt, und eine seiner Hauptrollen auf dem
films played along and one of his main roles on the
acted

Theater war jener verdammte Schwächling gewesen, der
theater was that damned weakling been the

Prinz von Homburg, den jeder wahre Nationalsozialist nur
prince of Homburg who each true national socialist only

anspucken kann. Max Harteisen hatte also allen Anlaß,
spit on can Max Harteisen had thus all occasion

sehr vorsichtig zu sein; eine Zeitlang war es ja sehr
very careful to be a time-long was it yes very
while indeed

zweifelhaft, ob er unter den braunen Herren
doubtful whether he under the brown gentlemen
brown-shirted

überhaupt noch spielen durfte.
at all still play was allowed
act

Aber das hatte dann ja schließlich doch geklappt.
But that had then yes finally still worked
indeed

Natürlich mußte der gute Junge eine gewisse
of course must the good young man a certain

Zurückhaltung üben und erst einmal echt braun gefärbten
restraint practice and first once real brown painted

Schauspielern den Vortritt lassen, wenn sie auch lange
actors the step forward let when they also long

nicht soviel konnten wie er. Aber grade an dieser
not so much could as he But right on this

Zurückhaltung hatte er es fehlen lassen; der ahnungslose
restraint had he it lack let the unsuspecting

Knabe hatte so gespielt, daß dies sogar dem Minister
lad had so played that this even the minister

Goebbels aufgefallen war. Ja, der Minister hatte sogar
Goebbels noticed was Yes the minister had even
had

einen Narren an dem Harteisen gefressen. Und was es
a fool on the Harteisen eaten and what it
became a great fan of Harteisen

mit solchen Vorlieben des Ministers auf sich hatte, das
with such preferences of the Minister on himself had that

wußte ja jedes Kind, denn es gab keinen launischeren,
knew yes indeed each child then it gave no more capricious

unberechenbareren Menschen als den Doktor Joseph
more unpredictable person as the doctor Joseph

Goebbels.
Goebbels

Zuerst hatte es wie eitel Freude und Glanz ausgesehen,
First had it as vain joy and radiance looked

denn wenn der Minister jemanden zu verehren geruhte, so
then when the minister someone to worship deigned so

machte er keinen Unterschied, ob dies eine Frau oder
made he no difference whether this a woman or

ein Mann war. Wie bei einer Geliebten hatte Doktor
a man was As with a lover had doctor

Goebbels jeden Morgen bei dem Schauspieler Harteisen
Goebbels every morning with the actor Harteisen

angerufen, er hatte sich nach seinem Schlaf erkundigt, er
called he had himself after his sleep informed he

hatte ihm wie einer Diva Blumen und Konfekt gesandt,
had him like a diva flowers and confectionery sent

und es durfte kein Tag vergehen, ohne daß der
and it was allowed no day to pass without that the

Minister wenigstens kurze Zeit mit Harteisen zusammen
minister at least short time with Harteisen together

war. Ja, er nahm den Schauspieler sogar nach Nürnberg
was Yes he took the actor even to Neuremberg

auf den Parteitag mit, er erklärte ihm den
on the Party day along he explained him the
CPAC

Nationalsozialismus »richtig«, und der Harteisen verstand
National Socialism correctly and the Harteisen understood

auch alles, was er verstehen sollte.
also everything what he understand should

Er verstand nur nicht, daß zum richtigen
He understood only not that to the true

Nationalsozialismus auch gehört, daß ein einfacher
National Socialism also heard that a simple
befits

Volksgenosse einem Minister nicht widerspricht. Denn ein
people's subject a minister not contradicts Then a

Minister ist schon einfach durch die Tatsache, daß er
minister is already simply through the fact that he

Minister ist, zehnmal klüger als jeder andere. Bei
minister is ten times more intelligent as each other (person) At

irgendeiner ganz belanglosen Filmfrage widersprach
some completely inconsequential film question contradicted

Harteisen seinem Minister und behauptete gradezu, es sei
Harteisen his minister and claimed downright it be

Quatsch, was der Herr Goebbels da geredet habe. Es
nonsense what the Mr Goebbels there said have It

soll dahingestellt bleiben, ob die wirklich belanglose
should put aside stay whether the really irrelevant

und dazu auch noch rein theoretische Filmfrage den
and there-to also still clean theoretical film question the

Schauspieler in so zornigen Eifer gerissen hatte, oder
actor in so angry zeal ripped had or

ob ihm die verstiegene Anhimmelei des Ministers
whether him the exaggerated adulation of the minister

einfach über war, und ob er darum einen Bruch
simply over was and whether he therefore a break

wünschte. Jedenfalls blieb er, trotz mancher Ermahnung,
wished Anyhow remained he despite many admonition

bei seinem Satz, Quatsch sei es und Quatsch bleibe es,
at his sentence nonsense be it and nonsense remain it

ob Minister oder nicht, ganz egal!
whether minister or not completely equal

Oh, wie änderte sich da die Welt für Max Harteisen!
Oh how changed itself there the world for Max Harteisen

Keine morgendlichen Erkundigungen mehr nach der Güte
No morning inquiries (any)more after the quality

seines Schlafes, keine Pralinen, keine Blumen, keine
of his sleep no chocolates no flowers no

Besuche bei Herrn Doktor Goebbels mehr, auch nichts
visit at Mr. doctor Goebbels (any)more also nothing

mehr von Belehrungen über den richtigen
(any)more from instructions over the true

Nationalsozialismus! Ach, das wäre alles noch zu
National Socialism Oh that would be everything still to

ertragen gewesen, ja, vielleicht war es sogar erwünscht,
endure been yes perhaps was it even wished

aber plötzlich gab es für den Harteisen auch keine
but suddenly gave it for the Harteisen also no
were there

Engagements mehr, schon fest abgeschlossene
engagements (any)more already firmly completed

Filmverträge zerplatzten, Gastspiele zerrannen in nichts,
film contracts broke up guest performances ran away in nothing

es gab nichts mehr zu tun für den Schauspieler
it gave nothing (any)more to do for the actor
there was

Harteisen.
Harteisen

Da Harteisen ein Mann war, der seinen Beruf nicht
There Harteisen a man was who his occupation not
Since

nur des Geldverdienens halber schätzte, sondern da er
only of the earning money half appreciated but there he

ein wirklicher Schauspieler war, dessen Leben seine
a real actor was whose life his

Höhepunkte auf der Bühne, vor der Kamera finden
high-point on the stage before the camera find

mußte, so war er über diese erzwungene Untätigkeit
must so was he over this forced inaction

ganz verzweifelt. Er konnte und wollte es nicht
completely desperate He could and wanted it not

glauben, daß der Minister, der anderthalb Jahre lang sein
believe that the minister who one and a half years long his

bester Freund gewesen war, nun zu einem so
most best friend been was now to a such

bedenkenlosen, ja gemeinen Feind geworden war, daß er
thoughtless yes mean enemy become was that he

die Macht seiner Stellung dazu benutzte, wegen eines
the power of his position there-to used because of of a

Widerspruches einem andern alle Lebensfreude zu nehmen.
contradiction an other all enjoyment of life to take (away)
joie de vivre

(Er hatte im Jahre 1940 noch immer nicht begriffen, der
He had in the years 1940 still always not understood the

gute Harteisen, daß jeder Nazi zu jeder Zeit bereit war,
good Harteisen that each nazi at each time ready was

jedem Deutschen, der eine von seiner abweichende
each German who a from his own different

Meinung hatte, nicht nur alle Lebensfreude, sondern auch
opinion had not only all enjoyment of life but also
joie de vivre

das Leben selbst zu nehmen.)
the life itself to take

Aber wie die Zeit dahinging und keinerlei
But as the time passed away and none at all

Arbeitsmöglichkeit auftauchte, mußte Max Harteisen
job opportunity showed up must Max Harteisen

schließlich daran glauben. Freunde berichteten ihm, daß
finally to it believe Friends reported him that

der Minister auf einer Filmkonferenz erklärt hatte, der
the minister on a film conference explained had the

Führer wolle diesen Schauspieler nie wieder im Rock
leader wanted this actor never again in the jacket

eines Offiziers auf der Leinwand sehen. Nicht viel später
of an officer on the cloth-wall see Not much later
movie screen

hieß es schon, der Führer wolle diesen Schauspieler
was called it already the leader wanted this actor

überhaupt nicht mehr sehen, und dann wurde ganz
at all not (any)more see and then became completely

offiziell erklärt, der Schauspieler Harteisen sei
officially explained the actor Harteisen were

»unerwünscht«. Aus, zu Ende, mein Lieber, mit
undesirable From to end my rather with

sechsunddreißig Jahren auf die Schwarze Liste gesetzt –
thirty-six years on the black list set –

für ein ganzes Tausendjähriges Reich!
for a whole thousand-year (long) realm

Jetzt hatte der Schauspieler Harteisen wirklich Butter auf
Now had the actor Harteisen really butter on

dem Kopf! Aber er ließ nicht nach, er bohrte und fragte,
the head But he let not to he drilled and asked

er wollte um jeden Preis erfahren, ob diese
he wanted for every price experience whether these
at

vernichtenden Urteile wirklich vom Führer ausgingen,
devastating judgments really from the leader went out

oder ob sie sich der kleine Mann nur ausgedacht
or whether they themselves the little man only made up
(Goebbels)

hatte, um einen Feind zu erledigen. Und an diesem
had for an enemy to take care of and on this

Montag war Harteisen nun völlig siegesgewiß zu seinem
Monday was Harteisen now totally winning-certain triumphantly to his

Anwalt Toll gestürzt und hatte gerufen: »Ich hab's! Ich
lawyer Toll rushed and had called I have it I

hab's, Erwin! Der Schurke hat gelogen. Der Führer hat
have it Erwin The villain has lied The leader has

den Film, in dem ich den preußischen Offizier spiele,
the movie in which I the Prussian officer play

überhaupt nicht gesehen, und er hat nie ein Wort gegen
at all not seen and he has never a word against

mich geäußert.«
me expressed.

Und er berichtete eifrig, daß diese Nachricht ganz
And he reported zealously that this message completely

gewiß sei, denn sie stamme von Göring selbst. Eine
true be then she stem from Goering himself A

Freundin seiner Frau habe eine Tante, und deren
(female) friend of his woman have an aunt and whose

Kusine sei zu Görings nach Karinhall eingeladen gewesen.
cousin was at Göring's to Karinhall invited been

Da habe sie den Fall zur Sprache gebracht, und Göring
There have she the case to the talk table brought and Goering

habe sich wie berichtet geäußert.
have himself as reported uttered spoken out

Der Anwalt sah den Aufgeregten ein wenig spöttisch an.
The lawyer saw the excited a little mocking at

»Nun, Max, und was ist dadurch geändert?«
Now Max and what is there-through changed
through that

Der Schauspieler murmelte ganz verdutzt: »Aber dieser
The actor murmured completely stunned But this

Goebbels hat doch gelogen, Erwin!«
Goebbels has indeed lied Erwin!

»Und? Hast du je geglaubt, alles, was Hinkebeinchen
And Have you then believed everything what little Stumbleleg
the little lame guy

sagt, sei wahr?«
says is true

»Nein, das natürlich nicht. Aber wenn man den Fall vor
No that of course not But when one the case before

den Führer bringt ... Er hat doch den Namen des
the leader brings He has indeed the name of the

Führers mißbraucht!«
leader abused

»Ja, und weil er das getan hat, wird der Führer einen
Yes and because he that done has will the leader an

alten Parteigenossen und Propami rausschmeißen, bloß
old party comrade and true friend kick out just

weil er dem Harteisen Kummer gemacht hat!«
because he the Harteisen grief done has

Der Schauspieler sah den überlegenen, spöttischen Anwalt
The actor saw the superior mocking lawyer

hilfeflehend an. »Aber es muß doch was geschehen
pleading for help at But it must indeed something happen

in meiner Sache, Erwin!« sagte er. »Ich will doch
in my case Erwin said he I want but

arbeiten! Und der Goebbels hindert mich zu Unrecht
work And the Goebbels prevents me to injustice
wrongly

daran!«
there-on
to that

»Ja«, sagte der Anwalt. »Ja!« Und schwieg wieder. Als
Yes said the lawyer Yes And was silent again As

aber Harteisen ihn so erwartungsvoll ansah,
however Harteisen him so expectant looked at

fuhr er fort: »Du bist ein Kind, Max, ein richtiges, groß
drove he away You are a child Max a real large
continued he

gewordenes Kind!«
become child

Der Schauspieler, der stets viel von seiner
The actor who all the time much from his

Weltläufigkeit gehalten hatte, warf unmutig den Kopf
cosmopolitanism held had threw angrily the head
expected

zurück.
back

»Wir sind ja hier unter uns, Max«, fuhr der Anwalt fort,
We are yes here under us Max drove the lawyer away
between friends continued the lawyer

»diese Tür ist gut gepolstert, wir können also offen
this door is well padded we can thus open

miteinander sprechen. Du wußtest doch auch, wenigstens
with each other speak You knew indeed also at least

ein ganz klein bißchen, wieviel schreiendes, blutiges,
a completely small bit how much screaming bloody

herzzerreißendes Unrecht heute in Deutschland geschieht –
heartbreaking injustice today in Germany happens

und kein Hahn kräht danach. Im Gegenteil, sie rühmen
and no rooster crows there-after In the contrary they boast
nobody cares about it On the

sich noch laut ihrer Schande. Aber weil der
themselves still loud their shame But because the

Schauspieler Harteisen ein ganz kleines Wehwehchen
actor Harteisen a completely little boo-boo

hat, entdeckt er plötzlich, daß Unrecht in der Welt
has discovers he suddenly that injustice in the world

geschieht, und schreit nach Gerechtigkeit, Max!«
happens and cries after justice Max

Harteisen sagte niedergedrückt: »Aber was soll ich denn
Harteisen said depressed But what should I then

tun, Erwin? Es muß doch etwas geschehen!«
do Erwin It must indeed something happen
There

»Was du tun sollst? Nun, das ist doch ganz klar! Du
What you do should Now that is indeed completely clear You

ziehst dich mit deiner Frau an einen hübschen Ort auf
pull yourself with your wife on a pretty place on

dem Lande zurück und hältst dich fein stille. Vor
the countryside back and keep yourself fine quiet Before
well

allem hörst du mit diesem unsinnigen Gerede über
all hear you with this nonsensical talk over
(hörst auf; stop)

›deinen‹ Minister auf und unterläßt die Verbreitung des
your minister up and under-let the distribution of the
leave behind

Göring-Interviews. Sonst kann es geschehen, daß dir
Göring interviews Otherwise can it happen that (to) you

der Minister noch etwas ganz anderes antut.«
the minister still something completely else does

»Aber wie lange soll ich denn da tatenlos auf dem
But how long should I then there idle on the

Lande sitzen?«
countryside sit

»Die Launen eines Ministers kommen und gehen. Sie
The whims of a minister come and go They

gehen auch, Max, sei sicher. Eines Tages wirst du wieder
go also Max be sure One day will you again

in Glanz und floribus sein.«
in radiance and bloom be

Der Schauspieler schauderte. »Nicht das!« bat er. »Nur
The actor shivered Not that bade he Just

nicht das!« Er stand auf. »Und du meinst wirklich nicht,
not that He stood up And you mean really not
believe

daß du in meiner Sache etwas tun kannst?«
that you in my case something do can

»Nicht das geringste!« meinte der Anwalt lächelnd. »Es
Not the least meant the lawyer smiling It
opinioned

sei denn, du hättest den Wunsch, als Märtyrer für deinen
be then you had the wish as martyr for your

Minister ins KZ zu gehen.«
minister in the concentration camp to go
(Konzentrationslager)

Drei Minuten darauf stand der Schauspieler Max Harteisen
Three minutes there-on stood the actor Max Harteisen
after that

im Treppenhaus des Bürogebäudes und hielt verwirrt
in the stairwell of the office building and held confused

eine Karte in der Hand: »Mutter! Der Führer hat mir
a card in the hand Mother The leader has me

meinen Sohn ermordet ...«
my son murdered

Um des Himmels willen! dachte er. Welcher Mensch
For of the heaven's will thought he Which human

schreibt denn so was? Er muß wahnsinnig sein! Er
writes then so what He must insane be He

schreibt sich ja um seinen Kopf! Unwillkürlich drehte er
writes himself yes for his head Involuntarily turned he
to death

die Karte um. Aber dort stand kein Absender oder
the card around But there stood no return address or

Empfänger, sondern: »Gebt diese Karte weiter, daß viele
receiver but Give this card further that many

sie lesen! – Stiftet nichts für das Winterhilfswerk! –
her read donate nothing for the winter aid organization

Arbeitet langsam, noch langsamer! Tut Sand in die
Work slowly still slower Do sand in the
Put

Maschinen! Jeder Handschlag weniger getan hilft diesen
machinery Each handshake less done helps this

Krieg früher beenden!«
war earlier end

Der Schauspieler sah hoch. Lichterglänzend fuhr der
The actor saw high Shiny drove the
up

Fahrstuhl an ihm vorbei. Er hatte das Gefühl, daß viele
elevator to him past He had the feeling that many

Augen auf ihn sahen.
eyes on him saw

Rasch steckte er die Karte in die Tasche, und rascher
Quickly stuck he the card in the pocket and faster

noch riß er sie wieder hervor. Er wollte sie schon auf
still ripped he her again forth He wanted her already on

die Fensterbank zurücklegen - und Bedenken überkamen
the window sill lay back and thoughts came over
(return) doubts

ihn. Vielleicht hatten ihn die vom Fahrstuhl aus hier
him Perhaps had him those from the elevator from here

stehen sehen, die Karte in der Hand - und sein Gesicht
stand see the card in the hand and his face

kannten viele. Die Karte wurde gefunden, es fanden sich
knew many The card became found it found itself

welche, die beeideten, er habe sie hingelegt. Er hatte sie
such who swore he have she laid down He had her

ja wirklich hingelegt, wieder hingelegt, hieß das.
indeed really laid down again laid down was called that

Aber wer würde ihm glauben, grade jetzt, wo er diesen
but who would him believe right now where he this

Streit mit dem Minister hatte? Er hatte so viel Butter
conflict with the minister had he had so much butter

auf dem Kopfe, und nun dies noch!
on the head and now this still

Schweiß trat auf seine Stirn, plötzlich begriff er, daß
Sweat stepped on his forehead suddenly understood he that
appeared

nicht nur der Kartenschreiber, daß auch er in naher
not only the card writer that also he in closer

Lebensgefahr war, er vielleicht am meisten. Seine Hand
life's-danger was he perhaps at the most his hand
risk of death

zuckte; er wollte die Karte hinlegen, er wollte sie doch
twitched he wanted the card lie down he wanted her indeed

lieber fortnehmen, er wollte sie zerreißen, hier an Ort
rather take away he wanted her tear apart here on place

und Stelle ... Aber vielleicht stand einer oben auf der
and spot But perhaps stood (some)one above on the

Treppe und beobachtete ihn? Er hatte in den letzten
stairs and observed him He had in the last

Tagen schon ein paarmal das Gefühl gehabt, beobachtet zu
days already a few times the feeling had observed to

werden, er hatte es für Nervosität gehalten, wegen
become he had it for nervousness held because of

dieser Gehässigkeit von Minister Goebbels ...
this spite from minister Goebbels

Und vielleicht war das Ganze eine Falle dieses
And perhaps was the whole (thing) a trap (of) this

Mannes, für ihn zurechtgebaut, daß er sich ganz
man for him built up that he himself completely

gründlich fing? Um aller Welt zu beweisen, wie recht der
thoroughly caught For all the world to prove how right the

Minister mit der Beurteilung des Schauspielers Harteisen
minister with the evaluation of the actor Harteisen

hatte? O Gott, er war ja schon wahnsinnig, er sah
had o god he was yes already insane he saw
was

Gespenster! Das tat doch ein Minister nicht! Oder tat er
ghosts That did indeed a minister not Or did he

grade das?
exactly that

Aber er konnte hier nicht ewig stehenbleiben. Er mußte
But he could here not eternally stand remain He must

sich entschließen; er hatte jetzt keine Zeit, an Goebbels
himself decide he had now no time on of Goebbels

zu denken, er mußte nur an sich denken!
to think he must only on of himself think

Er stürmt die halbe Treppe wieder hinauf, niemand steht
He storms the half stairs again up nobody stands

dort und beobachtet ihn. Aber er klingelt schon beim
there and observes him But he rings already at the

Rechtsanwalt Toll. Er stürmt an der Vorzimmerdame vorbei,
lawyer Toll He storms on the hall lady past

er knallt die Karte auf den Tisch des Anwalts, er ruft:
he bangs the card on the table of the lawyer he calls

»Da! Was ich hier eben im Treppenhaus gefunden habe!«
There What I here just in the stairwell found have

Der Anwalt wirft nur einen kurzen Blick auf die Karte.
The lawyer throws only a short glance on the card

Dann steht er auf und schließt sorgfältig die Doppeltür
Then stands he up and closes carefully the double door

seines Büros, die der Aufgeregte offengelassen hat. Er
of his office which the excited one open let has He

kehrt zu seinem Schreibtischplatz zurück. Er nimmt die
turns to his desk space back He takes the

Karte wieder auf und liest sie lange und sorgfältig,
card again up and reads her long and carefully

während Harteisen auf und ab läuft und ungeduldig Blicke
while Harteisen on and off runs and impatient glances

auf ihn wirft.
at him throws

Jetzt läßt Toll die Karte sinken und fragt: »Wo, sagtest
Now lets Toll the card sink and asks Where said

du, hast du die Karte gefunden?«
you have you the card found

»Hier auf der Treppe, eine halbe Treppe tiefer.«
Here on the stairs a half stairs deeper.

»Auf der Treppe! Auf den Stufen also?«
On the stairs On the steps then

»Sei nicht so wortklauberisch, Erwin! Nein, nicht auf den
Be not so word-stealing Erwin No not on the
precise with words

Stufen, sondern auf der Fensterbank!«
steps but on the window sill!

»Und darf ich dich fragen, warum du mir dieses reizende
And may I you ask why you me this enticing

Angebinde auf mein Büro schleppen mußtest?«
tie up on my office haul must
bundle

Die Stimme des Anwalts klingt schärfer, der Schauspieler
The voice of the lawyer sounds sharper the actor

sagt bittend: »Aber was sollte ich denn tun? Die Karte
says pleading But what should I then do The card

lag da, ich habe sie ganz gedankenlos aufgenommen.«
lay there I have her completely thoughtless taken up

»Und warum hast du sie nicht zurückgelegt? Das wäre
And why have you her not laid back That would

doch das Selbstverständlichste gewesen!«
indeed the most obvious been

»Ein Fahrstuhl fuhr an mir vorbei, während ich las. Ich
An elevator drove on me past while I read I

hatte das Gefühl, beobachtet zu werden. Mein Gesicht ist
had the feeling observed to become My face is

so bekannt!«
so famous

»Noch besser!« sagte der Anwalt bitter. »Und dann bist
Even better said the lawyer bitter And then are

du vermutlich mit dieser Karte offen in der Hand zu mir
you probably with this card open in the hand to me

gelaufen?« Der Schauspieler nickte düster. »Nein, mein
ran The actor nodded dark No my

Freund«, sagte Toll entschlossen und hielt ihm die Karte
friend said Toll decided and held him the card

wieder hin, »bitte, nimm sie wieder. Ich will damit
again away sorry take her again I want there-with

nichts zu schaffen haben. Wohlgemerkt, du kannst dich
nothing to do have Mind well you can yourself

nicht auf mich berufen. Ich habe diese Karte nie
not on me call I have this card never

gesehen. Nimm sie doch endlich wieder!«
seen Take her indeed finally again

Harteisen starrte den Freund mit blassem Gesicht an. »Ich
Harteisen stared the friend with (a) pale face at I

denke«, sagte er dann, »du bist nicht nur mein Freund,
think said he then you are not only my friend

du bist auch mein Anwalt, du nimmst meine Interessen
you are also my lawyer you take my interests

wahr!«
true

»Nicht dies, oder sagen wir besser: nicht mehr. Du bist
Not this or say we better not (any)more You are

ein Unglückshuhn, du hast ein unglaubliches Talent, in die
a bad luck chicken you have a unbelievable talent in the

schlimmsten Geschichten zu tappen. Du wirst auch andere
worst stories to tap You will also others
situations step

ins Unglück reißen. Also nimm endlich deine Karte
in the misfortune tear Thus take finally your card

zurück!«
back

Er bot sie ihm wieder an.
He offered her him again to

Aber Harteisen stand noch immer da, mit weißem
But Harteisen stood still always there with white

Gesicht, die Hände in die Taschen gebohrt.
face the hands in the pockets drilled
stuffed

Nach einem langen Schweigen sagte er leise: »Ich traue
After a long silence said he softly I trust

mich nicht. Ich habe in den letzten Tagen schon
myself not I have in the last days already

mehrfach das Gefühl gehabt, beobachtet zu werden. Tu
multiple times the feeling had observed to become Do

mir den Gefallen und zerreiß die Karte. Wirf sie unter
me the favor and tear the card Throw her under

das andere Zeug in deinem Papierkorb!«
the other stuff in your waste paper bin

»Zu gefährlich, mein Lieber! Der Bürobote oder eine
Too dangerous my dear The office messenger or a

schnüffelnde Reinmachefrau, und ich säße drin!«
sniffing clean up woman and I would sit inside
in prison

»Verbrenne sie!«
Burn her

»Du vergißt, daß wir hier Zentralheizung haben!«
You forget that we here central heating have

»Nimm ein Streichholz, verbrenne sie über deinem
Take a match burn her over your

Aschenbecher. Niemand würde es wissen.«
ashtray Nobody would it know

»Du würdest es wissen.«
You would it know

Mit blassen Gesichtern starrten sie sich an. Sie
With pale faces stared they each other on They

waren alte Freunde, schon aus der Schulzeit, aber nun
were old friends already from the schooldays but now

war die Angst zwischen sie gekommen, und die Angst
was the fear between them come and the fear

hatte das Mißtrauen mit sich gebracht. Sie sahen
had the mistrust with itself brought They looked

einander stumm an.
each other mutely at

Er ist ein Schauspieler, dachte der Anwalt. Vielleicht hat
He is an actor thought the lawyer Perhaps has

er mir hier was vorgespielt, will mich hineinreißen.
he me here what something pretended want me tear into frame

Kommt im Auftrag, meine Zuverlässigkeit auf die Probe
Comes in the mission my reliability on the test

zu stellen. Neulich, bei dieser unglückseligen Verteidigung
to place Newly with this unfortunate defense
The other day

vor dem Volksgerichtshof, bin ich mit knapper Not noch
before the people's court am I with tight need still

durchgekommen. Aber seitdem wird mir mißtraut ...
passed through But since then becomes me distrusted
am I

Inwiefern ist Erwin eigentlich mein Anwalt? dachte
In what way is Erwin actually my lawyer thought

unterdes finster der Schauspieler. In der Sache mit dem
under-that darkly the actor In the thing with the
meanwhile

Minister will er mir nicht helfen, und jetzt will er sogar
minister wants he me not help and now wants he even

gegen die Wahrheit aussagen, er hätte die Karte nie
against the truth say out he had the card never

gesehen. Er nimmt nicht meine Interessen wahr.
seen He takes not my interests true
(nimmt wahr; guards)

Er handelt gegen mich. Wer weiß, ob nicht diese
He acts against me Who knows whether not this

Karte - überall hört man von Fallen, die den Leuten
card everywhere hears one from cases which the people

gestellt werden. Aber Unsinn, er ist immer mein Freund
set become But nonsense he is always my friend

gewesen, ein zuverlässiger Mensch ...
been a more reliable human

Und beide besannen sich, beide sahen sich an, beide
And both reconsidered themselves both looked himself at both

fingen an zu lächeln.
caught on to smile
started

»Wir sind wahnsinnig gewesen, wir haben einander
We are insane been we have each other
have

mißtraut!«
distrusted

»Wir, die wir uns über zwanzig Jahre kennen!«
We who we us over twenty years know

»Die ganze Penne miteinander!«
The whole flophouse together

»Ja, wir haben es herrlich weit gebracht!«
Yes we have it wonderfully far brought

»Wie stehen wir da? Der Sohn verrät die Mutter, die
How stand we there The son betrays the mother the

Schwester den Bruder, der Freund die Freundin ...«
sister the brother the friend the (female) friend

»Aber wir uns nicht!«
But we us not

»Wir wollen überlegen, was am besten mit dieser Karte
We want to consider what at the best with this card

geschieht. Es wäre wirklich unvernünftig, wenn du mit
happens It would be really senselss when you with

ihr in der Tasche auf die Straße gingest, da du dich
her in the pocket on the street went there since you yourself

beobachtet fühlst.«
observed feels

»Es kann reine Nervosität gewesen sein. Gib mir die
It can pure nervousness been have been be Give me the

Karte, ich schaffe sie schon irgendwie fort!«
card I do her already somehow away

»Du mit deinem unheilvollen Hang zu Unbesonnenheiten!
You with your ominous tendency to rash actions

Nein, die Karte bleibt hier!«
No the card remains here

»Du hast Frau und zwei Kinder, Erwin. Dein Büropersonal
You have wife and two children Erwin Your office personnel

ist vielleicht auch nicht durchweg zuverlässig. Wer ist
is perhaps also not throughout always reliable Who is

denn heute noch zuverlässig? Gib mir die Karte. Ich rufe
then today still reliable Give me the card I call

dich in einer Viertelstunde an und melde dir, daß sie
you in a quarter of an hour on and report you that she

fort ist.«
away is

»Um Gottes willen! Das bist wieder einmal du, Max.
For god's will That are again once you Max

Wegen so etwas ein Telefongespräch führen! Warum
because of so something a phone call lead Why

rufst du nicht gleich Himmler an? Das geht dann doch
call you not immediately Himmler up That goes then indeed

schneller!«
more quickly

Und wieder sehen sie sich an, ein wenig getröstet,
And again look they each other at a little consoled

daß sie noch nicht ganz allein sind, daß sie doch
that they still not completely alone are that they indeed

noch einen zuverlässigen Freund besitzen.
still a trusted friend possess

Plötzlich schlägt der Anwalt zornig auf die Karte. »Was
Suddenly beats the lawyer angrily on the card What

dieser Idiot sich wohl gedacht hat, als er dieses Ding
this idiot himself well thought has as he this thing

schrieb und hier ins Treppenhaus legte! Andere Leute
wrote and here in the stairwell put Other people

aufs Schafott bringen!«
on the scaffold bring!

»Und wegen was? Was schreibt er eigentlich? Nichts,
And because of what What writes he actually Nothing

was jeder von uns nicht schon weiß! Es muß ein
what each from us not already knows It must a

Wahnsinniger sein!«
crazy person be

»Dieses ganze Volk ist ein Volk von Wahnsinnigen
This whole people is a people from insane

geworden, einer steckt den andern an!«
become one sticks the other on
(sticks an; infects)

»Wenn man diesen Kerl erwischte, der andere in solche
When one this chap caught who others in such

Schwierigkeiten bringt! Ich würde mich direkt freuen ...«
difficulties brings I would me directly enjoy

»Ach, laß doch! Du würdest dich bestimmt nicht
Oh leave (it) indeed You would you definitely not

freuen, wenn noch einer mehr sterben würde. Aber wie
enjoy (it) when still one more die would But how

kommen wir aus diesen Schwierigkeiten heraus?«
come we out this difficulties away out

Der Anwalt sah nachdenklich wieder auf die Karte. Dann
The lawyer saw thoughtful again on the card Then

griff er zum Telefon. »Wir haben hier irgend so einen
grabbed he to the phone We have here any so a

Politischen Leiter im Hause«, sagte er erklärend zum
political ladder in the home « said he explaining to the

Freund. »Ich werde ihm die Karte offiziell übergeben, den
friend i will him the card officially overgiven the

Sachverhalt schildern, wie er tatsächlich war, im übrigen
case-relation paint as he indeed was in the rest
story of the case

aber der Sache keine große Wichtigkeit beimessen. Du
but the thing no great importance during the meal you

bist deiner Aussage sicher?«
are your statement sure

»Völlig.«
completely

»Und deiner Nerven?«
and your annoy

»Ganz gewiß, mein Lieber. Auf der Bühne habe ich noch
all certainly my rather on the stage have i still

nie Lampenfieber gehabt. Vorher immer! Was für eine Art
never stage fright had before always what for a way

Mann ist dieser Politische Leiter?«
man is this political ladder

»Keine Ahnung. Ich erinnere mich nicht, ihn je gesehen
no idea i remember me not him the seen

zu haben. Wahrscheinlich irgend so ein kleiner Bonze.
to have probably any so a little boss

Jedenfalls rufe ich ihn jetzt an.«
anyhow call i him now

Aber das Männlein, das kam, sah nicht sehr nach Bonze
but the little men the came saw not very to boss

aus, eher nach einem Fuchs, der sich aber sehr
from before to a fox the himself but very

geschmeichelt fühlte, als er den berühmten Schauspieler
flattered felt as he the famous actor

kennenlernte, den er so oft schon im Film gesehen.
got to know the he so often already in the movie seen

Und aus dem Stegreif nannte er sechs Filme; in keinem
and from the impromptu called he six movies in no

davon hatte der Schauspieler je mitgespielt. Max
there-from had the actor the played along max

Harteisen bewunderte das Gedächtnis des Männleins, dann
admired the memory of the manly then

gingen sie zum geschäftlichen Teil des Besuches über.
went she to the entrepreneurial part of the visit over

Das Füchslein las die Karte, und seinem Gesicht war
the little fox read the card and his face was

nicht abzulesen, was der Mann dabei empfand. Es war
not read what the man there-by felt it was

nur schlau. Dann hörte er den Bericht von dem Auffinden
only smart then heard he the message from the find up
find out

der Karte, der Ablieferung hier auf dem Büro.
the card the delivery here on the office

»Sehr gut. Sehr korrekt!« lobte der Leiter. »Und wann
very good very correctly praised the ladder and when

war das etwa?«
was the about

Einen Augenblick stutzte der Anwalt, warf einen
a moment stopped short the lawyer threw a

raschen Blick auf den Freund. Besser nicht lügen, dachte
quick glance on the friend better not lies thought

er. Sie haben ihn mit der Karte in der Hand sehr erregt
he she have him with the card in the hand very excited

hereinkommen sehen.
enter see

»Vor einer guten halben Stunde«, meinte der Anwalt.
before a good half hour thought the lawyer

Das Männlein zog die Augenbrauen hoch. »So lange?«
the little men pulled the eyebrows high so long

fragte er mit leisem Erstaunen.
asked he with quiet astonishment

»Wir hatten noch anderes zu besprechen«, erklärte der
we had still other to explained the

Anwalt. »Wir legten der Sache keine große Wichtigkeit bei.
lawyer we laid the thing no great importance at

Oder ist sie wichtig?«
or is she important

»Wichtig ist alles. Wichtig wäre es gewesen, diesen
important is everything important would be it been this

Burschen, der die Karte niederlegte, zu fangen. Aber jetzt
lad the the card resigned to catch but now

nach einer halben Stunde ist es natürlich dafür viel zu
to a half hour is it of course therefore much to

spät.«
late

Jedes seiner Worte klang von einem leichten Vorwurf
each his words sounded from a light accusation

gegen dieses »Zu spät« wider.
against this to against

»Ich bedaure diese Verspätung«, sagte der Schauspieler
i deplore this delay said the actor

Harteisen tönend. »Sie entstand durch meine Schuld. Ich
resounding you arose through my guilt i

nahm meine Angelegenheit wichtiger als dieses -
took my matter more important as this -

Geschmier!«

»Ich hätte es besser wissen müssen«, sagte der Anwalt.
i had it better know have to said the lawyer

Das Füchslein lächelte beschwichtigend. »Nun, meine
the little fox smiled soothing now my

Herren, was zu spät ist, bleibt zu spät. Es freut mich
gentlemen what to late is remains to late it enjoys me

jedenfalls, daß ich auf diese Weise den Vorzug genossen
anyhow that i on this manner the preference enjoyed

habe, Herrn Harteisen persönlich kennenzulernen. Heil
have gentleman personally get to know hail

Hitler!«
hitler"

Sehr stark, aufspringend: »Heil Hitler!«
very strong jumping up hail hitler"

Und als sich die Tür hinter ihm geschlossen hatte, sahen
and as himself the door behind him closed had saw

sich die beiden Freunde an.
himself the both friends on

»Gott sei Dank, wir sind diese unselige Karte los!«
god be thanks we are this unfortunate (one) card away
come on

»Und er hat keinen Verdacht auf uns!«
and he has no suspicion on us

»Nicht wegen der Karte! Daß wir aber zwischen
not because of the card that we but between

Ablieferung und Nichtablieferung geschwankt haben, das
delivery and non-delivery have the

hat er sehr wohl begriffen.«
has he very well understood.

»Glaubst du, daß noch etwas nach der Sache kommt?«
»believe you that still something to the thing

»Nein, eigentlich nicht. Im schlimmsten Falle eine
no actually not in the worst case a

belanglose Vernehmung, wo und wann und wie du die
irrelevant interrogation where and when and as you the

Karte gefunden hast. Und da gibt es ja nichts zu
card found have and there gives it yes nothing to

verheimlichen.«

»Weißt du, Erwin, im Grunde bin ich jetzt ganz froh,
know you erwin in the ground am i now completely happy

aus dieser Stadt eine Weile herauszukommen.«
from this city a while

»Siehst du!«
see you

»Man wird schlecht in dieser Stadt!«
one will bad in this city

»Man wird es! Man ist es schon! Und das kräftig!«
one will it one is it already and the strong!

Unterdes war das Füchslein auf seine Ortsgruppe gefahren.
under-that was the little fox on his location group driven
meanwhile

Ein Braunhemd hielt jetzt die Karte in der Hand.
a brown shirt held now the card in the hand

»Das geht nur die Gestapo an«, sagte das Braunhemd.
that goes only the gestapo said the brown shirt

»Du fährst am besten selbst damit hin, Heinz. Warte,
you drive at the best himself there-with away heinz wait

ich gebe dir ein paar Zeilen mit. Und die beiden
i give you a few lines with and the both

Herren?«
gentlemen

»Völlig außer Frage! Natürlich, politisch zuverlässig sind
completely except question of course politically reliable are

sie beide nicht. Ich sage dir, sie haben Blut und Wasser
she both not i say you she have blood and water

geschwitzt, als sie mit der Karte anfangen mußten.«
sweated as she with the card start had to.

»Der Harteisen soll bei Minister Goebbels in Ungnade
the should at minister goebbels in unfortunate

sein«, meinte das Braunhemd nachdenklich.
be thought the brown shirt thoughtful

»Trotzdem!« sagte das Füchslein. »Er würde so was nie
nevertheless said the little fox he would so what never

wagen. Hat viel zuviel Angst. Ich habe ihm ins Gesicht
cart has much too much fear i have him in the face

sechs Filme genannt, in denen er nie aufgetreten ist,
six movies called in which he never occurred is

und habe seine Meisterleistung bewundert. Er hat eine
and have his masterpiece he has a

Verbeugung nach der andern gemacht und gestrahlt vor
bow to the other made and blasted before

Dankbarkeit. Dabei habe ich direkt gerochen, wie er vor
thankfullness there-by have i directly smelled as he before

Angst geschwitzt hat!«
fear sweated has

»Alle haben sie Angst!« entschied das Braunhemd
all have she fear decided the brown shirt

verächtlich. »Warum eigentlich? Es ist ihnen doch so
contemptuous why actually it is them indeed so

leicht gemacht, sie brauchen nur zu tun, was wir ihnen
easy made she need only to do what we them

sagen.«
say

»Das ist, weil die Leute das Denken nicht lassen
that is because the people the think not let

können. Sie glauben immer, mit Denken kommen sie
can she believe always with think come she

weiter.«
further

»Sie sollen bloß gehorchen. Das Denken besorgt der
you should just obey the think concerned the

Führer.«
leader

Das Braunhemd tippte auf die Karte: »Und der hier? Was
the brown shirt tapped on the card and the here what

meinst du zu dem, Heinz?«
mean you to the heinz?
believe

»Was soll ich dazu sagen? Wahrscheinlich hat er
what should i there-to say probably has he

wirklich den Sohn verloren ...«
really the son lost «

»I wo! Die so was schreiben und tun, das sind immer
»i where the so what write and do the are always

bloß Hetzer. Die wollen was für sich erreichen. Söhne
just agitator the want what for himself reach sons

und ganz Deutschland, das ist ihnen alles ganz
and completely germany the is them everything completely

egal. Irgend so ein alter Sozi oder Kommunist ...«
equal any so a old soci or communist «

»Glaube ich nicht. Glaube ich nie und nimmer im
(i) believe i not believe i never and never in the

Leben. Die können doch von ihren Phrasen nicht lassen,
life the can indeed from her phrases not let

Faschismus und Reaktion und Solidarität und Prolet - aber
fascism and reaction and solidarity and prolet - but

von all diesen Schlagworten steht nicht eins auf der
from all this key words stands not one on the

Karte. I wo, was ein Sozi ist oder ein Kommunist, das
card i where what a soci is or a communist the

rieche ich auf zehn Kilometer gegen den Wind!«
smell i on ten kilometers against the wind

»Und ich glaub's doch! Die haben sich jetzt alle
and i believe it indeed the have himself now all

getarnt ...«
camouflaged «

Aber die Herren auf der Gestapo waren auch nicht der
but the gentlemen on the gestapo were also not the

Meinung des Braunhemdes. Übrigens wurde der Bericht
opinion of the by the way became the message

des Füchsleins dort mit heiterer Ruhe aufgenommen.
of the little fox there with more cheerful rest taken up

Dort war man immerhin schon andere Dinge gewohnt.
there was one after all already other things used

»Na ja«, sagten sie. »Schön und gut. Werden ja sehen.
now yes said she beautiful and good become yes see

Wenn Sie sich vielleicht noch zu Kommissar Escherich
when she himself perhaps still to commissioner escherich

bemühen wollen, wir verständigen ihn telefonisch, der wird
endeavor want we make understand him by phone the will

die Sache bearbeiten. Geben Sie ihm noch einmal genauen
the thing to edit give she him still once exact

Bericht, wie sich die beiden Herren verhielten. Natürlich
message as himself the both gentlemen kept of course

geschieht im Augenblick nichts gegen sie, nur als
happens in the moment nothing against she only as

Material für etwaige spätere Fälle kann so was nützlich
material for any later cases can so what useful

sein, Sie verstehen doch ...?«
his she understand indeed «

Kommissar Escherich, ein langer, schlenkriger Mann mit
commissioner escherich a long more dangling man with

einem losen, sandfarbenen Schnurrbart, in einem hellgrauen
a loose sand-colored moustache in a light gray

Anzug – alles an diesem Menschen war so farblos, daß
suit – everything on this people was so colorless that

man ihn gut für eine Ausgeburt des Aktenstaubes halten
one him good for a birth of the file dust hold

konnte -, also, Kommissar Escherich drehte die Karte
could -, thus commissioner escherich turned the card

zwischen den Händen hin und her.
between the hands away and away

»Eine neue Platte«, meinte er dann. »Die habe ich noch
one new plate thought he then the have i still

nicht in meiner Sammlung. Schwere Hand, hat nicht viel
not in my collection heavy hand has not much

geschrieben in seinem Leben, immer mit der Hand
written in his life always with the hand

gearbeitet.«
worked.

»Ein Kapediste?« fragte das Füchslein.
a kapediste? asked the little fox

Der Kommissar Escherich kicherte: »Machen Sie doch
the commissioner escherich giggled make she indeed

keine Witze, Herr! So was und ein Kapediste! Sehen Sie,
no jokes mr so what and a kapediste see she

wenn wir eine richtige Polizei hätten und die Sache
when we a right police had and the thing

wäre es wert, so wäre der Schreiber da in
would be it worth so would be the scribblers there in

vierundzwanzig Stunden hinter Schloß und Riegel.«
twenty four hours behind closed and bars

»Und wie würden Sie das machen?«
and as would she the make

»Das ist doch ganz einfach! Ich ließe überall in
that is indeed completely simply i lets everywhere in

Berlin recherchieren, wem in den letzten zwei, drei
berlin do research whom in the last two three

Wochen ein Sohn gefallen ist, ein einziger Sohn
weeks a son fallen is a single son

wohlgemerkt, denn der Schreiber hat nur einen Sohn
mind you then the scribblers has only a son

gehabt!«
had!

»Woran sehen Sie denn das?«
»at what see she then that

»Das ist doch ganz einfach! Im ersten Satz, wo
that is indeed completely simply in the first sentence where

er von sich spricht, sagt er so. Im zweiten, bei den
he from himself speaks says he so in the second at the

andern, spricht er von Söhnen. Na, und auf die das dann
other speaks he from sons now and on the the then

zutrifft mit den Recherchen – es können gar nicht so
applies with the research - it can at all not so

viel sein in Berlin –, auf die hätte ich dann mein
much his in berlin –, on the had i then my

Augenmerk, und schon säße der Schreiber drin!«
attention and already would sit the scribblers inside!

»Aber warum tun Sie's nicht?«
but why do they it not

»Ich hab's Ihnen doch schon gesagt, weil wir den
i have it them indeed already said because we the

Apparat dazu nicht haben, und weil's die Sache nicht
machine there-to not have and because it the thing not

wert ist. Sehen Sie, es gibt zwei Möglichkeiten. Entweder
worth is see she it gives two possibilities either

schreibt er noch zwei, drei Karten, und dann hat er's
writes he still two three cards and then has he it

über. Weil's ihm zuviel Mühe macht oder weil das
over because it him too much trouble makes or because the

Risiko ihm zu groß ist. Dann hat er nicht viel Schaden
risk him to large is then has he not much harm

angerichtet, man hat aber auch nicht viel Arbeit von ihm
done (had) one has but also not much work from him

gehabt.«
had.

»Glauben Sie denn, daß hier alle Karten abgegeben
believe she then that here all cards delivered

werden?«
become

»Alle nicht, aber die meisten doch. Das deutsche Volk ist
all not but the most indeed the german people is

schon recht zuverlässig ...«
already right reliable «

»Weil sie alle Angst haben!«
because she all fear to have

»Nein, das habe ich nicht gesagt. Ich glaube zum Beispiel
no the have i not said i believe to the example

nicht, daß dieser Mann«, er klopfte mit dem Knöchel auf
not that this man he knocked with the ankle on
husband

die Karte, »daß dieser Mann Angst hat. Sondern ich
the card that this man fear has but i

glaube, es tritt die zweite Möglichkeit ein: der Mann wird
believe it steps the second possibility a the man will

immer weiterschreiben. Laß ihn, je mehr er schreibt,
always keep writing let him the (any)more he writes

um so mehr verrät er sich. Jetzt hat er nur ein
for so (any)more betrays he himself now has he only a

kleines bißchen von sich verraten, nämlich, daß er einen
little bit from himself betrayed namely that he a

Sohn verloren hat. Aber mit jeder Karte wird er mir ein
son lost has but with each card will he me a

bißchen mehr von sich verraten. Ich brauche gar
bit (any)more from himself betrayed i need at all

nicht viel dazu zu tun. Ich brauche nur hier zu sitzen,
not much there-to to do i need only here to sit

ein bißchen aufzupassen und – schnapp! – habe ich ihn!
a bit take care and – snap – have i him

Wir hier auf unserer Abteilung brauchen nur Geduld zu
we here on our department need only patience to

haben. Manchmal dauert es ein Jahr, manchmal noch
have sometimes takes it a year sometimes still

mehr, aber schließlich kriegen wir unsere Leute alle.
(any)more but finally get we our people all

Oder fast alle.«
or almost all

»Und was dann?«
and what then

Der Staubfarbige hatte einen Stadtplan von Berlin
the dust-colored had a map from berlin

vorgeholt und an der Wand festgemacht. Nun steckte er
brought forward and on the wall fixed now stuck he

ein rotes Fähnchen ein, genau dort, wo das Bürohaus
a red flag a exactly there where the office building

in der Neuen Königstraße stand. »Sehen Sie, das ist
in the new koenigstrasse stood see she the is
look

alles, was ich im Augenblick tun kann. Aber in den
everything what i in the moment do can but in the

nächsten Wochen werden immer mehr Fähnchen
next weeks become always (any)more flag

dazukommen, und dort, wo sie am dicksten sitzen, da
join in and there where she at the thickest sit there

steckt mein Klabautermann. Weil er nämlich mit der Zeit
sticks my klabautermann because he namely with the time

abstumpft, und weil es ihm den weiten Weg nicht
dulls and because it him the wide way not

mehr lohnt wegen einer Karte. Sehen Sie, an diese
(any)more worth it because of a card see she on this

Karte denkt der Klabautermann nicht. Und ist doch so
card thinks the klabautermann not and is indeed so

einfach! Und schnapp mache ich noch einmal und habe
simply and snap make i still once and have

ihn auch so fest!«
him also so firmly

»Und was dann?« fragte das Füchslein, von einer
and what then asked the little fox from a

lüsternen Neugier angetrieben.
curiosity

Kommissar Escherich sah ihn ein bißchen spöttisch an.
commissioner escherich saw him a bit mocking on

»Hören Sie's so gerne? Na, ich tu Ihnen den Gefallen:
listen they it so gladly now i do them the fallen

Volksgerichtshof und weg mit der Rübe! Was geht das
people's court and way with the turnip what goes the

mich an? Was zwingt den Kerl, so 'ne blöde Karte zu
me on what swings the chap so a stupid card to

schreiben, die kein Mensch liest und kein Mensch lesen
write the no human reads and no human read

will! Nee, das geht mich nichts an. Ich bezieh mein
want no the goes me nothing on i rel my

Gehalt, und ob ich dafür Marken verkaufe oder
salary and whether i therefore brands sell or

Fähnchen einpieke, das ist mir ganz egal. Aber ich
flag poke in the is me completely equal but i

werde an Sie denken, ich werde nicht vergessen, daß Sie
will on she think i will not forgotten that she

mir die erste Meldung gebracht haben, und wenn ich den
me the first notice brought have and when i the

Kerl gefaßt habe, und es ist soweit, so schicke ich Ihnen
chap taken have and it is so far so send i them

eine Einladungskarte für die Hinrichtung.«
a invitation card for the execution

»Nee, danke wirklich. So war das nicht gemeint!«
no thank really so was the not meant

»Natürlich war es so gemeint. Warum genieren Sie sich
of course was it so meant why embarrass she himself

denn vor mir?! Vor mir braucht sich kein Mensch zu
then before me before me needs himself no human to

genieren, ich weiß, was mit den Menschen los ist! Wenn
embarrass i knows what with the people loose is when

wir hier das nicht wüßten, wer soll's denn sonst
we here the not knew who will it then otherwise

wissen? Nicht mal der liebe Gott! Also, abgemacht, ich
know not once the love god thus agreed i

schicke Ihnen eine Karte zur Hinrichtung. Heil Hitler!«
send them a card to the execution hail hitler"

»Heil Hitler! Und vergessen Sie es auch nicht!«
hail hitler and forgotten she it also not

Ein halbes Jahr danach: Quangels

A half year after: Quangels

Ein halbes Jahr später war den beiden Quangels das
A half year later was the both Quangels the

sonntägliche Schreiben der Postkarten bereits zur
Sunday writing the postcards already to the

Gewohnheit geworden, zu einer heiligen Gewohnheit freilich,
habits become to a holy habits indeed

die ein Bestandteil ihres täglichen Lebens war wie die
which a component of their daily life was as the

tiefe Ruhe, die sie umgab, oder die eiserne
deep rest which them surrounded or the iron

Sparsamkeit um jeden Groschen. Es waren die schönsten
thrift for every dime It were the most beautiful

Stunden der Woche, wenn sie beide an den Sonntagen
hours the week when they both on the Sundays

beisammensaßen, sie in der Sofaecke, mit irgendeiner
together-sat she in the sofa corner with some

Flick- oder Stopfarbeit beschäftigt, er steif auf dem Stuhl
sweep or darn-work occupied he stiff on the chair

am Tisch, den Federhalter in der großen Hand, langsam
at the table the penholder in the large hand slowly

Wort für Wort hinmalend.
word for word forth-painting

Quangel hatte seine anfängliche Leistung von einer Karte
Quangel had his initial performance from a card

pro Woche jetzt verdoppelt. Ja, an guten Sonntagen
per week now doubled Yes on good Sundays

brachte er es sogar auf drei Karten. Nie aber schrieb
brought he it even on to three cards Never however wrote

er eine Karte gleichen Inhalts. Sondern beide Quangels
he a card (with the) same content But both Quangels

entdeckten, je mehr sie schrieben, um so mehr Fehler
discovered the more they wrote for so more failures

des Führers und seiner Partei. Dinge, die ihnen, als sie
of the leader and his party Things which them as she

geschahen, kaum als tadelnswert zum Bewußtsein
happened hardly as reprehensible to the awareness

gekommen waren, wie die Unterdrückung aller anderen
come were as the oppression of all other

Parteien, oder die sie nur als zu weitgehend und zu
parties or which they only as to far-going and too

roh durchgeführt verurteilt hatten, wie die
raw carried through judged had as the

Judenverfolgungen - diese Dinge bekamen jetzt, da sie
Jews-prosecutions these things got now when they

zu Feinden des Führers geworden waren, ein ganz
to enemies of the leader become were a completely

anderes Gesicht und Gewicht. Sie bewiesen ihnen die
other face and weight They proved them the

Verlogenheit der Partei und ihrer Führer. Und wie alle
mendacity of the party and its leader And as all

frisch Bekehrten hatten sie das Bestreben, andere zu
fresh converted (ones) had they the striving others to

bekehren, und so wurde der Ton, in dem diese Karten
convert and so became the tone in which these cards

geschrieben wurden, nie monoton, und an Themen gab es
written became never monotonous and on themes gave it
was there

keinen Mangel.
no lack

Anna Quangel hatte nun längst ihren stillen Zuhörerposten
Anna Quangel had now long her quiet listener role

aufgegeben, sie saß lebhaft da im Sofa, sprach mit,
given up she sat lively there in the sofa spoke along

schlug Themen vor und dachte Sätze aus. Sie
struck themes before and thought sentences out They
proposed subjects

arbeiteten in der schönsten Gemeinsamkeit, und diese
worked in the most beautiful unity and this

tiefe, innere Gemeinsamkeit, die sie nach so langer
deep inner unity which they after so long

Ehe jetzt erst kennenlernten, wurde ihnen zu einem
marriage now first learned to know became them to a

großen Glück, das über die ganze Woche hin sein Licht
large happiness which over the whole week away its light

ausstrahlte. Sie sahen sich mit einem Blick an, sie
beamed out They looked each other with a glance at they

lächelten, jedes wußte von dem andern, es hatte jetzt an
smiled each knew from the other it had now on

die nächste Karte gedacht oder an die Wirkung dieser
the next card thought or on the effect of this

Karten, an die ständig wachsende Zahl ihrer Anhänger,
card on the constantly growing number of their supporters

und daß schon mit Begier auf die nächste Nachricht von
and that already with eagerness on the next message from
for by

ihnen gewartet wurde.
them waited became

Beide Quangels zweifelten nicht einen Augenblick daran,
Both Quangels doubted not a moment to it

daß ihre Karten jetzt in den Betrieben heimlich von Hand
that their cards now in the companies secretly from hand

zu Hand gingen, daß Berlin von diesen Bekämpfern zu
to hand went that Berlin from these fighting to

sprechen anfing. Sie waren sich klar darüber, daß ein
speak began They were themselves clear about it that a

Teil der Karten der Polizei in die Hände fiel, aber sie
part the cards the police in the hands fell but they

nahmen an: höchstens jede fünfte oder sechste Karte. Sie
took on at most each fifth or sixth card They
assumed

hatten so oft an diese Wirkung gedacht und von ihr
had so often on this effect thought and from her

gesprochen, daß die Weiterverbreitung ihrer Nachrichten,
spoken that the farther-widening of their messages
spread

das Aufsehen, das sie erregten, ihnen ganz
the sensation that they excited them completely

selbstverständlich erschien, eine Tatsache, die man nicht
self-understandably appeared a fact which one not
self-evidently

bezweifeln konnte.
doubted could

Dabei hatten beide Quangels nicht den geringsten
There-by had both Quangels not the least

tatsächlichen Anhaltspunkt dafür. Ob Anna Quangel nun
actual hold-point therefore Whether Anna Quangel now
clue

vor einem Lebensmittelladen in der Schlange anstand,
before a food-shop in the snake stood-on
row stood

ob der Werkmeister sich stumm mit seinen scharfen
whether the work-master himself mutely with his sharp
foreman

Augen zu einer Gruppe von Schwätzern stellte und eben
eyes to a group of chatterboxes set and just

nur durch sein Dortstehen ihr Geschwätz zum Aufhören
only through his there-standing their babble to the stop

brachte - niemals hörten sie ein Wort von dem neuen
brought never heard they a word from the new

Kämpfer gegen den Führer, von den Botschaften, die er
warriors against the leader from the messages which he

in die Welt sandte. Aber dieses Schweigen über ihre
in the world sent But this silence about their

Arbeit konnte sie nicht wankend machen in dem festen
work could them not wavering make in the firm

Glauben, daß doch von ihr geredet wurde, daß sie ihre
believe that indeed from her talked became that she her

Wirkung tat. Berlin war eine sehr große Stadt, und die
effect did Berlin was a very large city and the
had

Verteilung der Karten erstreckte sich auf ein weites
division of the cards spread itself on a wide

Gebiet, es brauchte seine Zeit, bis das Wissen von ihnen
area it needed its time until the knowledge from them

überall einsickerte. Kurz, den Quangels erging es wie
everywhere filtered in (In) short the Quangels happened it as

allen Menschen: sie glaubten, was sie hofften.
all people they believed what they hoped

Von den Vorsichtsmaßregeln, die Quangel zu Beginn seiner
From the precautions that Quangel at start his

Arbeit für nötig gehalten hatte, war er nur bei den
work for necessary held had was he only at the

Handschuhen abgewichen. Genaue Überlegungen hatten ihm
gloves deviated Exact considerations had him

gesagt, daß diese störenden Dinger, die seine Arbeit so
said that this disturbing things which his work so
not handy

verlangsamten, nichts nützten. Seine Karten gingen
slowed down nothing used His cards went
for nothing served

vermutlich,	ehe	mal	wirklich	eine	bei	der	Polizei	landete,
probably	before	once	really	one	at	the	police	landed

durch	so	viele	Hände,	daß	auch	der	gewiegteste
through	so	many	hands	that	also	the	most cradled
							smartest

Polizeibeamte	nicht	mehr	ausmachen	konnte,	was	des
police officer	not	(any)more	out-make	could	what	of the
			discern			

Schreibers	Abdrücke	waren.	Natürlich	beobachtete	Quangel
writer's	prints	were	Of course	observed	Quangel

weiter	die	äußerste	Vorsicht.	Vor	dem	Schreiben	wusch
further	the	outermost	caution	Before	the	writing	washed

er	sich	stets	die	Hände,	er	faßte	die	Karten	nur
he	himself	all the time	the	hands	he	seized	the	cards	only

sachte	und	sehr	an	den	Rändern	an,	und	beim	Schreiben
softly	and	very	on	the	edges	on	and	at the	writing

lag	stets	ein	Löschblatt	unter	der	Schreibhand.
lay	all the time	a	blotting sheet	under	the	write-hand

Was	das	Ablegen	der	Karten	selbst	in	den	großen
What	the	lay off	of the	cards	themselves	in	the	large
		drop off						

Bürohäusern	anging,	so	hatte	es	längst	den	Reiz	der
office houses	concerned	so	had	it	long	the	rise	of the
							arousing	

Neuheit	verloren.	Dieses	Ablegen,	das	ihnen	zuerst	so
newness	lost	this	lay off	the	them	first	so
			drop off				

gefahrvoll erschienen war, hatte sich mit der Zeit als
danger-full appeared was had himself with the time as
dangerous

der leichteste Teil der Aufgabe erwiesen. Man ging in ein
the lightest part the task bestowed one went in a
easiest

solches belebtes Haus, man wartete den richtigen
such lived in house one waited the right

Augenblick ab, und schon stieg man wieder die Treppe
moment ~~off~~ and already rose one again the stairs

hinunter, ein bißchen erleichtert, von einem Druck in der
down a bit lightened from a press in the

Magengegend befreit, den Gedanken »Wieder einmal gut
stomach-area freed the thoughts Again once good
ok

gegangen« im Kopf, aber nicht sonderlich aufgeregt.
went in the head but not especially excited

Zuerst hatte Quangel diese Karten allein abgelegt, die
First had Quangel these cards alone laid off the
dropped off

Begleitung Annas war ihm sogar unerwünscht erschienen.
escort of Anna was him even undesirable appeared

Aber dann machte es sich von selbst, daß auch dabei
But then made it itself from itself that also there-by
happened automatically

Anna tätige Mithelferin wurde. Quangel hielt genau darauf,
Anna active along-helper became Quangel held exactly thereupon
helper

daß die Karten, ob nun eine oder zwei oder gar drei
that the cards whether now one or two or at all three

geschrieben waren, stets am folgenden Tage aus dem
written were all the time at the following days from the

Hause kamen. Aber manchmal konnte er wegen seiner
house came But sometimes could he because of of his

von Rheumaschmerzen geplagten Beine schlecht gehen,
from Rheuma-pains plagued legs bad go
troubled walk

zum andern forderte die Vorsicht, daß die Karten in weit
to the other requested the attention that the cards in far

voneinander entfernten Stadtteilen verbreitet wurden. Das
from each other distanced city-parts spread became That

bedingte zeitraubende Bahnfahrten, die an einem
demanded time consuming rail-journeys which on one

Vormittag durch eine Person kaum zu bewältigen waren.
morning through one person hardly to master were
by

So übernahm Anna Quangel ihren Anteil auch an dieser
So took over Anna Quangel her part also on this

Arbeit. Zu ihrer Überraschung entdeckte sie, daß es sehr
work To her surprise discovered she that it very

viel aufregender und nervenquälender war, vor einem
much more exciting and nerve-racking was before a

Hause zu stehen und auf den Mann zu warten, als die
house to stand and on the man to wait than the
for

Karten selbst abzulegen. Dabei war sie stets die
cards herself off to lay There-by was she all the time the
to drop off

Ruhe selbst. Sobald sie ein derartiges Haus betreten
rest himself As soon as she one such house entered
calmness

hatte, fühlte sie sich sicher in dem Getriebe der
had felt she herself sure in the drive of the
bustle

treppan und treppab Steigenden, sie wartete geduldig auf
stairs-up and stairs-down rising she waited patiently on
for

ihre Gelegenheit und legte dann rasch die Karten hin. Sie
her opportunity and put then quickly the cards away she

war sich ganz sicher, daß sie niemals bei diesem
was herself completely sure that she never at this

Ablegen beobachtet war, daß keiner sich ihrer erinnern
lay off observed was that none himself her remember
drop off

und eine Beschreibung ihrer Person geben konnte. In
and a description of her person give could In

Wahrheit war sie auch viel weniger auffallend als ihr
truth was she also much less strikingly as her

Mann mit dem scharfen Vogelgesicht. Sie war eine kleine
man with the sharp bird-face She was a little

Bürgersfrau, die eben mal rasch zum Doktor lief.
citizen-woman who just once quickly to the doctor ran

Nur ein einziges Mal waren die Quangels bei ihrer
Only one single time were the Quangels at their

sonntäglichen Schreiberei gestört worden. Aber auch bei
Sunday writing disturbed become But also at

dieser Störung hatte es nicht die geringste Aufregung
this disturbance had it not the least (state of) excitement

und Verwirrung gegeben. Wie viele Male schon besprochen,
and confusion given As many times already discussed

war Anna Quangel bei dem Klingeln leise an die Flurtür
was Anna Quangel at the ringing softly to the floor door

geschlichen und hatte nach den Besuchern Ausschau durch
snuck and had to the visitor view through

das Guckloch gehalten. Unterdes hatte Otto Quangel das
the peephole held Under-that Meanwhile had Otto Quangel the

Schreibzeug fortgepackt und die angefangene Karte in ein
writing material away-packed and the began card in a

Buch gelegt. Es standen auch hier erst die Worte:
book laid It stood also here first the words

»Führer, befiehl - wir folgen. Jawohl, wir folgen, wir sind
Leader order we follow Yes we follow we are

eine Herde Schafe geworden, die unser Führer auf jede
a herd (of) sheep become who our leader on each

Schlachtbank treiben darf. Wir haben das Denken
butcher-bench drive may We have the thinking

aufgegeben ...«
given up

Die Karte mit diesen Worten hatte Otto Quangel in ein
The card with these words had Otto Quangel in a

Radiobastelbuch seines gefallenen Sohnes gelegt, und als
radio-craft-book of his fallen son laid and as

nun Anna Quangel mit den beiden Besuchern, einem
now Anna Quangel with the both visitors a

kleinen Buckligen und einer dunklen, langen, müden Frau,
small hunchback and a dark tall tired woman

eintrat, saß Otto bei seiner Schnitzerei und bosselte an
in-stepped sat Otto at his cutting and whittled at
occurred

der Büste des Jungen, die schon ziemlich weit
the bust of the boy who already rather far

vorgeschritten war und auch nach Ansicht Anna Quangels
advanced was and also after opinion (of) Anna Quangel

immer ähnlicher wurde. Es erwies sich, daß der kleine
always more similar became It proved himself that the little

Bucklige ein Bruder Annas war; die Geschwister hatten
hunchback a brother (of) Anna was The siblings had

sich fast dreißig Jahre nicht mehr gesehen. Der
each other almost thirty years not (any)more seen The

kleine Buckel hatte stets in Rathenow bei einer
little humpback had all the time in Rathenow at a

optischen Fabrik gearbeitet und war erst vor kurzem
optical factory worked and was first before (a) short (while)

nach Berlin geholt worden, um als Spezialist in einer
to berlin fetched become for as specialist in a

Fabrik zu arbeiten, die irgendwelches Gerät für
factory to work which some kind of material for

Unterseeboote herstellte. Die müde, dunkle Frau war
undersea-boatssubmarines manufactured The tired dark woman was

Annas noch nie gesehene Schwägerin. Otto Quangel hatte
Anna's still never seen sister-in-law Otto Quangel had

diese beiden Verwandten bisher noch nicht kennengelernt.
these both relatives until-here still not know-learned
until now gotten to know

An diesem Sonntag wurde es mit der weiteren Schreiberei
On this Sunday became it with the further writing

nichts, die begonnene Karte blieb unvollendet in dem
nothing the started card remained unfinished in the

Radiobastelbuch Ottochens liegen. So sehr Quangels
radio-craft-book of the little Otto lie So much (as) (the) Quangels

auch sonst gegen alle Besuche, gegen Freundschaft und
also otherwise against all visits against friendship and

Verwandtschaft eingestellt waren, um der Ruhe willen, in
relationship set were for the rest will in

der sie leben wollten, dieser da so unvermutet
which they live wanted this there so unexpected

hereingeschneite Bruder und seine Frau mißfielen ihnen
snowed in brother and his wife miss-fell them
displeased

nicht. Heffkes waren in ihrer Art auch stille Leute,
not Heffkes were in their way also quiet people

irgendeiner religiöser Sekte angehörend, die, nach einer
some religious sect belonging which after an

Andeutung zu schließen, von den Nazis verfolgt wurde.
hint (of) to close from the nazi's persecuted became
order disband by

Aber sie sprachen kaum davon, wie überhaupt alles
But they spoke hardly there-of like at all everything

Politische ängstlich vermieden wurde.
political fearfully avoided became
anxiously

Aber Quangel hörte staunend, wie die beiden, Anna und
But Quangel heard amazed how the both Anna and

ihr Bruder Ulrich Heffke, Kindheitserinnerungen
her brother Ulrich Heffke childhood-memories

austauschten. Zum erstenmal hörte er es, daß Anna auch
exchanged For the first time heard he it that Anna also

einmal ein Kind gewesen war, ein Kind mit Übermut,
once a child been was a child with high spirits

Unarten und Streichen. Er hatte seine Frau erst
vices and tricks He had his woman first

kennengelernt, als sie schon ein älteres Mädchen gewesen
know-learned when she already a older girl been
gotten to know

war; er hatte nie daran gedacht, daß sie einmal
was he had never there-on thought that she once

ganz anders ausgesehen hatte, vor ihrem arg
completely different looked had before her rather

geplagten, freudlosen Dienstmädchendasein, das ihr so viel
plagued cheerless servant girl existence which her so much

von ihrer Kraft und ihrer Hoffnung genommen hatte.
from her strength and her hope taken had

Nun sah er, während die Geschwister miteinander
Now saw he while the siblings with each other

plauderten, das kleine, arme märkische Dorf vor sich;
chattered the little poor Brandenburg village before himself

er hörte, daß sie die Gänse hatte hüten müssen, daß
he heard that she the geese had look after must that

sie sich vor der verhaßten Arbeit des Kartoffelbuddelns
she herself before the hated work of the potato-digging

stets versteckt und viele Schläge deswegen bekommen
all the time hidden and many blows because of that become

hatte, und er erfuhr, daß sie im Dorfe recht beliebt
had and he experienced heard that she in the village right loved

gewesen war, weil sie sich, trotzig und couragiert,
been was because she herself defiant and brave

gegen alles aufgelehnt hatte, was ihr nach
against everything rebelled had what her after

Ungerechtigkeit schmeckte. Hatte sie doch sogar einem
injustice tasted Had she indeed even an

ungerechten Schullehrer dreimal hintereinander mit einem
unjust schoolteacher three times behind each other with a

Schneeball den Hut vom Kopfe geworfen – und sie war
snow-ball the hat from the head thrown and she was

nie als die Täterin entdeckt worden. Nur sie und Ulrich
never as the perpetrator discovered become Only she and Ulrich

hatten davon gewußt, Ulrich aber petzte nie.
had there-from known Ulrich but snitched never

Nein, dies war kein unangenehmer Besuch, obwohl zwei
No this was no unpleasant visit although two

Karten weniger als sonst geschrieben wurden. Quangels
cards less as otherwise written became Quangels

meinten es auch ganz aufrichtig, als sie den Heffkes
thought it also completely honestly as they the Heffkes

beim Abschied einen Gegenbesuch versprachen. Sie hielten
at the goodbye a reciprocal visit promised They held

auch das Versprechen. Etwa fünf oder sechs Wochen
also the promise About five or six weeks

später suchten sie die Heffkes in einer kleinen
later searched she the Heffkes in a small

Notwohnung auf, die ihnen im Westen in der Nähe
emergency-quarters up which them in the west in the proximity

des Nollendorfplatzes frei gemacht worden war. Die
of the Nollendorf-square free made become was The

Quangels benutzten diesen Besuch, um endlich auch mal
Quangels used this visit for finally also once

im Westen eine Karte abzulegen; obwohl es Sonntag und
in the west a card off to lay although it sunday and
to drop off

das Bürohaus wenig belebt war, ging alles gut.
the office building little lively was went everything well

Von da an folgten die gegenseitigen Besuche sich in
From there on followed the mutual visits themselves in

etwa sechswöchentlichem Abstand. Sie waren nicht weiter
about six-weekly distance They were not further

aufregend, aber sie brachten doch ein wenig andere Luft
exciting but they brought indeed a little other air

in das Leben der Quangels. Meist saßen Otto und seine
in the life of the Quangels Mostly sat Otto and his

Schwägerin schweigend am Tisch und lauschten auf das
sister in law in silence at the table and listened on the

leise Gespräch der beiden Geschwister, die nicht müde
softly conversation of the both siblings which not tired

wurden, von ihrer Kindheit zu plaudern. Es tat Quangel
became from their childhood to chat It did Quangel

gut, auch diese andere Anna kennenzulernen; freilich fand
good also this other Anna to get to know indeed found

er nie eine Brücke zwischen der Frau, die heute an
he never a bridge between the woman who today on

seiner Seite lebte, und jenem Mädchen, das die Landarbeit
his side lived and that girl that the land-work

verstand, mutwillige Streiche verübte und trotzdem als
understood wanton pranks committed and in spite of that as

beste Schülerin der kleinen Landschule galt.
best student of the small countryside-school was seen

Sie erfuhren, daß Annas Eltern noch immer in ihrem
They experienced that Anna's parents still always in their
heard

Geburtsort lebten, sehr alte Leute - der Schwager
place of birth lived very old people the brother in law

erwähnte beiläufig, daß er den Eltern monatlich zehn
mentioned casually that he the parents monthly ten

Mark sandte. Anna Quangel war schon drauf und dran,
mark sent Anna Quangel was already on it and there-on
{money}

dem Bruder zu sagen, daß sie das von nun an auch tun
the brother to say that she that from now on also do

würden, aber sie fing noch zur rechten Zeit einen
would but she caught still to the right time a

warnenden Blick ihres Mannes auf und schwieg.
warning glance from her man ~~on~~ and was silent
husband

Erst auf dem Heimweg sagte er dann: »Nein, besser
First on the way home said he then No better

nicht, Anna. Wozu solch alte Leute verwöhnen? Sie
not Anna To which such old people spoil They

haben doch ihre Rente, und wenn der Schwager dazu
have indeed their pension and when the brother in law there-to

noch alle Monate zehn Mark schickt, ist das genug.«
still all months ten mark sends is that enough
{money}

»Wir haben doch soviel Geld auf der Sparkasse!« bat
We have indeed so much money on the savings bank bade

Anna. »Wir werden es nie aufbrauchen. Früher haben wir
Anna We will it never use up Before have we

gedacht, es wäre mal für Ottochen, aber jetzt ... Laß es
thought it would be once for little Otto but now Let it

uns tun, Otto! Und wenn es nur fünf Mark sind alle
us do Otto And when it only five mark {money} are all

Monate!«
months

Ungerührt antwortete Otto Quangel: »Jetzt, wo wir in
Untouched answered Otto Quangel Now where we in

der großen Sache drin sind, wissen wir nicht, wozu
the large affair there in are know we not to which

wir unser Geld eines Tages noch brauchen werden.
we our money one day still need become

Vielleicht werden wir jede einzelne Mark gebrauchen,
Perhaps will we each single mark {money} use

Anna. Und die alten Leute haben bisher auch ohne uns
Anna And the old people have until-here until now also without us

gelebt, warum nicht weiter so?«
lived why not further so

Sie schwieg, ein wenig gekränkt, vielleicht nicht so sehr
She was silent a little hurt perhaps not so very

in ihrer Liebe zu den Eltern, denn sie hatte kaum je
in her love to the parents then she had hardly before

an die alten Leute gedacht und ihnen nur einmal im
on the old people thought and them only once in the of

Jahre aus Pflichtgefühl zu Weihnachten einen Brief
years from feeling of duty at Christmas night a letter

geschrieben. Aber sie kam sich vor dem Bruder
written But she came himself before the brother

etwas blamiert und schäbig vor. Der Bruder sollte doch
something blamed and shabby before The brother should indeed

nicht denken, sie könnten nicht das, was er konnte.
not think they could not that what he could

Anna sagte hartnäckig: »Der Ulrich wird denken, wir
Anna said persistent The Ulrich will think we

können's nicht, Otto. Er wird von deiner Arbeit gering
can it not Otto He will from your work small

denken, daß sie nur so wenig einbringt.«
think that she only so little brings in

»Es ist doch ganz egal, was andere von mir
It is indeed completely equal (not important) what others from me

denken«, versetzte Quangel. »Ich hole nun einmal für so
think retorted Quangel I get now once for so

was kein Geld von der Kasse.«
what no money from the bank

Anna fühlte, dieser letzte Satz war unumstößlich. Sie
Anna felt this last sentence was irrevocable She

schwieg, sie fügte sich wie immer, wenn solch ein
was silent she suited herself as always when such a

Satz von Otto gesprochen wurde, aber ein bißchen
sentence from Otto spoken became but a bit

gekränkt war sie doch, daß der Mann nie Rücksicht auf
hurt was she indeed that the man never consideration on

ihre Gefühle nahm. Doch vergaß Anna Quangel diese
her feelings took Indeed forgot Anna Quangel this

Kränkung rasch bei der Weiterarbeit am großen Werk.
insult quickly at the further-work to the large work

Ein halbes Jahr danach: Kommissar Escherich

A half year after: Commissary Escherich

Ein halbes Jahr nach Empfang der ersten Karte stand
A half year after reception of the first card stood

der Kommissar Escherich, seinen sandfarbenen Schnurrbart
the commissioner Escherich his sand-colored moustache

streichend, vor der Karte Berlins, auf der er mit roten
stroking before the map of Berlin on which he with red

Fähnchen die Fundpunkte von Quangels Karten markiert
little flags the find-points of (the) Quangels cards marked

hatte. Es steckten jetzt vierundvierzig solcher Fähnchen
had It stuck now four-and-forty such little flags
There forty four

auf dem Blatt; von den achtundvierzig Karten, die
on the leaf from the eight-and-forty cards the
page forty eight

Quangels in diesem halben Jahr geschrieben und
Quangels in this half year written and

ausgetragen hatten, waren nur vier bei der Gestapo nicht
carried out had were only four at the Gestapo not

gelandet.
landed

Und auch diese vier waren wohl kaum in den Betrieben
And also these four were well hardly in the companies

von Hand zu Hand gegangen, wie es sich die
from hand to hand gone as it themselves the

Quangels erhofft, sondern sie waren, kaum gelesen, schon
Quangels hoped but they were hardly read already

angstvoll zerrissen, weggespült oder verbrannt worden.
fearfully torn up flushed away or burned become

Die Tür geht, und Escherichs Vorgesetzter, der
The door goes and Escherichs before-sitter boss the

SS-Obergruppenführer Prall, kommt herein: »Heil Hitler,
ss-over-groups-leader (ss officer) Prall comes in Hail hitler

Escherich! Nun, warum beißen Sie so auf Ihrem Bart
Escherich Now why bite you so on your beard

herum?«
around

»Heil Hitler, Herr Obergruppenführer! Das ist der
Hail hitler mr over-groups-leader That is the

Kartenschreiber, der Klabautermann, wie ich ihn bei mir
card writer the kobold how I him at me

nenne.«
name call

»Nanu? Warum denn Klabautermann?«
Well now Why then kobold

»Weiß nicht. Fiel mir so ein. Vielleicht, weil er die
Know not Fell me so in Maybe because he the

Leute graulich machen will.«
people afraid make wants

»Und wie weit sind wir damit, Escherich?«
And how far are we there-with Escherich

»Tja!« sagte der Kommissar gedehnt. Er sah wieder
Well said the commissioner stretched He looked again

nachdenklich auf die Karte. »Nach der Verbreitung zu
thoughtful at the card After the widening to
spread

schließen, muß er irgendwo nördlich vom Alexanderplatz
close must he somewhere northern from the Alexanderplatz
conclude

sitzen, da sind die meisten Vorkommen. Aber auch
sit there are the most occurred But also

Osten und Zentrum sind ganz gut bepflastert. Der
(the) east and center are completely good paved The

Süden gar nicht, im Westen, etwas südlich vom
south at all not in the west something southern from the

Nollendorfplatz, sind zwei Vorkommen – da muß er
Nollendorfplatz are two occurrances there must he

irgendwie gelegentlich zu tun haben.«
somehow occasionally to do have

»Gut deutsch: Aus der Karte läßt sich noch gar nichts
Good german From the card lets itself still at all nothing

sagen! Damit kommen wir nicht einen Schritt weiter!«
say There-with come we not a step further

»Abwarten! Ein halbes Jahr später, wenn mein
Wait off A half year later when my

Klabautermann bis dahin keinen andern Schwupper macht,
kobold until there to no other whoosh [failure] makes

wird die Karte schon viel mehr Aufschluß geben.«
will the cards already much more revelation give

»Halbes Jahr! Sie sind ja prächtig, Escherich! Ein halbes
Half year You are yes wonderful Escherich A half

Jahr wollen Sie dieses Schwein noch wühlen und grunzen
year want you this swine still stir and grunt

lassen und nichts tun, als in aller Gemütsruhe Ihre
let and nothing do as in all mood's rest [calmness] your

Fähnchen einpieken?«
little flags in-stick

»Bei unserer Arbeit muß man Geduld haben, Herr
At our work must one patience have Mr

Obergruppenführer. Das ist, wie wenn Sie auf dem
Over-groups-leader That is as when you on the

Anstand sitzen und auf den Bock warten. Sie müssen
on-stand [raised hideout] sit and for the buck [male deer] wait You must

eben warten. Ehe er kommt, können Sie nicht schießen.
just wait Before he comes can you not shoot

Aber wenn er kommt, da schieß ich, verlassen Sie sich
But when he comes there shoot I leave you yourself

darauf!«
there-on

»Ich hör immerzu Geduld, Escherich! Glauben Sie denn,
I hear always patience Escherich Believe you then

die Herren über uns haben soviel Geduld? Ich fürchte,
the gentlemen above us have so much patience I fear

wir kriegen bald einen reingehängt, an dem wir lange
we get soon one hung in on which we long

kauen werden. Bedenken Sie, in einem halben Jahr
chew become Think you in a half year

vierundvierzig Karten, das sind in jeder Woche fast zwei
forty-four cards that are in each week almost two

Karten, die bei uns eintrudeln, das sehen doch die
cards which at us roll in that see indeed the

Herren. Da fragen sie mich: Na, und? Noch nicht
gentlemen There ask they me Now and Still not

gefaßt? Warum noch nicht gefaßt? Was tut ihr eigentlich?
caught Why still not caught What do you actually

Fähnchen pieken und Daumen drehen, antworte ich. Und
Little flags stick and thumbs rotate answer I And

dann kriege ich meinen reingewürgt und den Befehl, den
then get I mine choked in and the order the

Mann in zwei Wochen zu fassen.«
man in two weeks to catch

Kommissar Escherich grinste unter seinem sandfarbenen
Commissioner Escherich grinned under his sand-colored

Bart. »Und dann würgen Sie mir einen rein, Herr
beard And then choke you me one there in Mr

Obergruppenführer, und geben mir den dienstlichen Befehl,
Over-groups-leader and give me the service order

den Mann in einer Woche zu fassen!«
the man in one week to catch

»Grinsen Sie nicht so albern, Escherich! Über so einen
Grin you not so silly Escherich Over such an

Fall, wenn der zum Beispiel dem Himmler zu Ohren
affair when it for ~~the~~ example the himmler to ears

kommt, kann man sich die schönste Karriere
comes can one himself the most beautiful carreer

verpfuschen, und vielleicht denken wir beide im
botch and perhaps think we both in the

KZ Sachsenhausen eines Tages noch trübselig
concentration camp (konzentrationslager) sachsenhausen one day still gloomily

darüber nach, wie schön doch die Zeiten waren, als
there-about ~~after~~ how beautiful indeed the times were when

wir noch rote Fähnchen einpieken durften.«
we still red little flags in stick could

»Keine Bange, Herr Obergruppenführer! Ich bin ein alter
No fear Mr Over-group-leader I am an old

Kriminalist und weiß, keiner kann was Besseres
criminologist and know none can what better
something

machen als wir tun: warten. Die sollen uns doch einen
do then we do wait They should us indeed a

besseren Weg vorschlagen, die Klugscheißer, wie man an
better way propose the smart-shitters how one on

meinen Klabautermann rankommt. Aber natürlich wissen die
my kobold onto comes But of course know they

auch keinen.«
also none

»Escherich, bedenken Sie, wenn vierundvierzig bei uns
Escherich think you when forty four at us

eingetrudelt sind, so heißt es, daß mindestens ebensoviel,
rolled in are so is called it that at least as many

vielleicht aber über hundert Karten heute in Berlin
perhaps but over hundred cards today in Berlin

umlaufen, Unzufriedenheit säen, Sabotage stiften. Das kann
run around discontent sow sabotage raise That can

man doch nicht ruhig mit ansehen!«
one indeed not calm along look at

»Hundert Karten im Umlauf!« lachte Escherich. »Haben
Hundred cards in the running laughed Escherich Have

Sie eine Ahnung vom deutschen Volk, Herr
you an idea of the German people Mr

Obergruppenführer! Bitte tausendmal um Entschuldigung,
Over-groups-leader Ask thousand time(s) for (an) apology

Herr Obergruppenführer, so wollte ich es wirklich nicht
Mr Over-groups-leader so wanted I it really not

sagen, es ist mir nur so rausgerutscht! Natürlich haben
say it is me only so out-rushed Of course has

Herr Obergruppenführer viel Ahnung vom deutschen
Mr Over-groups-leader much idea from the German

Volk, mehr als ich wahrscheinlich, aber die Leute haben
people more as I probably but the people have

jetzt doch solche Angst! Die liefern ab - mehr als zehn
now indeed such fear They deliver off more then ten

Karten sind bestimmt nicht im Umlauf!«
cards are definitely not in the around-walk
circulation

Nach einem zornigen Blick wegen des beleidigenden
After an angry glance because of of the insulting

Ausrufes von Escherich (diese Leute, die von der
exclamation from Escherich these people the from the

Kripo kamen, waren ein bißchen reichlich dumm und
criminal-police came were a bit richly stupid and

taten viel zu kollegial!) und einem rügenden Vorschnellen
did much too familiar and (with) a reprimanding before rush

des Armes sagte jetzt der Obergruppenführer: »Aber zehn
of the arms said now the over-groups-leader But ten

sind auch noch zuviel! Eine ist noch zuviel! Gar keine
are also still too much One is still too much At all none

darf mehr umlaufen! Sie müssen den Mann fassen,
may (any)more run around You must the man grab
circulate

Escherich – und schnell!«
Escherich and fast

Der Kommissar stand stumm da. Er hob den Blick nicht
The commissioner stood mutely there He raised the glance not

von den glänzenden Stiefelspitzen des Obergruppenführers,
from the shining boot-toes of the Over-groups-leader

er strich gedankenvoll den Schnurrbart und schwieg
he stroke thoughtful the moustache and was silent

hartnäckig.
stubborn

»Ja, da stehen Sie und schweigen!« rief Prall ärgerlich.
Yes there stand you and are silent called Prall annoyed

»Und ich weiß auch, was Sie denken. Sie denken nämlich
And I know also what you think You think namely

grade, daß ich auch so ein Klugscheißer bin, der wohl
right that I also such a smart-shitter am which well

Rüffel austeilen kann, aber nichts Besseres vorzuschlagen
telling-offs distribute can but nothing better to propose

weiß.«
knows

Rot werden konnte der Kommissar Escherich schon lange
Red become could the commissioner Escherich already long

nicht mehr. Aber er war in diesem Augenblick, da er
not (any)more But he was in this moment there he

genau über seinen heimlichen Gedanken erwischt worden
exactly over his secret thoughts caught become

war, dem Erröten so nahe wie nur möglich. Und
was the becoming red so close as only possible And

verlegen war er auch, was ihm seit endlosen Zeiten nicht
shy was he also what him since endless times not

mehr passiert war.
(any)more happened was

Obergruppenführer Prall merkte das alles wohl. Heiter
Over-groups-leader Prall noticed that everything well Cheerful

sagte er: »Nun, ich will Sie gewiß nicht in Verlegenheit
said he Now I want you certainly not in embarrassment

bringen, Escherich, ich gewiß nicht! Und ich will Ihnen
bring Escherich I certainly not And I want you

auch keine guten Ratschläge geben. Sie wissen, ich bin
also no good advice give You know I am

kein Kriminalist, ich bin in diesen Laden nur kommandiert
no criminologist I am in this shop only commanded
ordered

worden. Aber unterrichten Sie mich mal ein bißchen. Ich
become But teach you me once a bit I

werde in den nächsten Tagen bestimmt über diesen Fall
will in the next days definitely over this case

berichten müssen, da wüßte ich gerne genau Bescheid.
report must there would know I gladly exactly information
more

Der Mann ist nie beim Ablegen der Karten beobachtet
The man is never at the lay off (of) the cards observed
drop off

worden?«
become

»Nie.«
Never

»Und kein Verdacht geäußert in den Häusern, wo die
And no suspicion uttered in the houses where the
spoken out

Karten aufgefunden wurden?«
cards found became

»Verdacht? Verdacht über Verdacht! Verdacht gibt's heute
Suspicion Suspicion over suspicion Suspicion gives it today
is there

überall. Aber es steckt nirgends mehr dahinter als ein
everywhere But it sticks nowhere (any)more there behind as a

bißchen Wut auf den Nachbarn, Spitzeltum,
bit (of) anger on the neighbors snitching

Denunziantenfieber. Nein, daher kommt keine Spur!«
denouncer-fever No there-from comes no trail

»Und die Auffinder selbst? Alle unverdächtig?«
And the finders themselves All unsuspected

»Unverdächtig?« Escherich verzog den Mund. »Ach Gott,
Unsuspected Escherich pulled the mouth Oh god

Herr Obergruppenführer, unverdächtig ist heutzutage
Mr over-groups-leader unsuspected is these days

keiner.« Und nach einem raschen Blick auf das Gesicht
no one And after a quick glance on the face

seines Vorgesetzten: »Oder alle. Aber wir haben hier
of his supervisor Or all But we have here

sämtliche Finder gesiebt und noch mal gesiebt. Mit dem
all finders sifted and still once sifted With the

Schreiber der Karten hat keiner was zu tun.«
writer of the cards has none what to do

Der Obergruppenführer seufzte. »Sie hätten Pfarrer werden
The over-groups-leader sighed You had parson become

sollen. Sie können so wunderbar trösten, Escherich!« sagte
should You can so wonderful console Escherich said

er. »Bleiben also noch die Karten. Und wie steht es da
he Remain thus still the cards And how stands it there

mit den Anhaltspunkten?«
with that on-hold-points
clues

»Dürftig. Sehr dürftig!« sagte Escherich. »Nee, lieber nicht
Meager Very meager said Escherich No rather not

Pfarrer, aber die Wahrheit für Sie, Herr
parson but the truth for you Mr

Obergruppenführer! Nach dem ersten Schwupper, den er
over-groups-leader After the first whoosh which he
failure

gemacht hat mit dem einzigen Sohn, habe ich gedacht, er
made has with the only son have I thought he

würde sich mir selbst ans Messer liefern. Aber der
would himself me himself to the knife deliver But that one

ist schlau.«
is sly

»Sagen Sie mal, Escherich«, rief Prall plötzlich, »haben
Say you once Escherich called Prall suddenly have

Sie je daran gedacht, daß es auch eine Frau sein
you indeed there-on thought that it also a woman be

könnte? Mir fiel das eben so ein, als Sie vom einzigen
could Me fell that just so in as you from the only

Sohn sprachen.«
son spoke

Der Kommissar sah einen Augenblick seinen Vorgesetzten
The commissioner looked a moment his supervisor

überrascht an. Er dachte nach. Dann sagte er, bekümmert
surprised at He thought ~~after~~ Then said he troubled

den Kopf schüttelnd: »Damit ist's auch nichts, Herr
the head shaking There-with is it also nothing Mr
With that

Obergruppenführer. Das ist vielmehr grade einer der
over-groups-leader That is much more right one of the

Punkte, die ich für absolut sicher ansehe. Mein
points the I for absolutely sure on-see My

Klabautermann ist ein Witwer oder jedenfalls ein Mann,
kobold is a widow or anyhow a man

der ganz für sich allein lebt. Wäre ein Weib in
who completely for himself alone lives Would be a woman in

der Sache, das hätte längst inzwischen ein bißchen
the thing that had long in the meantime a bit

Geschwätz gegeben. Bedenken Sie: ein halbes Jahr, so
babble given Think you a half year so

lange hält keine Frau dicht!«
long holds no woman close
shuts up

»Aber eine Mutter, die den einzigen Sohn verloren hat?«
But a mother who the only son lost has

»Auch nicht. Grade die nicht!« entschied Escherich.
Also not Right that one not decided Escherich

»Wer Kummer hat, will getröstet werden, und um Trost
Who sorrow has want consoled become and for consolation

zu bekommen, muß man reden. Nein, bestimmt ist keine
to become must one talk No definitely is no

Frau in der Sache. Von der weiß nur einer, und
woman in the thing From that one knows only one and

der kann schweigen.«
that one can remain silent

»Wie gesagt: Pfarrer! Und was sonst für Anhaltspunkte?«
As said parson And what otherwise for on-hold-points
clues

»Dürftig, Herr Obergruppenführer, sehr dürftig. Ziemlich
Meager Mr over-groups-leader very meager Rather

sicher ist der Mann geizig oder hat irgendwann mal
sure is the man avaricious or has at some time once

Krach mit dem Winterhilfswerk gehabt. Denn
noise with the winter help workwinter aid organization had Then
Since

auf den Karten mag stehen, was da will, noch nicht
on the cards may stand what there wants still not

einmal hat er die Mahnung vergessen: Gebt nichts für das
once has he the warning forgotten Give nothing for the

WHW!«
winter-help-work

»Na, wenn wir nach einem in Berlin suchen sollen, der
Now when we after one in Berlin search should who

nicht gerne fürs WHW spendet, Escherich ...«
not gladly for the winter help work (winterhilfswerk) spends Escherich

»Sage ich auch, Herr Obergruppenführer. Zu wenig. Zu
Say I also Mr over-groups-leader Too little Too

dürftig.«
meager

»Und sonst?«
And otherwise

Der Kommissar zuckte die Achseln. »Wenig, nichts«, sagte
The commissioner shrugged the shoulders Little nothing said

er. »Wir können vielleicht noch mit ziemlicher Sicherheit
he We can perhaps still with quite a lot of certainty

annehmen, daß der Kartenableger keinen festen Beruf
on-take that the card-layer no firm occupation
assume fulltime

hat, denn die Karten sind zu allen Tageszeiten aufgefunden
has then the cards are at all times of day found
since

worden, zwischen morgens acht und abends neun Uhr.
become between morning eight and in the evening nine hour
o'clock

Und bei der Belebtheit der Treppenhäuser, die mein
And at the liveliness of the staircases which my

Klabautermann benutzt, ist wohl anzunehmen, daß jede
kobold used is well to assume that each

Karte ziemlich rasch nach ihrem Ablegen gefunden ist.
card rather quickly after their lay off found is
drop off

Sonst? Ein Handarbeiter, der wenig geschrieben hat in
Otherwise A hand-worker who little written has in

seinem Leben, aber mit nicht schlechter Schulbildung,
his life but with not worse education

macht kaum je einen Schreibfehler,
makes hardly indeed one write-failure

drückt sich nicht ungewandt aus ...«
presses himself not awkward out
expresses himself not awkwardly

Escherich schwieg, beide schwiegen sie ziemlich lange,
Escherich was silent both remained silent they rather long

wobei sie gedankenlos auf die Karte mit den roten
where-by they thoughtless on the map with the red

Fähnchen starrten.
little flags stared

Dann sagte der Obergruppenführer Prall: »Eine harte Nuß,
Then said the over-groups-leader Prall One hard nut

Escherich. Hart für uns beide.«
Escherich Hard for us both

Der Kommissar meinte tröstend: »Es gibt keine Nuß, die
The commissioner thought consoling It gives no nut which

so hart ist – ein Nußknacker schafft sie doch!«
so hard is a nut-cracker manages it in any case

»Mancher klemmt sich auch die Finger dabei,
Many (a person) jams himself also the finger there-by

Escherich!«
Escherich

»Nur Geduld, Herr Obergruppenführer, bloß ein bißchen
Only patience Mr over-groups-leader just a bit

Geduld!«
(of) patience

»Wenn die andern oben sie bloß haben,
If the others above she just have
that had

an mir liegt's nicht, Escherich. Na, martern Sie Ihr
on me lays it not Escherich Now torture you your
it's not me

Köpfchen mal ein bißchen, Escherich, vielleicht fällt Ihnen
little head once a bit Escherich perhaps falls you

doch noch was Besseres ein als diese blöde Warterei.
indeed still what better in as this stupid waiting
something

Heil Hitler, Escherich!«
Hail hitler Escherich

»Heil Hitler, Herr Obergruppenführer!«
Hail hitler Mr over-groups-leader

Allein geblieben, stand der Kommissar Escherich noch eine
Alone remained stood the commissioner Escherich still a

Weile vor der Karte, gedankenvoll den hellen Schnurrbart
while before the map thoughtful the bright moustache

streichelnd. Es war ja nicht ganz so, wie er seinen
stroking It was yes not completely so as he his

Vorgesetzten hatte glauben machen wollen. In diesem Falle
supervisor had believe make want in this case

war er nicht nur der abgebrühte Kriminalist, den nichts
was he not only the callous criminologist who nothing

mehr aufregen kann. Sondern er hatte Interesse
(any)more excite can But he had interest

gefunden an diesem stummen, ihm leider noch
found on this mute him unfortunately still

gänzlich unbekannten Kartenschreiber, der sich da
completely unknown card writer who himself there

schonungslos und doch so vorsichtig, so klug berechnend
ruthless and indeed so carefully so sensibly calculating

in einen fast aussichtslosen Kampf gestürzt hatte. Dieser
in an almost out-see-less fight rushed had This
hopeless

Fall Klabautermann war zuerst nur einer von vielen
case kobold was first only one from many

gewesen. Dann hatte er ihn warm gemacht. Er mußte
been Then had he him warm made He must
it

diesen Mann finden, der da mit ihm unter den
this man find who there with him under the

zehntausend Dächern von Berlin saß, er mußte ihn von
ten-thousand roofs of Berlin sat he must him from

Angesicht zu Angesicht sehen, ihn, der dem Kommissar
face to face see him who the commissioner

allwöchentlich mit der Regelmäßigkeit einer Maschine zwei,
all-weekly with the regularity of a machine two

drei Postkarten am Montagabend, spätestens am
three postcards at the Monday evening no later than at the

Dienstagvormittag auf den Schreibtisch sandte.
Tuesday before afternoon on the desk sent

Escherich war längst weit entfernt von jener Geduld, die
Escherich was long far removed from that patience which

er dem Obergruppenführer eben noch so sehr empfohlen
he the over-groups-leader just still so very advised

hatte. Escherich jagte – dieser alte Kriminalist war ein
had Escherich hunted this old criminologist was a

echter Jäger. Das steckte ihm im Blut. Er hetzte
real hunter That stuck him in the blood He rushed
hounded

Menschen, wie andere Jäger Schweine hetzten. Daß die
people like other hunters swine hounded That the
boars

Schweine und die Menschen am Schluß der Jagd
swine and the people at the end of the hunt
boars

sterben mußten, das rührte ihn nicht. Es war dem
die must that touched him not It was the

Schwein bestimmt, auf diese Art zu sterben, wie es auch
swine defined on this way to die like it also

den Menschen, die solche Karten schrieben, bestimmt war.
the people who such cards wrote definitely was

Er hatte sich längst den Kopf zermartert, wie er
He had himself long the head tormented how he

schneller an den Klabautermann herankommen könnte –
faster on the kobold to-on-come could
come upon

so was brauchte ihm der Obergruppenführer Prall
so what needed him the over-group-leader Prall
something like that

nicht erst zu empfehlen. Aber er fand keinen Weg, denn
not first to advise But he found no way then

es gab hier nur Geduld. Man konnte nicht wegen einer
it gave here only patience One could not because of a

solch unbedeutenden Sache den ganzen Polizeiapparat in
such insignificant thing the whole police-machine in

Bewegung setzen, jede Wohnung in Berlin durchsuchen
movement set each house in Berlin through-search

lassen – ganz abgesehen davon, daß er nicht solche
let completely aside there-from that he not such

Beunruhigung in die Stadt tragen durfte. Er mußte
unrest in the city carry was allowed He must

immer weiter Geduld haben ...
always further patience have

Und wenn man genug Geduld gehabt hatte, da geschah
And when one enough patience had had there happened

es dann plötzlich: fast immer geschah etwas. Der
it then suddenly almost always happened something The

Verbrecher beging einen Fehler, oder der Zufall spielte
criminal committed a failure or the coincidence played

ihm einen Streich. Auf eines von diesen beiden mußte
him a prank On one of these both must

man warten, auf den Zufall oder auf den Fehler. Eines
one wait on the coincidence or on the failure One

geschah immer oder fast immer. Escherich hoffte, daß es
happened always or almost always Escherich hoped that it

in diesem Falle kein »fast immer« geben würde. Er war
in this case no almost always give would He was

interessiert, oh, er war stark interessiert. Im Grunde war
interested oh he was strong interested In the ground was

es ihm ganz egal, ob er hier einem Verbrecher das
it him completely equal whether he here a criminal the

Handwerk legte oder nicht. Escherich, es ist schon gesagt
hand-werk laid stopped or not Escherich it is already said

worden, Escherich jagte. Nicht um des Bratens willen,
become Escherich hunted Not for of the roast's will

sondern weil das Jagen eine Lust ist. Er wußte, im
but because the hunt a desire is He knew in the

gleichen Augenblick, wo das Wild
same moment where the wild (animal)

zur Strecke gebracht, der Verbrecher gefangen und ihm
to the distance caught is brought the criminal caught and him

seine Verbrechen hinreichend bewiesen waren – in dem
his crimes sufficiently proved were in the

gleichen Moment würde Escherichs Interesse an diesem
same moment would Escherich's interest on this

Fall aufhören. Das Wild war erlegt, der Mann saß in
case stop The wild (animal) was put down the man sat in

Untersuchungshaft - die Jagd war zu Ende. Auf ein
research-arrest the hunt was to end On a

Neues!
new (one)

Escherich hat den farblosen Blick von der Karte gewendet.
Escherich has the colorless glance from the map turned

Er sitzt jetzt an seinem Schreibtisch und ißt langsam und
He sits now at his desk and eats slowly and

gedankenvoll seine Frühstücksstullen. Als das Telefon
thoughtfully his breakfast-sandwiches As the phone

klingelt, greift er nur zögernd danach. Noch ganz
rings grabs he only hesitating there-after Still completely

gleichgültig hört er die Meldung: »Hier Polizeirevier
indifferent hears he the notice Here police-station

Frankfurter Allee. Kommissar Escherich?«
Frankfurter avenue Commissioner Escherich

»Am Apparat.«
At the machine

»Sie bearbeiten den Fall: Karte Unbekannt?«
You work on the case Card Unknown

»Ja. Was gibt's? Schnell ein bißchen!«
Yes What gives it Fast a little
is it

»Wir haben mit ziemlicher Sicherheit den Kartenverteiler
We have with quite a certainty the card-distributer

gefaßt.«
caught

»Bei der Verteilung?«
At the distribution

»Nahezu. Er leugnet natürlich.«
Near-to(it) he lies of course

»Wo haben Sie ihn?«
Where have you him

»Noch bei uns auf dem Revier.«
Still with us on the bureau

»Behalten Sie ihn dort, ich bin mit meinem Wagen in
Keep you him there I am with my car in

zehn Minuten bei Ihnen. Und: nicht weiter vernehmen!
ten minutes with you And not further interrogate

Den Mann in Ruhe lassen! Ich will mit ihm selber
The man in rest leave I want with him self

sprechen. Verstanden?«
speak Understood

»Zu Befehl, Herr Kommissar!«
At (your) order Mr commissioner!

»Ich komme dann!«
I come then

Einen Augenblick stand Kommissar Escherich fast reglos
A moment stood commissioner Escherich almost motionless

über dem Telefon. Der Zufall – der gnädige, gute
over the phone The coincidence the gracious good

Zufall! Er hatte es ja gewußt, nur Geduld mußte
coincidence He had it yes indeed known only patience must

man haben!
one have

Er ging rasch zur ersten Vernehmung des
He went quickly to the first interrogation of the

Kartenverteilers.
card distributor

Ein halbes Jahr danach: Enno Kluge

A half year after: Enno Kluge

Der Feinmechaniker Enno Kluge saß ungeduldig wartend
The precision mechanic Enno Kluge sat impatiently waiting

im Vorzimmer eines Arztes. Er saß dort mit noch
in the antechamber of a doctor He sat there with still

andern dreißig oder vierzig Wartenden. Eine stets
other thirty or fourty waiting An all the time

gereizte Sprechstundenhilfe rief eben die Nummer 18 aus,
irritated speak-hour-help called just the number 18 out
receptionist

Enno aber hatte die Nummer 29. Er würde noch über
Enno however had the number 29. He would still over

eine Stunde sitzen müssen, und in der Kneipe »Ferner
an hour sit must and in the pub Further

liefen« wartete man schon auf ihn.
walk waited one already on him

Enno Kluge konnte es nicht länger beim Sitzen aushalten.
Enno Kluge could it not longer at the sitting out-hold
with the bear

Er wußte gut, er durfte nicht eher gehen, bis der
he knew good he was allowed not before to go until the
well

Arzt da vorn ihn krank geschrieben hatte, sonst
doctor there in the front him sick written had otherwise

gab es Stunk in der Fabrik. Aber eigentlich konnte er
gave it stink in the factory But actually could he

gar nicht länger warten, sonst war es zu spät, noch
at all not longer wait otherwise was it too late still

seine Rennwetten abzuschließen.
his run-betting to close off
horse racing bets to make

Enno will im Wartezimmer auf und ab gehen. Aber
Enno wants in the waiting-room up and down go But

dafür ist es viel zu voll, er wird angeschnauzt. So
therefore is it much too full he becomes snapped at So
for that

zieht er sich auf den Flur zurück, und als ihn die
pulls he himself on the hall back and as him the

Sprechstundenhilfe dort entdeckt und sehr gereizt
speak-hours-help there discovers and very irritated

auffordert, ins Wartezimmer zurückzugehen, fragt er sie
demands in the waiting-room back to go asks he her

nach der Toilette.
after the toilet
for

Sie zeigt sie ihm widerspenstig genug, und sie will auch
She shows her him unwilling enough and she want also
it

abwarten, bis der Mann wieder herauskommt. Aber dann
off-wait until the man again comes out but then
to await

geht die Flurklingel ein paarmal kurz nacheinander, und
goes the floor-bell a few times short after each other and

sie muß den 43., den 44., den 45. Patienten empfangen,
she must the 43rd the 44th the 45th patient receive

sie	hat	Personalien	aufzunehmen,	Kartothekkarten
she	has	personal details	to take up	index cards
			to register	

auszufüllen,	Krankenscheine	zu	stempeln.
to fill out	sick-certificates	to	stamp
	health certificates		

So	geht	das	vom	frühen	Morgen	bis	in	die	späte
so	goes	that	from the	early	morning	until	in	the	late

Nacht.	Sie	ist	halbtot,	der	Arzt	ist	halbtot,	und	nie
night	She	is	half dead	the	doctor	is	half dead	and	never

verläßt	sie	mehr	dieser	unselige	Zustand	dauernder
leaves	she	(any)more	this	unfortunate	condition	of enduring
						of permanent

Gereiztheit,	in	dem	sie	nun	schon	Wochen	und	Wochen
irritation	in	which	she	now	already	weeks	and	weeks

ist.	In	diesem	Zustand	hat	sie	einen	wahren	Haß	auf
is	In	this	condition	has	she	a	true	hate	on
									for

diesen	immer	weiter	fließenden	Strom	von	Patienten
this	always	further	flowing	flow	from	patients

geworfen,	die	sie	nie	mehr	zur	Ruhe	kommen
thrown	which	she	never	(any)more	to the	rest	come

lassen,	die	schon	morgens	um	acht	Uhr,	wenn	sie
let	which	already	in the morning	around	eight	hour	when	she
				at		o'clock		

kommt,	geduldig	an	der	Tür	stehen,	und	die	noch
comes	patiently	on	the	door	stand	and	which	still

abends um zehn im Wartezimmer herumhocken, es
in the evening around ten in the waiting-room around-squat it
at

mit ihren üblen Gerüchen erfüllend: alles Drückeberger von
with their foul smells filling all shirkers from

der Arbeit, Drückeberger von der Front, Menschen, die
the work shirkers from the front people who

sich auf eine ärztliche Bescheinigung mehr
themselves on a doctor's certificate more

Lebensmittel, bessere Lebensmittel erschleichen wollen. Alles
food better food creep in want All
sneakily acquire

Leute, die sich von ihren Pflichten drücken wollen, sie
people who themselves from her duties press want she
shirk

aber kann das nicht. Sie muß hier aushalten, darf nicht
however can that not She must here hold-out may not
endure

krank sein (was finge denn der Doktor ohne sie an?), sie
sick be what catch then the doctor without her on she

muß noch freundlich sein zu diesen Heuchlern, die
must still friendly be to this hypocrites who

alles schmutzig machen, vollschleimen, vollkotzen! Auf
everything dirty make full slime full vomit On

der Toilette liegt immer alles voll Zigarettenasche.
the toilet lies always everything full (of) cigarette ash

Dabei fällt ihr der kleine Schleicher ein, dem sie
There-by falls her the little sneak in which she

vorhin die Toilette hat zeigen müssen. Sicher sitzt der
a while ago the toilet has show must Sure sits that one

noch immer da und qualmt Zigaretten. Sie springt auf,
still always there and smokes cigarettes She jumps up

rennt hinaus, rüttelt an der Tür.
runs out shakes on the door

»Besetzt!« ruft es von drinnen.
Occupied calls it from inside

»Wollen Sie wohl machen, daß Sie da runterkommen!«
Want you well make that you there under come
get out

fängt sie zornig zu schelten an. »Denken Sie, Sie können
catches she angrily to scold on Think you you can
starts

da Stunden und Stunden sitzen? Andere Leute möchten
there hours and hours sit Other people might
would like

auch die Toilette benutzen!«
also the toilet use

Sie wirft dem an ihr vorbeischleichenden Kluge zornig die
She throws the to her past-sneaking Kluge angrily the

Worte nach: »Natürlich alles wieder vollgequalmt! Ich
words after Of course everything again full smoked I

werde dem Herrn Doktor erzählen, wie krank Sie sind!
will the gentleman doctor tell how sick you are

Sie sollen mal was erleben!«
You should once what experience
something

Entmutigt lehnt Enno Kluge im Sprechzimmer gegen die
Discouraged leans Enno Kluge in the speak-room against the
waiting room

Wand – sein Stuhl ist unterdes auch besetzt worden. Der
wall his chair is under-that also occupied become The
meanwhile

Arzt ist inzwischen bis Nummer 22 gekommen.
doctor is in the meantime until number 22 come

Wahrscheinlich ganz sinnlos, hier noch weiter zu
Probably completely senseless here still further to

warten. Das Biest da draußen ist imstande, den Arzt
wait The beast there outside is able the doctor

aufzuhetzen, daß er ihn wirklich nicht krank schreibt. Und
to incite that he him really not sick writes And

was dann? Dann funkt es draußen in der Fabrik! Er fehlt
what then Then sparks it outside in the factory He misses

nun schon mal wieder den vierten Tag; die sind imstande
now already once again the fourth day they are able

und schicken ihn wirklich noch in eine Strafkompanie oder
and send him really still in a criminal company or

in ein KZ – imstande sind die Brüder dazu!
in a concentration camp able are the brothers there-to
(konzentrationslager)

Ja, er muß heute noch einen Krankenschein kriegen, und
yes he must today still a sick-certificate get and
health certificate

es ist am schlauesten, er wartet hier weiter, da er nun
it is at the slyest he waits here further there he now
smartest

schon so lange gewartet hat. Bei einem andern Arzt ist
already so long waited has At an other doctor is

es ebenso voll, er muß bis in die Nacht sitzen, und von
it likewise full he must until in the night sit and from

diesem hier hat er wenigstens gehört, daß er leicht krank
this here has he at least heard that he easy sick

schreibt. Wird er heute eben mal nicht auf Pferde wetten,
writes Will he today just once not on horses bet

muß es eben heute mal ohne den Enno gehen, hilft
must it just today once without the Enno go helps

nichts ...
nothing

Er lehnt hüstelnd gegen die Wand, ein schwächliches
He leans coughing against the wall a weak

Etwas. Besser ein Garnichts. Von jener Abreibung durch
Something Better a nothing at all From that abrasion through
beating by

den SS-Mann Persicke hat er sich nie ganz erholen
the ss man Persicke has he himself never completely heal

können. Jawohl, mit der Arbeit war es nach ein paar
been able Yes with the work was it after a few

Tagen besser geworden, obwohl seine Hände nicht wieder
days better become although his hands not again

die alte Geschicklichkeit erlangten. Es reichte jetzt gerade
the old skill acquired He reached now just

zu einem Durchschnittsarbeiter. Nie wieder würde er die
to a regular worker Never again would he the

alte Handfertigkeit erlangen, ein angesehener Mann in
old hand-skill reach an respected man in

seinem Fach werden.
his profession become

Vielleicht war es das, was ihm die Arbeit so gleichgültig
Perhaps was it that what him the work so indifferent

machte, vielleicht lag es aber auch daran, daß er
made perhaps lay it however also there-on that he

auf die Länge überhaupt nicht gerne mehr arbeitete. Er
on the length at all not gladly (any)more worked He
in the long run

sah den Sinn und den Zweck der Arbeit nicht so recht
saw the reason and the purpose of the work not so right

ein. Wozu sich so anstrengen, wenn man auch ohne
in To which himself so strain when one also without

Arbeit ausreichend leben konnte! Etwa für den Krieg? Die
work sufficiently live could About for the war They
Maybe

sollten ihren Scheißkrieg gut und gerne alleine führen, ihn
should their shit-war good and gladly alone lead him

interessierte der nicht. Vielleicht schickten die mal ihre
interested it not Perhaps sent they once their

ganzen fetten Bonzen an die Front, dann würde der
whole fat big bosses to the front then would the

Krieg schnell aus sein!
war fast out be
ended

Nein, es war aber auch nicht die Frage nach dem
No it was however also not the question after the

Sinn seiner Arbeit, die ihm alle Tätigkeit verhaßt
reason of his work which him all activity hated

machte. Es war der Umstand, daß Enno zur Zeit ohne
made It was the fact that Enno at the time without

Arbeit leben konnte. Ja, er war schwach gewesen, er
work live could Yes he was weak been he

gestand es sich jetzt ein, er war wieder zu den Weibern
confessed it himself now in he was again to the women

gegangen, erst zu Tutti, dann zu Lotte, und die waren
gone first to Tutti then to Lotte and they were

auch ganz bereit gewesen, diesen kleinen,
also completely ready been this small

anschmiegsamen Mann eine Weile durchzuschleppen. Und
cuddly man a while through-to-drag And

sobald man sich mit den Weibern einließ, war es mit
as soon as one himself with the women let in was it with

jeder geregelten Arbeit aus. Schon morgens schimpften
each regular work out Already in the morning scolded

sie, wenn er um sechs Uhr seinen Kaffee und das
they when he at six hour his coffee and the
o'clock

Frühstück verlangte, was das wohl heißen sollte? Um diese
breakfast desired what that well mean should At this

Zeit schlief jeder Mensch, und ob er es denn nötig
time slept every human and whether he it then necessary

habe? Er solle doch ruhig wieder ins warme Bett
have He should indeed calm again in the warm bed

kriechen!
crawl

Nun, ein- oder zweimal bestand man ein solches Gefecht
Now once or twice held out one a such battle

siegreich, aber, wenn man ein Enno Kluge war, kein
victorious but when one an Enno Kluge was not

drittes Mal. Man gab nach, kroch zu der Frau in die
(a) third time One gave after in crept to the woman in the

Betten und schlief noch ein oder zwei oder sogar noch
bed and slept still one or two or even still

drei Stunden.
three hours

War es so spät, ging er überhaupt nicht mehr in die
Was it so late went he at all not (any)more in the

Fabrik, sondern machte den Tag blau. Oder war es noch
factory but made the day blue Or was it still

früher, kam man eben ein bißchen zu spät zur Arbeit,
earlier came one just a bit too late to the work

mit irgendeiner lahmen Entschuldigung, wurde angeschnauzt
with some lame apology became snapped at

(aber das war man ja schon lange gewohnt, da hörte
but that was one yes already long used to there heard

man gar nicht mehr hin), tat ein paar Stunden was
one at all not (any)more away did a few hours something

und ging heim, wieder vom Geschimpfe empfangen:
and went home again from the scoldings received

Wozu man denn einen Mann im Haus hielte, wenn er
To which one then a man in the house held when he

den ganzen Tag fort war? Wegen der paar Mark! Die
the whole day away was Because of the few mark {money} They

wären gewiß leichter zu verdienen! Nein, wenn es Arbeit
were certainly easier to earn No when it work

sein mußte, wäre er besser in seinem engen
be must would be he better in his narrow

Hotelzimmerchen geblieben, Weiber und Arbeit, das ließ
hotel room remained women and work that let

sich nicht vereinigen. Bei einer ja, bei der Eva – und
himself not unite At one yes at the Eva and

natürlich hatte Enno Kluge auch wieder einen Versuch
of course had Enno Kluge also again a try

gemacht, bei seiner Frau, der Briefbestellerin,
made at his wife the postal worker

unterzukriechen. Aber da erfuhr er von der Frau
under-to-crawl But there experienced heard he from the woman

Gesch, daß die Eva verreist war. Die Gesch hatte einen
Gesch that the Eva out of town was The Gesch had a

Brief von ihr gekriegt, sie saß irgendwo im Ruppinschen
letter from her received she sat somewhere in the Ruppinsch

bei Verwandten. Jawohl, sie, die Gesch, hatte jetzt die
at relatives Yes she the Gesch had now the

Schlüssel zu der Wohnung, aber sie dachte nicht daran,
key to the house but she thought not there-on

sie dem Enno Kluge auszuhändigen. Wer schickte
she the Enno Kluge to hand over Who sent

regelmäßig die Miete: er oder seine Frau? Nun also,
regularly the rent he or his wife Now thus

gehörte die Wohnung doch ihr, nicht ihm! Sie hatte
belonged to the house indeed her not him She had

sich seinetwegen schon genug Ungelegenheiten gemacht,
himself because of him already enough inconveniences made

sie dachte gar nicht daran, ihm die Wohnung freizugeben.
she thought at all not there-on him the house free to give

Übrigens, wenn er durchaus was für seine Frau tun
By the way when he throughout something for his woman do
at all

wolle, so sollte er doch mal auf die Post gehen. Die
wanted so should he indeed once on the mail go They

hatten schon ein paarmal nach Frau Kluge geschickt, und
had already a few times after woman Kluge sent and

vor kurzem war auch eine Vorladung vor irgendein
before (a) short (while) was also an invitation before any

Parteigericht gekommen; die Gesch hatte sie einfach mit
party-court come the Gesch had them simply with

dem Vermerk »Empfänger unbekannt verreist« zurückgehen
the note Receiver unknown traveled return

lassen. Aber das auf der Post sollte er ruhig mal regeln.
let But that on the mail should he calm once arrange

Seine Frau hatte da sicher noch Ansprüche.
His wife had there sure still claims (for salary)

Das mit den Ansprüchen hatte ihn gezwickt; schließlich
That with the claims had him pinched finally

konnte er sich als rechtlicher Ehemann ausweisen, Evas
could he himself as rightful husband identify Eva's

Ansprüche waren auch seine Ansprüche. Aber der Weg
claims were also his claims But the way

erwies sich als Fehlweg; auf der Post nahmen sie ihn
proved itself as wrong way on the mail (office) took they him

mächtig in die Zange. Die Eva mußte irgendwas mit der
powerfully in the pliers The Eva must something with the
greatly

Partei angestellt haben, die waren wütend auf sie!
(political) party engaged have they were furious on her

Er hatte es gar nicht mehr eilig, sich als rechtlicher
He had it at all not (any)more hurried himself as rightful

Ehemann Evas auszuweisen - im Gegenteil, er gab sich
husband of Eva out-to-show in the contrary he gave himself
to identify

die größte Mühe, nachzuweisen, daß er schon länger von
the greatest trouble after-to-point that he already longer from
to prove

der Eva getrennt lebe und keine Ahnung von ihrem
the Eva parted live and no idea from her

Tun und Lassen hatte.
do and let had
doings

Schließlich ließen sie ihn laufen. Was war aus solchem
Finally let they him walk What was from such

kleinen Männchen auch herauszuholen, das immer bereit
(a) small little man also out to drag that always ready
who

war, gleich loszuheulen, und das bei jedem Anpfiff zu
was immediately away to howl and that at each on-whistle to
who scolding

zittern anfing? Also, er konnte gehen, er sollte machen,
tremble began Thus he could go he should make

daß er fortkam, und wenn er seine Frau doch mal
that he came away and when he his wife indeed once

wiedersah, so sollte er sie sofort hierher aufs Amt
again-saw so should he her immediately hereto on the bureau

schicken. Oder besser noch: Er solle denen einen Wink
send Or better still He should those a nudge

geben, wo sie wohnte, das Weitere würden sie von hier
give where she lived the further would they from here

aus erledigen.
out take care of

Auf seinem Heimweg zur Lotte grinste Enno Kluge
On his way home to the Lotte grinned Enno Kluge

wieder. Also die tüchtige Eva saß auch in der Klemme,
again So the efficient eva sat also in the clamp

war ins Ruppinsche zu ihren Verwandten ausgerissen und
was in the Ruppinsche to her relatives ripped out and

wagte nicht mehr, sich in Berlin sehen zu lassen! So
dared not (any)more herself in Berlin see to let So

dumm war Enno natürlich nicht gewesen, den Postleuten
stupid was Enno of course not been the mail-people

zu verraten, wohin die Eva gereist war; so schlau wie
to betray where-to the Eva traveled was so smart as

die Gesch war er auch. Es bliebe ein letzter
the Gesch was he also It would remain a last
There

Ausweg, wenn es hier in Berlin für ihn mal ganz
way out when it here in Berlin for him once completely

schiefgehen sollte, so konnte er immer noch bei der Eva
go wrong should so could he always still at the Eva

auftauchen, vielleicht nahm sie ihn doch auf. Sie würde
duck up perhaps took she him indeed up She would
appear

sich auch vor den Verwandten genieren, allzu scharf
herself also before the relatives embarrass all too sharp

gegen ihn aufzutreten. Eva gab noch was auf Ansehen
against him to step up Eva gave still something on on-look
cared for respect

und guten Ruf. Und schließlich hatte er sie ja durch
and good call standing And finally had he her yes through

Karlemanns Heldentaten in der Schraube; sie würde es
Karlemann's hero-deeds in the screw she would it

nie leiden, daß er davon ihren Verwandten erzählte,
never suffer that he there-from her relatives told

lieber noch nahm sie ihn in Kauf.
rather still took she him in purchase tolerated she him

Ein letzter Ausweg, wenn wirklich alles schiefging.
A last way out when really everything crooked went

Vorläufig hatte er noch seine Lotte. Sie war wirklich
For now had he still his Lotte She was really

ganz nett, bis auf die Schnauze, die sie nicht eine
completely nice until on the snout which she not a

Sekunde halten konnte, und bis auf ihre verdammte
second hold could and until on her damned

Angewohnheit, ewig Männer auf die Bude zu bringen. Er
habit eternally men on the digs to bring He

mußte dann die halbe, manchmal sogar die ganze Nacht
must then the half sometimes even the whole night

in der Küche hocken - und am nächsten Tag war es
in the kitchen crouch and at the next day was it

wieder nichts mit der Arbeit.
again nothing with the work

Es war nie mehr ganz das Rechte mit der Arbeit,
It was never (any)more completely the right with the work

und es würde auch nie mehr richtig werden, das
and it would also never (any)more right become that

wußte er. Aber vielleicht ging dieser Krieg schneller zu
knew he But perhaps went this war faster to

Ende, als man jetzt dachte, und es gelang ihm doch
end as one now thought and it succeeded him indeed

noch, die solange hinzuhalten. So war er wieder ganz
still it so long away-to-hold So was he again completely

allmählich ins Bummeln und ins Blaumachen gekommen.
gradually in the slacking and in the blue-making come
skipping work

Der Meister kriegte schon einen wutroten Kopf, wenn er
The master got already a anger-red head when he

ihn nur sah. Dann hatte es einen zweiten Anpfiff von
him only saw Then had it a second on-whistle from
scolding

der Leitung gegeben, aber dieses Mal hatte er nicht
the management given but this time had he not

lange vorgehalten. Enno Kluge sah doch auch, was hier
long reproached Enno Kluge saw indeed also what here

gespielt wurde, die brauchten jeden Tag Arbeiter, so leicht
played became they needed every day worker so easy

warfen die ihn nicht raus!
threw they him not out

Dann waren ganz rasch drei Bummeltage hintereinander
Then were completely quickly three slack-days behind each other

gekommen. Er hatte da so eine reizende Witwe
come He had there so an enticing widow

kennengelernt, nicht mehr ganz jung, ein bißchen
know-learned not (any)more completely young a bit
gotten to know

sehr aus dem Leim gegangen, aber entschieden etwas
very from the glue gone but decidedly something

Besseres als seine bisherigen Weiber. Hatte sie doch ein
better as his previous women Had she indeed a
than

gutgehendes Tiergeschäft in der Nähe des Königstors!
good-going animal-business in the proximity of the King's-gate
pet-shop

Sie handelte mit Vögeln und Fischen und Hunden, sie
She dealt with birds and fish and dogs she

hatte Futter und Halsbänder und Sand und Hundekuchen
had fodder and neck-bands and sand and dog-cookies
collars

und Mehlwürmer. Es gab Schildkröten bei ihr, Laubfrösche,
and mealworms It gave turtles at her tree frogs

Salamander, Katzen ... Ein Geschäft, das wirklich was
salamanders cats A business that really something

trug, und sie war eine tüchtige Frau, eine richtige
carried and she was an efficient woman a true

Geschäftsfrau.
business women

Er hatte sich ihr gegenüber als Witwer ausgegeben, er
He had himself her opposite as widow given out he
pretended

hatte sie auch glauben gemacht, Enno sei sein Nachname,
had her also believe made Enno be his last name

sie nannte ihn Hänschen. Bestimmt, er hatte Chancen bei
she called him little Hans Definitely he had opportunities at

der Frau, das hatte er während der drei Bummeltage,
the woman that had he during the three slack-days

die er ihr im Geschäft half, gut gesehen. So ein
which he her in the business helped good seen So a

Männlein, das nach einem bißchen Zärtlichkeit verlangte,
little man that after a bit (of) tenderness desired

war ihr grade recht. Sie war in den Jahren, da einer
was (to) her straight right She was in the years then a
needed when

Frau angst wird, ob sie für ihre alten Tage noch
woman fear becomes whether she for her old days still
fearful

einen Mann abkriegt. Natürlich würde sie ihn heiraten
a man gets off Of course would she him marry
gets

wollen, aber das Ding konnte er auch schon irgendwie
want but that thing could he also already somehow

hindrehen, daß es paßte. Schließlich gab es jetzt
turn away that it suited In the end gave it now
were there

Kriegstrauungen, wo die Unterlagen so genau nicht
war marriages where the under-layers so exactly not
background

geprüft wurden, und wegen der Eva brauchte er keine
checked became and because of the Eva needed he no

Bedenken zu haben. Die würde froh sein, ihn für
doubts to have That one would happy be him for

immer loszuwerden, die würde den Mund schon halten!
always to get rid of that one would the mouth already hold
keep shut

Da war plötzlich brennend in ihm der Wunsch
There was suddenly burning in him the wish

aufgetaucht, sich erst einmal ganz von der Fabrik frei
duck-up himself first once completely from the factory free
surfaced

zu machen. Er mußte ja sowieso krank spielen, da er
to make He must yes anyway sick play there he
pretend

schon drei Tage ohne Entschuldigung gefehlt hatte. Da
already three days without (an) apology missed had There

wollte er auch richtig krank sein! Und während dieser
wanted he also right sick be And during this

Krankheit würde er die Sache mit der Witwe Hete
illness would he the thing with the widow Hete

Häberle schon richtig zum Klappen bringen. Jetzt ekelte
Haberle already right to the banging bring Now disgusted
end

es ihn bei der Lotte; er konnte diese Wirtschaft nicht
it him at the lotte he could this economics not
(household)

länger ertragen, ihr Gequassel nicht, ihre Männer nicht
longer endure her jabbering not her men not

und am wenigsten ihre Zärtlichkeit, wenn sie angetrunken
and at the least her tenderness when she drunk
most of all

war. Nein, in drei, vier Wochen wollte er verheiratet sein
was No in three four weeks wanted he married be

und eine ordentliche Wirtschaft haben! Dazu mußte ihm
and a neat economics have There-to must him
(household)

der Arzt verhelfen.
the doctor help to

Erst Nummer 24, es dauert immer noch eine halbe
Only number 24 it takes always still a half

Stunde, bis Enno drankommt. Ganz mechanisch steigt
hour until Enno there-on-comes Completely mechanically rises
Enno's turn comes up

er über all die Füße weg und steht wieder auf dem Flur.
he over all the feet away and stands again on the hall

Trotz der bissigen Sprechstundenhilfe wird er noch eine
Despite the snappy speak-hours-help will he still a
assistant

Zigarette auf dem Klo stoßen. Er hat Glück, er gelangt
cigarette on the toilet bump He has fortune he reaches
smoke

ungesehen auf die Toilette, aber kaum hat er die ersten
unseen on the toilet but hardly has he the first

paar Züge gemacht, so rüttelt dieses Weibsbild doch
few pulls made so shakes this female-image indeed
wench

wieder an der Tür.
again on the door

»Sie sind ja schon wieder auf der Toilette! Sie rauchen
You are yes already again on the toilet You smoke
indeed

ja schon wieder!« schreit sie. »Ich weiß genau, daß
yes already again cries she I knows exactly that
indeed

Sie es sind! Wollen Sie wohl machen, daß Sie
you it are Wnat you well make that you

rauskommen, oder muß ich erst den Herrn Doktor
come out or must I first the gentleman doctor

holen?«
fetch

Wie sie schreit, wie ekelhaft sie schreit! Da gibt er
How she cries how horrible she cries There gives he

lieber gleich nach, wie er stets lieber nachgibt als
rather immediately to as he all the time rather to-gives as
in gives in than

widersteht. Er läßt sich von ihr in den Warteraum jagen,
withstands He lets himself from her in the waiting room chase

er sagt nicht ein Wort zu seiner Entschuldigung. Und da
he says not a word to his apology And there

lehnt er nun wieder gegen die Wand und wartet, daß
declines he now again against the wall and waits that

seine Nummer drankommt. Die wird ihn schön beim
his number there-on-comes That one. will him nicely at the
comes up

Arzt verklagen, diese verdammte Kreuzotter, die!
doctor complain to this damned viper that one
accuse

Die Sprechstundenhilfe hat den kleinen Enno Kluge auf
The speak-hours-help has the small enno kluge on
assistant

seinen Platz gejagt, sie geht zurück über den Flur. Dem
his place hunted she goes back over the hall That one

hat sie es aber besorgt!
has she it but delivered
indeed given to

Da sieht sie eine Karte am Boden liegen, etwas
There sees she a card on the ground lay somewhat

entfernt vom Briefkastenschlitz. Die Karte hat vor fünf
removed from the mailbox slit The card has before five

Minuten noch nicht hier gelegen, als sie dem letzten
minutes still not here laid as she the last

Patienten öffnete, das weiß sie genau. Und es hat gar
patient opened that knows she exactly And it has at all

nicht geklingelt, jetzt ist doch überhaupt nicht die Zeit
not rung now is indeed at all not the time

für Postzustellung.
for mail delivery

All das hat die Hilfe flüchtig gedacht, während sie sich
All that has the help fleetingly thought while she herself

nach der Karte bückt, und später weiß sie es auch
to the card stoops and later knows she it also

ganz genau, daß sie schon da, ehe sie die Karte in
completely exactly that she already there before she the card in

Händen hielt, ehe sie noch gesehen hatte, was mit ihr
(the) hands held before she still seen had what with her
it

los war, daß sie da schon das Gefühl hatte, dieser
loose was that she there already the feeling had this
wrong

kleine schleichende Mann habe etwas damit zu
little creeping man have something there-with to

schaffen.
create
do

Sie wirft nur einen Blick auf den Text, liest ein paar
She throws only a glance on the text reads a few

Worte und stürzt aufgeregt zum Arzt in das
words and rushes excited to the doctor in the

Behandlungszimmer. »Herr Doktor! Herr Doktor! Was ich
treatment room Mr doctor Mr doctor What I

da eben auf unserm Flur gefunden habe!«
there just on our hall found have

Sie unterbricht die Konsultation, sie erreicht, daß der
She interrupts the consultation she reached that the
succeeds

halbausgezogene Patient in ein Nebenzimmer geschickt
half undressed patient in a side room sent

wird, dann gibt sie dem Arzt die Karte zu lesen. Sie
becomes then gives she the doctor the card to read She

kann es kaum abwarten, daß er zu Ende gelesen hat,
can it hardly off-wait that he to end read has
to await

und schon berichtet sie von ihrem Verdacht: »Es kann
and already reported she from her suspicion It can

wirklich kein anderer gewesen sein als dieser kleine
really no other been be as this little
have

Schleicher! Gleich war er mir unsympathisch mit seinem
sneaker Immediately was he me unsympathetic with his

scheuen Blick! Und das verkörperte schlechte Gewissen,
shy glance And the embodied bad conscience

nicht einen Augenblick hat er sich ruhig halten können,
not a moment has he himself calm hold can
been able

immer auf den Flur raus, zweimal hab ich ihn von der
always on the hall out twice have I him from the

Toilette gejagt! Und wie ich das zum zweitenmal tat, da
toilet chased And as I that for the second time did there

hat hinterher die Karte auf dem Flur gelegen! Von außen
has after the card on the hall lied From outside

kann sie gar nicht eingeworfen sein, dafür hat sie viel
can she at all not thrown in be therefore has she much

zu weit ab vom Briefkastenschlitz gelegen! Herr Doktor,
too far off from the mailbox slit lain Mr doctor

rufen Sie gleich die Polizei an, ehe der Kerl
call you immediately the police on before the chap
up

wegschleicht! O Gott, er kann jetzt schon weg sein, ich
away sneaks O god he can now already away be I

muß gleich einmal nachsehen ...«
must immediately once after-see
check

Damit stürzt sie aus dem Behandlungszimmer, die Tür
There-with rushes she from the treatment room the door

hinter sich weit offen lassend.
behind herself wide open letting
leaving

Der Arzt steht da, die Karte noch immer in der Hand.
The doctor stands there the card still always in the hand

Es ist ihm äußerst peinlich, daß so was grade in seiner
it is him extremely painful that so what right in his

Sprechstunde passieren muß! Gottlob, daß die Hilfe die
speak-hour pass must Praise god that the help the
consultation hour assistant

Karte fand und daß er nachweisen kann, daß er seit
card found and that he after-point can that he since
prove

zwei Stunden sein Zimmer nicht verlassen hat, nicht
two hours his room not left has not

einmal auf der Toilette ist er gewesen. Das Mädchen hat
once on the toilet is he been The girl has
even is

recht, das beste ist, gleich die Polizei anzurufen. Er
right the best is immediately the police to call He

fängt an, im Telefonbuch nach der Nummer seines
catches on in the phone book to the number of his
starts for

Reviers zu suchen.
district to search

Das Mädchen sieht durch die offengebliebene Tür. »Er ist
The girl sees through the open-remained door He is
looks

noch da, Herr Doktor!« flüstert sie. »Er denkt natürlich,
still there Mr Doctor whispers she He thinks of course

so kann er den Verdacht von sich ablenken. Aber ich
so can he the suspicion from himself deflect But I

bin ganz sicher ...«
am completely sure

»Es ist gut«, unterbricht der Arzt die Aufgeregte.
It is good interrupts the doctor the excited one

»Machen Sie bitte die Tür zu. Ich spreche jetzt mit der
Make you please the door close I speak now with the

Polizei.«
police

Er erstattet seine Meldung, bekommt die Weisung, den
He states his report gets the instruction the

Mann unbedingt festzuhalten, bis jemand vom Revier
man absolutely fast to hold until someone from the district

kommt, gibt diese Weisung an die Hilfe weiter, sagt ihr,
comes gives this instruction to the help further says her

sie solle ihn sofort rufen, wenn der Mann Anstalten
she should him immediately call when the man moves

macht zu gehen, und setzt sich wieder in seinen
makes to go and set himself again in his

Schreibtischstuhl. Nein, die Behandlungen kann er jetzt
write-table-chair No the treatments can he now
desk chair

nicht fortsetzen, er ist zu erregt. Daß gerade ihm
not continue he is too excited That just him

so was passieren mußte, warum nur gerade ihm?
so what pass must why only right him
something like that happen

Ein gewissenloser Kerl, dieser Kartenschreiber, er brachte
A conscience-less chap this cards writer he brought
unscrupulous

die Leute in die größte Bedrängnis! Dachte er gar nicht
the people in the greatest distress Thought he at all not

an die Schwierigkeiten, die er ihnen mit seiner
on the difficulties which he them with his
of

verdammten Karte machte?
cursed cards make

Wahrhaftig, diese Karte hatte gerade noch zum Glück des
Truly this card had just still to the fortune of the

Arztes gefehlt! Jetzt war die Polizei zu ihm unterwegs,
doctor's missed Now was the police to him on the way

vielleicht geriet er doch in Verdacht, man machte eine
perhaps became he indeed in suspicion one made a

Haussuchung, und wenn sich dann auch erwies, daß der
house search and when itself then also proved that the

Verdacht falsch war, so fand man hinten in der
suspicion false was so found one in the back in the

Dienstbotenkammer ...
Servants room

Der Arzt stand auf, er mußte ihr wenigstens Bescheid
The doctor stood up he must her at least information

sagen ...
say

Und setzte sich wieder. Wie konnte er denn in Verdacht
And (he) set himself again How could he then in suspicion

geraten? Und außerdem, selbst wenn man sie fand, so
gotten And in addition himself when one her found so

war sie eben seine Hausdame, wie es ja auch ihre
was she just her house-lady how it yes also her

Papiere aussagten. All das war ja hundertfach bedacht
papers out-said showed All that was yes hunderd-times considered

und besprochen worden, seit er sich vor gut einem
and discussed become since he himself before good a

Jahr von seiner Frau, einer Jüdin, hatte scheiden lassen
year from his wife a Jewish lady had separate divorce let

müssen – unter dem Druck der Nazis. Er hatte es
must under the pressure of the nazi's He had it

getan, hauptsächlich auf ihre Bitten hin, um den Kindern

done mainly on her demand away for the children

wenigstens eine Existenz zu sichern. Später hatte er dann,

at least an existence to secure insure Later had he then

nachdem er die Wohnung gewechselt, seine ehemalige Frau

after he the house exchanged his former wife

mit falschen Papieren als seine Hausdame zurückgeholt.

with false papers as his house-lady back-gotten

Eigentlich konnte garnichts passieren, so jüdisch sah sie

Actually could nothing at all pass so Jewish looked she

gar nicht aus ...

at all not out

Diese unselige Karte! Daß sie grade auf ihn treffen

This unblessed unfortunate card That she it right on him meet

mußte! Aber wahrscheinlich war es so, daß sie überall,

must But probably was it so that she everywhere

wohin sie auch kam, Schrecken und Angst erregte. Jeder

where-to she also came fright and fear excited Each

hatte in diesen Zeiten etwas zu verbergen!

had in these times something to hide

Vielleicht war es grade der Zweck dieser Karte, Angst

Perhaps was it right the purpose of this card fear

und Schrecken zu erregen? Vielleicht wurde diese Karte

and fright to arouse Perhaps became this card

mit teuflischem Vorbedacht unter den Verdächtigen verteilt,
with devilish forethought under the suspects distributed

um festzustellen, wie sich die verhielten? Vielleicht
for to ascertain how themselves they kept up Perhaps
acted

stand er schon länger unter Beobachtung, und dies war
stood he already longer under observation and this was

nur eines der Mittel, um festzustellen, ob der
only one of the means for to ascertain whether the

Verdächtige sich keine Blöße gab?
suspect himself no nakedness gave
not bare

Er hatte sich jedenfalls korrekt benommen. Fünf Minuten
He had himself anyhow correct behaved Five minutes

nach Auffinden der Karte hatte er die Polizei verständigt.
after find up the card had he the police notified
find out

Und er konnte ihr sogar einen Verdächtigen präsentieren,
And he could her even a suspect present
them

vielleicht einen armen Teufel, der gar nichts mit der
perhaps a poor devil who at all nothing with the

Sache zu tun hatte. Nun, er konnte da nicht helfen,
thing to do had Now he could there not help

sollte der selber sehen, wie er aus der Geschichte
should that one self see how he from the story

herauskam! Die Hauptsache war, er blieb verschont.
came out The main thing was he remained spared

Und obwohl diese Erwägungen den Arzt ruhiger gemacht
And although these weighings the doctor calmer made
considerations

haben, steht er auf und macht sich rasch und sicher
have stands he on and makes himself quickly and surely

eine kleine Morphiumspritze. Die wird ihn instand
a little morphine syringe That one will him in state

setzen, diesen Herren, die da zu ihm im Anmarsch
set these gentlemen who there to him in the march

sind, ruhig und sogar ein bißchen gelangweilt zu
are calm and even a bit bored to

begegnen. Diese kleine Spritze ist das Hilfsmittel, zu dem
meet This little syringe is the help-means to which
tool

der Arzt seit der Schande seiner Scheidung, wie er
the doctor since the shame of his divorce how he

diesen Schritt innerlich noch immer nennt, häufiger seine
this step internally still always calls more often his

Zuflucht nimmt. Er ist noch kein Morphinist, weit
refuge takes He is still no addict to morphine far

entfernt, er kommt manchmal fünf, sechs Tage ohne
removed he comes sometimes five six days without

Morphium aus, aber wenn Schwierigkeiten auf seinem
morphine out but when difficulties on his

Lebensweg auftauchen, und diese Schwierigkeiten häufen
life's road duck up and these difficulties accumulate
appear

sich jetzt während des Krieges immer mehr, so nimmt
himself now while of the war always more so takes

er Morphium. Das allein hilft ihm noch, ohne diese
he morphine That alone helps him still without this

künstliche Hilfe verliert er seine Nerven. Nein, noch ist er
artificial help loses he his nerves No still is he

kein Morphinist! Aber er ist auf dem besten Wege, einer
no morphine addict But he is on the best road one

zu werden. Ach, wenn nur erst dieser Krieg vorbei wäre,
to become Oh when only first this war past would be

daß man aus diesem elenden Lande hinaus könnte! Mit
that one from this miserable country out could With

dem kleinsten Hilfsarztposten draußen im Ausland
the smallest assistant-doctor's post outside in the foreign country

würde er zufrieden sein.
would he satisfied be

Einige Minuten darauf empfängt ein blasser, etwas
Some minutes thereupon receives a pale somewhat

müder Arzt die beiden Herren von der Polizeiwache.
more tired doctor the both gentlemen from the police guard

Der eine ist nur ein uniformierter Wachtmeister zur
The one is only a uniformed guard-master officer to the

Aufsicht über die Flurtür hierher kommandiert. Er löst
oversight over the floor door hereto commanded He dissolves relieves

sofort die Sprechstundenhilfe ab.
immediately the speak-hour-help assistant off

Der andere ist ein Zivilist, Kriminalassistent Schröder - in
The other is a civilian criminal-assistent Schroeder in

seinem Behandlungszimmer übergibt ihm der Arzt die
his treatment room over-gives him the doctor the

Karte. Was er aussagen könne? Nun er kann eigentlich
card What he say out could Now he can actually
state

nichts aussagen, er habe seit über zwei Stunden hier
nothing say out he have since over two hours here
state

schon ohne Unterbrechung Patienten abgefertigt, etwa
already without under-breaking patients worked off about
pause

zwanzig oder fünfundzwanzig hintereinander. Aber er werde
twenty or twenty five behind each other But he will

sofort die Sprechstundenhilfe holen.
immediately the speak-hours-help get
assistant

Die Hilfe kommt, und sie hat viel auszusagen. Sehr viel.
The help comes and she has much out-to-say Very much
to state

Sie schildert diesen Schleicher, wie sie ihn nur nennt, mit
She paints this sneaker as she him only calls with

einem Haß, der zwei harmlosen Rauchereien auf der
a hate which two harmless smokings on the

Toilette gegenüber völlig unbegreiflich ist. Der Arzt
toilet opposite totally incomprehensible is The doctor

beobachtet sie genau, wie sie da erregt, mit oft
observes her exactly how she there excited with often

versagender Stimme aussagt. Er denkt: Ich muß jetzt mal
failing voice testifies He thinks I must now once

sehen, daß sie wirklich was Ernstliches gegen ihren
see that she really what serious against her

Basedow unternimmt. Es wird immer schlimmer mit
Basedow undertakes It becomes always worse with
(some accused)

ihr. So erregt, wie sie jetzt spricht, ist sie eigentlich
her So excited as she now speaks is she actually

schon nicht mehr voll zurechnungsfähig.
already not (any)more full accountable
sane

Der Kriminalassistent scheint Ähnliches zu denken. Mit
The criminal-assistent seems similar to think With

einem kurzen »Danke! Ich weiß jetzt vorläufig genug«,
a short Thanks I know now for now enough

unterbricht er ihre Aussagen. »Zeigen Sie mir jetzt noch,
interrupts he her saying out Show you me now still
statements

Fräulein, wo die Karte auf dem Flur gelegen hat. Aber
miss where the card on the floor lied has But

bitte möglichst genau!«
please as possible precise
most

Das Fräulein, die Hilfe, legt die Karte auf eine Stelle, die
The miss the help lays the card on a spot that

sie vom Briefkastenschlitz, wie es scheint, unmöglich
she from the letter-box-slit as it seems impossible
mailbox

erreichen kann. Aber der Assistent probiert, vom
reach can But the assistent tries by the

Wachtmeister unterstützt, so lange das Einwerfen der
officer supported so long the throw in of the

Karte, bis sie nahezu auf dem von der Hilfe bezeichneten
card until she close on the from the help shown

Platz zu liegen kommt. Nahezu, etwa zehn Zentimeter
place to lie comes Close about ten centimeters

fehlen ...
lack

»Da könnte sie doch auch gelegen haben, Fräulein?« fragt
There could she indeed also lied have young lady asks

der Assistent.
the assistent

Die Sprechstundenhilfe ist sichtlich entrüstet, daß dem
The speak-hours-help is visibly indignant that the
doctor's assistant

Assistenten dies Experiment geglückt ist. Sie erklärt mit
assistant this experiment succeeded is she explained with

Entschiedenheit: »Nein, so nah an der Tür kann die Karte
decisiveness No so near on the door can the card

unmöglich gelegen haben! Eher noch weiter in den
impossible lied have Before still further in the
More likely

Flur hinein, als ich vorhin zeigte. Ich glaube jetzt, sie
hall inside as I a while ago showed I believe now she

lag hier direkt bei dem Stuhl.« Und sie zeigt einen Fleck,
lay here directly at the chair And she shows a spot

der noch einen halben Meter weiter vom Einwurf
which still a half meter further from the in-throw

entfernt liegt. »Ich bin fast sicher, daß ich gegen diesen
removed lies I am almost sure that I against this

Stuhl beim Aufheben gestoßen habe.«
chair at the lift up bumped have

»Soso«, sagt der Assistent und mustert kühl die Zornige.
Well well says the assistant and inspects coolly the angry one

Im Innern macht er einen Strich durch alle ihre
In the inside makes he a stroke through all her

Aussagen. Die ist ja hysterisch, denkt er. Der
say out statements That one is indeed hysterical thinks he That one

fehlt natürlich ein Mann. Na ja, wo alle im Felde
lacks of course a man Now yes where all in the field

sind, und sehr verlockend sieht sie auch nicht aus.
are and very alluring sees looks she also not out

Er wendet sich laut an den Arzt: »Ich möchte jetzt wie
He turns himself loud to the doctor I may now like

ein beliebiger Patient drei Minuten im Wartezimmer
a regular patient three minutes in the waiting-room

sitzen und mir den beschuldigten Herrn erst einmal so
sit and me the accused gentleman first once so

ansehen, ohne daß er weiß, wer ich bin. Das läßt sich
look at without that he knows who I am That lets itself

doch machen?«
indeed do

»Natürlich läßt sich das machen. Fräulein Kiesow wird
Of course lets itself that do Miss Kiesow will

Ihnen sagen, wo er sitzt.«
them say where he sits

»Steht!« erklärt die Hilfe ärgerlich. »So einer setzt
Stands clears up the help annoyed So one sits
stands up assistant

sich doch nicht! Der tritt lieber den andern auf den
himself indeed not That one steps rather the others on the

Füßen herum! Dem läßt sein schlechtes Gewissen doch
feet around That one lets his bad conscience indeed

keine Ruhe! Dieser Schleicher ...«
no rest This sneaker

»Also, wo steht er?« unterbricht sie der Assistent wieder
So where stands he interrupts she the assistant again

und nicht sehr höflich.
and not very courteous
polite

»Vorhin stand er beim Spiegel am Fenster«, antwortet sie
Before stood he at the mirror at the window answers she

ihm gekränkt. »Aber ich kann natürlich nicht sagen, wo
him hurtfully But I can of course not say where

er jetzt steht, so unruhig, wie der ist!«
he now stands so restless as that one is

»Ich werde ihn schon finden«, meint der Assistent
I will him already find means the assistant

Schröder. »Sie haben ihn mir ja beschrieben.«
Schroeder You have him me indeed described

Und er geht ins Wartezimmer.
And he goes in the waiting room

Dort herrscht einige Erregung. Seit über zwanzig Minuten
There prevails some excitement Since over twenty minutes

ist kein Patient zum Arzt gerufen worden – wie lange
is no patient to the doctor called become how long

sollen sie hier noch sitzen? Sie haben wahrhaftig
should they here still sit They have truly

anderes zu tun! Wahrscheinlich fertigt der Doktor vorne
other (things) to do Probably readies finishes the doctor in front

gut zahlende Privatpatienten ab, und die Kassenpatienten
good paying private patients off and the fund-patients

hier können sitzen, bis sie schwarz werden! Aber so
here can sit until they black become But so

machen es doch alle Ärzte, mein lieber Herr, da können
do it indeed all doctors my dear sir there can

Sie hingehen, wo Sie wollen! Überall hat das Geld
you go away where you want Everywhere has the money

den Vortritt!
the step forward
priority

Während die Berichte über die Käuflichkeit der Ärzte
While the messages over the venality of the doctors

immer höhere Wellen schlagen, mustert der Assistent
always higher waves strike inspects the assistant

schweigend seinen Mann. Er hat ihn sofort erkannt.
in silence his man He has him immediately recognized

Der Mann ist weder so unruhig noch so schleicherisch,
The man is neither so restless nor so sneaky

wie ihn die Hilfe geschildert hat. Er steht da ganz
as him the help painted has He stands there completely
described

ruhig an seinem Spiegel, an der Unterhaltung der andern
calm at his mirror on the conversation of the others

beteiligt er sich nicht. Er scheint nicht einmal auf das
involves he himself not He seems not once on that
even

zu hören, was die sagen, und das tut man sonst doch
to hear what they say and that does one otherwise indeed
listen

gerne, eine langweilige Wartezeit sich zu verkürzen. Er
gladly a boring waiting time himself to shorten he

schaut ein bißchen stumpfsinnig und ein bißchen ängstlich
stares a bit dumb and a bit fearfully
anxiously

darein. Kleiner Arbeiter, entscheidet der Assistent. Nee, ein
therein Little worker decides the assistant No a

bißchen besser, die Hände sehen geschickt aus,
bit better the hands see fine out

Arbeitsspuren, aber nicht nach schwerer Arbeit ... Anzug
work-traces but not after heavy work Suit

und Mantel mit großer Sorgfalt instand gehalten, was
and coat with great care in state held what

freilich nicht über ihr Abgetragensein hinwegtäuscht. Im
indeed not over her worn out being away deceives In the

ganzen nichts von dem Mann, den man sich nach dem
whole nothing from the man that one himself after the

Ton der Karte vorstellt. Der schreibt doch einen
tone the card imagines That one writes indeed a

ganz kräftigen Stil, und nun dieses sorgenvolle
completely powerful style and now this worryful

Kaninchen ...
little rabbit

Aber der Assistent weiß längst, daß die Menschen oft
But the assistant knows long that the people often

sehr anders sind, als sie aussehen. Und dieser Mann ist
very different are than they look And this man is

immerhin durch die Aussage der Zeugin so schwer
after all through the statement of the witness so heavy

belastet, daß man die Angelegenheit wenigstens nachprüfen
accused that one the matter at least after-proof
double check

muß. Dieser Kartenschreiber muß die Herren oben ein
must This card writer must the gentlemen above a

bißchen nervös gemacht haben, erst neulich gab's da
bit nervous made have first the other day gave it there

wieder unter »Geheim! Streng geheim!« einen Befehl, daß
again under secret strict secret an order that

auch der kleinsten Spur in dieser Sache unverzüglich
also the smallest trace in this thing immediately

nachzugehen sei.
to check be

Wär ganz schön, wenn ich da einen kleinen Erfolg
Were completely beautiful when I there a small success

hätte! denkt der Assistent. Es wird höchste Zeit mit
had thinks the assistant It becomes highest time with

einer kleinen Beförderung.
a little promotion

In dem allgemeinen Geschimpfe geht er fast unbeachtet
In the general scolding goes he almost unwatched

an den kleinen Mann beim Spiegel heran, tippt ihn auf
to the small man at the mirror near taps him on

die Schulter und sagt: »Kommen Sie doch mal einen
the shoulder and says Come you indeed once a

Augenblick auf den Flur. Ich möchte Sie mal was
moment on the hall I may you once something

fragen.«
ask

Gehorsam folgt ihm Enno Kluge, wie er jedem Befehl
Obediently follows him Enno Kluge as he each order

gehorsam folgt. Aber während er schon hinter dem
obediently follows But while he already behind the

unbekannten Herrn dreingeht, erfaßt ihn Angst: Was
unknown gentleman there in goes grasps him fear What

soll das? Was will der von mir? Der sieht doch
should that What wants that one from me That one looks indeed

wie ein Bulle aus, und er spricht auch ganz wie ein
like a cop out and he speaks also completely like a

Bulle. Was habe ich mit der Kripo zu tun – ich
cop What have I with the criminal-police to do I

habe doch gar nichts getan!
have indeed at all nothing done

Im gleichen Augenblick fällt ihm der Einbruch bei der
In the same moment falls him the burglary at the

Rosenthal ein. Es ist kein Zweifel, der Borkhausen ist
rosenthal in It is no doubt the Borkhausen is

hochgegangen und hat ihn verpfiffen. Und die Angst
went up blown and has him whistled betrayed And the fear

wird stärker in ihm, er hat doch geschworen, er will
becomes stronger in him he has indeed sworn he wants

nichts aussagen und wenn er nun doch aussagt, wird ihn
nothing say out and when he now indeed testifies will him
tell

dieser Kerl von der SS wieder vornehmen und vertrimmen,
this chap from the ss again take in front and trim down
take apart beat up

und diesmal noch viel schlimmer! Er darf nichts aussagen,
and this time still much worse He may nothing say out
tell

aber wenn er nichts aussagt, nimmt ihn sich dieser
but when he nothing testifies takes him himself this

Bulle vor, und dann schwatzt er doch. Hier Verderben,
cop before and then chatters he indeed Here ruin

dort Verderben ... Oh, diese Angst!
there ruin Oh this fear

Als er auf den Flur tritt, sehen ihn vier Gesichter
As he on the hall steps look him four faces

erwartungsvoll an – aber er sieht sie gar nicht, er sieht
expectantly at but he sees them at all not he sees

nur die Uniform des Schupos und weiß, daß er mit
only the uniform of the bobbies and knows that he with
(Schutz-Polizei)

seiner Angst recht gehabt hat, daß er nun wirklich
his fear right had has that he now really

zwischen Verderben und Verderben steht.
between ruin and ruin stands

Und diese Angst verleiht Enno Kluge Eigenschaften, die er
And this fear loans Enno Kluge properties that he

sonst nicht besitzt, nämlich Entschlußkraft, Stärke und
otherwise not possesses namely determination strength and

Schnelligkeit. Er wirft den überraschten Assistenten, der
speed He throws the surprised assistant which

dies nie von dem kleinen Schwächling erwartet hätte,
this never from the small weakling expected had

gegen den Schupo, läuft an Arzt und Hilfe vorbei,
against the bobby runs at doctor and help past
(Schutz Polizei)

reißt die Flurtür auf und ist schon auf der Treppe ...
rips the floor door up and is already on the stairs
open

Aber hinter ihm trillert die Pfeife des Schupos, und
But behind him trills the whistle of the bobbies and

diesem langbeinigen jungen Mann ist er im Tempo nicht
this long-legged young man is he in the tempo not
speed

gewachsen. Auf der untersten Treppe wird er eingeholt,
grown On the lowest stairs becomes he overtaken
good enough for

der Schupo versetzt ihm einen Schlag, der ihn gleich
the bobby sets him a strike which him immediately
gives

auf die Stufen niederschickt, und als er vor drehenden
on the steps down sends and as he before turning

Sonnen und Feuerkreisen wieder sehen kann, sagt der
suns and fire crosses again see can says the

Schupo freundlich lächelnd: »Na, streck mal deine süße
bobby friendly smiling Now stretch once your sweet

Pfote her! Will dir lieber ein Armband schenken. Das
paws away here Want you dear a bracelet give The

nächste Mal machen wir so 'nen Spaziergang gemeinsam,
next time make we so a walk together

was?«
what

Und schon hat die Stahlfessel um sein Handgelenk
And already has the steel-shackle around his wrist

geklirrt, und es geht wieder treppauf, zwischen dem
clinked and it goes again up the stairs between the

schweigsamen, finster blickenden Bullen und dem vergnügt
silent dark looking cop and the pleased

lächelnden Schupo, dem dieser kleine Ausreißer nur
smiling bobby (Schutz Polizei) which this little runaway only

Spaß macht.
fun makes

Oben, wo die Patienten auf dem Flur stehen und gar
Above where the patients on the hall stand and at all

nicht mehr böse sind über die lange Wartezeit bei
not (any)more angry are over the long waiting time at

ihrem Doktor, denn eine Verhaftung ist immer etwas
their doctor then an arrest is always something

Interessantes, und wie die Sprechstundenhilfe erzählt hat,
interesting and as the speak-hours-help told has

ist dies sogar ein Politischer, ein Kommunist, und diesen
is this even a political a communist and these

Brüdern geschieht es ganz recht - oben also geht es
brothers happens it completely right above thus goes it

an all diesen Gesichtern vorbei in das Behandlungszimmer
on all these faces past in the treatment room

des Arztes. Das Fräulein Kiesow wird gleich von
of the doctor's The miss Kiesow becomes immediately by

dem Assistenten hinausgeschickt, der Arzt aber darf bei
the assistant sent out the doctor however may at

der Vernehmung dabeibleiben und hört, wie der Assistent
the interrogation remain and hears how the assistant

sagt: »So, mein Sohn, nun setz dich erst mal hier auf
says So my son now set you first once here on

den Stuhl und ruh dich von deiner Rennerei aus. Du
the chair and rest yourself from your runnings out You

machst ja ordentlich einen abgehetzten Eindruck!
make indeed properly a heated impression

Wachtmeister, Sie können dem Herrn erst einmal die
Guard you can the gentleman first once the

Fessel wieder abnehmen. Der rennt uns nicht noch
shackles again take off That one runs us not another

einmal weg - oder?«
once away or

»Nein, nein!« versichert Enno Kluge verzweifelt, und schon
No no assures Enno Kluge desperately and already

rollen die Tränen über sein Gesicht.
roll the tears over his face

»Würde ich dir auch nicht geraten haben! Das nächste
Would I you also not advised have The next

Mal knallt's, und ich kann schießen, Sohn!« Der Assistent
time bangs it and I can shoot son The assistant

bleibt dabei, den wohl zwanzig Jahre älteren Kluge mit
remains there-by the well twenty years older kluge with

»Sohn« anzureden. »Na, weine man bloß nicht so! So
son to address Now cry one just not so So

schlimm wird's ja gar nicht gewesen sein, was du
bad will it indeed at all not been be what you

ausgefressen hast. Oder?«
out-eaten have Or
get up to

»Gar nichts habe ich ausgefressen!« stößt Enno Kluge
At all nothing have I out-eaten utters Enno Kluge
get up to

unter Tränen hervor. »Rein gar nichts!«
under tears forth Clean at all nothing

»Aber natürlich, Sohn!« stimmt der Assistent zu. »Darum
But of course son agrees the assistant ~~to~~ Therefore

rennst du ja auch so schnell wie ein Hase, sobald
run you indeed also so fast like a hare as soon as

du die Uniform von einem Wachtmeister siehst! Doktor,
you the uniform from a police officer see Doctor

haben Sie nicht irgendwas, womit Sie diesem
have you not anything where-with you this
with which

Jammergestell wieder ein bißchen auf die Beine helfen
whine rack again a bit on the legs help
whiner

können?«
can

Jetzt, da der Arzt fühlt, alle Gefahr ist von seinem
Now there the doctor feels all danger is from his

eigenen Haupt abgewendet, sieht er mit herzlichem
own head turned away sees he with heartily

Mitleid auf dieses unglückselige Männlein. Auch so ein
compassion on this unfortunate little man Also so a

Geschlagener des Lebens ist das, den jedes Hindernis
beaten by the life is that who each obstacle

umwirft. Der Doktor ist in der Versuchung, dem Kleinen
throws over The doctor is in the temptation the small one

auch eine Spritze Morphium zu bewilligen, in leichtester
also a syringe morphine to indulge in (the) lightest

Dosierung. Er wagt es aber nicht recht wegen des
dose He dares it however not right because of of the
really

Kriminalbeamten. Lieber ein bißchen Brom ...
criminal officials Rather a bit bromine
detectives

Aber während er das Bromsalz noch im Wasser auflöst,
But while he the bromine salt still in the water disolves

sagt Enno Kluge: »Ich brauch nichts. Ich will nichts
says Enno Kluge I need nothing I want nothing

einnehmen. Ich lasse mich nicht vergiften. Ich will lieber
take in I let myself not poison I want rather

aussagen ...«
say out
make a statement

»Na also!« sagt der Kriminalbeamte. »Wußte ich doch, daß
Now so says the criminal official Knew I indeed that
then detective

du vernünftig werden würdest, Sohn! Dann erzähle also
you sensible become would son Then tell also

mal ...«
once

Und Enno Kluge wischt sich die Tränen von den Backen
And Enno Kluge wipes himself the tears from the jaws

und fängt an zu erzählen ...
and catches on to tell
starts

Als er nämlich mit Weinen anfing, hat er ganz echte
As he namely with crying began has he completely real

Tränen geweint, einfach weil ihn seine Nerven
tears cried simply because him his nerves

im Stich ließen. Wenn es aber auch ganz echte
in the sting let When it however also completely real
let down

Tränen waren, so weiß Enno doch längst aus seinem
tears were so knows Enno indeed long from his

Umgang mit den Frauen, daß man beim Weinen sehr gut
dealing with the women that one at the crying very good

nachdenken kann. Und bei diesem Nachdenken ist er
pondering can And at this pondering is he

darauf gekommen, daß es doch sehr unwahrscheinlich ist,
thereupon come that it indeed very improbable is

daß die ihn aus dem Sprechzimmer eines Arztes heraus
that they him from the speak-room of a doctor out
consultation room

wegen Einbruchs verhaften. Wenn die ihn wirklich
because of burglary arrest When they him really

beschattet haben, dann konnten sie ihn auch auf der
shadowed have then could they him also on the

Straße oder im Treppenflur verhaften, da brauchten sie
street or in the stairway arrest there needed they

ihn nicht erst zwei Stunden im Wartezimmer
him not first two hours in the waiting room

sitzenzulassen ...
sitting to let

Nein, diese Sache hat wahrscheinlich nicht das geringste
No this thing has probably not the least

mit dem Einbruch bei der Frau Rosenthal zu tun.
with the burglary at the woman Rosenthal to do

Wahrscheinlich liegt der Verhaftung ein Irrtum zugrunde,
Probably lies the arrest a mistake to ground

und dunkel ahnt Enno Kluge, daß sie irgendwas mit der
and dark suspects Enno Kluge that she something with the

bösartigen Sprechstundenhilfe zu tun hat.
malicious speak-hours-help to do has
doctor's assistant

Aber nun ist er einmal getürmt, und nie wird er so
But now is he once towered and never will he so
arrested

einem Bullen einreden können, daß er nur aus Nervosität
a cop talk in be able that he only from nervousness

weggelaufen ist, einfach, weil er jede Besinnung beim
run away is simply because he each sense at the

Anblick einer Uniform verliert. So was nimmt ihm solch
sight of a uniform loses So what takes him such
believes

ein Bulle nie ab. Er muß also schon was Glaubhaftes,
a cop never off He must thus already what believable

Nachzuprüfendes gestehen, und was das sein soll, das
provable confess and what that be should that

weiß er auch gleich. Es ist zwar schlimm, darüber zu
knows he also immediately It is indeed bad about it to

sprechen, und die Folgen sind nicht abzusehen, aber
speak and the consequences are not to be foreseen but

von zwei Übeln ist solch ein Geständnis gewiß das
from two bad things is such a confession certainly the

kleinere.
smaller

Als er also jetzt zum Reden aufgefordert ist, trocknet er
As he thus now to the talking asked is dries he

sich die Tränen ab und beginnt mit leidlich fester
himself the tears off and begins with tolerable more firmly

Stimme von seiner Arbeit als Feinmechaniker zu sprechen,
voice from his work as precision mechanic to speak

und wie er so viel krank gewesen ist, daß die Herren
and how he so much sick been is that the gentlemen

dort böse auf ihn geworden sind, und nun wollen sie ihn
there angry on him become are and now want they him

entweder ins KZ oder in eine Strafkompanie
either in the concentration camp (Konzentrationslager) or in a criminal company

stecken. Natürlich erzählt Enno Kluge nichts von seiner
stick Of course told Enno Kluge nothing from his

Arbeitsscheu, aber er denkt, das wird der Bulle auch so
work-shyness but he thinks that will the cop also so

kapieren.
understand

Und damit hat er sogar recht, der Bulle kapiert das
And there-with has he even right the cop understands that

ganz gut, was für ein windiges Früchtchen dieser Enno
completely well what for a windy little fruit this Enno

Kluge ist. »Ja, Herr Kommissar, und wie ich Sie da sah
Kluge is Yes Mr commissioner and as I you there saw

und die Uniform von dem Herrn Wachtmeister, und ich
and the uniform from the gentlemen police officers and I

saß doch gerade beim Doktor, um mich krank schreiben
sat indeed just at the doctor for me sick to write

zu lassen, da habe ich gedacht, nun ist es soweit, nun
to let there have I thought now is it so far now

holen sie dich ins KZ, und da bin ich
get they you in the concentration camp (Konzentrationslager) and there am have I

denn losgelaufen ...«
then run away

»Soso«, sagt der Assistent. »Soso!« Er überlegt eine Weile
Soso says the assistant Soso He considers a while

und sagt dann: »Aber es scheint mir, Sohn, daß du gar
and says then But it seems to me son that you at all

nicht mehr so recht glaubst, daß wir deswegen hier
not (any)more so right believe that we because of that here

sind.«
are

»Nein, eigentlich nicht«, gibt Kluge zu.
No actually no gives Kluge to admits Kluge

»Und warum glaubst du das nicht mehr, Sohn?«
And why believe you that not (any)more son

»Weil Sie mich da doch viel einfacher in der Fabrik
Because you me there indeed much simpler in the factory

oder in meiner Wohnung festnehmen könnten.«
or in my house fast-take arrest could

»Also, 'ne Wohnung hast du auch, Sohn?«
So a house have you also son

»Aber natürlich, Herr Kommissar. Meine Frau ist doch bei
But of course Mr commissioner My wife is indeed at

der Post, ich bin richtig verheiratet. Meine beiden Jungen
the mail I am rightly married My both boys

stehen im Felde, der eine ist bei der SS in Polen. Ich
stand in the field the one is at the ss in Poland I

habe auch Papiere hier, ich kann Ihnen alles beweisen,
have also papers here I can you everything prove

was ich gesagt habe, wegen der Wohnung und wegen
what I said have because of the house and because of

meiner Arbeitsstelle.«
my job position

Und Enno Kluge zieht sein schäbiges, abgegriffenes
And Enno Kluge pulls his shabby worn

Brieftäschchen hervor und fängt an, Papiere vorzusuchen.
briefcase forth and catches on papers to search
starts

»Deine Papiere laß mal jetzt stecken, Sohn«, sagt der
Your papers let once now stick son says the

Assistent abweisend. »Das hat später auch noch Zeit ...«
assistant dismissive That has later also still time

Er versinkt in Nachdenken, und alles schweigt nun.
He sinks in pondering and everything is silent now

Der Arzt aber hinter seinem Schreibtisch fängt eilig
The doctor however behind his desk catches hurriedly
starts

an zu schreiben. Vielleicht hat er doch Gelegenheit,
on to write Perhaps has he indeed opportunity

diesem kleinen Männlein da, das von einer Angst in die
this small little men there that from one fear in the

andere gejagt wird, einen Krankenschein zuzustecken.
other hunted becomes a health certificate to stick to

Gallenleiden hat er gesagt, nun also. Das sind doch
Gallbladder disease has he said now then That are indeed

Zeiten, wo man dem andern helfen muß, wenn's nur
times where one the other help must if it only

irgend geht!
any goes

»Was schreiben Sie denn da, Doktor?« fragt der Assistent,
What write you then there doctor asks the assistant

plötzlich aus seinem Nachdenken hochfahrend.
suddenly from his pondering high-going
rising up

»Krankengeschichten«, erklärt der Arzt. »Ich will die Zeit
Sick-stories explained the doctor I want the time

ein bißchen nutzbringend verwenden, ein Haufen Menschen
a bit useful use a heap (of) people

sitzt da noch in meinem Sprechzimmer.«
sit there still in my consultation room

»Richtig, Doktor«, sagt der Assistent und steht auf. Er hat
Right doctor says the assistant and stands up He has

seinen Entschluß gefaßt. »Da wollen wir Sie auch nicht
his decision taken There want we you also not

länger aufhalten.«
longer hold up

Die Geschichte dieses Enno Kluge kann wahr sein, sie ist
The story of this Enno Kluge can true be she is

sogar höchstwahrscheinlich wahr, aber der Assistent wird
even highly probably true but the assistant becomes

das Gefühl nicht los, daß da noch irgend etwas
the sense not rid of that there still any something
somewhere something

anderes dahintersteckt, daß er nicht die ganze Geschichte
else behind it sticks that he not the whole story

zu hören bekommen hat. »Na, denn komm, mein Sohn!
to hear become has Now then come my son

Du begleitest uns doch noch ein paar Schritte? O nein,
You (will) escort us indeed still a few steps Oh no

nicht bis zum Alex, nur hierher auf unser Revier.
not until to the Alex only hereto on our district
to the Gestapo on Alexanderplatz

Ich will mich doch gerne noch ein bißchen mit dir
I want myself indeed gladly still a bit with you

unterhalten, mein Sohn, so ein munterer Knabe wie du
converse my son so a lively lad as you

bist, und den Onkel Doktor dürfen wir hier auch nicht
are and the uncle doctor may we here also not

länger aufhalten.« Er sagt zum Wachtmeister: »Nein, keine
longer hold up He says to the guard-master No no
police officer

Fessel. Er geht schon so fein brav mit, ist ja ein
shackles He goes already so fine brave with is yes an
good obeying along indeed

kluges Kind. Heil Hitler, Herr Doktor, und schönen
intelligent child Hail hitler Mr Doctor and beautiful

Dank!«
thanks

Sie sind schon an der Tür, es sieht alles genauso
They are already at the door it looks everything just as

aus, als wollten sie wirklich gehen. Aber da zieht der
out as wanted they really go But there pulls the

Assistent plötzlich die Karte, die Quangelsche Karte, aus
assistant suddenly the card the Quangel's card from

der Tasche, hält sie dem Enno Kluge unter die Nase und
the pocket holds her the Enno Kluge under the nose and

sagt zu dem Überraschten scharf: »Da, lies uns das mal
says to the surprised (one) sharply There read us that once

vor, Sohn! Aber ganz schnell, ohne zu zucken und
before son But completely fast without to flinch and
to

zu stottern!«
to stutter

So sagt er ganz bullenmäßig.
So says he completely bullish
like a cop

Aber schon, als der Assistent sieht, wie der Kluge die
But already as the assistant sees how the Kluge the

Karte anfaßt, wie sein glotzendes Auge immer
card takes on how his gawking eye always

verständnisloser wird, wie Kluge dann zu stammeln
less understanding becomes as kluge then to stammer

anfängt: »Deutscher, vergiß es nicht! Mit dem Anschluß
begins Germans forget it not With the joining

von Österreich fing es an. Es folgte Sudetenland und
from Austria caught it on It followed Sudetenland and
began There

die Tschechoslowakei. Polen wurde überfallen, Belgien,
the Czechoslovakia Poland became ambushed Belgium

Holland« - schon da weiß der Assistent mit ziemlicher
Holland already there knows the assistant with quite a

Gewißheit: Dieser Mann hat die Karte noch nie in
certainty This man has the card still never in the

Händen gehabt, hat nie ihren Inhalt gelesen, geschweige
hands had has never her content read be silent
let alone

denn ihn schreiben können - der ist ja viel zu blöd
then it write been able that one is yes much to dumb

für so was!
for so what
for something like that

Und ärgerlich reißt er dem Enno Kluge die Karte wieder
And annoyed rips he the Enno Kluge the card again

aus der Hand, sagt kurz: »Heil Hitler!« und verläßt mit
from the hand says shortly Hail hitler and leaves with

dem Schupo und seinem Festgenommenen das
the bobby and his arrested (one) the
(schutz polizei)

Behandlungszimmer.
treatment room

Langsam zerreißt der Arzt wieder den für Enno Kluge
Slowly tears up the doctor again the for Enno Kluge

vorbereiteten Behandlungsschein. Es war keine
prepared treatment certificate It was no
There

Gelegenheit, ihm den zuzustecken. Schade! Aber
opportunity him it towards to stick Pity But
put in

wahrscheinlich hätte er ihm doch nichts geholfen, vielleicht
probably had he him indeed nothing helped perhaps

war dieser Mann, der den Schwierigkeiten der heutigen
was this man who the difficulties of the today's

Zeit so wenig gewachsen schien, doch bereits zum
time so little grown seemed indeed already to the
up to it

Untergang verurteilt. Vielleicht konnte ihm keine Hilfe von
under-going sentenced Perhaps could him no help from
doom

außen wirklich helfen, weil nichts Festes in ihm war.
outside really help because nothing firm in him was

Schade ...
Pity

Das Verhör

The interrogation

Wenn der Kriminalassistent trotz seiner festen
When the criminal-assistent despite his firm

Überzeugung, der Enno Kluge komme weder als Schreiber
conviction the Enno Kluge come neither as writer

noch als Verbreiter der Karten in Frage, wenn er
nor as distributor of the cards in question when he

trotzdem in seiner telefonischen Meldung beim Kommissar
although in his phone notice at the commissioner
to the

Escherich durchblicken ließ, der Kluge sei doch wohl
Escherich through-glance let the Kluge be indeed well
drop

Verbreiter dieser Pamphlete, so tat er es darum, weil
distributor of this pamphlet so did he it therefore because

ein kluger Untergebener nie die Ansichten seines
a smart subordinate never the views of his

Vorgesetzten vorwegnehmen soll. Gegen den Kluge lag
supervisor away take should Against the Kluge lay

eine feste Anzeige der Sprechstundenhilfe Fräulein Kiesow
a firm report of the speak-hours-help miss Kiesow
assistant

vor, und ob die nun begründet war oder nicht, das
before and whether that now justified was or not that

mochte der Herr Kommissar selber herausfinden.
might the Mr commissioner (him)self find out

War sie begründet, so war der Assistent ein fähiger Mann
Was she justified so was the assistant a capable man

und des Wohlwollens des Kommissars sicher. War sie
and of the well-willing of the commissary sure Was she
assured

aber nicht begründet, so war der Kommissar klüger
however not justified so was the commissioner more intelligent

als der Assistent, und so ein Klügersein des Vorgesetzten
as the assistant and so a smarter-be of the supervisor

ist für den Untergebenen oft bekömmlicher als alle
is for the subordinate often more beneficial as all

Tüchtigkeit.
proficiency

»Nun?« sagte der lange, graue Escherich und storchte
Now said the tall gray Escherich and storked
stepped long

hinein in das Revier. »Nun, Kollege Schröder? Wo
inside in the police station Now colleague Schroeder Where

haben Sie denn Ihren Fang?«
have you then your catch

»In der hintersten Zelle links, Herr Kommissar.«
In the most backward cell left Mr commissioner

»Hat der Klabautermann gestanden?«
Has the kobold confessed

»Wer? Klabautermann? Ach so, ich verstehe! Nein, Herr
Who Kobold Oh so I understand No Mr

Kommissar, ich habe ihn natürlich nach unserm
commissioner I have him of course after our

Telefongespräch sofort abführen lassen.«
phone call immediately carry off let

»Gut!« lobte Escherich. »Und was weiß er von den
Good praised Escherich And what knows he from the

Karten?«
cards

»Ich habe«, sagte der Assistent vorsichtig, »ihn die
I have said the assistant carefully him the

aufgefundene Karte einmal vorlesen lassen. Den Anfang,
found card once read aloud let The beginning

heißt das.«
is called that
just to be clear

»Eindruck?«
Impression

»Ich möchte da nicht vorgreifen, Herr Kommissar«, sagte
I may there not anticipate Mr commissioner said

der Assistent.
the assistant

»Nicht zu ängstlich, Kollege Schröder! Eindruck?«
Not too fearful colleague Schroeder Impression

»Mir erscheint es jedenfalls unwahrscheinlich, daß er der
Me appears it anyhow improbable that he the

Schreiber dieser Karte ist.«
writer of this card is

»Warum?«
Why

»Ist nicht sehr helle. Außerdem furchtbar verängstigt.«
Is not very bright In addition terribly fearful

Der Kommissar Escherich strich unzufrieden über seinen
The commissioner Escherich stroke dissatisfied over his

sandfarbenen Schnurrbart. »Nicht sehr helle - furchtbar
sand-colored moustache Not very bright terribly

verängstigt«, wiederholte er. »Na, mein Klabautermann ist
fearful repeated he Now my kobold is

helle und bestimmt nicht verängstigt. Wieso glauben Sie,
bright and definitely not scared How so believe you

daß Sie den Rechten gefaßt haben? Berichten Sie mal!«
that you the right (one) taken have Report you once
Tell me indeed

Der Assistent Schröder tat es. Vor allen Dingen
The assistant Schroeder did it Before all things

wiederholte er stark die Beschuldigungen der
repeated he strong the accusations of the

Sprechstundenhilfe und betonte auch den Fluchtversuch.
speak-hours-help and stressed also the fleeing attempt
assistant

»Ich konnte es nicht anders machen, Herr Kommissar.
I could it not different make Mr commissioner
do

Nach den ergangenen Befehlen mußte ich ihn festhalten.«
After the received orders must I him firm-hold
arrest

»Richtig, Kollege Schröder. Ganz richtig gehandelt. Hätt
Right colleague Schroeder Completely right handled Had
correctly acted

ich auch nicht anders gemacht.«
I also not different made
done

Escherichs Mut hatte sich durch diesen Bericht wieder
Escherich's courage had itself through this message again

etwas verstärkt. Der klang besser als »nicht sehr helle«
somewhat strengthened It sounded better as not very bright

und »stark verängstigt«. Vielleicht ein Kartenverteiler,
and strongly fearful Perhaps a card-distributer

trotzdem der Kommissar bisher fest angenommen hatte,
although the commissioner until-here firmly taken on had
until now assumed

der Klabautermann habe keine Mitwisser.
the kobold have no confidantes

»Haben Sie seine Papiere schon durchgesehen?«
Have you his papers already through-seen
checked

»Hier liegen sie. Bestätigen im allgemeinen, was er sagt.
Here lie they Confirm in the general what he says
in

Ich habe den Eindruck, Herr Kommissar, das ist so ein
I have the impression Mr commissioner that is so a
he

Arbeitsscheuer, Angst vor der Front, keine Lust zum
work-shy one fear for the front no desire to the
of

Arbeiten, Pferdewetter ist er auch - ich habe einen
work horsebetter is he also I have a

ganzen Packen Rennzeitungen und Berechnungen bei ihm
whole stack course-papers and calculations with him
of horse racing papers

gefunden. Und dann noch ziemlich gewöhnliche Briefe von
found And then still rather ordinary letters from

kommunen Weibern, so ein Früchtchen, verstehen Sie, Herr
communal women so a little fruit understand you Mr
prostitutes

Kommissar. Aber immerhin an die Fünfzig heran.«
commissioner But after all on the fifty on
reaching years

»Schön, schön«, sagte der Kommissar, fand es aber gar
Beautiful beautiful said the commissioner found it but at all

nicht schön. Weder der Kartenschreiber noch ein etwaiger
not beautiful Neither the card writer nor a sort of
any

Verteiler konnte viel mit Weibern zu tun haben. Das
distributer could much with women to do have That

stand für ihn fest. Seine eben erst wiederbelebte
stood for him firm his just first again-lived
was certain re-experienced

Hoffnung begann von neuem schwächer zu werden. Aber
hope began from new weaker to become But
again

dann dachte Escherich an seinen Vorgesetzten, den
then thought Escherich on his supervisor the
of

Obergruppenführer Prall, und an die noch höheren
over-groups-leader Prall and on the still higher

Vorgesetzten bis zu Himmler hinauf. Die würden ihm in
supervisor until to Himmler away-up They would him in

der nächsten Zeit das Leben verdammt schwer machen,
the next time the life damned heavy make
difficult

wenn gar keine Spur vorlag. Hier aber war eine
when at all no trace before-lay Here however was a
was present

Spur, wenigstens lagen hier starke Beschuldigungen und
trace at least lay here robust accusations and

verdächtiges Benehmen vor. Man konnte diese Spur
suspicious behavior before One could this trace

verfolgen, auch wenn man sie im geheimsten Innern
follow also when one her in the most secret inside

nicht ganz für die richtige hielt. Man gewann Zeit,
not completely for the right (one) held One won time

weiter geduldig zu warten. Niemand geschah ein Leid
further patiently to wait Nobody happened a suffering
experienced harm

dadurch. Was kam es schließlich auf solch ein
there-through What came it finally on such a
through that did it actually matter

Früchtchen an!
little fruit on

Escherich stand auf. »Ich geh mal hinten zu den Zellen,
Escherich stood up I go once in the back to the cells

Schröder. Geben Sie mir mal die neue Karte, und warten
Schroeder Give you me once the new card and wait

Sie hier.«
you here

Der Kommissar ging ganz leise, er hielt die Schlüssel
The commissioner went completely quietly he held the key

fest in der Hand, damit sie nicht klapperten. Ganz
firmly in the hand there-with she not rattled Completely

vorsichtig schob er die Blende vom Spion und sah
carefully pushed he the cover from the spy (hole) and looked

in die Zelle.
into the cell

Der Inhaftierte saß auf einem Schemel. Er hatte den
The imprisoned (one) sat on a stool He had the

Kopf in die Hand gestützt und seine Augen auf die Tür
head in the hand supported and his eyes on the door
leaning

gerichtet. Es machte ganz den Eindruck, als sähe
directed It made completely the impression as would see

der Mann grade in das lauernde Auge des Kommissars.
the man right in the lurking eye of the commissioner

Aber der Gesichtsausdruck Kluges verriet, daß er nichts
But the facial expression (of) Kluge betrayed that he nothing

sah. Der Mann war nicht zusammengeschreckt, als die
saw The man was not together-scared startled as the

Blende bewegt worden war, sein Gesicht hatte auch nichts
cover moved become had was his face had also nothing

Gespanntes, wie es sonst stets bei einem ist, der
anxious as it otherwise all the time at one is who

sich beobachtet fühlt.
himself observed feels

Sondern er sah so einfach vor sich hin, kaum in
But he saw so simply before himself away hardly in

Gedanken verloren, eher dösend, von trüben Ahnungen
thoughts lost before more like dozing from clouded premonitions

voll.
full

Der Kommissar am Guckloch wußte es jetzt mit
The commissioner at the peephole knew it now with

Bestimmtheit: Dies war weder der Klabautermann noch ein
determination This was neither the kobold nor a

Helfershelfer. Sondern dies war einfach ein Mißgriff – die
helper's helper But this was simply a miss grab the

Beschuldigungen mochten gelautet haben, wie sie wollen,
accusations might sounded have as they want

und das Verhalten mochte noch so verdächtig
and the behaviour might still so suspicious

gewesen sein.
been be
have been

Aber Escherich dachte auch wieder an seine Vorgesetzten,
But Escherich thought also again on his supervisor
of

er kaute an seinem Bart, er überlegte, wie man diese
he chewed on his beard he considered how one this

Sache recht lange hinziehen könnte, bis entdeckt wurde,
thing right long through-pull could until discovered became

dies war der Falsche. Blamieren durfte er sich ja
this was the false Blame might he himself yes
indeed

auch nicht dabei.
also not there-by
for it

Er schloß mit einem Ruck die Zelle auf und
He closed with a jerk the cell up and
aufschliessen: open

trat ein. Der Verhaftete war bei dem Klirren des
stepped in The imprisoned (one) was at the clattering of the
had

Schlosses zusammengefahren, starrte erst verwirrt auf den
lock together-moved stared first confused on the
flinched

Eintretenden, dann machte er einen Versuch aufzustehen.
in stepping one then made he a try to get up
person entering

Aber Escherich drückte ihn gleich auf den Schemel
But Escherich pushed him immediately on the stool

zurück.
back

»Bleiben Sie sitzen, Herr Kluge, bleiben Sie sitzen. In
Remain you sit Mr Kluge remain you sit In

unserem Alter kommt man nicht mehr so leicht hinten
our age comes one not (any)more so light back
easily

hoch!«
high
up

Er lachte, und dieser Kluge machte auch Anstalten,
He laughed and this Kluge made also moves

mitzulächeln, aus purer Höflichkeit ein bißchen kläglich
along-to-grin from pure courtesy a bit plaintive

mitzulächeln.
along-to-grin

Der Kommissar klappte das Bett von der Wand und setzte
The commissioner clapped (swung) the bed from the wall and set

sich darauf. »Na, Herr Kluge«, sagte er und sah
himself thereupon Now Mr Kluge said he and looked

aufmerksam in das blasse Gesicht mit dem schwachen
attentively in the pale face with the weak

Kinn, dem merkwürdig dicklippigen roten Mund und den
chin the strange thick-lipped red mouth and the

hellen Augen, die ständig zwinkerten. »Na, Herr Kluge,
bright eyes which constantly blinked Now Mr Kluge

und nun erzählen Sie mal, was Sie auf dem Herzen
and now tell you once what you on the heart

haben. Ich bin der Kommissar Escherich von der
have I am the commissioner Escherich from the

Geheimen Staatspolizei.« Er fuhr sanft zuredend fort, als
secret state police He drove softly to-talking coaxing on as

er den andern schon bei der Nennung der Geheimen
he the other already at the mention of the secret

Staatspolizei ängstlich zurückzucken sah: »Sie brauchen
state police fearfully back-jerk saw You need

keine Angst zu haben. Wir fressen keine kleinen Kinder.
no fear to have We eat no small children

Und Sie sind doch bloß ein kleines Kind, das sehe ich
And you are indeed just a little child that see I

doch ...«
indeed

Bei dem Hauch von Anteilnahme, der aus diesen Worten
At the breath of sympathy which from these words

vernehmlich wurde, füllten sich Kluges Augen sofort
noticeable became filled themselves Kluge's eyes immediately

wieder mit Tränen, sein Gesicht zuckte, die Backenmuskeln
again with tears his face twitched the back-muscles

arbeiteten krampfhaft.
worked spasmodically

»Na, na!« sagte Escherich und legte seine Hand auf die
Now now said Escherich and put his hand on that

des kleinen Mannes. »So schlimm wird's ja nicht sein.
of the small man So bad will it indeed not be

Oder ist es so schlimm?«
Or is it so bad

»Es ist alles verloren!« rief Enno Kluge verzweifelt.
It is everything lost called Enno Kluge desperately
Everything is

»Ich bin ja doch hin! Ich hab keinen Krankenschein, und
I am yes indeed gone I have no sick-certificate and
health certificate

ich müßte zur Arbeit. Und hier sitze ich fest, und da
I must to the work And here sit I fixed and there
caught

schicken die mich ins KZ, da gehe ich
send they me in the concentration camp there go I
(konzentrationslager)

gleich hops, das halte ich keine vierzehn Tage aus!«
immediately hop that hold I no fourteen days out
(dead)

»Nu, nu!« sagte der Kommissar wieder wie zu einem
Now now said the commissioner again as to a

Kind. »Das mit Ihrer Fabrik, das wird sich ja regeln
child That with your factory that will itself yes arrange
indeed

lassen. Wenn wir jemand festhalten, und es stellt sich
let When we someone firm hold and it puts itself
arrest

heraus, es ist ein ordentlicher Mann, so sorgen wir auch
out it is an orderly man so worry we also
reputable

dafür, daß er keinen Schaden von dem Festhalten hat.
therefore that he no harm from the firm holding has
arrest

Sie sind doch ein ordentlicher Kerl, Herr Kluge - was?«
You are indeed an orderly chap Mr Kluge what

Wieder arbeitete es in Kluges Gesicht, dann entschloß er
Again worked it in Kluge's face then decided he

sich diesem sympathischen Mann gegenüber zu einem
himself this sympathetic man opposite to a

Teilgeständnis. »Ich arbeite denen ja nicht genug!«
partial confession I work for those yes not enough
indeed

»Na, und was meinen Sie selbst, Herr Kluge? Arbeiten Sie
Now and what mean you self Mr Kluge Work you
think

Ihrer Ansicht nach genug - oder?«
your opinion after enough or (what)
according to your opinion

Wieder überlegte Kluge. »Ich bin doch so viel krank«,
Again considered Kluge I am indeed so much sick

sagte er kläglich. »Aber die sagen nur, jetzt ist keine
said he plaintive But they say only now is no

Zeit zum Kranksein.«
time to the sick being

»Sie sind doch nicht immer krank? Nun, und wenn Sie
You are indeed not always sick Now and when you

nun nicht krank sind und arbeiten - tun Sie dann genug?
now not sick are and work do you then enough

Wie denken Sie darüber, Herr Kluge?«
How think they about it Mr Kluge

Wieder entschloß sich Kluge. »Ach Gott, Herr
Again decided himself Kluge Oh god Mr

Kommissar«, klagte er an, »die Weiber laufen mir doch
commissioner complained he on the women run me indeed
accused he

so nach!«
so after

Es klang ebenso kläglich wie eitel.
It sounded likewise plaintive as vain

Der Kommissar schüttelte bedauernd mit dem Kopf hin
The commissioner shook regretful with the head away
left

und her, als sei das freilich schlimm.
and back as be that indeed bad
right

»Das ist nicht gut, Herr Kluge«, meinte er dann. »In
That is not good Mr Kluge thought he then In

unsern Jahren läßt man ja nicht gerne was aus, nicht
our years lets one yes not gladly what out not

wahr?«
true

Kluge sah ihn nur mit einem schwachen Lächeln an,
Kluge looked him only with a weak smile on

froh, bei diesem Mann Verständnis gefunden zu haben.
happy at this man understanding found to have

»Ja«, sagte der Kommissar. »Und wie steht's da mit der
Yes said the commissioner And how stands it there with the
are you

Kasse?«
cashbox

»Ich wett manchmal ein bißchen«, gestand Kluge. »Nicht
I bet sometimes a little bit confessed Kluge Not

viel und nicht hoch, Herr Kommissar. Nie mehr als
much and not high Mr commissioner Never more as

höchstens mal fünf Mark, wenn ein Tip ganz sicher
at most once five mark {money} when a tip completely sure

ist, das schwöre ich Ihnen, Herr Kommissar!«
is that swear I you Mr commissioner!

»Und wovon bezahlen Sie das, Herr Kluge, die Weiber
And where-from pay you that Mr Kluge the women

und die Wetten? Wenn Sie doch nicht viel arbeiten?«
and the bet When you indeed not much work

»Aber die Weiber bezahlen doch mich, Herr Kommissar!«
But the women pay indeed me Mr commissioner!

sagte Kluge fast ein wenig gekränkt über soviel
said Kluge almost a little hurt over so much

Unverstand. Er lächelte eitel. »Weil ich doch so tüchtig
misunderstanding He smiled vain Because I indeed so capable

bin!« setzte er hinzu.
am set he there-to
added

In diesem Augenblick legte der Kommissar Escherich die
In this moment put the commissioner Escherich the

Beschuldigung, dieser Enno Kluge habe auch nur das
accusation this Enno Kluge have also only the

geringste mit der Abfassung oder Verbreitung der Karten
least with the creation or distribution of the cards

zu tun, endgültig zu den Akten. Dieser Kluge war zu
to do finally to the files This Kluge was to
archive

so was einfach nicht imstande, alle Voraussetzungen
so what simply not in-the-stand all requirements
such a thing capable

fehlten ihm dafür. Aber befragen mußte er ihn
were missing him there-for But ask must he him
for that

deswegen	doch,	denn	er	mußte	ja	ein	Protokoll
because of that	indeed	then	he	must	yes	a	protocol

anfertigen	über	dieses	Verhör,	ein	Protokoll	für	die
ready make	over	this	interrogation	a	protocol	for	the
draw up							

Herren	Vorgesetzten,	damit	die	erst	mal
gentlemen	supervisor	there-with	that one	first	once

Ruhe	hielten,	ein	Protokoll,	das	den	Kluge	weiter	unter
rest	held	a	protocol	that	the	Kluge	further	under
calmed down								

Verdacht	hielt,	Schritte	gegen	ihn	begründete	…
suspicion	held	steps	against	him	grounded	
					based on	

So	zog	er	denn	die	Karte	aus	der	Tasche,	legte	sie
So	pulled	he	then	the	card	from	the	pocket	put	her
										it

vor	Kluge	hin	und	sagte	ganz	gleichgültig:	»Sie
before	Kluge	before	and	said	completely	indifferent	You

kennen	diese	Karte,	Herr	Kluge?«
know	this	card	Mr	Kluge

»Ja«,	sagte	Enno	Kluge	erst	ganz	gedankenlos,	aber
Yes	said	Enno	Kluge	first	completely	thoughtless	but

zusammenschreckend	verbesserte	er	sich:	»Das	heißt
together-scaring	corrected	he	himself	That	is called
startling					

natürlich	nein.	Ich	habe	sie	vorhin	vorlesen	müssen,	den
of course	no	I	have	she	a while ago	read aloud	must	the
				it				

Anfang heißt das. Sonst kenn ich die Karte nicht!
beginning is called that Otherwise know I the card not
that is

Heilig wahr, Herr Kommissar!«
Holy true Mr commissioner
truth

»Na, na!« tat Escherich zweiflerisch. »Herr Kluge, wo
Now now did Escherich doubtful Mr Kluge where
now that

wir über so 'ne große Sache wie über Ihre Arbeiterei
we about such a great thing as about your work

und das KZ klargeworden sind, wo ich selbst
and the concentration camp clear-become are where I even
(konzentrationslager)

zu Ihren Herren hingehen und die Sache für Sie
to your masters go away and the thing for you

ordnen werde, da werden wir uns doch über so 'ne
order will there will we us indeed over such a
will fix then

kleine Sache wie diese Karte einig werden!«
little thing as this card agreed become

»Ich hab nichts damit zu tun, gar nichts, Herr
I have nothing there-with to do at all nothing Mr

Kommissar!«
commissioner

»Ich geh ja nicht so weit, Herr Kluge«, sagte der
I go yes not so far Mr Kluge said the

Kommissar, ungerührt von diesen Beteuerungen, »ich geh
commissioner untouched from these assertions I go
by

ja nicht so weit wie mein Kollege, der Sie für den
yes not so far as my colleague who you for the
indeed

Kartenschreiber hält, und der Sie durchaus vor den
card writer holds and who you throughout before the
at all

Volksgerichtshof schleppen will und dann: Rübe ab, Herr
people's court drag wants and then Turnip off Mr
Head

Kluge!«
Kluge

Der kleine Mann erzitterte, und sein Gesicht wurde
The little man trembled and his face became

aschfahl.
ash-pale
ashen

»Nein«, sagte der Kommissar beruhigend und legte seine
No said the commissioner soothing and put his

Hand wieder auf die des andern. »Nein, für den
hand again on that of the other No for the

Kartenschreiber halte ich Sie nicht. Aber ... daß die Karte
card writer hold I you not But that the card

auf dem Flur des Arztes lag, und Sie haben sich
on the floor of the doctor lay and you have yourself
landing

doch verdächtig viel auf dem Flur zu schaffen gemacht,
indeed suspicious much on the floor to create made
landing held up

und dann Ihre Unruhe, Ihr Weglaufen. Und für alles
and then your unrest your away-walking And for everything
nervosity running away

sind gute Zeugen da – nein, Herr Kluge, es ist schon
are good witnesses there no Mr Kluge it is already

besser, Sie sagen mir die Wahrheit. Ich möchte doch
better you tell me the truth I may indeed

nicht, daß Sie sich selbst ins Unglück stürzen!«
not that you yourself self in the misfortune rush

»Die Karte muß von außen reingesteckt sein, Herr
The card must from outside in-stuck be Mr

Kommissar. Ich habe mit ihr nichts zu schaffen, heilig
commissioner I have with her nothing to create holy
it do

wahr, Herr Kommissar!«
true Mr commissioner!
truth

»Kann ja gar nicht von außen reingesteckt sein, so
Can yes at all not from outside in-stuck be so
indeed

wie die gelegen hat! Und fünf Minuten vorher ist sie
as that one lain has And five minutes before is she

noch nicht dagewesen, das wird das Fräulein vom Arzt
still not there-been that will the miss from the doctor

beschwören. In der Zwischenzeit waren Sie aber auf der
swear In the meantime were she but on the

Toilette. Oder wollen Sie behaupten, es war noch jemand
toilet or want she claim it there was still someone

anders aus dem Wartezimmer auf dem Klo?«
different from the waiting-room on the toilet

»Nein, glaube ich nicht, Herr Kommissar. Nein, bestimmt
No believe I not Mr commissioner no definitely

nicht. Wenn's um fünf Minuten geht, dann bestimmt nicht.
not if it for five minutes goes then definitely not

Ich wollte nämlich schon eine ganze Weile rauchen, und
I wanted namely already a whole while smoke and

darum habe ich aufgepaßt, ob einer auf die Toilette
therefore have I watched out whether one on the toilet

ging.«
went

»Na also!« sagte der Kommissar, anscheinend sehr
Now so then said the commissioner apparently very

befriedigt. »Da sagen Sie es ja selbst: Nur Sie, nur Sie
satisfied There say you it yes yourself Just you just you

allein können die Karte auf den Flur gelegt haben!«
alone can the card on the hall laid have

Kluge starrte ihn mit weit aufgerissenen, jetzt wieder
Kluge stared him with far open-ripped now again
wide opened

völlig erschreckten Augen an.
totally scared eyes on

»Nachdem Sie das also eingestanden haben ...«
After you that so admitted have

»Ich habe nichts eingestanden, nichts! Ich habe nur
I have nothing admitted nothing I have only

gesagt, in den letzten fünf Minuten ist niemand vor mir
said in the last five minutes is nobody before me

auf dem Klo gewesen!«
on the toilet been

Kluge schrie das fast.
Kluge cried that almost

»Aber, aber!« sagte der Kommissar und schüttelte
But but said the commissioner and shook

mißbilligend den Kopf. »Sie werden doch ein eben
disapproving the head You will indeed a just

abgelegtes Geständnis nicht gleich widerrufen wollen,
laid-off confession not immediately recall want
offered

dafür sind Sie doch ein viel zu vernünftiger Mann. Ich
therefore are you indeed a much too reasonable man I

müßte den Widerruf auch ins Protokoll nehmen, Herr
must the recall also in the protocol take Mr

Kluge, und so was sieht nie hübsch aus.«
Kluge and so what sees never handsome out
never looks good

Kluge starrte ihn verzweifelt an. »Ich habe doch nichts
kluge stared him doubting on I have indeed nothing

gestanden ...« flüsterte er tonlos.
stood whispered he without tone
confessed

»Wir werden uns darüber schon noch einig werden«,
We will us about it already still agreed become

meinte Escherich beruhigend. »Nun sagen Sie mir erst
thought Escherich soothing Now say you me first
opined

mal: Wer hat Ihnen die Karte zur Ablage gegeben? War's
once Who has you the card to the lay-off given Was it

ein guter Bekannter, ein Freund, oder hat Sie jemand auf
a good acquaintance a friend or has you someone on

der Straße angesprochen und Ihnen ein paar Mark
the street talked to and you a few mark
{money}

dafür gegeben?«
therefore given

»Nichts! Nichts!« schrie wieder Kluge. »Ich habe die Karte
Nothing Nothing cried again Kluge I have the card

nicht in der Hand gehabt, mit keinem Auge habe ich sie
not in the hand had with no eye have I her
it

gesehen, ehe sie mir Ihr Kollege gab!«
seen before her me your colleague gave
it

»Aber, aber, Herr Kluge! Sie haben vorhin selber
But but Mr Kluge You have a while ago (your)self
Now now

zugegeben, daß Sie die Karte auf den Flur gelegt haben
admitted that you the card on the hall laid have

...«

»Nichts habe ich zugegeben! So was habe ich nie
Nothing have I admitted So what have I never

gesagt!«
said

»Nein«, sagte Escherich, strich sich über den Bart und
No said Escherich stroke himself over the beard and

wischte damit ein Lächeln fort. Es machte ihm jetzt
wiped there-with a smile away It made him now
did

schon viel Vergnügen, diesen feigen, jammernden Hund ein
already much pleasure this cowardly wailing dog a

bißchen tanzen zu lassen. Das wurde noch ein ganz
little dance to let That became still a completely

nettes Protokoll mit starkem Verdacht - für die
nice protocol with strong suspicion for the
report

Vorgesetzten. »Nein«, sagte er, »in der Form haben Sie es
supervisor No said he in the form have you it
literally

nicht gesagt. Sondern Sie haben nur gesagt, daß nur Sie
not said But you have only said that only you

die Karte dort abgelegt haben können, daß niemand außer
the card there laid off have been able that nobody except
put down

Ihnen dort gewesen ist, und das bedeutet wohl
you there been is and that means well

ebensoviel.«
equal-as-much

Enno starrte ihn mit weit offenen Augen an. Dann sagte
Enno stared him with wide open eyes on Then said

er plötzlich mürrisch: »Das habe ich auch nicht gesagt. Es
he suddenly grumpily That have I also not said It

können übrigens auch andere Leute auf die Toilette
can by the way also other people on the toilet

gegangen sein, nicht nur die vom Wartezimmer.«
gone be not only those from the Waiting-room

Er setzte sich wieder; in der Erregung vorhin, bei den
He sat himself again in the excitement a while ago at the

falschen Beschuldigungen war er aufgesprungen.
false accusations was he jumped up
had

»Aber ich sage gar nichts mehr aus. Ich verlange
But I speak at all nothing (any)more out I desire

einen Anwalt. Und ein Protokoll unterschreibe ich auch
a lawyer And a protocol undersign I also
report

nicht.«
not

»Aber, aber«, sagte Escherich. »Habe ich denn schon von
But but said Escherich Have I then already from
Now now

Ihnen verlangt, Herr Kluge, daß Sie ein Protokoll
you required Mr Kluge that you a protocol
report

unterschreiben? Habe ich mir auch nur eine Notiz
under-write Have I me also only a notice
sign

gemacht von dem, was Sie ausgesagt haben? Wir sitzen
made from that what you out-said have We sit
spoken out

doch hier wie zwei alte Freunde, was wir hier reden,
indeed here as two old friends what we here talk

geht keinen was an.«
goes nobody what on
is nobody's business

Er stand auf, öffnete die Zellentür weit.
He stood on opened the cell door wide

»Sehen Sie, niemand auf dem Gang, der horcht. Und da
See you nobody on the hallway who listens And there

machen Sie mir solche Schwierigkeiten wegen so einer
make you me such difficulties because of such a

albernen Karte? Sehen Sie, ich lege ja gar keinen Wert
stupid card See you I lie yes at all no value

auf diese Karte. Das ist ja ein Idiot, der die geschrieben
on this card That is yes an idiot who it written

hat! Aber wo die Sprechstundenhilfe und mein Kollege
has But where the speak-hours-help assistant and my colleague

doch so viel Aufhebens davon machen, muß ich der
indeed so much upheaval there-from make must I the

Sache nachgehen! Seien Sie kein Frosch, Herr Kluge,
thing to go after Are you no frog Mr kluge

sagen Sie mir einfach: Ein Herr auf der Frankfurter
say you me simply A gentleman on the Frankfurter

Allee hat sie mir gegeben, er will dem Doktor einen
avenue has her it me given he wants the doctor a

kleinen Streich spielen, hat er gesagt. Und zehn Mark
little prank play has he said And ten mark {money}

hat er Ihnen dafür gezahlt. Sie haben doch einen
has he you therefore paid You have indeed a

ganz neuen Zehnmärker in der Tasche gehabt, den
completely new ten mark note in the pocket had that one

habe ich doch schon gesehen. Sehen Sie, wenn Sie mir
have I indeed already seen See you when you me

das jetzt erzählen, dann sind Sie mein Mann. Dann
that now tell then are you my man Then

machen Sie mir keine Schwierigkeiten, dann kann ich
make you me no difficulties then can I

beruhigt nach Haus gehen.«
calmed down to house go
home

»Und ich? Wohin geh ich? In die Plötze! Und dann Kopf
And I Where-to go I I the roach And then head

ab! Nee, Herr Kommissar, das sage ich nie und nie
off No Mr commissioner that say I never and never

aus!«
out

»Sie, wohin Sie gehen, Herr Kluge, wenn ich nach Haus
You where-to you go Mr Kluge when I to house

gehe? Sie gehen doch auch nach Haus, haben Sie das
go You go indeed also to house have you that

denn immer noch nicht begriffen? Sie sind frei, so oder
then always still not understood You are free so or

so, ich laß Sie laufen ...«
so I let you walk

»Wahr, Herr Kommissar, heilig wahr? Ich kann gehen auch
True Mr commissioner holy true I can go also

ohne Aussage, ohne Protokoll?«
without statement without protocol
report

»Aber natürlich können Sie gehen, Herr Kluge, jetzt auf
But of course can you go Mr Kluge now on

der Stelle können Sie gehen. Nur eines überlegen Sie
the spot can you go Only one (thing) consider you

sich noch mal, ehe Sie gehen ...«
herself still once before you go

Und er tippte dem erregt Aufgesprungenen, schon nach
And he tapped the excited jumped up (one) already to

der Tür Hingewendeten auf die Schulter.
the door turned towards on the shoulder

»Sehen Sie, ich regle das in Ihrer Fabrik für Sie, den
See you I fix that in her factory for you that

Gefallen tu ich Ihnen. Das habe ich Ihnen versprochen,
pleasure do I you That have I you promised

und ich halte Wort. Aber nun denken Sie auch mal
and I keep (my) word But now think you also once

einen Augenblick an mich, Herr Kluge. Denken Sie mal an
one moment on of me Mr Kluge Think you once on

all die vielen Schwierigkeiten, die ich von meinem
all the many difficulties that I from my

Kollegen kriege, wenn ich Sie laufenlasse: Der
colleague get when i you let walk That one

verklatscht mich doch bei meinem Vorgesetzten, ich kann
tattles on me indeed at to my supervisor I can

die größten Schwierigkeiten davon haben. Es wäre
the greatest difficulties there-from have It would be

wirklich anständig von Ihnen, Herr Kluge, wenn Sie mir
really decent from you Mr Kluge when you me

das von dem Mann in der Frankfurter Allee
that from the man in the Frankfurter avenue

unterschreiben würden, da ist doch für Sie gar kein
under-write would there is indeed for you at all no
sign

Risiko dabei. Der Mann kann ja gar nicht aufgefunden
risk there-by The man can indeed at all not found

werden, also, Herr Kluge!«
become so Mr kluge

So sanft bohrendem Zureden war Enno Kluge eigentlich
So soft (with) penetrating talking to was Enno Kluge actually

nie in seinem Leben gewachsen gewesen. Er stand
never in his life grown been He stood
strong enough for

zweifelnd da. Die Freiheit lockte, und mit der Fabrik
hesitating there The freedom lured and with the factory

würde auch alles in Ordnung kommen, wenn er diesen
would also everything in order come when he this

Mann da nicht vor den Kopf stieß. Er hatte eine
man there not before the head bumped He had a

schreckliche Angst davor, diesen netten Kommissar vor
horrible fear therefore this nice commissioner before

den Kopf zu stoßen. Dann bearbeitete womöglich der Bulle
the head to bump Then worked at possibly the cop

den Fall weiter, und der würde ihn eines Tages doch
the case further and that one would him one day indeed

noch dazu bringen, den Einbruch bei der Rosenthal zu
still there-to bring the burglary at the rosenthal to

gestehen. Dann war Enno Kluge verloren, der SS-Mann
confess Then was Enno Kluge lost the SS man

Persicke ...
Persicke

Er konnte wirklich dem Kommissar den Gefallen tun -
He could really the commissioner the pleasure do

was war dabei? Es war so 'ne Quatschkarte,
what was there-by It was so a nonsense card
wrong with that

irgendwas Politisches, mit dem er nie was zu tun
something political with which he never what to do
anything

gehabt hatte, wovon er nichts verstand. Und der Mann
had had where-from he nothing understood And the man

in der Frankfurter Allee würde wirklich nie zu finden
in the Frankfurter avenue would really never to find

sein, weil es ihn einfach nicht gab. Ja, er wollte dem
be because it him simply not gave Yes he wanted the
he existed

Kommissar den Gefallen tun und unterschreiben.
commissioner the pleasure do and under-write
sign

Aber dann warnte ihn wieder seine angeborene Vorsicht,
But then warned him again his inborn attention

seine Ängstlichkeit. »Ja«, sagte er, »und wenn ich
his fearfulness Yes said he and when I

unterschrieben habe, dann lassen Sie mich doch nicht
signed have then let you me indeed not

frei.«
free

»Aber! Aber!« sagte der Kommissar Escherich und sah
But But said the commissioner Escherich and saw
Now Now

sein Spiel schon so gut wie gewonnen. »Wegen so 'ner
his play already so good as won Because of such a

Dreckskarte, und wo Sie mir doch einen Gefallen tun.
shit-card and where you me indeed a pleasure do
when

Ich gebe Ihnen mein Ehrenwort, Herr Kluge, als
I give you my word of honor Mr Kluge as

Kriminalkommissar und als Mensch: Sobald Sie das
detective inspector and as human As soon as you the

Protokoll unterschrieben haben, sind Sie frei.«
protocol signed have are you free
report

»Und wenn ich nicht unterschreibe?«
And when I not sign

»Sind Sie natürlich auch frei!«
Are you of course also free

Enno Kluge entschloß sich. »Also, ich werd es
Enno Kluge decided himself So I will it

unterschreiben, Herr Kommissar, damit Sie keine
sign Mr commissioner there-with you no

Unannehmlichkeiten haben, und ich tu Ihnen auch mal
inconveniences have and I do you also once

einen Gefallen. Aber Sie vergessen das nicht mit meiner
a pleasure But you forget that not with my

Fabrik?«
factory

»Wird heute noch erledigt, Herr Kluge. Heute noch!
Becomes today still finished Mr Kluge Today still

Lassen Sie sich da morgen mal ein bißchen sehen,
Let you yourself there tomorrow once a bit see

und unterlassen Sie überhaupt diese blöde Krankschreiberei.
and under-let you at all this stupid sick-writing
refrain from

Mal einen Tag blau, sagen wir einmal in der Woche, da
Once a day blue say we once in the week there

wird niemand mehr ein Wort sagen, wenn ich mit
will nobody (any)more a word say when I with

denen gesprochen habe. Soll es so recht sein, Herr
them spoken have Should it so right be Mr

Kluge?«
Kluge

»Aber natürlich! Ich bin Ihnen sehr dankbar, Herr
But of course I am you very grateful Mr

Kommissar!«
commissioner!

So sprechend, waren sie über den Zellengang wieder in
So speaking were they over the cell-hallway again in

der Stube angelangt, wo der Assistent Schröder wartend
the room arrived where the assistant Schroeder waiting

saß, gespannt, wie das Verhör ausgefallen sein würde,
sat anxiously how the interrogation fallen out be would
turned out

und im voraus schon in sein Schicksal ergeben, wenn
and in the in front already in his fate surrendered when
weary

es doch etwas setzte. Er sprang auf, als die beiden
it indeed something set He jumped up as the both

eintraten.
stepped in

»Na, Schröder«, sagte der Kommissar lächelnd und deutete
Now Schroeder said the commissioner smiling and pointed

mit dem Kopf auf Kluge, der klein und ängstlich bei ihm
with the head on Kluge who small and fearfully with him
anxiously

stand, denn der Bulle sah ihn schon wieder
stood then the cop saw him already again

furchteinflößend an. »Da haben Sie unsern Freund. Er hat
fear-inducing at There have you our friend He has

mir eben zugegeben, daß er die Karte bei dem Doktor
me just admitted that he the card at the doctor

auf den Flur gelegt hat, er hat sie von einem Herrn
on the hall laid has he has her from a gentleman
it

auf der Frankfurter Allee bekommen ...«
on the Frankfurter avenue become

Der Brust des Assistenten entrang sich ein Laut wie
(From) the chest of the assistant wrang itself a sound like

Stöhnen. »Den Donner!« sagte er dann. »Aber er kann
moaning The thunder said he then But he can
rascal

doch gar nicht ...«
indeed at all not

»Und jetzt«, fuhr der Kommissar unberührt fort, »und jetzt
And now drove the commissioner ontouched on and now
emotionless

machen wir beide hier nur ein kleines Protokoll, und dann
make we both here only a little protocol and then
report

geht der Herr Kluge nach Haus. Ist frei. Stimmt's, Herr
goes the Mr Kluge to house is free Is that right Mr

Kluge, oder stimmt's nicht?«
Kluge or is that right not

»Ja«, antwortete Kluge, aber nur ganz leise, denn die
Yes answered Kluge but only completely softly then the

Gegenwart des Bullen flößte ihm immer neue Bedenken
presence of the cop induced him always new doubts

und neue Angst ein. Der Assistent aber stand ganz
and new fear in The assistant however stood completely

dämlich da. Der Kluge hatte die Karte nicht hingelegt,
stupid there The Kluge had the card not laid down

nie und nie im Leben, das stand für ihn fest. Und
never and never in the life that stood for him firm And
were true

nun war der Kluge doch bereit, das Gegenteil zu
now was the Kluge indeed ready the contrary to

unterschreiben.
sign

Was für ein Fuchs, dieser Escherich! Wie er das wohl
What for a fox this Escherich How he that well

erreicht haben mochte? Schröder gestand sich – nicht
reached have might Schroeder confessed himself not
done

ohne Neid – ein, daß dieser Escherich ihm weit
without envy in that this Escherich him far

überlegen war. Und dann, nach solchem Geständnis, den
over-laid was And then after such (a) confession the
better than

Burschen auch noch freilassen! Nicht zu verstehen, nicht
lad also still free-let Not to understand not

zu durchschauen! Na, es gab eben immer noch Klügere,
to see through Well it gave just always still smarter ones

so schlau man sich auch vorkam.
so smart one oneself also appeared

»Hören Sie, Kollege«, sagte Escherich, der jetzt die
Hear you colleague said Escherich who now the

Verblüffung des Assistenten genug genossen hatte, »Sie
amazement of the assistant enough enjoyed had you

könnten eigentlich einen Gang für mich tun, jetzt gleich,
could actually a course for me do now immediately

aufs Präsidium.«
on the praesidium

»Zu Befehl, Herr Kommissar!«
To order Mr commissioner

»Sie wissen, ich habe da doch diesen Fall – wie
You know I have there indeed this case how

hieß er doch gleich? –, ach ja, diesen Fall
was called he it indeed immediately oh yes this case

Klabautermann. Sie erinnern sich doch, Kollege?«
kobold you remember yourself indeed colleague

Die Augen beider trafen sich und verstanden sich.
The eyes of both found each other and understood each other

»Also, Herr Schröder, Sie gehen für mich aufs Präsidium
So Mr Schroeder you go for me on the Praesidium

und sagen dem Kollegen Linke – aber setzen Sie sich
and tell the colleague Linke however set you yourself

doch, Herr Kluge, entschuldigen Sie, ich will dem Kollegen
indeed Mr Kluge apologize you I want the colleague
forgive

nur noch ein paar Worte sagen.«
only still a few words say

Er ging mit dem Assistenten zur Tür. Er flüsterte:
He went with the assistant to the door He whispered

»Fordern Sie dort zwei Leute an. Sollen sofort
Demand you there two people on Should immediately
Get ready

hierherkommen, tüchtige Leute zum Beschatten. Dieser
here come efficient people to the shadowing This

Kluge wird vom Verlassen des Reviers an ohne
Kluge will from the leaving of the district on(wards) without

Unterbrechung beschattet. Meldung über seine Wege alle
under-breaking shadowed Notice over his ways all
pause

zwei, drei Stunden, wie's paßt, telefonisch zu mir auf die
two three hours how it suits by phone to me on the

Gestapo. Deckwort: Klabautermann. Zeigen Sie den beiden
gestapo Deck-word kobold Show you the both
Codeword

Leuten den Mann, sie sollen sich ablösen. Und
people the man they should each other relieve And

kommen Sie wieder hier rein, wenn die Männer
come you again here in when the men

bereitstehen. Dann laß ich das Häschen laufen.«
ready stand Then let I the little hare run

»Geht alles in Ordnung, Herr Kommissar. Heil Hitler!«
Goes everything in order Mr commissioner Hail Hitler

Die Tür klappte, der Bulle war gegangen. Neben Enno
The door clapped (swung) the cop was gone Beside Enno

Kluge setzte sich der Kommissar und sagte: »Also den
Kluge sat himself the commissioner and said So that one

wären wir los! Den mögen Sie wohl nicht sehr gerne,
were are we loose rid off That one like you well not very much

Herr Kluge?«
Mr Kluge

»Nicht so sehr wie Sie, Herr Kommissar!«
Not so much as you Mr commissioner!

»Haben Sie gesehen, was der für Augen machte, als er
Have she seen what that one for eyes made as he

hörte, ich lasse Sie laufen? Der hat jetzt eine schöne
heard I let you run That one has now a beautiful

Wut im Bauch! Deswegen habe ich ihn ja grade
anger in the belly Because of that have I him indeed immediately

weggeschickt, den kann ich bei unserm kleinen Protokoll
sent away that one can I at our small protocol report

nicht brauchen. Hätte uns immerzu reingeredet. Ich lasse
not need Had us always in-talked I let

nicht einmal ein Tippfräulein kommen, kliere die paar
not once a typing-lady come muck the few

Zeilen lieber allein. Ist ja doch nur eine Abmachung
lines rather alone Is yes indeed only a agreement

unter uns, damit ich vor meinen Vorgesetzten wegen
under us there-with I before my supervisor because of

Ihrer Freilassung ein bißchen gedeckt bin.«
your free-letting a bit covered am

Und nachdem er so den kleinen Angstpeter wieder
And after he so the small fearful rabbit again

beruhigt hatte, nahm er die Feder und begann zu
calmed down had took he the feather and began to

schreiben. Manchmal sagte er laut und deutlich, was er
write sometimes said he loud and clearly what he

schrieb (wenn er das schrieb, was er laut sagte, was bei
wrote when he that wrote what he loud said what at

einem so gerissenen Kriminalisten, wie es der Escherich
a such ripped cunning criminologist like it the Escherich

war, nicht einmal so ganz sicher war), manchmal
was not once so completely sure was sometimes

murmelte er nur. Kluge konnte nicht recht verstehen, was
murmured he only Kluge could not right really understand what

er sagte.
he said

Er sah nur, es wurden nicht nur ein paar Zeilen, es
He saw only it became not only a few lines it

wurden drei, es wurden fast vier Aktenseiten. Aber das
became three it became almost four file pages But that

interessierte ihn im Augenblick noch nicht einmal so
interested him in the moment still not once so

sehr, ihn interessierte bloß, ob er jetzt wirklich
much him interested just whether he now really

gleich freikam. Er sah nach der Tür hin. Mit einem
immediately free came He saw to the door away With a

raschen Entschluß stand er auf, ging zu ihr hin und
quick decision stood he up went to her away and

öffnete sie ein wenig ...
opened her a little

»Kluge!« rief es hinter ihm, aber nicht befehlend. »Herr
Kluge called it behind him but not commanding Mr

Kluge, ach bitte!«
kluge oh please

»Ja?« fragte er und sah zurück. »Ich darf wohl doch
Yes asked he and saw back I may well indeed

nicht gehen?« Er lächelte ängstlich.
not go He smiled fearfully anxiously

Der Kommissar sah ihn, den Federhalter in der Hand,
The commissioner looked him the penholder in the hand

mit einem Lächeln an. »Also reut Sie's schon wieder,
with a smile at So regret you it already again

Herr Kluge, was wir besprochen hatten? Was Sie mir fest
Mr Kluge what we discussed had What you me firmly

versprochen hatten? Nun, schön, habe ich den Kohl
promised had Now beautiful have I the cabbage

umsonst gekliert!« Er legte die Feder energisch weg.
for nothing clinched He put the feather energetically away

»Aber gehen Sie doch, Kluge - freilich, das sehe ich nun,
But go you indeed Kluge indeed that see I now

daß Sie kein Mann von Wort sind. Also gehen Sie schon,
that you no man of word are So go you already

ich weiß doch, Sie unterschreiben nicht! Ist auch gut,
I know indeed you sign not Is also good

meinethalben ...«
for my sake

Und auf diese Weise erreichte es der Kommissar, daß
And on this manner reached managed it the commissioner that

Enno Kluge wirklich das Protokoll unterschrieb. Ja, Kluge
Enno Kluge really the protocol report signed Yes Kluge

verlangte nicht einmal, daß es ihm vorher laut und
desired not once that it him before loud and

deutlich vorgelesen wurde. Er unterschrieb ahnungslos.
clearly read to became He signed without a clue

»Und jetzt darf ich gehen, Herr Kommissar?«
And now may I go Mr commissioner

»Natürlich. Besten Dank auch, Herr Kluge, haben Sie gut
Of course Best thanks also Mr Kluge have you well

gemacht. Auf Wiedersehen. Das heißt, besser nicht hier,
done On to see again That is called better not here
Until we meet again means

besser nicht an dieser Stelle. Ach, einen Augenblick noch,
better not on this spot Oh one moment still

Herr Kluge ...«
Mr Kluge

»Ich darf also doch nicht gehen?«
I may thus indeed not go

Im Gesicht Kluges zitterte es schon wieder.
In the face of Kluge trembled it already again

»Aber gewiß doch! Trauen Sie mir schon wieder nicht
But certainly indeed Trust you me already again not

mehr? Sind Sie aber ein mißtrauischer Mensch, Herr
(any)more Are you but a mistrustful human Mr
indeed

Kluge! Doch ich denke, Sie würden gerne Ihre Papiere
Kluge Indeed I think you would gladly your papers

und Ihr Geld mitnehmen? Na, sehen Sie! Also wollen wir
and your money take along Now see you So want we

mal schauen, ob auch alles da ist, Herr Kluge ...«
once see whether also everything there is Mr Kluge

Und sie fingen an zu vergleichen: Arbeitsbuch, Wehrpaß,
And they caught on to compare Work-book defense-pass
began

Geburtsurkunde, Trauschein ...
birth-certificate marriage-proof

»Wozu schleppen Sie eigentlich all die Papiere mit sich
Where-to haul you actually all these papers with yourself

rum, Kluge? Wenn die Ihnen mal verlorengehen!«
around Kluge When those you once lost go

... Polizeiliche Anmeldung, vier Lohntüten ...
Police notice four pay-sacks

»Viel verdienen Sie aber nicht, Herr Kluge! Ach so, ja
Much earn you however not Mr Kluge Oh so yes

richtig, ich sehe, jede Woche nur drei, vier Tage
right I see each week only three four days

gearbeitet, Sie kleiner Drückeberger, Sie!«
worked you little shirker you

... Drei Briefe ...
Three letters

»Nee, lassen Sie nur, die interessieren mich gar nicht!«
No let you only those interest me at all not

... 37 Reichsmark in Scheinen und 65 Reichspfennig in
37 reichsmark in notes and 65 reichspennies in
(money)

Münzen ...
coins

»Sehen Sie, da haben wir ja auch den
See you there have we indeed also the

Zehnmarkschein, den Sie von dem Herrn bekommen
ten mark note which you from the gentleman become

haben, den nehme ich wohl lieber zu den Akten. Aber,
have that one take I well rather to the files But

warten Sie, Sie sollen dadurch keinen Verlust haben, ich
wait you you should there-through no loss have I
through that

gebe Ihnen zehn Mark von mir als Ersatz ...«
give you ten mark from myself as replacement
{money}

So trieb es der Kommissar so lange, bis der Assistent
So drove it the commissioner so long until the assistant
continued

Schröder wieder hereinkam: »Befehl ausgeführt, Herr
Schroeder again came in Order executed Mr

Kommissar. Und ich soll melden, der Kommissar Linke
commissioner And I should report the commissioner Linke

möchte Sie auch noch gerne wegen des Falls
may you also still gladly because of of the case

Klabautermann sprechen.«
kobold speak

»Schön, schön. Danke auch bestens, Kollege. Ja, wir hier
Beautiful beautiful Thank also best colleague Yes we here

sind fertig. Also denn auf Wiedersehen, Herr Kluge.
are ready So then on see again Mr Kluge
to

Schröder, zeigen Sie dem Herrn Kluge doch mal den
Schroeder show you the gentleman Kluge indeed once the

Weg. Also, Herr Schröder geht mit durch die
way So Mr Schroeder goes along through the

Revierstube. Nochmals auf Wiedersehen, Herr Kluge. Die
district room Again on see again Mr Kluge The
police station room to

Fabrik vergesse ich nicht. Nein, nein! Heil Hitler!«
factory forget I not No no Hail Hilter

»Na, denn nichts für ungut, Herr Kluge«, sagte Schröder,
Now then nothing for un-good Mr Kluge said Schroeder

stand auf der Frankfurter Allee und schüttelte ihm die
stood on the Frankfurter avenue and shook him the

Hand. »Sie wissen, Beruf ist Beruf, und manchmal
hand You know occupation is occupation and sometimes

müssen wir auch ein bißchen derb zufassen. Aber ich
must we also a bit coarse grab on But I

habe Ihnen gleich wieder die Handfessel abnehmen
have you immediately again the handcuffs take off

lassen. Von dem Puff, den Ihnen der Wachtmeister gab,
let From the bang which you the guard-master gave
hit officer

spüren Sie doch nichts mehr?«
feel you indeed nothing (any)more

»Nein, gar nichts. Und ich verstehe auch alles ...
No at all nothing And I understand also everything

Entschuldigen Sie bloß die Mühe, die ich Ihnen gemacht
Apologize you just the trouble which I you made
Forgive me

habe, Herr Kommissar.«
have Mr commissioner

»Also denn: Heil Hitler, Herr Kluge!«
So then Hail Hitler Mr Kluge

»Heil Hitler, Herr Kommissar!«
Hail Hitler Mr commissioner

Und der kleine, schmächtige Enno Kluge trabte los. Er
And the little slender Enno Kluge trotted loose He

lief in einem richtigen Zuckeltrab durch die Menschen auf
ran in a true jog-trot through the people on

der Frankfurter Allee, und der Assistent Schröder sah
the Frankfurter avenue and the assistant Schroeder looked

ihm nach. Er überzeugte sich noch, daß die beiden
him after He convinced himself still that the both

Leute, die er angesetzt hatte, richtig auf seiner Spur
people who he set on had right on his trace

waren, nickte dann und ging zurück auf die Wache.
were nodded then and went back on the guard

Kommissar Escherich bearbeitet die Sache Klabautermann

Commissary Escherich works on the case Kobold

»Da, lesen Sie!« sagte der Kommissar Escherich zu dem
There read you said the commissioner Escherich to the

Assistenten Schröder und gab ihm das Protokoll in die
assistant Schroeder and gave him the protocol in the
report

Hand.
hand

»Tja«, antwortete Schröder und reichte die Bogen zurück.
Well answered Schroeder and reached the sheet back
handed

»Da hat er es also doch gestanden und ist nun reif für
There has he it also indeed stood and is now ripe for
declared

den Volksgerichtshof und den Scharfrichter. Ich hätte es
the people's court and the executioner I had it

nicht gedacht.« Er setzte nachdenklich hinzu: »Und
not thought He set thoughtful there-to And
added

so was läuft frei auf der Straße rum!«
so what runs free on the street around
something like that

»Jawohl!« sagte der Kommissar, legte das Protokoll in
Yes said the commissioner put the protocol in
report

einen Aktendeckel und den Aktendeckel wieder in seine
a file cover and the file cover again in his

Ledertasche. »Jawohl, so was läuft nun frei auf der
leather bag Yes so what runs now free on the
something like that

Straße rum – aber doch wohl ordentlich beschattet von
street around but indeed well properly shadowed from
followed by

unseren Leuten?«
our people

»Selbstverständlich!« beeilte sich Schröder zu versichern.
Of course hastened himself Schroeder to assure

»Ich habe mich selbst davon überzeugt: sie waren ihm
I have me myself there-from convinced they were him

beide gut auf der Spur.«
both good on the track
trail

»Und da läuft er rum«, fuhr der Kommissar
And there runs he around drove the commissioner
continued

Escherich, nachdenklich seinen Schnurrbart streichelnd, fort,
Escherich thoughtful his moustache stroking away
on

»läuft und läuft, und unsere Leute laufen hinter ihm
runs and runs and our people run behind him

drein! Und eines Tages – heute oder in einer Woche oder
there-in And one day today or in a week or

in einem halben Jahr – läuft unser kleiner, fieser Herr
in a half year runs our little nasty Mr

Kluge zu seinem Kartenschreiber, zu dem Mann, der ihm
Kluge to his card writer to the man who him

den Auftrag gab: Leg sie da und dort ab. Zu dem
the mission gave Lay her there and there off To that one
Drop it

führt er uns so sicher, wie das Amen in der Kirche
leads he us so sure as the poor in the church

kommt. Und da mache ich schnapp, und dann erst sind
come And there make I snap and then first are
then will I snap my fingers

die beiden richtig reif für die Plötze und so weiter und
these both right ripe for the roach and so further and

so fort.«
so away
on

»Herr Kommissar«, sagte der Assistent Schröder, »ich
Mr commissioner said the assistant Schroeder I

kann's noch immer nicht ganz glauben, daß der Kluge
can it still always not completely believe that the Kluge

die Karte hingelegt hat. Ich hab's doch gesehen, wie ich
the card laid down has I have it indeed seen how I

sie ihm in die Hand gab, der hat noch nie was
her him in the hand gave that one has still never what
it anything

von der Karte gewußt! Das hat sich alles bloß dieses
from the card known That has herself everything just this

hysterische Frauenzimmer, die Sprechstundenhilfe,
hysterical woman the speak-hours-help
assistant

ausgedacht.«
thought up

»Aber es steht doch im Protokoll, daß er sie hingelegt
But it stands indeed in the protocol that he her laid down
report it

hat«, wandte der Kommissar ein, doch ohne besonderen
has turned the commissioner in indeed without special
countered the commissioner

Nachdruck. »Im übrigen möchte ich Ihnen raten, in
emphasis In the rest may I you advise in
For the

Ihrem Bericht nichts vom hysterischen Frauenzimmer zu
your message nothing from the hysterical woman to

schreiben. Keine persönlichen Vorurteile, rein sachlich.
write No personal prejudices clean businesslike

Wenn Sie wollen, können Sie ja noch den Arzt
when you want can you yes still the doctor
indeed

wegen der Glaubwürdigkeit seiner Hilfe befragen. Ach
because of the credibility his help ask Oh

nein, lassen Sie das man auch lieber. Das wird auch
no let you that one also rather That becomes also

wieder so ein persönliches Urteil, das können wir dem
again such a personal judgement that can we (to) the

Untersuchungsrichter überlassen, wie er die einzelnen
examining magistrate leave over as he the single

Aussagen bewertet. Wir arbeiten nur rein sachlich,
out-sayings rates We work only clean businesslike
declarations

nicht wahr, Schröder, ohne jedes Vorurteil.«
not true Schroeder without each prejudice
isn't it

»Selbstverständlich, Herr Kommissar.«
Of course mr commissioner

»Wenn da eine Aussage steht, so steht da eben eine
if there a statement stands so stands there just a

Aussage, und an die halten wir uns. Wie und
statement and on that (one) keep we ourselves As and

warum sie zustande gekommen ist,
why she to-stand come is
it in existence

das geht uns nichts an. Wir sind ja keine Psychologen,
that goes us nothing on We are yes no psychologists
that's unimportant to us indeed

wir sind Kriminalisten. Crime, Verbrechen zu deutsch,
we are criminologists Crime crimes to German
(English) in

Schröder, nur das Verbrechen interessiert uns. Und wenn
schroeder only the crimes interest us And when

einer gesteht, er hat ein Verbrechen begangen, so
one confesses he has a crime committed so

genügt uns das. Das ist wenigstens meine Ansicht von
is sufficient to us that That is at least my opinion from

der Sache, oder denken Sie anders darüber, Schröder?«
the case or think you different about it Schröder

»Aber selbstverständlich nicht, Herr Kommissar!« rief der
But self-understandably not mr commissioner! called the
self-evidently

Assistent Schröder aus. Es klang, als sei er maßlos
assistant schroeder out It sounded as be he measureless

erschrocken über den Gedanken, er könne irgend etwas
frightened over the thoughts he could any something

anders auffassen als sein Vorgesetzter. »Genau, was ich
different understand as his before-sitter boss Exactly what I

denke! Immer gegen das Verbrechen!«
think always against the crime

»Ich wußte es ja«, sagte der Kommissar Escherich und
I knew it yes indeed said the commissioner Escherich and

streichelte seinen Bart. »Wir alten Kriminalisten sind doch
petted stroke his beard We old criminologists are indeed

immer einer Meinung. Wissen Sie, Schröder, es arbeiten
always (of) one opinion Know you Schroeder it there work

jetzt viele Außenseiter in unserm Beruf, aber wir halten
now many outsiders in our occupation but we hold keep

doch stets zusammen, und davon haben wir ja
indeed all the time together and there-from have we yes indeed

denn auch manches Gute. Also, Schröder«, dieses rein
then also much good Thus Schroeder this saying it clean

dienstlich, »ich bekomme dann heute noch Ihren Bericht
official formal I get then today still your message

über die Verhaftung des Kluge und das Protokoll mit den
over the arrest of the Kluge and the protocol report with the

Aussagen der Sprechstundenhilfe und des Arztes. Ja,
declarations of the speak-hours-help and of the doctor Yes
assistant

richtig, Sie hatten ja auch einen Wachtmeister mit,
right you had yes also a guard-master along
officer

Schröder ...«
Schroeder

»Oberwachtmeister Dubberke hier vom Revier ...«
Chief constable Dubberke here from the district

»Kenn ich nicht. Soll aber auch einen Bericht machen
Know I not Should however also a message make
Don't know him report

über das Ausreißen des Kluge. Kurz, sachlich, kein
over the tear out of the Kluge Short businesslike no
catching

Geschwafel, keine persönlichen Urteile, verstanden, Herr
gobbledygook no personal judgments understood mr

Schröder?«
Schröder

»Zu Befehl, Herr Kommissar!«
To order Mr commissioner!
At your command

»Also denn, Schröder! Wenn Sie die Berichte abgegeben
So then Schroeder when you the messages delivered
reports

haben, werden Sie ja mit dieser Sache nicht mehr
have become you yes with this thing not (any)more

befaßt werden, höchstens mal irgendeine Aussage vor
deals become at most once some statement before

einem Richter oder bei uns auf der Gestapo ...« Er
a judge or at us on the gestapo He

betrachtete seinen Untergebenen sinnend. »Wie lange sind
regarded his subordinate pondering How long are

Sie schon Assistent, Herr Schröder?«
you already assistant Mr Schröder

»Schon dreieinhalb Jahre, Herr Kommissar.«
Already three and a half years Mr commissioner

Das Auge des »Bullen«, wie es jetzt auf dem Kommissar
The eye of the cops as it now on the commissioner

lag, hatte etwas Rührendes.
lay had something touching
emotional

Aber der Kommissar sagte nur: »Ja, dann wird's ja
But the commissioner said only Yes then becomes it yes
indeed

auch allmählich Zeit«, und verließ das Revier.
also gradually time and left the district
(hinting on promotion)

In der Prinz-Albrecht-Straße ließ er sich dann sofort
In the Prinz-Albrecht-straße let he himself then immediately

bei seinem direkten Vorgesetzten, dem
at his direct supervisor the

SS-Obergruppenführer Prall, melden. Er mußte fast eine
SS-over-groups-leader Prall announce He must almost an
(SS officer)

Stunde warten; nicht, daß Herr Prall grade sehr
hour wait not that Mr Prall right very

beschäftigt gewesen wäre, oder doch, er war grade sehr
occupied been would be or indeed he was right very

beschäftigt. Escherich hörte das Klirren von Gläsern, das
occupied Escherich heard the clattering from glasses the

Schnalzen der Pfropfen, er hörte Gelächter und Geschrei:
snapping of the stoppers he heard laughter and shouting

eine der häufigen Zusammenkünfte höherer Führer also.
one of the frequent meetings of higher leaders thus

Geselligkeit, Umtrunk, heitere Zwanglosigkeit, Erholung nach
Conviviality drinks cheerful unconstraint recreation after

der schweren Mühe, Mitmenschen zu quälen und an den
the heavy trouble fellow humans to hurt and to the

Galgen zu bringen.
gallows to bring

Der Kommissar wartete ohne Ungeduld, obwohl er an
The commissioner waited without impatience although he on

diesem Tage noch viel vorhatte. Er kannte die
this day still much intended He knew the

Vorgesetzten im allgemeinen, und er kannte diesen
supervisor in the general and he knew this

Vorgesetzten im besonderen. Da half kein Drängeln,
supervisor in the special especially There helped no jostle

und wenn halb Berlin in Flammen stand, wenn der
and when half Berlin in flames stood when that one

saufen wollte, so soff er erst mal. Das war so!
drink wanted so drank he first once That was so

Nach einem Stündchen wurde Escherich dann aber doch
After a little hour became Escherich then but indeed

vorgelassen. Das Zimmer mit den deutlichen Spuren eines
previous The room with the clear traces of a

Trinkgelages sah ziemlich wüst aus, und der Herr Prall,
drinking bout saw rather wild out and the Mr Prall

dunkelrot von Armagnac glühend, sah auch ziemlich wüst
dark red from Armagnac glowing saw also rather wild

aus. Aber er sagte leutselig: »Da, Escherich! Schenken Sie
out But he said affable There Escherich Pour you

sich doch auch ein Glas ein! Das sind die Früchte
yourself indeed also a glass in Those are the fruits

unseres Sieges über Frankreich: echter Armagnac: zehnmal
(of) our victory over France real Armagnac ten times

besser als Kognak. Zehnmal? Hundertmal! Warum trinken
better as cognac Ten times (A) hundred times Why drink

Sie nicht?«
you not

»Bitte um Verzeihung, Herr Obergruppenführer, ich habe
Ask for forgiveness Mr over-groups-leader I have

heute noch ziemlich viel zu tun, möchte einen klaren
today still rather much to do may a clear

Kopf behalten. Übrigens bin ich das Trinken nicht mehr
head keep By the way am I the drinking not (any)more

gewohnt.«
used to

»Ach was, nicht gewohnt! Klarer Kopf, Flausen! Wozu
Oh what not used Clear head fluff To which

brauchen Sie einen klaren Kopf? Lassen Sie jemand anders
need you a clear head Let you someone else

Ihre Arbeit tun und schlafen Sie sich aus. Prost,
your work do and sleep you yourself out Cheers

Escherich – auf unsern Führer!«
Escherich on our leader

Escherich prostete mit, weil er mußte. Er prostete auch
Escherich toasted along because he must He toasted also

noch ein zweites und ein drittes Mal mit, und dachte
still a second and a (a) third time along and thought

dabei, wie die Gesellschaft seiner Kameraden, zusammen
there-by how the company of his comrades together

mit dem Alkohol, diesen Mann verändert hatte. Prall war
with the alcohol this man changed had Prall was

sonst eigentlich immer ganz erträglich, nicht halb so
otherwise actually always completely bearable not half so

schlimm wie hundert andere Burschen, die mit ihren
bad as hundred other lads who with their

schwarzen Uniformen in diesem Bau herumliefen,
black uniforms in this construction building ran around

sondern eher ein bißchen zweiflerisch, eben nur
but before rather a little hesitant just only

»kommandiert«, wie er mal gesagt hatte, keineswegs von
commanded as he once said had in no way of

allem überzeugt.
everything convinced

Aber unter dem Einfluß von Kameraden und Alkohol wurde
But under the influence of comrades and alcohol became

er wie die: unberechenbar, brutal, sprunghaft und
he like them unpredictable brutal by leaps and bounds and

bereit, jede andere Ansicht sofort mit Stumpf und Stiel
ready each other opinion immediately with root and stem

auszurotten, und sei es nur eine andere Ansicht über
to eradicate and be it only even if it was just an other opinion over

das Trinken von Schnaps. Hätte ihm Escherich das
the drinking of schnapps Had him Escherich the

Anstoßen ernstlich verweigert, so wäre er so sicher
clinging (of glasses) seriously refused so would be he so sure

verloren gewesen, wie wenn er den schlimmsten
lost been as when he the worst

Verbrecher hätte laufenlassen. Ja, eigentlich wäre so was
criminal had let run Yes actually would be so what

noch unverzeihlicher gewesen, weil es an eine
still unpardonable been because it on a

persönliche Beleidigung grenzte, wenn der Untergebene
personal insult bordered when the subordinate

nicht so viel und so oft mit dem Vorgesetzten anstieß,
not so much and so often with the supervisor clang
toasted

wie der wünschte.
as that one wished

Escherich stieß also an, stieß mehrmals an und trank
Escherich bumped thus on bumped multiple times on and drank
clang his glass clang

mit.
along

»Also, was gibt's, Escherich?« sagte dann Prall und
So what gives it Escherich said then Prall and
is happening

versuchte, an seinem Schreibtisch möglichst grade zu
tried at his desk as possible straight to

stehen, an ihm und durch ihn. »Was haben Sie denn
stand at him and through him What have you then
it because of it

da?«
there

»Ein Protokoll«, erklärte Escherich. »Von mir aufgenommen
A protocol explained Escherich Of me taken up
report

in Sachen meines Klabautermanns. Ein paar andere
in things of my Klabautermann A few other

Berichte und Protokolle folgen noch, aber dieses ist das
messages and protocols follow still but this is the
reports reports

wichtigste. Bitte, Herr Obergruppenführer.«
most important Ask, Mr obergruppenführer
Here you go

»Klabautermann?« fragte Prall, scharf nachdenkend. »Das
Klabautermann asked Prall sharp reflecting That

ist doch der Kerl mit den Karten. Na, ist Ihnen da
is indeed the chap with the (post)cards Now is them there

doch was eingefallen, Escherich, wie ich Ihnen befohlen
indeed what occurred Escherich as I you ordered

habe?«
have

»Zu Befehl, Herr Obergruppenführer. Wenn Herr
To order Mr over-groups-leader When Mr

Obergruppenführer das Protokoll lesen würde?«
over-groups-leader the protocol read would
report

»Lesen? Nee, nicht jetzt. Später vielleicht mal. Lesen Sie
Read No not now Later perhaps once Read you

jetzt mal vor, Escherich!«
now once before Escherich
aloud

Aber er unterbrach die Vorlesung nach den ersten drei
But he interrupted the lecture at the first three

Sätzen. »Wollen erst noch mal einen genehmigen. Prost,
sentences Want first still once one authorize take Cheers

Escherich! Heil Hitler!«
Escherich Hail Hitler"

»Heil Hitler, Herr Obergruppenführer!«
Hail Hitler Mr over-groups-leader

Und nachdem er ausgetrunken hatte, fing Escherich
And after he drunk out had caught started Escherich

wieder mit Vorlesen an.
again with reading aloud on

Aber nun war dem alkoholisierten Prall ein neckisches
But now was the alcoholized Prall a teasing

Spiel eingefallen. Immer, wenn Escherich drei, vier Sätze
play occurred Always when Escherich three four sentences

gelesen hatte, unterbrach er ihn mit einem »Prost!«, und
read had interrupted he him with a Cheers and

Escherich mußte, nachdem er auch geprostet hatte, wieder
Escherich must after he also toasted had again

von vorn anfangen. Nie ließ Prall ihn über die
from the front the beginning start Never let Prall him over the

erste Seite hinauskommen, schon unterbrach er ihn mit
first side come out already interrupted he him with

einem neuen »Prost!« Er sah wohl – trotz all seiner
a new Cheers He saw well despite all his

Besoffenheit –, wie es in dem Manne arbeitete, wie das
drunkenness how it in the man worked how the

scharfe Getränk ihm widerstand, daß er zehnmal die Lust
sharp drink him stood against that he ten times the desire
revolted

hatte, das Protokoll hinzulegen und fortzugehen, und wie
had the protocol to lay down and to go away and how
report

er es nicht wagte, weil der andere eben der Vorgesetzte
he it not dared because the other just the superimposed
boss

war, wie er kuschen mußte, sich den Zorn nicht merken
was who he kiss must himself the anger not notice

lassen durfte ...
let was allowed

»Prost, Escherich!«
Cheers Escherich

»Danke gehorsamst, Herr Obergruppenführer! Prost!«
Thanks obediently Mr over-groups-leader Cheers

»Na, nun lesen Sie doch weiter, Escherich! Nee, fangen
Now now read you indeed further Escherich No catch
start

Sie noch mal wieder von vorne an. Die eine Stelle
you still once again from in front on That one spot
the beginning line

ist mir noch nicht ganz aufgegangen. Immer ein
is me still not completely gone up Always a
become clear

langsamer Denker gewesen ...«
slow thinker been

Und Escherich las. Ja, jetzt wurde er genauso gequält,
And Escherich read Yes now became he exactly so tormented

wie er vor zwei Stunden den schmächtigen Kluge
as he before two hours the lanky Kluge
two hours earlier

gequält hatte, genau wie den plagte auch ihn nur das
tormented had exactly as the plagued also him only the
tortured one

Verlangen, aus der Tür herauszukommen. Aber er mußte
desire from the door to come out But he must

lesen, lesen und trinken, trinken und lesen, solange das
read read and drink drink and read as long (as) the

dem andern beliebte. Er fühlte schon, wie es flockig,
the other pleased He felt already as it flaky

wolkig in seinem Kopf zog – seine gute Arbeit, ade!
cloudy in his head pulled his good work goodbye

Verdammte Zucht!
Damned breed

»Prost, Escherich!«
Cheers Escherich

»Prost, Herr Obergruppenführer!«
Cheers Mr over-groups-leader

»Na, denn lesen Sie noch mal von Anfang an!«
Now then read you still once from beginning on

Bis dieses Spiel dem Prall plötzlich langweilig wurde, bis
Until this play the Prall suddenly boring became until

er grob sagte: »Ach, lassen Sie doch diese blöde
he rough said Oh let you indeed this stupid

Vorleserei! Sie sehen doch, ich bin besoffen, wie soll ich
reading aloud You see indeed I am drunk how should I

denn da das Zeugs kapieren? Wollen sich wohl mit
then there that stuff understand Want yourself well with

Ihrem geistreichen Protokoll dicketun, was? Andere Berichte
your witty protocol report show off what Other reports

folgen, sind nicht so wichtig wie der vom großen
follow are not so important as the one from the large

Kriminalisten Escherich! Wenn ich schon so was höre!
criminologist Escherich When I already so what hear

Kurz und Furz: Haben Sie den Kartenschreiber
Short and fart Have you the card writer

geschnappt?«
snatched

»Zu Befehl, nein, Herr Obergruppenführer. Aber ...«
To order no Mr over-groups-leader But «

»Und warum kommen Sie denn da zu mir? Warum
And why come you then there to me Why

stehlen Sie mir meine kostbare Zeit und saufen mir den
steal you me my costly time and drink me the

schönen Armagnac weg?« Dies war nun schon reines
beautiful Armagnac away This was now already pure

Gebrüll. »Sie sind wohl ganz wahnsinnig geworden,
roaring You are well completely insane become

Herr? Aber mit Ihnen werde ich jetzt in einem andern
sir But with you will I now in an other

Ton reden, Herr! Bin viel zu gutmütig gewesen, habe
tone talk sir Am much to good-natured been have

Sie zu frech werden lassen, verstanden?«
you too fresh become let understood
cheeky

»Zu Befehl, Herr Obergruppenführer!« Und rasch, ehe das
To order Mr over-groups-leader And quickly before the

Geschrei von neuem losging, stieß Escherich hervor:
shouting from new went off bumped Escherich forth
again started

»Aber ich habe jemanden gefaßt, der die Karten verteilt
But I have someone taken who the cards distributed

hat. Ich denke wenigstens.«
has I think at least

Diese Nachricht besänftigte Prall ein bißchen. Er sah den
This message appeased Prall a little He saw the

Kommissar mit stieren Augen an und sagte: »Vorführen
commissioner with staring eyes on and said Before lead

den Mann! Soll mir sagen, wer ihm die Karten gegeben
the man Should me say who him the cards given

hat. Werde ihn zwiebeln – bin grade in der Stimmung
has Will him harass am right in the mood

dazu!«
to it

Einen Augenblick schwankte Escherich. Er hätte sagen
One moment swayed Escherich He had say

können, daß der Mann noch nicht in der
can that the man still not in the

Prinz-Albrecht-Straße war, daß er ihn holen würde – und
Prinz-Albrecht-straße was that he him get would and

dann würde er ihn wirklich holen, nämlich von der Straße
then would he him really get namely from the street

her oder aus seiner Wohnung, mit Hilfe der Beschatter.
away or from his house with help of the tail follower

Oder aber er würde ruhig aus der Ferne abwarten, bis
Or however he would calm from the distance off-wait await until

der Obergruppenführer seinen Rausch ausgeschlafen hatte.
the over-groups-leader his trance slept in had

Dann würde er wahrscheinlich alles vergessen haben.
Then would he probably everything forgotten have

Aber weil Escherich eben der Escherich war, nämlich ein
But because Escherich just the Escherich was namely one

in seinen Sünden gesottener Kriminalist, nämlich nicht
in his sins boiled criminologist namely not

feige, sondern er war mutig, und aus dem Mut heraus
cowardly but he was brave and from the courage out

sagte er (es komme, was da wolle): »Ich habe den
said he it come what there wanted I have the

Mann wieder auf freien Fuß gesetzt, Herr
man again on free foot set Mr

Obergruppenführer!«
over-groups-leader

Gebrüll – nein, du lieber Himmel, was für ein tierisches
(A) roar no you dear heaven what for an animalistic

Gebrüll! Der sonst wirklich für einen höheren Führer
roar The otherwise really for a high leader

recht gesittete Prall vergaß sich doch so weit, daß er
right well-mannered Prall forgot himself indeed so far that he

seinen Kommissar vor der Brust faßte, ihn hin und her
his commissioner before the breast seized him away and away
on there here

schüttelte und dabei schrie: »Freigelassen? Freigelassen?
shook and there-by cried Released Released

Weißt du, was ich nun mit dir machen werde, du
Know you what I now with you do will you

Schwein? Jetzt werde ich dich einstecken, jetzt sollst du
swine Now will I you plug in now will you

mal sitzen! Warte, eine Tausendwattlampe hänge ich dir
once sit Wait a thousand watt lamp hang I you

vor deinen Schnurrbart, und wenn du einschläfst, lasse
before your moustache and when you fall asleep let

ich dich wachprügeln, du Aas ...«
I you awake beat you carrion

So ging es noch eine ganze Weile weiter. Escherich ließ
So went it still a whole while further Escherich let

sich schütteln und beschimpfen, er hielt ganz still.
himself shake and insult he held completely quiet

Jetzt war es vielleicht doch ganz gut, daß er Alkohol
Now was it perhaps indeed completely good that he alcohol

getrunken hatte. Ein wenig betäubt durch den Armagnac
drunk had A little dazed through the Armagnac

empfand er alles, was geschah, nur undeutlich, als sei
felt he everything what happened only indistinct as be

es mehr ein Traumgeschehen.
it more a dream event
rather

Schrei du nur! dachte er. Je lauter du schreist, um so
Scream you only thought he The louder you scream for so

eher wirst du heiser. Mach's nur so weiter, gib's dem
before become you hoarse Make it only so further give it the
Do it just

alten Escherich tüchtig!
old Escherich thoroughly

Und wirklich, nachdem er sich heiser geschrien, ließ
And really after he himself hoarse shouted let

Prall seinen Untergebenen los. Er goß sich ein
Prall his subordinate loose He poured himself an

weiteres Glas Armagnac ein, musterte Escherich mit bösem
additional glass Armagnac a looked at Escherich with evil

Blick und krächzte: »Nun melden Sie gefälligst, warum Sie
glance and croaked Now report you kindly why you

diese Riesendummheit gemacht haben!«
this giant stupidity done have

»Zuerst möchte ich melden«, sagte Escherich leise, »daß
First may I report said Escherich softly that

der Mann ständig durch zwei unserer besten Leute vom
the man constantly through two of our best people from the

Präsidium beschattet wird. Ich denke, früher oder später
praesidium shadowed will I think sooner or later

wird er doch seinen Auftraggeber, den Kartenschreiber,
will he indeed his client the card writer

aufsuchen. Jetzt leugnet er, ihn zu kennen. Der bekannte
seek out Now denies he him to know The known

große Unbekannte.«
great unknown

»Ich hätte den Namen schon aus ihm rausgepreßt. Diese
I had the name already from him squeezed out This

Beschatterei – womöglich verlieren die noch den Mann!«
tailing possibly lose they still the man

»Die nicht! Die tüchtigsten Leute vom Alex!«
They not The most efficient people from the Alex

»Na, na!« Aber ersichtlich zog bei Prall wieder besseres
Now now But evidently pulled at Prall again better

Wetter auf. »Sie wissen, ich will diese Eigenmächtigkeiten
weather up You know I want these idiosyncrasies

nicht haben! Ich hätte den Mann lieber in meinen
not have I had the man rather in my

Fingern!«
fingers

Das möchtest du! dachte Escherich. Und in einer halben
That would like you thought Escherich and in a half

Stunde hast du raus, daß der gar nichts mit den
hour have you there out that that one at all nothing with the
out of him he

Karten zu tun hat, und fängst wieder an, mich zu
(post)cards to do has and catch again on me to
start

hetzen ...
hurry
press

Laut aber sagte er: »Das ist ein so verängstigtes kleines
Aloud however said he That is a so frightened little

Geschöpf, Herr Obergruppenführer. Wenn Sie den
creature Mr over-groups-leader When you that one

zwiebeln, der sagt Ihnen alles aus, was Sie wollen,
harass that one says you everything out what you want

und wir laufen hinter hundert Lügen her. So führt er
and we run behind hundred lies away So leads he
This way

uns glatt zum Kartenschreiber.«
us smoothly to the card writer

Der Obergruppenführer lachte: »Na ja, Sie oller Fuchs,
The over-groups-leader laughed Now yes you old (one) fox
(alter)

also trinken wir noch einen!«
then drink we still one

Also tranken sie noch einen.
Thus drank they still one

Der Obergruppenführer sah den Kommissar prüfend an.
The over-groups-leader looked the commissioner examining at

Sichtlich hatte sein Zornesausbruch ihm gutgetan, hatte ihn
Visibly had his anger him well done had him

etwas nüchterner gemacht.
somewhat soberer made

Er überlegte, dann sagte er: »Von dem Protokoll da, Sie
He considered then said he Of the protocol there you
report

wissen schon ...«
know already

»Zu Befehl, Herr Obergruppenführer!«
To order Mr over-groups-leader

»... von dem Protokoll da lassen Sie mir ein paar
of the protocol there let you me a few
report

Abschriften anfertigen. Stecken Sie Ihr geistreiches
transcripts ready make Stick you your witty
draw up

Machwerk wieder ein.« Beide grinsten. »Hier gerät es
make-work again in Both grinned Here ends up it
homework

womöglich doch noch in den Armagnac ...«
possibly indeed still in the Armagnac

Escherich tat das Protokoll wieder in den Aktendeckel und
Escherich did the protocol again in the file cover and
put report

den Deckel in die Mappe.
the cover in the portfolio

Unterdes hatte sein Vorgesetzter in einer
Under-that had his before-sitter in a
Meanwhile boss

Schreibtischschublade gekramt und kam jetzt zurück, eine
desk drawer rummaged and came now back a

Hand auf dem Rücken. »Sagen Sie mal, Escherich, haben
hand on the back Say you once Escherich have

Sie eigentlich schon das Kriegsverdienstkreuz?«
you actually already the war merit cross

»Nein, Herr Obergruppenführer.«
No Mr obergruppenführer

»Irrtum, Escherich! Da haben Sie's!« Und er streckte
Error Escherich There have you it And he extended

überraschend die bisher verborgene Hand aus, auf deren
surprised the until-here hidden hand from on whose
as a surprise until now

Fläche das Kreuz lag.
surface the cross lay
palm

Der Kommissar war so überwältigt, daß er nur einzelne
The commissioner was so overwhelmed that he only single

Worte stammeln konnte. »Aber, Herr Obergruppenführer!
words stammer could But Mr over-groups-leader

Nicht verdient ... Finde keine Worte ...«
Not earned Find no words

Alles hatte er während des Anpfiffs fünf Minuten
Everything had he during of the kickoff five minutes

zuvor erwartet, sogar ein paar Tage und Nächte im
before expected even a few days and nights in the

Bunker hatte er für möglich gehalten, aber daß ihm
bunker had he for possible held but that him
cell

direkt darauf das Verdienstkreuz überreicht werden würde
directly thereupon the cross of merit presented become would

...

»... Jedenfalls danke ich gehorsamst.«
Anyhow thank I obediently

Der Obergruppenführer Prall weidete sich an der
The over-groups-leader Prall grazed himself on the

Überraschung des Dekorierten.
surprise of the decorated

»Na ja, Escherich«, sagte er dann. »Sie wissen ja, ich
Now yes Escherich said he then You know yes I
well

bin gar nicht so. Und schließlich sind Sie ja doch ein
am at all not so And finally are you yes indeed a
well

ganz tüchtiger Beamter. Man muß Sie nur manchmal
completely efficient civil servant One must you only sometimes

ein bißchen auf den Trab bringen, sonst schlafen Sie
a bit on the trot bring otherwise sleep you

mir noch ganz ein. Wollen noch mal einen genehmigen.
me still completely in Want still once one authorize
take

Prost, Escherich, auf Ihr Kreuz!«
Cheers Escherich on your cross

»Prost, Herr Obergruppenführer! Und nochmals meinen
Cheers Mr over-groups-leader And again my

gehorsamsten Dank!«
most obedient thanks

Der Obergruppenführer fing an zu schwatzen: »Eigentlich
The over-groups-leader caught on to babble Actually
started

war das Kreuz gar nicht für Sie bestimmt, Escherich.
was the cross at all not for you destined Escherich

Eigentlich sollte es Ihr Kollege, der Rusch, kriegen, für
actually should it your colleague the Rusch get for

eine ganz zackige Sache, die er mit einer ollen
a completely jagged thing that he with an old

Jüdin gedreht hat. Aber Sie kamen eben eher.« Er
Jewish lady turned has But you came just earlier He
done

schwatzte noch eine Weile weiter, drehte dann das Rotlicht
chatted still a while further turned then the red light

über seiner Tür an, was bedeutete: »Wichtige
over his door on what meant Important
which

Besprechung! Nicht stören!«, und legte sich zum Schlafen
meeting Not disturb and put himself to the sleep
Do not

auf eine Couch.
on a couch

Als Escherich, das Verdienstkreuz noch immer in der
As Escherich the cross of merit still always in the

Hand, sein Büro betrat, saß da sein Vertreter am
hand his office entered sat there his representative at the

Apparat und rief: »Was denn? Fall Klabautermann? Ist das
machine and called What then Case kobold Is that

kein Irrtum? Hier liegt kein Fall Klabautermann vor!«
no mistake Here lies no case kobold in front

»Geben Sie her!« sagte Escherich und faßte nach dem
Give you here said Escherich and grabbed after the

Hörer. »Und verdimensionieren Sie sich schleunigst!«
listener And oversize you yourself hurry

Er rief in den Apparat: »Ja, hier, Kommissar Escherich!
He called in the machine Yes here commissioner Escherich

Was ist mit Klabautermann? Wollen wohl Meldung
What is with kobold Want well notice

erstatten?«
make

»Melde gehorsamst, Herr Kommissar, daß wir den Mann
Report obediently Mr commissioner that we the man

leider aus den Augen verloren haben, nämlich ...«
unfortunately from the eyes lost have namely

»Was haben Sie?«
What have you

Escherich war nahe daran, einen Zornesausbruch folgen zu
Escherich was close there-on an anger-outbreak follow to
to it

lassen, wie ihn eine Viertelstunde zuvor sein Vorgesetzter
let as him a quarter of an hour before his before-sitter
boss

gehabt hatte. Aber er bezwang sich: »Wie hat denn das
had had But he defeated himself How has then that
done held in

geschehen können? Ich denke, Sie sind ein tüchtiger
happened been able I think you are an efficient

Mann, und der Observierte ist doch bloß ein Männeken!«
man and the observed one is indeed just a little man

»Ja, das sagen Sie so, Herr Kommissar. Aber er kann
Yes that say you so Mr commissioner But he can

laufen wie ein Wiesel, und in dem Gedränge auf dem
run like a weasel and in the crowd on the

U-Bahnhof Alexanderplatz war er plötzlich weg. Er muß
subway station Alexanderplatz was he suddenly gone He must

gemerkt haben, daß wir ihn beschatteten!«
noticed have that we him shadowed

»Auch das noch!« stöhnte Escherich. »Hat's gemerkt! Ihr
Also that still groaned Escherich Hat it noticed Your

Hornochsen habt mir meinen ganzen Film verkorkst! Nun
horn oxes have me my whole movie messed up Now

kann ich euch nicht mehr schicken, er kennt euch ja.
can I you not (any)more send he knows you yes

Und neue kennen ihn wieder nicht!« Er überlegte: »Also
And new know him again not He considered So

schnellstens zurück aufs Präsidium! Jeder von euch
as soon as possible back on the praesidium Each from you

beiden holt sich einen Ersatzmann. Und der eine von
both gets himself a substitute And the one from

euch nimmt irgendwo in der nächsten Nähe seiner
you takes somewhere in the next proximity of his

Wohnung Posto, aber gut bedeckt, wohlverstanden?! Daß
house post but good covered well-understood That

er euch nicht noch mal ausreißt! Ihr habt nur die
he you not still once tears off escapes You have only the

Aufgabe, euerm Ersatzmann den Kluge zu zeigen, und
task your substitute the Kluge to show and

dann schwirrt ihr ab. Der andere geht zur Fabrik, wo
then whir go you off away The other goes to the factory where

er arbeitet, und meldet sich dort bei der Leitung.
he works and reports himself there at the management

Warten Sie doch, Sie großer Held, Sie müssen doch erst
Wait you indeed you great hero you must indeed first

die Adresse von der Wohnung haben!« Er suchte sie
the address from the house have He searched her

heraus und gab sie durch. »So, und nun schnellstens
out and gave her through So and now as soon as possible

auf eure Posten! In die Fabrik kann übrigens der
on your post In the factory can by the way the

Ersatzmann allein gehen, und das erst morgen früh. Da
substitute alone go and the first morning early There

werden sie ihm den Mann schon zeigen! Ich sage dort
will they him the man already show I say there

Bescheid. Und in einer Stunde bin ich selbst in seiner
information And in an hour am I myself in his

Wohnung ...«
house

Er hatte aber so viel zu diktieren und zu telefonieren,
He had however so much to dictate and to phone

daß er erst sehr viel später zur Wohnung der Eva
that he first very much later to the house of the Eva

Kluge kam. Seine Leute sah er nicht, und an der Tür
Kluge came His people saw he not and on the door

klingelte er umsonst. So blieb auch ihm nur die
resounded he for nothing So remained also him only the

Nachbarin, die Gesch.
neighbor the Gesch

»Der Kluge? Sie meinen den Kluge? Nee, der wohnt hier
The Kluge You mean the Kluge No he lives here

nich. Hier wohnt bloß seine Frau, lieber Mann, die
not Here lives just his wife dear man that one him

läßt den schon längst nicht mehr in die Wohnung.
lets that one she already long not (any)more in the house

Die ist aber verreist. Wo er wohnt? Wie soll ich
That one is however out of town Where he lives How should I

das wissen, lieber Mann? Der treibt sich doch nur so
that know dear man That one drives himself indeed only so

rum, immer mit Weibern. Ich hab wenigstens mal so was
around always with women I have at least once so what

gehört, aber ich will nischt gesagt haben. Die Frau hat
heard but I want nuthin' (nichts) said have The woman has

mir schon Vorwürfe genug gemacht, weil ich dem Mann
me already reproaches enough made because I the man

mal in ihre Wohnung geholfen habe.«
once in her house helped have

»Hören Sie mal, Frau Gesch«, sagte Escherich und war in
Hear you once Mrs Gesch said Escherich and was in

den Flur der Wohnung eingetreten, da sie ihm die Tür
the hall of the house stepped in there she him the door

vor der Nase zuschlagen wollte. »Nun erzählen Sie mir
before the nose to-strike wanted Now tell you me
slam shut

mal reineweg alles, was Sie von den Kluges wissen!«
once cleanly everything what you from the Kluges know

»Wie komm ich denn dazu, lieber Mann, und wie
How come I then there-to dear man and how

kommen Sie dazu, hier einfach in meine Wohnung ...«
come you there-to here simply in my house

»Ich bin nämlich der Kommissar Escherich von der
I am namely the commissioner Escherich from the

Geheimen Staatspolizei, und wenn Sie meinen Ausweis
secret state police and when you my identification card

sehen wollen ...«
see want

»Nee, nee!« rief die Gesch abwehrend und war
No no called the Gesch defensive and was

erschrocken bis an die Wand der Küche zurückgewichen.
frightened until on the wall of the kitchen backed away
up to

»Nischt will ich sehn, nischt will ich hören! Und von den
Nuthin' want I see nuthin' want I hear and from the
Nothing nothing

Kluges habe ich Ihnen schon alles gesagt, was ich
Kluges have I you already everything said what I

weiß!«
know

»Nun, ich denke, das werden Sie sich noch überlegen,
Now I think that will you yourself still consider

Frau Gesch, wenn Sie mir hier nämlich nichts erzählen
Mrs Gesch when you me here namely nothing tell

wollen, dann müßte ich Sie nach der Prinz-Albrecht-Straße
want then must I you to the Prinz-Albrecht-straße

auf die Gestapo einladen zu einem richtigen Verhör. Das
on the gestapo invite to a true interrogation That

würde Ihnen bestimmt keinen Spaß machen. Hier
would you definitely no fun make Here

unterhalten wir uns doch nur ein bißchen in aller
conversed we us indeed only a little in all

Gemütlichkeit, nichts wird aufgeschrieben ...«
coziness nothing becomes written down

»Ja doch, Herr Kommissar. Aber ich habe wirklich nichts
Yes indeed Mr commissioner But I have really nothing

mehr zu erzählen. Ich weiß doch von denen gar
(any)more to tell I know indeed from them at all

nichts.«
nothing

»Wie Sie wollen, Frau Gesch. Machen Sie sich dann
How you want Mrs Gesch Make you yourself then

fertig, ich habe unten ein paar Leute, Sie können
ready I have down a few people you can
downstairs

gleich mitkommen. Und legen Sie Ihrem Mann – Sie
immediately coming along And put you for your man You
husband

haben doch einen Mann? Aber natürlich haben Sie einen
have indeed a man But of course have you a
husband

Mann! –, also legen Sie Ihrem Mann mal einen Zettel
man so put you for your man once a note
husband

hin: ›Bin auf der Gestapo. Rückkunft unbestimmt.‹ Also
away Am on the gestapo Return indeterminate So

los, Frau Gesch! Schreiben Sie den Zettel!«
loose Mrs Gesch Write you the note

Die Gesch war blaß geworden, ihre Glieder flogen, die
The Gesch was pale become her members flew the
had arms and legs

Zähne klapperten in ihrem Mund.
teeth rattled in her mouth

»So was werden Sie doch nicht tun, lieber, lieber Herr!«
So what will you indeed not do dear dear sir

fleht sie.
begs she

Er antwortete mit gespielter Grobheit: »Natürlich werde ich
He answered with played coarseness Of course will I

so was tun, Frau Gesch, wenn Sie mir nämlich weiter
so what do Mrs Gesch when you me namely further

eine selbstverständliche Auskunft verweigern. Also seien Sie
a self-evident notice refuse Also are you

vernünftig, setzen Sie sich hierher und erzählen Sie mir
sensible set she yourself hereto and tell you me

alles, was Sie von den Kluges wissen. Wie ist denn die
everything what you from the Kluges know How is then the

Frau?«
woman

Natürlich nahm die Gesch Vernunft an. Im Grunde war
Of course took the Gesch reason up In the ground was

er ein sehr lieber Herr, dieser Herr von der
he a very dear gentleman this gentleman from the

Gestapo, ganz anders, als sie sich solche Herren
gestapo completely different as she herself such gentlemen

vorgestellt hatte. Und natürlich erfuhr Kommissar
imagined had And of course experienced heard commissioner

Escherich alles, was es eben bei der Gesch zu erfahren
Escherich everything what it just at the Gesch to experience

gab. Sogar von dem SS-Mann Karlemann hörte er, denn
gave Even from the SS man Karlemann heard he then

was die Eckkneipe wußte, das wußte die Gesch natürlich
what the corner pub knew that knew the Gesch of course

auch. Der tüchtigen Ex-Briefträgerin Eva Kluge hätte es
also The sound ex-letter carrier ex-postal worker Eva Kluge had it

das Herz abgedrückt, wenn sie gehört hätte, wie sehr sie
the heart squeezed when she heard had how much she

und ihr ehemaliger Liebling Karlemann in der Leute
and her former darling (sweet son) Karlemann in the people

Munde waren.
mouth were

Als Kommissar Escherich von der Gesch schied, ließ er
As commissioner Escherich from the Gesch parted let he

nicht nur ein paar Zigarren für den Mann zurück, sondern
not only a few cigars for the man back but

er hatte auch der Gestapo eine eifrige, unbezahlte und
he had also the gestapo an eager unpaid and

unbezahlbare Spionin gewonnen. Sie würde nicht nur auf
priceless spy won She would not only on

die Wohnung der Kluges ständig ein Auge haben,
the house of the Kluges constantly an eye have

sondern auch überall im Haus und in den Schlangen
but also everywhere in the house and in the lines

vor den Geschäften lauschen und den lieben
in front of the businesses listen and the dear
shops

Kommissar stets sofort anrufen, wenn sie was
commissioner all the time immediately call when she what
something

erfuhr, was er brauchen konnte.
experienced what he need could
heard

In Verfolg dieser Unterhaltung rief Kommissar Escherich
In track of this conversation called commissioner Escherich

seine beiden Leute wieder ab. Die Wahrscheinlichkeit, daß
his both people again off The probability that

man den Kluge in der Wohnung seiner Frau erwischte,
one the Kluge in the house of his woman caught

war nach dem Erfahrenen ganz gering, außerdem
was to the experiences quite small in addition

paßte die Gesch auf die Wohnung auf. Dann ging
fitted the Gesch on the house on Then went
took the Gesch care of the house

Kommissar Escherich noch auf das Postamt und zu der
commissioner Escherich still on the post office and to the

Parteidienststelle und zog weitere Erkundigungen über
party office and pulled further inquiries over

diese Frau Kluge ein. Nie konnte man wissen, wozu
this Mrs Kluge in Never could one know where-to
for which

so was gut war.
so what good was
something like that

Escherich hätte denen auf der Post und Partei
Escherich had those on the mail and (political) party

ganz gut sagen können, daß er einen Zusammenhang
completely good tell can that he a context

zu kennen glaubte zwischen dem Parteiaustritt der Frau
to know believed between the party resignation of the Mrs

Kluge und den Schandtaten ihres Sohnes in Polen. Er
Kluge and the outrages of her son in Poland He
(child murders)

hätte auch die Adresse von Frau Kluge im Ruppinschen
had also the address from Mrs Kluge in the Ruppinsch

verraten können, hatte er sich doch von dem Brief von
betrayed can had he himself indeed from the letter of

der Kluge an die Gesch, als sie die Schlüssel schickte,
the Kluge on the Gesch as she the key sent

die Anschrift notiert. Aber Escherich tat das nicht, er
the address written down But Escherich did that not he

fragte viel, aber Auskünfte gab er nicht. Wohl war das
asked much but information gave he not Well was that

die Partei und das Postamt, also etwas Amtliches,
the (political) party and the post office also something official

aber die Gestapo ist nicht dafür da, andern in ihren
but the gestapo is not therefore there others in their

Geschäften zu helfen. Dafür ist sie sich zu gut – und
businesses affairs to help Therefore is she herself too good and

in diesem Punkte wenigstens teilte Kommissar Escherich
in this point at least shared commissioner Escherich

die allgemeine Gestapo-Einbildung vollkommen.
the general gestapo conceit perfectly

Das mußten auch die Herren in der Fabrik erfahren. Sie
That must also the gentlemen in the factory experience They

trugen Uniform, und sie waren in der Rangstufe und
carried uniform and they were in the rank and

auch vom Gehalt aus gesehen sicher etwas sehr viel
also from the salary out seen certainly some very much

Höheres als der farblose Kommissar. Aber er blieb
higher than the colorless commissioner But he remained

dabei: »Nein, meine Herren, was gegen den Kluge
there-by No my gentlemen what against the Kluge

vorliegt, das ist allein Sache der Geheimen Staatspolizei.
lies before that is alone thing of the secret state police

Darüber sage ich nichts. Ihnen eröffne ich nur, daß Sie
There-about say I nothing You open reveal I only that you

den Kluge anstandslos kommen und gehen lassen, wie er
the Kluge without objection come and go let how he

Lust hat, daß es keine Anschnauzereien und
desire has that it no snarks and

Verängstigungen mehr gibt, und daß Sie den durch
scares (any)more gives and that you the through

mich ausgewiesenen Beamten anstandslos Zulaß in
me designated officials without objection admittance in

Ihrem Betrieb geben und ihre Arbeit, soweit das in Ihrer
their operation give and their work so far that in your

Macht steht, unterstützen werden. Haben wir uns nun
power stands support will Have we ourselves now
lies

verstanden?«
understood

»Ich bitte um eine schriftliche Bestätigung dieser
I ask for a written confirmation of these

Anordnungen!« rief der Offizier. »Und das heute noch!«
arrangements called the officer And that today still

»Heute noch? Das wird ein bißchen spät. Aber vielleicht
Today still That becomes a little late But perhaps

morgen. Vor morgen kommt der Kluge bestimmt nicht.
tomorrow Before tomorrow comes the Kluge definitely not

Wenn er überhaupt wieder hierher kommt! Also dann, Heil
When he at all again hereto comes Thus then hail

Hitler, meine Herren!«
hitler my gentlemen

»Gottverdammich!« knirschte der Offizier. »Diese Kerle
God damn gnashed the officer These guys

werden immer anmaßender! Die ganze Gestapo soll der
become always more pretentious The whole gestapo should the

Henker holen! Die denken, weil sie jeden Deutschen
hangman get Those think because they every German

einstecken können, dürfen sie sich alles erlauben.
plug in jail can may they themselves everything permit

Aber ich bin Offizier, ich bin sogar Berufsoffizier ...«
But I am officer I am even professional officer

»Was ich noch sagen wollte ...« der Kopf Escherichs
What I still say wanted the head of Escherich

erschien wieder im Türspalt, »hat der Mann vielleicht
appeared again in the door gap has the man perhaps

hier noch Papiere, Briefe, persönliches Eigentum?«
here still papers letters personal property

»Da müssen Sie seinen Meister nach fragen! Der hat
There must you his master after ask That one has

einen Schlüssel zu seinem Schrank ...«
a key to his closet

»Also schön«, sagte Escherich und sank auf einen Stuhl.
Also beautiful said Escherich and sank on a chair

»Da fragen Sie denn also den Meister danach, Herr
There ask you then also the master there-after Mr

Oberleutnant! Aber wenn es Ihnen nicht zuviel Mühe
over-lieutenant But when it you not too much trouble

macht, ein bißchen schnell, ja?«
makes a bit fast yes

Einen Augenblick tauschten die beiden Blicke. Die Augen
One moment exchanged they both looks The eyes

des spöttischen farblosen Escherich und die vor Zorn
of the mocking colorless Escherich and the for of anger

dunklen des Oberleutnants führten einen Kampf
dark ones of the lieutenant led a fight

miteinander. Dann schlug der Offizier die Hacken
with each other Then struck the officer the heels

zusammen und verließ eilig den Raum, die gewünschte
together and left hurriedly the space the desired

Auskunft zu besorgen.
information to deliver

»Ulkige Kruke das!« sagte Escherich zu dem plötzlich
Funny stone jar fellow that said Escherich to the suddenly

eifrig an seinem Schreibtisch beschäftigten Parteibonzen.
zealously on his desk employed party boss

»Wünscht die Gestapo zum Henker. Möchte gerne wissen,
Wishes the gestapo to the hangman May gladly know

wie lange ihr hier noch sicher sitzen würdet, wenn wir
how long you here still sure sit would when we

nicht wären. Letzten Endes: der ganze Staat, das ist die
not were existed Last endes the whole country that is the

Gestapo. Ohne uns bräche alles zusammen – und ihr
gestapo Without us breaks everything together and you

ginget alle zum Henker!«
went all to the hangman

Frau Hete beschließt

Mrs Hete decides

Dem Kommissar Escherich wie seinen beiden Spionen
The commissioner Escherich as his both spies

vom Alex wäre es wohl recht seltsam zu
from the Alex (Alexanderplatz) would be it well right strangely to

vernehmen gewesen, daß der kleine Enno Kluge gar
hear been that the little Enno Kluge at all

nichts davon geahnt hatte, daß er beschattet wurde.
nothing there-from suspected had that he shadowed became

Sondern von dem Augenblick an, als ihn Assistent
But from the moment onwards as him assistant

Schröder endgültig in die Freiheit entließ, hatte er nur
Schroeder finally in the freedom let go had he only

den einen Gedanken: Bloß fort von hier und zur Hete!
the one thought Just away from here and to the Hete

Er lief durch die Straßen und sah keine Menschen, er
He ran through the streets and saw no people he

ahnte nicht, wer hinter und wer neben ihm war. Er sah
guessed not who behind and who beside him was He looked

nicht hoch, er dachte bloß: Hin zu Hete!
not up he thought just Away to Hete

Der Schacht der U-Bahn verschluckte ihn. Er stieg in

The shaft tunnel of the subway swallowed him He mounted in

einen Zug und entrann so für dieses Mal dem Kommissar

a train and escaped so for this once the commissioner

Escherich, den Herren vom Alex und der ganzen

Escherich the gentlemen from the Alex (Alexanderplatz) and the whole

Gestapo.

gestapo

Enno Kluge hatte sich entschlossen: Er fuhr erst noch

Enno Kluge had himself decided He drove went first still

einmal zur Lotte und holte seine Sachen. Er wollte

one-time to the Lotte and got his things He wanted

gleich mit seinem Koffer bei der Hete anrücken, da

immediately with his suitcases at the Hete approach there then

sah er denn, ob sie ihn wirklich liebte, und er bewies

saw he then whether she him really loved and he proved

ihr, daß er mit seinem alten Leben Schluß machen wollte.

her that he with his old life end make wanted

So kam es, daß ihn seine Beschatter im Gedränge und

So came it that him his tail follower in the crowd and

schlechten Licht der U-Bahn aus dem Auge verloren. Er

bad light of the subway from the eye lost He

war ja wirklich nur ein Schatten, dieser schmächtige
was yes indeed really only a shade this slender

Enno! Wäre er aber gleich zu der Hete gegangen –
Enno Would be he however immediately to the Hete gone

und zum Königstor konnte er ja vom Alex
and to the king's gate could he yes indeed from the Alex (Alexanderplatz)

aus gut zu Fuß gehen, da brauchte er keine U-Bahn –,
from good at foot go there needed he no subway

so hätten sie ihn nicht verloren und hätten in der
so had they him not lost and had in the

kleinen Tierhandlung immer wieder einen Ausgangspunkt
small pet shop always again a starting point

für ihre Beobachtungen gehabt.
for their observations had

Mit der Lotte hatte er Glück. Sie war nicht zu Hause,
With the Lotte had he luck She was not at house home

und eilig packte er seine paar Sachen in den
and hurriedly packed he his few things in the

Handkoffer. Er widerstand sogar der Versuchung, ihre
suitcase He resisted even the temptation her

Sachen zu durchstöbern, ob er etwa einiges zum
things to browse through whether he about some to the

Mitnehmen Brauchbares fände – nein, diesmal sollte es
take along usable would find no this time should it

anders werden. Nie wieder wie damals sollte es
different become Never again as at that time should it

kommen, als er in das enge Zimmer des kleinen Hotels
come as he in the narrow room of the small hotel

einzog, nein, diesmal wollte er wirklich ein anderes Leben
moved in no this time wanted he really an other life

führen – wenn die Hete ihn aufnahm.
lead when the Hete him uptook

Immer langsamer ging er, je näher er dem Laden kam.
Always slower went he the closer he to the shop came

Immer häufiger setzte er den Koffer ab, und so schwer
Always more often set he the suitcases off and so heavy

war der gar nicht. Immer öfter wischte er den
was that one at all not Always more often wiped he the

Schweiß von der Stirn, und so heiß war es auch nicht.
sweat from the forehead and so hot was it also not

Dann stand er vor dem Laden und spähte durch die
Then stood he before the shop and spied through the

blanken Gitterstäbe der Vogelkäfige hinein: ja, Hete war
bare lattice bars the bird cages inside yes Hete was

an der Arbeit. Sie bediente grade; vier, fünf Kunden
at the work She served right at that moment four five customers

standen im Laden. Er stellte sich zu ihnen und sah
stood in the shop He set himself to them and looked

stolz und doch zitternden Herzens zu, wie geschickt sie
proud and indeed with trembling heart on how able she

die Kunden abfertigte, wie höflich sie mit ihnen sprach.
the customers dispatched how polite she with them spoke

»Indische Hirse gibt es nicht mehr, meine Dame. Das
Indian millet gives it not (any)more my lady That
is there

müßten Sie doch wissen, wo Indien zum Empire gehört.
must you indeed know where India to the empire belongs

Aber bulgarische Hirse habe ich noch, die ist viel
But Bulgarian millet have I still that one is much

besser.«
better

Und sagte mitten aus der Bedienung heraus: »Ach, Herr
And said middle from the service out Oh Mr

Enno, das ist nett, daß Sie mir ein bißchen helfen wollen.
Enno that is nice that you me a bit help want

Den Koffer setzen Sie am besten in die Stube. Und
The suitcases set you at the best in the room And

dann holen Sie mir bitte gleich Vogelsand aus dem
then get you me please immediately bird sand from the

Keller. Katzensand brauche ich auch. Und dann
basement Cat sand need I also And then

Ameiseneier ...«
ant eggs

Und während er mit diesen und anderen Aufträgen vollauf
And while he with this and other orders fully

beschäftigt war, dachte er: Sie hat mich gleich
occupied was thought he She has me immediately

gesehen, und sie hat auch sofort gesehen, daß ich
seen and she has also immediately seen that I

einen Koffer mit habe. Daß ich ihn in die Stube setzen
a suitcase along have That I him in the room set
it

durfte, ist ein gutes Zeichen. Aber sicher wird sie mich
was allowed is a good sign But sure will she me

erst ausfragen, sie nimmt alles so schrecklich genau.
first out-question she takes everything so terribly exact
interrogate

Aber ich werde ihr schon irgendeine Geschichte erzählen.
but I will her already some story tell

Und dieser Mann um die Fünfzig, dieser alt gewordene
And this man around the fifty (years) this old become

Herumtreiber, Nichtstuer und Weiberheld betete wie ein
tramp Nothing-doer and womanizer prayed like a

Schulkind: Ach, lieber Gott, laß mich doch noch einmal
schoolchild Oh dear god let me indeed still once

Glück haben, nur dieses einzige Mal noch! Ich will auch
luck have only this only once still I want also

ganz bestimmt ein anderes Leben anfangen, nur mach,
completely definitely an other life start only make

daß mich die Hete aufnimmt!
that me the Hete takes up

So betete, bettelte er. Und dabei wünschte er doch, daß
So prayed begged he And there-by wished he indeed that

es noch recht lange hin bis zum Ladenschluß sein
it still right long away until to the shop closure been

möchte, bis zu dieser ausführlichen Aussprache und
may until to this detailed declaration and

seinem Geständnis, denn irgend etwas gestehen mußte er
his confession then any something confess must he

der Hete, das war klar. Wie sollte er ihr sonst
the Hete that was clear How should he her otherwise

begreiflich machen, warum er hier mit Sack und Pack
understandable make why he here with bag and pack

angerückt kam, und mit einem so dürftigen Sack und
pulled up came and with a so poor bag and

Pack dazu! Er hatte doch vor ihr immer den großen
pack there-to He had indeed before her always the big

Mann gespielt.
man played

Und dann war es plötzlich soweit. Schon längst war die
And then was it suddenly so far Already long was the

Ladentür geschlossen, anderthalb Stunden hatte es dann
store door closed one and a half hours had it then

noch gekostet, all seine Bewohner mit frischem Wasser
still costed all its residents with fresh water

und Futter zu versehen und den Laden aufzuräumen. Nun
and fodder to supply and the shop clean up Now

saßen die beiden einander gegenüber an dem runden
sat they both each other opposite at the round

Sofatisch, hatten gegessen, ein wenig geplaudert, immer
sofa table had eaten a little chatted always

ängstlich das Hauptthema vermeidend, und plötzlich hatte
fearfully / anxiously the main topic avoiding and suddenly had

diese zerfließende, verblühte Frau den Kopf erhoben und
this deliquescent withered woman the head risen and

gefragt: »Nun, Hänschen? Was ist es? Was ist dir
asked Now little Hans What is it What is you

geschehen?«
happened

Kaum hatte sie diese Worte in einem ganz mütterlich
Hardly had she these words in a completely motherly

besorgten Ton gesprochen, da fingen bei Enno die
worried tone spoken there caught / started at Enno the

Tränen an zu fließen; erst langsam, dann immer
tears on to flow first slowly then always

reichlicher strömten sie über sein mageres, farbloses
more abundant streamed they over his lean colorless

Gesicht, dessen Nase dabei stets spitzer zu werden
face of which the nose there-by all the time sharper to become

schien.
seemed

Er stöhnte: »Ach, Hete, ich kann nicht mehr! Es ist zu
He groaned Oh Hete I can not (any)more It is to

schlimm! Die Gestapo hat mich vorgehabt ...«
bad The gestapo has me intended / has it in for me

Und er verbarg, laut aufschluchzend, den Kopf an ihrem
And he hid loud sobbing the head on her

großen, mütterlichen Busen.
large maternal bosom

Bei diesen Worten richtete Frau Hete Häberle den Kopf
At these words rose woman Hete haberle the head

auf, in ihre Augen kam ein harter Glanz, ihr Nacken
up in her eyes came a hard radiance her neck

steifte sich, und sie fragte fast hastig: »Was haben sie
stiffened itself and she asked almost hastily What have they

denn von dir gewollt?«
then from you wanted

Der kleine Enno Kluge hatte es – in nachtwandlerischer
The little Enno Kluge had it in nightwalker

Sicherheit – mit seinen Worten so gut, wie es nur
security with his words so good as it only

möglich war, getroffen. Mit all seinen andern Geschichten,
possible was hit With all his other stories

mit denen er sich an ihr Mitleid oder an ihre Liebe
with which he himself on her compassion or on her love

hätte wenden können, wäre es ihm nicht so gut
had turn been able would be it him not so good

ergangen wie mit diesem Wort Gestapo. Denn Witwe Hete
gone as with this word gestapo Then widow Hete

Häberle haßte Unordnung, und nie hätte sie einen
Haberle hated disarray and never had she a

liederlichen Herumtreiber und Zeittotschläger in ihr Haus
dissolute tramp and time deadbeat in her house

und in ihre mütterlichen Arme genommen. Aber das eine
and in her maternal arms taken But the one

Wort Gestapo öffnete ihm alle Pforten ihres mütterlichen
word gestapo opened him all gates of her maternal

Herzens, ein von der Gestapo Verfolgter war von
heart a from the gestapo persecuted one was from

vornherein ihres Mitleids und ihrer Hilfe sicher.
in advance of her pity and her help sure

Denn ihren ersten Mann, einen kleinen kommunistischen
Then her first husband a small communist

Funktionär, hatte die Gestapo schon im Jahre 1934 in
official had the gestapo already in the year 1934 in
to

ein KZ abgeholt, und nie wieder hatte sie
a concentration camp dragged off and never again had she
(konzentrationslager)

von ihrem Mann etwas gesehen und gehört, außer
from her man something seen and heard except from

einem Paket, das ein paar zerrissene und verschmutzte
a package that a few torn and soiled

Sachen von ihm enthielt. Obenauf hatte der Totenschein
things from him contained Over-up had the death certificate
On top

gelegen, ausgestellt vom Standesamt II, Oranienburg,
lied exhibited from the registry office II Oranienburg
given out by the

Todesursache: Lungenentzündung. Aber sie hatte später von
cause of death pneumonia But she had later from

andern Häftlingen, die entlassen worden waren, gehört,
other prisoners who dismissed become were heard

was sie in Oranienburg und in dem nahegelegenen
what they in Oranienburg and in the nearby

KZ Sachsenhausen unter Lungenentzündung
concentration camp (konzentrationslager) Sachsenhausen under pneumonia

verstanden.
understood

Und nun hatte sie wieder einen Mann in ihren Armen,
And now had she again a man in her arms

einen Mann, für den sie bisher seines schüchternen,
a man for whom she until-here until now of his shy

anschmiegenden, liebebedürftigen Wesens halber schon
clinging in need of love being half already

Sympathie empfunden, und wieder war er von der Gestapo
sympathy perceived and again was he from the gestapo

verfolgt.
persecuted

»Ruhig, Hänschen!« sagte sie tröstend. »Erzähle mir nur
Quiet little Hansl said she consoling Tell me only

alles. Wenn einer von der Gestapo verfolgt wird,
everything When one from the gestapo persecuted becomes

der kann von mir alles haben!«
that one can from me everything have

Diese Worte waren Balsam in seinen Ohren, und er hätte
These words were balsam in his ears and he had

ja nicht der mit Frauen erfahrene Enno Kluge sein
yes indeed not the with women experienced Enno Kluge been

müssen, wenn er nicht seine Gelegenheit benutzt hätte.
must when he not his opportunity used had

Was er da unter vielem Schluchzen und Tränen
What he there under many sobbing and tears

vorbrachte, war nun freilich ein sonderliches Gemisch von
uttered was now indeed a peculiar mixture from

Wahrheit und Lüge: er brachte es doch sogar fertig, die
truth and lie he brought it indeed even ready the

Mißhandlungen durch den SS-Mann Persicke seine neuesten
maltreatment through by the SS man Persicke his latest

Abenteuer einzuschmuggeln.
adventure to smuggle in

Aber was diese Erzählung an Unwahrscheinlichem haben
But what this narrative on unlikely have

mochte, das verdeckte für Hete Häberle der Haß auf die
might that covered for Hete Haberle the hate on the
of

Gestapo. Und schon begann ihre Liebe einen strahlenden
gestapo And already began her love a radiant

Glanz um den Nichtsnutz an ihrer Brust zu weben, sie
shine for the good-for-nothing on her bosom to weave she

sagte: »Du hast also das Protokoll unterschrieben und
said You have also the protocol signed and
report

dadurch den Täter gedeckt, Hänschen. Das war sehr
there-through the offender covered little Hans That was very
through that

mutig von dir, ich bewundere dich. Von zehn Männern
brave of you I admire you From ten men

hätte das kaum einer gewagt. Aber, das weißt du doch,
had that hardly one dared But that know you indeed

wenn sie dich kriegen, so bekommst du es schlimm, denn
when they you get so get you it bad then

daß sie dich mit diesem Protokoll für immer in der Falle
that they you with this protocol for always in the trap
report

haben, ist doch ganz klar.«
have is indeed completely clear

Er sagte, schon halb getröstet: »Oh, wenn du nur zu mir
He said already half consoled Oh when you only to me

hältst, werden die mich nie kriegen!«
keep will they me never get

Aber sie schüttelte leise und bedenklich den Kopf. »Ich
But she shook softly and thoughtful the head I

verstehe nicht, warum sie dich überhaupt wieder
understand not why they you at all again

losgelassen haben.« Plötzlich fiel es ihr schrecklich ein: »O
let go of have Suddenly fell it her terribly in Oh

Gott, wenn sie dir nachspioniert haben, wenn sie nur
god when they you spied upon have when they only

wissen wollten, wohin du gehst?«
know wanted where-to you go

Er schüttelte den Kopf. »Glaube ich nicht, Hete. Ich war
He shook the head Believe I not Hete I was

erst bei – ich war erst auf einer anderen Stelle, um
first at I was first on an other spot for

meine Sachen zu holen. Ich hätte es merken müssen,
my things to get I had it notice must

wenn jemand hinter mir her war. Und warum? Da
when someone behind me away was And why There

hätten sie mich doch gar nicht erst loszulassen
had they me indeed at all not first let go

brauchen.«
need

Aber sie hatte es schon überlegt: »Sie glauben, du kennst
But she had it already considered They believe you know

den Kartenschreiber und bringst sie auf die Spur. Und
the card writer and bring you on the trace And

vielleicht kennst du ihn wirklich und hast die Karte doch
perhaps know you him really and have the card indeed

selbst dorthin gelegt. Aber ich will es gar nicht wissen,
yourself there-to laid But I want it at all not know

das sollst du mir nie sagen!« Sie bückte sich zu ihm
that will you me never say She bent herself to him

und flüsterte: »Ich gehe jetzt eine halbe Stunde weg,
and whispered I go now a half hour away

Hänschen, und beobachte das Haus, ob vielleicht doch
little Hans and watch the house whether perhaps indeed

irgendwo ein Spitzel herumsteht. Nicht wahr, du wirst hier
somewhere a snitch stands around Not true you will here

ganz still im Zimmer bleiben?«
completely quiet in the room stay

Er sagte ihr, daß dieses Nachsehen ganz unnütz sei,
He told her that this to check completely useless be

niemand sei ihm gefolgt, bestimmt nicht.
nobody be him followed definitely not

Aber ihr stand es in zu schreckvoller Erinnerung, wie sie
But her stood it in to terrifying memory how she

ihr schon einmal den Mann aus der Wohnung und
her already once the man from the house and

damit aus dem Leben holten. Ihre Unruhe litt es
there-with from the life dragged Her unrest suffered it

nicht, sie mußte auf und hinaus, um nachzusehen.
not she must up and out for to see after
to double check

Und während sie langsam um den Block geht - sie hat
And while she slowly around the block goes she has

den Blacky aus dem Laden an einer Leine mitgenommen,
the blacky from the shop on a leash taken along

einen reizenden Scotch, und durch ihn sieht dieser
a lovely scotch and through him sees this

Abendweg doch ganz unverfänglich aus –, während sie
evening path indeed completely unevitable from while she

also um seiner Sicherheit willen langsam auf und ab
thus for his security's will slowly on and off
sake

schlendert, anscheinend nur mit dem Hund beschäftigt,
strolls apparently only with the dog occupied

aber die wachsamen Augen und Ohren überallhin gerichtet
but the watchful eyes and ears anywhere directed

- unterdes nimmt Enno mit vorsichtigen Händen ein
under-that takes Enno with careful hands a
meanwhile

rasches erstes Inventar ihrer Stube auf. Es kann nicht
quick first inventory of her room up It can not

mehr als nur ganz flüchtig sein, außerdem hat sie
(any)more as only completely fleeting be in addition has she

die meisten Möbelstücke verschlossen. Aber schon diese
the most furniture locked But already this

erste Durchsicht verrät ihm, daß er in seinem ganzen
first review betrays him that he in his whole

Leben so eine Frau noch nicht gehabt hat, eine Frau
life such a woman still not had has a woman

mit Bankkonto und sogar einem Postscheckkonto, wo
with bank account and even a post office checking account where

ihr Name ganz richtig gedruckt auf allen Formularen
her name completely right printed on all forms

steht!
stands

Und Enno Kluge beschließt wiederum bei sich, wirklich
And Enno Kluge decides again by himself really

ein ganz anderes Leben anzufangen, sich in dieser
a completely different life to start himself in this

Wohnung stets korrekt zu benehmen und nicht zu
house all the time correct to behave and not to

beschlagnahmen, was sie ihm nicht freiwillig gibt.
seize what she him not voluntarily gives

Sie kommt zurück und sagt: »Nein, ich kann nichts
She comes back and says No I can nothing

Auffälliges sehen. Aber vielleicht haben sie dich doch hier
noticeable suspicious see But perhaps have they you indeed here

hereingehen sehen und kommen morgen früh zurück. Ich
go inside see and come tomorrow early back I

gehe morgen gleich noch mal, ich werde den Wecker
go tomorrow immediately still once I will the waker alarm

auf sechs stellen.«
on six put

»Ist nicht nötig, Hete«, sagt er wieder. »Mir ist
Is not necessary Hete says he again Me is

bestimmt keiner gefolgt.«
definitely no one followed

Dann macht sie ihm ein Lager auf dem Sofa und legt
Then makes she him a bed on the sofa and lays

sich selbst ins Bett. Aber sie läßt die Tür zwischen
herself self in the bed But she lets the door between

den beiden Zimmern offen und horcht darauf, wie er
the both rooms open and listens thereupon how he

sich hin und her wirft, wie er stöhnt, und wie unruhig
himself away and away throws how he moans and how restless

er schläft, als er endlich wirklich eingeschlafen ist. Dann,
he sleeps as he finally really slept in (asleep fallen) is Then

sie ist eben grade selbst ein wenig eingedämmert, dann
she is just right herself a little dozed off then

wacht sie wieder davon auf, daß sie ihn weinen hört.
wakes she again there-from up that she him cry hears

Wieder weint er, ob nun im Wachen oder im
Again cries he whether now in the waking or in the

Schlaf. Frau Hete sieht im Dunkeln sein Gesicht deutlich
sleep Mrs Hete sees in the dark his face clearly

vor sich, dieses Gesicht, das trotz seiner fünfzig Jahre
before herself this face that despite his fifty years

immer noch etwas Kindliches hat – vielleicht durch das
always still something childish has perhaps through the

schwache Kinn und den vollippigen, sehr roten Mund.
weak chin and the full-lipped very red mouth

Eine Weile hört sie still auf dieses Weinen, das durch
A while listens she quietly to this crying that through

die Nacht klagelos immer weitergeht, als traure die
the night complaint-free always continues as mourns the

Nacht selbst über all den Kummer, den es jetzt auf der
night itself over all the sorrow that it now on the

Welt gibt.
world gives

Dann entschließt sich Frau Häberle, sie steht auf und
Then decides herself Mrs Haberle she stands up and

tastet sich im Dunkeln an sein Sofa.
gropes herself in the dark to his sofa

»Weine doch nicht so, Hänschen! Du bist ja in
Cry indeed not so little Hans You are yes indeed in

Sicherheit, du bist bei mir. Deine Hete hilft dir ...«
security you are with me Your Hete helps you

So spricht sie ihm tröstend zu, und als das Weinen
So speaks she him consoling to and as the crying

trotzdem nicht aufhört, beugt sie sich über ihn, sie
in spite of that not stops leans she herself over him she

schiebt ihren Arm unter seine Schultern, sie führt den
shoves her arm under his shoulders she leads the

Weinenden zu ihrem Bett, und dort nimmt sie ihn in ihre
crying to her bed and there takes she him in her

Arme, an ihre Brust ...
arms on her breast

Eine alternde Frau, ein ältlicher Mann, liebebedürftig wie
An aging woman an elderly man in need of love like

ein Kind, ein bißchen Trost, ein bißchen Leidenschaft,
a child a little consolation a little passion

ein klein wenig Glorienschein um das Haupt des
a small little glory shine around the head of the

Geliebten – und nicht einmal fällt es Frau Hete ein,
beloved and not once falls it woman Hete in

sich darüber klarzuwerden, wie dieses haltlose, weinerliche
herself about it to get clear how this baseless whiny

Wesen denn zu einem Kämpfer und Helden paßt.
being then to a warrior and hero suits

»Nun ist alles gut, nicht wahr, Hänschen?«
Now is everything good not true little Hans

Aber nein, diese eine Frage läßt den eben erst versiegten
But no this one question lets the just first dried up

Tränenstrom von neuem fließen, es schüttelt ihn in ihren
stream of tears from new again flow it shakes him in her

Armen.
arms

»Aber was ist denn, Hänschen? Hast du noch Sorgen,
But what is (it) then little Hans Have you still worries

von denen du mir noch nichts gesagt hast?«
from which you me still nothing said have

Und dies ist nun der Augenblick, auf den dieser alte
And this is now the moment on which this old

Frauenjäger seit Stunden hingearbeitet hat, denn er hat
woman hunter womanizer since hours worked towards has then he has

bei sich entschieden, daß es doch zu gefährlich und für
at himself decided that it indeed too dangerous and for

die Dauer auch unmöglich sei, sie ganz im unklaren
the duration also impossible be her completely in the unclear

über seinen wirklichen Namen und seine Ehe zu lassen.
over his real name and his marriage to leave

Er ist nun einmal im Gestehen, nun gut, wird er auch
He is now one time in the confessing now good will he also

dieses noch gestehen, sie wird es schon hinnehmen, ihn
this still confess she will it already accept him

darum nicht weniger lieben. Gerade jetzt, da sie ihn
therefore not less love Just now there she him

eben erst in ihre Arme genommen hat, wird sie ihn
just first in her arms taken has will she him

schon nicht wieder auf die Straße setzen!
already not again on the street set

Sie hat das Hänschen gefragt, ob es denn noch
She has the little Hans asked whether it then still

Sorgen gebe, von denen er ihr nichts gesagt hat. Nun
worries give from which he her nothing told has Now

gesteht er, weinend, verzweifelt, daß er gar nicht Hans
confesses he crying doubting that he at all not Hans

Enno heißt, sondern Enno Kluge, und daß er ein
Enno is called but Enno Kluge and that he a

verheirateter Mann ist, mit zwei großen Jungen. Ja, er
married man is with two large young ones Yes he

ist ein Lump, er hat sie belügen und betrügen wollen,
is a lump he has her lied to and cheat want

aber er bringt es nun doch nicht übers Herz, wo sie
but he brings it now indeed not over the heart where she

so gut zu ihm gewesen ist.
so good to him been is

Wie stets ist sein Geständnis nur ein Teilgeständnis,
As all the time is his confession only a partial confession

ein wenig Wahrheit mit viel Lüge untermischt. Er zeichnet
a little truth with much lies mixed He draws

das Bild seiner Frau, dieser harten, bösen Nazistin auf
the picture of his wife this hard bad nazi woman on

dem Postamt, die den Mann nicht bei sich dulden will,
the post office who the husband not at herself tolerate wants

weil er nicht in die Partei eintreten mag. Diese
because he not in the (political) party in-step may wants This

Frau, die seinen ältesten Sohn gezwungen hat, in die SS
woman who his oldest son forced has in the SS

einzutreten – und er berichtet von den Greueltaten
to enter and he reported from the atrocities

Karlemanns. Er entwirft ein Bild dieser ungleichen,
of Karlemann He designs a picture of this unequal

schlechten Ehe, der stille, geduldige, alles ertragende
bad marriage the quiet patient everything enduring

Mann und die böse, ehrgeizige, nazistische Frau. Sie
man and the angry ambitious nazi woman They

können ja nicht zusammen leben, sie müssen einander
can yes indeed not together live they must each other

ja hassen. Und nun hat sie ihn aus der Wohnung
yes indeed hate And now has she him from the house

hinausgetrieben! So hat er seine Hete belogen, aus
driven out So has he his Hete lied to from

Feigheit, weil er sie zu sehr liebt, weil er ihr keinen
cowardice because he her too much loves because he her no

Schmerz bereiten wollte!
pain prepare cause wanted

Aber jetzt hat er sich freigesprochen. Nein, jetzt weint
But now has he himself acquitted No now cries

er nicht mehr. Er wird aufstehen und seine Sachen
he not (any)more He wants to get up and his things

packen und von ihr gehen – in die schlimme Welt hinaus.
get and from her go in the bad world out

Er wird sich schon irgendwo vor der Gestapo verbergen,
He will himself already somewhere for the gestapo hide

und wenn die ihn doch erwischen, so macht das auch
and when they him indeed get so makes that also
matters

nicht viel aus. Jetzt, wo er Hetes Liebe, die einzige
not much out now where he Hete's love the only
-

Frau, die er wirklich im Leben geliebt hat, verlor!
woman who he really in the life loved has lost

Ja, er ist ein recht gerissener alter Frauenverführer, dieser
Yes he is a right torn old woman seducer this
crafty

Enno Kluge. Er weiß schon, wie man es anpacken muß
Enno Kluge He knows already how one it tackle must

bei diesen Weibern: Lieben und Lügen, das geht alles
with these women Love and lie that goes everything

in einem hin. Es muß nur ein bißchen Wahres dazwischen
in one away It must only a little truth in between

sein, sie muß nur ein bißchen von dem Zeug glauben
be she must only a bit from the stuff believe

können, das man erzählt, und vor allem muß man
be able that one tells and before all must one

stets die Tränen bereit halten und die Hilflosigkeit ...
all the time the tears ready hold and the helplessness

Frau Hete hat diesmal mit einem wahren Schrecken sein
Mrs Hete has this time with a true fright his

Geständnis gehört. Warum hat er sie nur so angelogen?
confession heard Why has he her only so lied to

Als sie sich kennenlernten, lag doch noch gar kein
As they each other learned to know lay indeed still at all no

Grund für solche Lügen vor! Hatte er denn damals
reason for such lies before Had he then at that time

schon Absichten auf sie gehabt? Dann können es nur
already intentions on her had Then can it only

schlimme Absichten gewesen sein, wenn sie zu solchen
bad intentions been be when they to such
have been

Lügen Anlaß wurden.
lies occasion became
reason

Ihr Instinkt sagt ihr, daß sie ihn wegschicken muß, daß
Her instinct says her that she him send away must that

ein Mann, der fähig ist, eine Frau vom ersten
a man who capable of is a woman from the first

Anfang an so bedenkenlos zu täuschen, auch stets
beginning on so without hesitation to deceive also all the time

bereit sein wird, sie später zu belügen. Und mit einem
ready be will her later to lie to And with a

Lügner kann sie nicht zusammen leben. Sie hat immer ein
liar can she not together live She has always a

sauberes Leben gelebt mit ihrem ersten Mann, und diese
clean life lived with her first husband and these

paar kleinen Geschichten, die es seit seinem Tode gab,
few small stories who it since his death gave

über so etwas lächelt eine erfahrene Frau nur.
over so something smiles an experienced woman only

Nein, aus ihren Armen noch würde sie ihn gehen lassen
No from her arms still would she him go let

– wenn sie ihn nicht grade dem Feind in die Arme jagte,
when she him not right the enemy in the arms chased

der verhaßten Gestapo. Denn sie ist fest überzeugt, daß
the hated gestapo Then she is firmly convinced that

sie das tut, wenn sie ihn jetzt gehen heißt. Diese ganze
she that does when she him now go is called This whole
lets

Verfolgung durch die Gestapo, die nimmt sie seit seiner
persecution through the gestapo that takes she since his

Erzählung am Abend für bare Münze. Sie kommt nicht
narrative at the evening for bare coin She comes not
truth

einmal auf den Gedanken, an ihrer Wahrheit zu zweifeln,
once on the thought on its truth to doubt
even

obwohl sie ihn doch eben erst als Lügner kennengelernt
although she him indeed just first as liar know-learned
gotten to know

hat.
has

Und dann ist da diese Frau ... Es ist nicht möglich,
And then is there this woman It is not possible

daß alles, was er über diese Frau gesagt hat, unwahr
that everything what he about this woman said has untrue

ist. So etwas denkt sich kein Mensch aus, da muß
is So something thinks himself no human out there must
up

etwas Wahres daran sein. Sie glaubt den Mann doch
something true there on be She believes the man indeed
to it

zu kennen an ihrer Seite, ein schwaches Geschöpf, ein
to know on her side a weak creature a

Kind, gutartig eigentlich: mit ein paar freundlichen Worten
child benign actually with a few friendly words

ist er zu leiten. Aber diese Frau, hart, ehrgeizig, diese
is he to lead But this woman hard ambitious this

Nazistin, die durch die Partei hochkommen will, für
nazi woman who through the (political) party up come wants for

die war natürlich ein solcher Mann nichts, ein Mann,
that one was of course a such man nothing a man

der die Partei haßte, vielleicht insgeheim gegen sie
who the (political) party hated perhaps secretly against her

arbeitete, ein Mann, der sich weigerte, in die Partei
worked a man who himself refused in the (political) party

einzutreten!
to enter

Konnte sie ihn zurückjagen zu solcher Frau? Der
Could she him chase back to such (a) woman The

Gestapo in die Arme?
gestapo in the arms

Sie konnte es nicht, und so durfte sie es auch nicht.
She could it not and so was allowed she it also not

Das Licht geht an. Da steht er schon neben ihrem Bett,
The light goes on There stands he already beside her bed

in einem viel zu kurzen blauen Hemdchen, stille Tränen
in a much too short blue shirt quiet tears

rinnen jetzt über sein blasses Gesicht. Er beugt sich
run now over his pale face He leans himself

über sie, er flüstert: »Adieu, Hete! Du bist sehr gut zu
over her he whispers Adieu Hete You are very good to
have

mir gewesen, aber ich verdiene es nicht, ich bin ein
me been but I deserve it not I am a

schlechter Mensch. Adieu! Ich gehe jetzt ...«
bad human Adieu I go now

Sie hält ihn fest. Sie flüstert: »Nein, du bleibst bei mir.
She holds him firmly She whispers No you stay with me

Ich habe es dir versprochen, und ich halte mein
I have it you promised and I hold my

Versprechen. Nein, sag nichts. Geh jetzt bitte auf das
promise No say nothing Go now please on the

Sofa und versuche, noch ein bißchen zu schlafen. Ich will
sofa and try still a little to sleep I want

überlegen, wie alles am besten einzurichten ist.«
to consider how everything at the best to set up is

Er schüttelt langsam und traurig den Kopf. »Hete, du bist
He shakes slowly and sad the head Hete you are

zu gut für mich. Ich will alles tun, was du sagst,
too good for me I want everything do what you say

aber wirklich, Hete, es ist besser, du läßt mich gehen.«
but really Hete it is better you let me go

Aber natürlich geht er nicht. Natürlich läßt er sich
But of course goes he not Of course lets he himself

überreden, zu bleiben. Sie wird alles überlegen,
persuade to stay She will everything consider

alles ordnen. Und natürlich erreicht er auch, daß die
everything order And of course achieves he also that the

Verbannung zum Sofa wieder aufgehoben wird, daß er
exile to the sofa again lifted up will that he

zurück zu ihr ins Bett darf. Ganz von ihrer
back to her in the bed may Completely from her

mütterlichen Wärme umschlossen, schläft er bald ein,
maternal warmth enclosed sleeps he soon in

dieses Mal ohne weiteres Weinen.
this once without additional crying

Sie aber liegt noch lange wach. Eigentlich liegt sie die
She however lies still long awake Actually lies she the

ganze Nacht wach. Sie hört auf sein Atmen, es ist
whole night awake She listens to his breathing it is

schön, wieder einen Mann bei sich atmen zu hören,
beautiful again a man with herself breathing to hear

ihn so nahe im Bett zu haben. Sie war so lange sehr
him so close in the bed to have She was so long very

allein. Nun hat sie wieder jemand, für den sie sorgen
alone Now has she again someone for whom she care

kann. Ihr Leben ist nicht mehr ohne allen Inhalt. O
can Her life is not (any)more without all content Oh
any meaning

ja, er wird ihr vielleicht mehr Sorgen machen als gut
yes he will her perhaps more worry make than good

ist. Aber solche Sorgen, Sorgen um einen Menschen, den
is But such worries worries for a human who

man liebhat, das sind gute Sorgen.
one beloved-has those are good worries

Frau Hete beschließt, stark für zwei zu sein. Frau Hete
Mrs Hete decides strong for two to be Mrs Hete

beschließt, ihn vor allen von der Gestapo drohenden
decides him before all from the gestapo threatening
everything

Gefahren zu behüten. Frau Hete beschließt, ihn zu
dangers to protect Mrs Hete decides him to

erziehen und aus ihm einen wahrhaftigen Menschen zu
educate and from him a truthful human to

machen. Frau Hete beschließt, das Hänschen, ach nein,
make Mrs Hete decides the little Hans oh no

nun heißt er ja Enno, Frau Hete beschließt, den Enno
now is called he yes Enno Mrs Hete decides the Enno

von dieser andern Frau, der Nazistin, freizukämpfen. Frau
from this other woman the nazi to fight free Mrs

Hete beschließt, in dieses Leben da, das nun bei ihr
Hete decides in this life there that now with her

liegt, Ordnung und Sauberkeit zu bringen.
lies order and cleanliness to bring
purity

Und Frau Hete hat keine Ahnung, daß dieser schwache
And Mrs Hete has no idea that this weak

Mann an ihrer Seite stark genug sein wird, Unordnung,
man on her side strong enough be will disarray

Leid, Selbstvorwürfe, Tränen, Gefahr in ihr Leben zu
suffering self-reproach tears danger in her life to

bringen. Frau Hete hat keine Ahnung, daß all ihre Stärke
bring Mrs Hete has no idea that all her strength

zu nichts wurde im gleichen Augenblick, als sie
to nothing will become in the (the) same moment as she

beschloß, diesen Enno Kluge bei sich zu behalten und
decided this Enno Kluge with herself to keep and

ihn gegen die ganze Welt zu verteidigen. Frau Hete hat
him against the whole world to defend Mrs Hete has

keine Ahnung, daß sie sich selbst mit dem ganzen
no idea that she herself self with the whole

kleinen Reich, das sie sich aufbaute, in höchste Gefahr
small kingdom that she herself built up in highest danger

gebracht hat.
brought has

Angst und Furcht

Anxiety and fear

Seit jener Nacht sind zwei Wochen vergangen. Frau Hete
Since that night are two weeks passed Mrs Hete
have

und Enno Kluge haben in dem engen Beieinanderleben
and Enno Kluge have in the narrow living together

eines das andere besser kennengelernt. Es war ja nun so,
one the other better know-learned It was yes now so
gotten to know

daß der Mann wegen der Furcht vor der Gestapo nicht
that the man because of the fear before the gestapo not

aus dem Hause durfte. Sie lebten wie auf einer Insel,
from the house was allowed They lived as on an island

nur sie zwei. Sie konnten sich nicht aus dem Wege
only they two They could each other not out the way

gehen, sich bei andern Menschen ein wenig frischen
go themselves with other people a little fresh

Wind um die Nase wehen lassen. Sie waren ganz
air for the nose blow let They were completely

aufeinander angewiesen.
on each other reliant
stuck with

In den ersten Tagen hatte sie es dem Enno nicht einmal
In the first days had she it the Enno not once

erlaubt, ihr im Laden zu helfen, in diesen ersten Tagen,
allowed her in the shop to help in these first days

da sie noch nicht ganz sicher war, ob nicht doch
there she still not completely sure was whether not indeed
when

ein Agent der Gestapo ums Haus schlich. Sie hatte
an agent of the gestapo around the house sneaked She had

ihm gesagt, daß er ganz still in der Stube bleiben
him told that he completely quiet in the room stay

müsse. Von niemandem dürfe er sich sehen lassen. Ein
must From no one may he himself see let A
By

wenig überrascht war sie, mit welcher Gelassenheit er
little surprised was she with which serenity he

diese Eröffnung aufnahm; ihr wäre es schrecklich
this disclosure took up her would be it terrible

gewesen, zu solchem untätigen Sitzen in der engen
been to such idle sitting in the narrow
small

Stube verurteilt zu sein. Aber er hatte nur gesagt:
room sentenced to be But he had only said
living room

»Nun gut, da werde ich mich ein bißchen pflegen!«
Now good there will I myself a little nurture

»Und was wirst du tun, Enno?« hatte sie gefragt. »So
And what will you do Enno had she asked Such

ein Tag ist lang, und ich kann mich nicht viel um dich
a day is long and I can myself not much for you

kümmern, und Grübeln trägt nichts ein.«
care and pondering carries nothing in
doesn't help

»Tun?« hatte er ganz erstaunt gefragt. »Wieso tun?
Do had he completely astonished asked How so do

Ach, du meinst arbeiten?« Er hatte es schon auf der
Ah you mean work He had it already on the

Zunge, daß er seiner Ansicht nach genug gearbeitet
tongue that he his opinion after enough worked
according to

hatte für eine lange Zeit, aber er war noch sehr
had for a long time but he was still very

vorsichtig bei ihr und sagte darum: »Natürlich würde ich
careful with her and said therefore Of course would I

gerne was arbeiten. Aber was kann ich denn hier im
gladly what work But what can I then here in the
work some

Zimmer arbeiten? Ja, wenn da 'ne Drehbank stünde!«
room work Yes when there a lathe would stand

Und er lachte.
And he laughed

»Aber ich weiß eine Arbeit für dich! Sieh mal her,
But I know a work for you Look once here
just

Enno!«
Enno

Sie trug einen großen Karton herein, ganz gefüllt
She carried a large cardboard in completely filled

mit allen möglichen Sämereien. Nun stellte sie ein
with all possible seeds Now put she a

Brettchen vor ihn hin, eines jener hölzernen Zahlbretter
little board before him away one of those wooden payment boards
down

mit Rand, wie sie auf vielen Ladentischen stehen. Und
with (a) rim as they on many counters stands And

sie nahm einen Federhalter zur Hand, in dem die Feder
she took a penholder to the hand in which the feather

verkehrt herum steckte. Diesen Halter wie eine Schaufel
wrong around stuck This holder like a shovel

benutzend, fing sie an, eine Handvoll Sämereien, die sie
using caught she on a handful of seeds which she
started -

auf das Zahlbrett geschüttet hatte, aufzuteilen in die
on the payment board poured had up to divide in the
to split

verschiedenen Sorten. Rasch und geschickt ging die Feder
different varieties Quickly and able went the feather

hin und her, teilte, schob in eine Ecke, sonderte
hither and thither divided pushed in a corner seperated

wieder, und dabei erklärte sie: »Das sind alles
again and there-by explained she Those are all

Futterreste, aus den Ecken zusammengefegt, aus
food remains from the corners swept together from

zerplatzten Tüten, das habe ich alles gesammelt, seit
broken up bags those have I all gathered since

Jahren. Jetzt da das Futter so knapp ist, kommt es mir
years Now there since the fodder so scarce is comes it me

zugute. Ich sortiere es ...«
benefit I sort it

»Aber warum sortierst du es? Das ist ja eine
But why sort you it That is yes indeed a

Riesenarbeit! Gib's den Vögeln doch so zu fressen, die
giant work Give it the birds indeed so to eat those

sortieren es sich schon selbst!«
sort it themselves already self

»Und veraasen dabei drei Viertel des Futters! Oder
And scavenge ruin there-by three quarters of the food Or

fressen Futter, das ihnen nicht bekommt, und
eat fodder that them not gets is good for and

gehen mir ein! Nein, die kleine Arbeit muß man sich
go me die in No that little work must one oneself

schon machen. Ich hab's meist am Abend getan und
already make do I have it mostly at the evening done and

am Sonntag, immer wenn ich ein bißchen Zeit hatte. An
at the Sunday always when I a little time had On

einem Sonntag habe ich einmal fast fünf Pfund sortiert,
one Sunday have I once almost five pound sorted

neben meiner Hausarbeit! Nun, wir werden ja sehen,
besides my housework Now we will yes indeed see

ob du meinen Rekord schlägst. Du hast ja jetzt
whether you my record beats You have yes indeed now

viel Zeit, und es denkt sich gut dabei nach. Sicher hast
much time and it thinks itself good there-by after Sure have

du viel nachzudenken. So, nun versuch du es einmal,
you much to think about So now try you it once

Enno!«
Enno

Sie gab ihm eine kleine Schaufel in die Hand und sah
She gave him a little shovel in the hand and looked

zu, wie er zu arbeiten anfing.
on how he to work began

»Du bist gar nicht ungeschickt!« lobte sie ihn. »Du hast
You are at all not clumsy praised she him You have

kluge Hände!«
deft hands

Und einen Augenblick später: »Aber du mußt besser
And a moment later but you must better

aufpassen, Hänschen – nein, Enno meine ich. Ich muß
watch out little hans – no enno my i i must

mich erst daran gewöhnen! Sieh mal, dies spitze
me first to it habituate look once this tip

glänzende Korn, das ist Hirse, und das stumpfe, schwarze,
shiny grain the is millet and the blunt black

das ist Raps. Das darfst du nicht durcheinanderbringen.
the is raps the may you not mess

Die Sonnenblumenkerne nimmst du am besten vorher mit
the sunflower seeds take you at the best before with

den Fingern heraus, das geht schneller als mit der Feder.
the fingers out the goes faster as with the feather

Warte, ich hole dir noch Schalen, in die du das fertig
wait i get you still shells in the you the ready

sortierte tun kannst!«
sorted do can

Sie war ganz Eifer, ihn für seine langweiligen Tage
She was completely zealous him for his boring days

mit Arbeit zu versorgen. Dann ging die Ladenklingel zum
with work to supply Then went the store bell for the

erstenmal, und von nun an riß es nicht ab mit Kunden,
first time and from now on ripped it not off with customers
stopped it not

sie konnte ihn immer nur für einen Augenblick besuchen.
she could him always only for a moment visit

Dann traf sie ihn träumend vor seinem Zahlbrett mit
Then hit she him dreaming before his payment board with
found

den Sämereien. Oder noch schlimmer war es, wenn er
the seeds Or still worse was it when he

sich eilig, vom Geräusch der Tür erschreckt, an
himself hurriedly from the sound of the door startled on

seinen Arbeitsplatz schlich wie ein Kind, das beim Faulsein
his workplace sneaked like a child that at the laziness
who

ertappt ist.
caught is

Sie sah bald, nie würde er ihren Rekord von fünf Pfund
She saw soon never would he her record of five pound

schlagen, er würde es nicht einmal auf zwei Pfund
beat he would it not one time on two pound

bringen. Und die würde sie auch noch einmal durchsehen
bring And these would she also still one time through-see
double check

müssen, so liederlich hatte er gearbeitet.
must so dissolute had he worked
bad

Sie war ein bißchen enttäuscht, aber sie gab ihm recht,
She was a little disappointed but she gave him right

als er sagte: »Nicht ganz zufrieden, Hete, was?« Er
as he said Not completely satisfied Hete what He

lachte verlegen. »Aber, weißt du, das ist keine richtige
laughed shy But know you that is no right

Arbeit für einen Mann. Gib mir 'ne richtige Arbeit für
work for a man Give me a right work for

einen Mann und du sollst mal sehen, wie ich loshaue!«
a man and you will once see how I loose chop
go for it

Natürlich hatte er recht, und am nächsten Tag setzte sie
Of course had he right and at the next day set she

ihm das Brett mit den Sämereien nicht mehr hin. »Du
him the board with the seeds not (any)more away before You

mußt eben sehen, wie du den Tag hinbringst, du Armer!«
must just see how you the day through-bring you poor guy

sagte sie tröstend. »Es muß schrecklich für dich sein.
said she consoling It must terrible for you be

Aber vielleicht liest du ein bißchen? Ich habe dort im
But perhaps read you a little I have there in the

Schrank noch viele Bücher von meinem Mann. Warte, ich
closet still many books from my husband Wait I

schließe dir gleich auf.«
close you immediately up

Er stand hinter ihr, als sie die Reihen musterte. »Er war
He stood behind her as she the rows looked at He was

Funktionär bei der KPD. Da, den Marx habe ich noch
official at the kpd There the Marx have I still

grade bei einer Haussuchung gerettet. Ich hatte ihn ins
right at a house search rescued I had him it in the

Ofenloch gesteckt, und grade wollte ein SA-Mann die
oven hole put and right wanted an SA man the

Ofentür aufmachen, da gab ich ihm rasch eine Zigarette,
oven door openmake (open) there gave I him quickly a cigarette

und er vergaß es.« Sie sah ihm ins Gesicht. »Aber das
and he forgot it She saw him in the face But those

sind wohl keine Bücher für dich, Lieber, was? Ich muß
are well no books for you rather what I must

dir gestehen, ich habe auch kaum hineingesehen, seit
you confess I have also hardly looked inside since

mein Mann tot ist. Vielleicht ist das falsch, jeder müßte
my husband dead is Perhaps is that wrong each must

sich um Politik kümmern. Hätten wir das alle
himself for politic(s) care Had we that all

rechtzeitig getan, so wäre es nicht gekommen, wie es
at the right time done so would be it not come as it

jetzt durch die Nazis geworden ist, das hat Walter immer
now through the nazi's become is that has Walter always

gesagt. Aber ich bin nur eine Frau ...«
said But I am only a woman

Sie brach ab, sie merkte, er hatte gar nicht hingehört.
She broke off she noticed he had at all not listened

»Aber da unten stehen noch ein paar Romane von mir.«
But there under stand still a few novels from me

»Am liebsten hätte ich einen richtigen Detektivroman, so
At the dearest had I a true detective novel so

was mit Verbrechen und Mord«, erklärte Enno.
what with crimes and murder explained Enno

»Ich glaube, so was ist nicht da. Aber hier habe ich ein
I believe so what is not there But here have I a

wirklich schönes Buch, das habe ich immer wieder
really beautiful book that have I always again

gelesen. Raabe: Chronik der Sperlingsgasse. Das versuch
read Raabe Chronicle of the Sperlingsgasse That try

mal, das wird dich freuen ...«
once that will you enjoy

Aber sie sah, wenn sie in die Stube kam, er las nicht
But she saw when she in the room came he read not

darin. Es lag aufgeschlagen auf dem Tisch, später war es
therein It lay struck up opened on the table later was it

beiseite geschoben.
to the side pushed

»Es gefällt dir nicht?«
It pleases you not

»Ach, weißt du, ich weiß nicht ... Das sind alles so
Oh know you I know not Those are all such

schrecklich gute Menschen, so was ist doch langweilig.
terribly good people so what is indeed boring

So ein richtig frommes Buch ist das. Kein Buch für
Such a right pious book is that No book for

einen Mann. Wir wollen mehr was Aufregendes, verstehst
a man We want more what exciting understand

du ...«
you

»Schade«, sagte sie. »Schade.« Und sie stellte das Buch
Pity said she Pity And she put the book

in den Schrank zurück.
in the closet back
bookcase

Es irritierte sie, wenn sie jetzt in die Stube kam, den
It irritated her when she now in the room came the

Mann da sitzen zu sehen, immer in der gleichen
man there sit to see always in the (the) same

schlaffen Haltung, vor sich hin dösend. Oder er schlief
slack stature before himself away dozing Or he slept

auch, den Kopf auf den Tisch gelegt. Oder er stand am
also the head on the table laid Or he stood at the

Fenster und starrte auf den Hof, immer die gleiche
window and stared on the court always the same

Melodie vor sich hin pfeifend. Es irritierte sie sehr.
melody before himself away whistling It irritated her much

Sie war immer eine tätige Frau gewesen, sie war es
She was always an active woman been she was it
had

noch, ein Leben ohne Arbeit wäre ihr sinnlos
still a life without work would be her senseless

erschienen. Am liebsten hatte sie es, wenn der ganze
appear At the dearest had she it when the whole

Laden voller Kunden stand, und sie hätte sich am
shop full of customers stood and she had herself at the

liebsten in zehn Stücke zerteilt.
dearest in ten pieces divided

Und da stand nun dieser Mann, stand, saß, hockte, lag,
And there stood now this man stood sat crouched lay

zehn Stunden, zwölf Stunden, vierzehn Stunden, und tat
ten hours twelve hours fourteen hours and did

nichts, rein gar nichts! Er stahl dem lieben Herrgott den
nothing clean at all nothing He stole of the dear lord god the

Tag! Was fehlte ihm denn? Er schlief genug, er aß mit
day What lacked him then He slept enough he ate with

Appetit, es ging ihm nichts ab, aber er arbeitete nicht!
apetite it went him nothing off but he worked not
failed -

Einmal riß ihr die Geduld, und sie sagte gereizt: »Wenn
Once ripped her the patience and she said irritated If
broke

du nur nicht immer dieselbe Melodie pfeifen wolltest,
you only not always the same melody whistle wanted

Enno! Seit sechs, acht Stunden pfeifst du schon: Kleine
Enno Since six eight hours whistle you already Little

Mädchen müssen schlafen gehn ...«
girl must sleep go

Er lachte verlegen. »Stört dich meine Pfeife? Na, ich
He laughed shy Disturbs you my whistle Now I

kann auch anders. Soll ich dir mal das Horst-Wessel-Lied
can also different Should I you once the Horst Wessel song
nazi song

pfeifen?« Und er fing an: Die Fahne hoch! Die Reihen
whistle And he caught on The flags high The rows
started

fest geschlossen ...
firmly closed

Ohne ein Wort ging sie in den Laden zurück. Diesmal
Without a word went she in the shop back This time

hatte er sie nicht nur irritiert, diesmal war sie ernstlich
had he her not only irritated this time was she seriously

verletzt.
injured

Aber das verging wieder. Sie war nicht nachtragend, und
But that passed again She was not resentful and

außerdem hatte auch er gemerkt, daß er etwas falsch
in addition had also he noticed that he something wrong

gemacht hatte, und hatte ihr als Überraschung eine neue
done had and had her as surprise a new

Lampe über dem Bett zurechtgebastelt. Ja, so was
lamp over the bed together fixed Yes so what
something like that

konnte er auch; wenn er wollte, war er geschickt genug,
could he also when he wanted was he able enough

aber meist wollte er nicht.
but mostly wanted he not

Übrigens gingen diese Tage seiner Verbannung in die
By the way went these days of his exile in the

Stube rasch vorüber. Frau Hete hatte sich bald davon
room quickly past Mrs Hete had herself soon there-from

überzeugt, daß wirklich kein Spitzel um das Haus
convinced that really no snitch around the house

herumstrich, und Enno konnte wieder im Laden helfen.
snuck around and Enno could again in the shop help

Auf die Straße freilich durfte er vorläufig überhaupt nicht,
On the street indeed may he for now at all not

immer konnte ihn ein Bekannter sehen. Aber im Laden
always could him an acquaintance see But in the shop

helfen, das konnte er, und da erwies er sich nun
help that could he and there proved he himself now

wieder recht nützlich und geschickt. Sie sah bald, daß ihn
again right useful and able She saw soon that him

eine längere Zeit gleichförmig hintereinander ausgeführte
a longer time uniform behind each other executed

Arbeit rasch ermüdete, so gab sie ihm jetzt dies, dann
work quickly tired so gave she him now this then

das zu tun.
that to do

Bald ließ sie ihn auch bei der Kundenbedienung helfen.
Soon let she him also at the customer service help

Er wurde gut mit der Kundschaft fertig, er war höflich,
He became good with the customers ready he was polite

schlagfertig, manchmal sogar auf eine schlafmützige Art
quick-witted sometimes even on a sleepy way

witzig.
funny

»Mit dem Herrn haben Sie aber einen guten Griff
With the gentleman have you but a good grab
indeed choice

getan, Frau Häberle«, sagten alte Kunden. »Wohl was
done Mrs Häberle said old customers Well what
someone

Verwandtes?«
related

»Ja, ein Vetter von mir«, log Frau Hete und war glücklich
Yes a cousin of me lied Mrs Hete and was happy

über dies Enno gespendete Lob.
over this (for) Enno spent praise

Eines Tages sagte sie zu ihm: »Enno, ich möchte heute
One day said she to him Enno I may today

nach Dahlem fahren. Du weißt doch, die Tierhandlung von
to Dahlem drive You know indeed the pet shop from

Löbe macht zu, weil er zur Wehrmacht muß. Ich kann
Löbe makes to because he to the army must I can
closes

seine Bestände kaufen. Er hat sehr viel liegen, es
his stocks buy He has very much lie it
laying around

würde eine große Hilfe für uns sein, wo die Ware
would a great help for us be where the goods

immer knapper wird. Glaubst du, daß du mit dem Laden
always tighter become Believe you that you with the shop

fertig wirst?«
ready become
can handle

»Aber selbstredend, Hete, selbstredend! So was erledige
But of course Hete of course So what do

ich doch spielend. Wie lange willst du denn fortbleiben?«
I indeed playing How long want you then stay away

»Na, ich würde gleich nach dem Mittagessen fahren,
Now I would immediately after the lunch drive

aber ich glaube nicht, daß ich bis Ladenschluß zurück
but I believe not that I until shop closure back

sein werde. Ich möchte dann auch gleich bei meiner
be will I may then also immediately with my

Schneiderin rangehen ...«
dressmaker to go

»Tu das, Hete. Von mir aus hast du Urlaub bis
Do that Hete From me from have you leave until

Mitternacht. Um den Laden hier mach dir keine Sorgen,
midnight For the shop here make you no worries

den erledige ich dir prima.«
that one manage I you fine

Er setzte sie noch in die U-Bahn. Es war Mittagspause,
He set her still in the subway It was lunch break
even

der Laden war geschlossen.
the shop was closed

Sie lächelte vor sich hin, als der Wagen schon fuhr.
She smiled before herself away as the carriage already drove
by herself

Das Leben zu zweien war doch ein ander Leben! Es
The life to two was indeed an other life It
with

war schön, wenn man so gemeinsam arbeitete. Dann erst
was beautiful when one so together worked Then first

hatte man abends das richtige Gefühl von Befriedigung.
had one in the evening the right feeling from satisfaction

Und er gab sich Mühe, entschieden gab er sich
And he gave himself trouble decidedly gave he himself
made an effort made

Mühe, es ihr recht zu machen. Er tat, was er konnte.
trouble it her right to make He did what he could
an effort good

Sicher war er kein energischer oder auch nur fleißiger
Sure was he no energetic or also only more diligent

Mensch, sie gestand es sich ein. Wenn er zu viel hatte
human she confessed it herself in When he too much had

laufen müssen, zog er sich gerne einmal in die Stube
run must pulled he himself gladly once in the room

zurück, der Laden mochte noch so voll stehen, er überließ
back the shop might still so full stand he let over

ihr die Kundschaft allein. Oder sie fand ihn nach langem
her the customers alone Or she found him after long

vergeblichem Rufen im Keller, wie er auf dem Rand
futile calling in the basement how he on the edge

der Sandkiste saß und vor sich hin döste; das halb
of the sandbox sat and before himself away dozed the half

mit Sand gefüllte Eimerchen stand vor ihm – und sie
with sand filled bucket stood before him and she

wartete schon zehn Minuten darauf!
waited already ten minutes thereupon

Er fuhr zusammen, wenn sie ihn ein wenig scharf anrief:
He drove together when she him a little sharp addressed
flinched

»Enno, wo bleibst du bloß? Ich warte mir die Seele
Enno where stay you just I wait me the soul
are now

aus dem Leibe!«
from the leibe

Wie ein erschrockener Schuljunge sprang er auf. »Ein
As a terrified school boy jumped he up A

bißchen eingedöst«, murmelte er verlegen und fing
little dozed off murmured he shy and caught
started

langsam zu schippen an. »Komme gleich, Frau Chefin,
slowly to shovel on Come immediately Mrs Cheffin
- I will come

soll auch nicht wieder passieren.«
should also not again happen

Mit solchen kleinen Scherzen versuchte er dann, sie zu
With such small jokes tried he then her to

versöhnen.
reconcile

Nein, in keiner Hinsicht ein großes Kirchenlicht, dieser
No in no view a large churchlight this

Enno, soweit sah sie jetzt schon klar, aber er tat, was er
Enno so far saw she now already clear but he did what he

konnte. Und dabei gut zu leiden, höflich, umgänglich,
could And there-by good to suffer polite social

anschmiegsam, ohne ersichtliche Laster. Daß er ein
cuddly without apparent vices That he a

bißchen sehr viel Zigaretten rauchte, das
little very many cigarettes smoked that

sah sie ihm nach. Sie rauchte selber gerne mal eine,
saw she him after She smoked herself gladly once one
tolerated she him

wenn sie abgespannt war ...
when she tensed was

Mit ihren Besorgungen aber hatte Frau Hete an diesem
With her errands however had Mrs Hete on this

Tage Pech. Das Geschäft von Löbe in Dahlem war
days bad luck The business from Löbe in Dahlem was

geschlossen, als sie hinkam, man konnte ihr auch nicht
closed as she there-came one could her also not

sagen, wann Herr Löbe zurückkam. Nein, eingezogen war
say when Mr Löbe came back No drafted in was

er noch nicht, aber er hatte jetzt wohl viel Gänge
he still not but he had now well many walkways

durch seine Einberufung. Vormittags ab zehn Uhr war
through his convocation Early afternoon off ten hour o'clock was

das Geschäft sonst immer geöffnet gewesen - vielleicht
the business otherwise always opened been perhaps

versuchte sie es morgen vormittag?
tried she it tomorrow morning

Sie dankte und fuhr zu ihrer Schneiderin. Vor dem
She thanked and drove to her dressmaker Before the

Hause aber blieb sie erschrocken stehen. In der Nacht
house however remained she frightened stand In the night

war eine Fliegerbombe hineingegangen, das Haus war nur
was an air bomb went in the house was only

noch eine Ruine. Die Leute gingen eilig daran vorüber,
still a ruin The people went hurriedly there-on past

manche mit absichtlich abgewandten Gesichtern, die das
many with intentionally averted faces who the

Grauen der Zerstörung nicht sehen wollten, oder die
grayness of the destruction not see wanted or the

Angst hatten, ihre Erbitterung nicht verbergen zu können,
fear had their bitterness not hide to been able

andere besonders langsam (Polizei sorgte dafür, daß
others particularly slowly police provided therefore that

niemand stehenblieb), entweder mit sorglos lächelnden,
nobody stopped either with carefree smiling

neugierigen Gesichtern oder mit einem finsteren, fast
curious faces or with a dark almost

drohenden Blick die Verwüstung musternd.
threatening glance the destruction mustering

Ja, Berlin wurde jetzt öfter in den Keller geschickt,
Yes Berlin became now more often in the basement sent

und jetzt fielen auch immer häufiger Bomben und die
and now fell also always more often bombs and the

gefürchteten Phosphorkanister. Immer öfter wurde jetzt
dreaded phosphor canister Always more often became now

auch das Wort Görings zitiert, er wolle Meier heißen,
also the word Göring's quoted he wanted Meier be called
was nowhere to be seen

wenn sich ein feindliches Flugzeug über Berlin sehen
when itself a hostile airplane over Berlin see

ließe. In der vergangenen Nacht hatte Frau Hete auch
let In the past night had Mrs Hete also

im Keller gesessen, allein, denn sie wollte nicht,
in the basement sat alone then she wanted not
air raid shelter

daß Enno schon jetzt als ihr offizieller Freund und
that Enno already now as her official friend and

Hausgenosse gesehen wurde. Sie hatte das Surren der
housemate seen became She had the whir of the

Flieger über sich gehört, dieses nervenzerrüttende
flyers over herself heard this nerve shattering
airplanes

Geräusch, wie wenn immer wieder eine Mücke sirrt und
sound as when always again a mosquito buzzes and

surrt. Das Geräusch von Einschlägen hatte sie nicht
buzzes The sound of strikes had she not

gehört, ihre Gegend war bisher noch ganz verschont
heard her area was until-here still completely spared
until now

geblieben. Die Leute erzählten ja, die Engländer wollten
remained The people told yes the Englishman wanted

den Arbeitern nichts tun, sie wollten nur die feinen
the workers nothing do they wanted only the fine
well to do

Familien im Westen erledigen ...
families in the west take care of

Die Schneiderin war kein reicher Mensch gewesen, nun
The dressmaker was no rich human been now

hatte sie es doch getroffen. Frau Hete Häberle suchte
had she it indeed hit Mrs Hete Haberle searched

von einem Schutzmann zu erfahren, wo die Schneiderin
from a defence man to experience where the dressmaker
guard

geblieben, ob ihr etwas geschehen sei. Der
remained whether her something happened be The

Schutzmann bedauerte, keine Auskunft geben zu können.
guard regretted no notice give to be able

Vielleicht ginge die Dame mal aufs Revier, oder sie
Perhaps went the lady once on the district or she

erkundigte sich auch auf der nächsten Stelle des
inquired herself also on the next spot of the

Luftschutzbundes?
air protection federation

Aber dazu hatte Frau Hete jetzt keine Ruhe. So leid
But there-to had Mrs Hete now no rest So (much) pity

ihr die Schneiderin auch tat, und so gerne sie etwas
her the dressmaker also did and so gladly she something

über ihr Ergehen erfahren hätte, es drängte Hete jetzt
about her goings experienced had it pushed Hete now

nach Haus. Immer, wenn man so etwas sah, drängte es
to house Always when one so something saw pushed it

einen nach Haus. Sofort mußte man sich dort
one to house Immediately must one himself there

überzeugen, daß auch alles in Ordnung war. Es war
convince that also everything in order was It was

töricht, man wußte es, aber man fuhr doch los. Man
foolish one knew it but one drove indeed loose One

mußte sich erst mit eigenen Augen überführen, daß dort
must oneself first with own eyes lead over convince that there

nichts geschehen war.
nothing happened was

Aber leider war doch etwas geschehen mit der
But unfortunately was indeed something happened with the

kleinen Tierhandlung am Königstor. Nichts Tragisches,
small pet shop at the King's gate Nothing tragic

gewiß nicht, und doch erschütterte es Frau Häberle tief,
certainly not and indeed shook it Mrs Haberle deep

tiefer als manches Erlebnis in vielen Jahren. Frau Häberle
deeper as much happening in many years Mrs Haberle

fand den Rollladen vor dem Laden heruntergelassen, und
found the roller shutter before the shop lowered and

an ihm war ein Schild festgemacht, ein Schild mit der
on him was a sign fixed a sign with the
it

dummen Inschrift, über die sie sich immer empört
dumb inscription over which she herself always outraged

hatte: »Komme gleich wieder.« Und darunter: »Frau
had Come immediately again And under it Mrs
Come back later

Hedwig Häberle.«
Hedwig Häberle

Daß unter diesem Zettel auch noch ihr Name stand, daß
That under this note also still her name stood that

sie mit ihrem guten Namen diese Liederei und
she with her good name this debauchery and

Pflichtvergessenheit decken mußte, das beleidigte sie fast
forgetting of duty cover must that offended her almost

ebenso tief wie der Vertrauensbruch, den Enno begangen
likewise deep as the breach of trust that Enno committed

hatte. Hinter ihrem Rücken fortgeschlichen, und hinter
had Behind her back crept away and behind

ihrem Rücken hätte er auch wieder aufgemacht, hätte ihr
her back had he also again opened had her

kein Wort davon gesagt, daß er sie belogen hatte. Und
no word there-from said that he her lied to had And

wie dumm dabei, wie überaus dumm, denn es war doch
how stupid there-by how extremely stupid then it was indeed

fast sicher, daß eine ihrer Stammkundinnen sie fragte:
almost sure that one of her regular customers her asked

»Gestern nachmittag zugehabt? Unterwegs gewesen, Frau
Yesterday afternoon closed On the way been Mrs

Häberle?«
Häberle

Sie kommt über den Hausflur in ihre Wohnung. Dann
She comes over the house floor in her house Then

zieht sie den Laden von ihrer Ladentür hoch, öffnet die
pulls she the shop from her store door high opens the

Tür. Sie wartet, bis der erste Kunde kommt, nein, sie
door She waits until the first customer comes no she

möchte jetzt gar nicht, daß er kommt. Solch ein Verrat
may now at all not that he comes Such a betrayal

hinter ihrem Rücken – in ihrer ganzen Ehe mit Walter
behind her back in her whole marriage with Walter

hat es nie so etwas gegeben. Immer hatten sie volles
has it never so something given happened Always had they full

Vertrauen zueinander, und nie hatte eines je das
trust to each other and never had one indeed the

Vertrauen des andern getäuscht. Und nun dies! Sie hatte
trust of the other deceived And now this She had

ihm doch nicht die geringste Veranlassung gegeben!
him indeed not the least motive given

Die erste Kundin kommt, sie wird von ihr bedient; aber
The first customer comes she becomes by her served but

als Hete ihr auf einen Zwanzigmarkschein herausgeben will
as Hete her on a twenty mark note out give want

und die Ladenkasse aufzieht, ist die leer. Es war
and the shop cashbox open pulls is it empty It was
cash register There

reichlich Wechselgeld in der Kasse, als sie fortging,
richly exchange-money in the cash register as she went away
change

an die hundert Mark. Sie bezwingt sich, sie holt aus
on the hundred mark She restrains herself she gets from
up to {money}

ihrer Handtasche Geld, gibt heraus, fertig! Die Ladentür
her handbag money gives out ready The store door

bimmelt.
jingles

Ja, jetzt möchte sie den Laden zuschließen und ganz
Yes now may she the shop close and completely

mit sich allein sein. Ihr fällt ein – während sie immer
with herself alone be Her falls a while she always

weiter Kundschaft abfertigt –, daß es ihr in den letzten
further customers dispatched that it her in the last

Tagen schon ein paarmal so vorgekommen war, als könne
days already a few times so occurred was as could

die Kasse nicht ganz stimmen, als müsse die
the cash register accounts not completely be correct as must the

Tageslosung höher sein. Damals hat sie solche Gedanken
daily sum higher be At that time had she such thoughts

unmutig verjagt. Was sollte Enno auch mit dem Geld
angrily chased away What should Enno also with the money

anfangen? Er kam ja gar nicht aus dem Hause, war
start He came yes at all not from the house was

immer unter ihren Augen!
always under her eyes

Aber jetzt denkt sie daran, daß die Toilette auf der
But now thinks she there-on of it that the toilet on the

halben Treppe liegt, und daß er viel mehr Zigaretten
half stairs lies and that he much more cigarettes

geraucht hat, als er in seinem Köfferchen mitgebracht
smoked has as he in his suitcase brought along

haben kann. Sicher hat er jemanden im Hause gefunden,
have can Sure has he someone in the house found

der ihm Zigaretten holt, schwarz gekaufte, ohne Karte,
who him cigarettes gets black purchased without card

hinter ihrem Rücken! Wie schmählich und gemein! Sie
behind her back How shameful and mean She

hätte ihn liebend gerne mit Zigaretten versorgt, er hätte
had him lovingly gladly with cigarettes taken care of he had

nur den Mund auftun müssen!
only the mouth open must

In diesen anderthalb Stunden bis zum Wiederauftauchen
In this one and a half hours until to the resurfacing

Ennos kämpft Frau Häberle einen schweren Kampf mit
of Enno fights woman Haberle a heavy fight with

sich. In den letzten Tagen hat sie sich daran gewöhnt,
herself In the last days has she herself there-on used
to it

daß wieder ein Mann im Hause ist, daß sie nicht
that again a man in the house is that she not

mehr allein ist, sondern für jemanden zu sorgen hat,
(any)more alone is but for someone to worry has

für jemanden, den sie gerne hat. Aber wenn der Mann so
for someone who she gladly has But when the man so

ist, wie es jetzt den Anschein hat, so muß sie die Liebe
is as it now the appearance has so must she the love

ausreißen aus ihrem Herzen! Besser allein sein als in
tear out from her heart Better alone be as in
than

solch ewigem Mißtrauen und in solcher grauenvollen Angst
such eternal mistrust and in such gruesome fear

leben! Sie kann ja nicht mehr um die Ecke
to live She can yes not (any)more around the corner
indeed

in den Grünkram gehen, schon muß sie Angst haben, er
in the green stall for groceries go already must she fear have he

betrügt sie wieder!
cheats her again

Und dann fällt Hete ein, daß es ihr auch so
And then falls Hete in that it her also so

vorgekommen ist, als lägen die Sachen nicht ganz
occurred is as lay the things not completely

richtig in ihrem Wäschespind. Nein, es muß sein, sie muß
right in her linen locker No it must be she must

ihn fortschicken, heute noch, so schwer es ihr auch fällt.
him send away today still so heavy difficult it her also falls

Später würde es noch schwerer sein.
Later would it still heavier more difficult be

Aber dann denkt sie daran, daß sie eine alternde Frau
But then thinks she there-on of the fact that she an aging woman

ist, daß dies vielleicht ihre letzte Gelegenheit ist, einem
is that this perhaps her last opportunity is a

einsamen Lebensabend zu entgehen. Nach diesem Erlebnis
lonely evening of life to escape After this experience

mit Enno Kluge wird sie sich kaum noch entschließen,
with Enno Kluge will she herself hardly still decide

mit einem andern Manne es aufs neue zu versuchen.
with an other man it on the new again to try

Nach diesem erschreckenden, zerschmetternden Erlebnis mit
After this terrifying smashing experience with

Enno!
Enno

»Ja, Mehlwürmer sind wieder da. Wieviel darf es denn
Yes mealworms are again there How much may it then

sein, meine Dame?«
be my lady

Eine halbe Stunde vor Ladenschluß kommt Enno. Es ist
A half hour before shop closure comes Enno It is

für ihren Gefühlszustand bezeichnend, daß sie erst jetzt
for her emotional state significant that she first now

daran denkt, daß er sich ja gar nicht auf der
there-on thinks that he himself yes at all not on the
of it indeed

Straße sehen lassen soll, in solcher Gefahr, wie er durch
street see let should in such danger as he through

die Gestapo war! Bisher hat sie daran gar nicht denken
the gestapo was Until-here has she there-on at all not think
Until now

können, so sehr war sie mit dem Verrat beschäftigt, den
been able so much was she with the betrayal occupied which

er an ihr begangen. Aber was helfen denn alle
he on her committed But what help then all

Vorsichtsmaßregeln, wenn er in ihrer Abwesenheit einfach
precautions when he in her absence simply

losläuft? Und vielleicht ist all das mit der Gestapo auch
runs off And perhaps is all that with the gestapo also

Lug und Trug? Bei diesem Manne ist alles möglich!
lies and tricks With this man is everything possible

Er hat natürlich schon an dem hochgezogenen Rolladen
He has of course already on the raised roller shutter

gemerkt, daß sie wieder im Laden ist. Er kommt von
noticed that she again in the shop is He comes from

der Straße herein, vorsichtig und behutsam schlängelt er
the street in carefully and carefully meanders he

sich durch die Kunden, lächelt ihr zu, als sei nicht das
himself through the customers smiles her to as be not the

geringste vorgefallen, und sagt, in der Stube
least happened and says in the room

verschwindend: »Ich komme gleich und helfe, Chefin!«
infinitesimal I come immediately and help Chief

Und er kommt wirklich sehr schnell zurück, und
And he comes really very fast back and

notgedrungen, um vor der Kundschaft das Ansehen zu
inevitably for before the customers the look to

bewahren, muß sie mit ihm sprechen, ihm Anweisungen
preserve must she with him speak him instructions

geben, tun, als sei nichts geschehen – und doch ist ihre
give do as were nothing happened and indeed is her

Welt eingestürzt! Aber sie läßt sich nichts merken, sie
world collapsed But she lets herself nothing notice she

geht sogar auf seine schwachen Witzchen ein, die er
goes even up his weak joke in which he

heute besonders reichlich bereithält, und nur, als er an
today particularly richly provides and only as he on

die Ladenkasse will, sagt sie scharf: »Bitte, die Kasse
the store checkout wants says she sharp Sorry the cash register

besorge ich!«
get I

Er ist etwas zusammengefahren, mit einem scheuen Blick
He is somewhat together-moved with a shy glance
flinched

sieht er sie von der Seite an – wie ein Hund, der
sees he her from the side on like a dog who

geschlagen wird, ja, genau wie ein verprügelter Hund,
struck becomes yes exactly like a beaten up dog

denkt sie. Dann hat sich seine Hand in die Tasche
thinks she Then has itself his hand in the pocket

getastet, ein Lächeln ist auf sein Gesicht getreten, jawohl,
grabbed a little smile is on his face stepped yes
become

er hat den Schlag schon wieder verwunden.
he has the strike already again wound
absorbed

»Zu Befehl, Chefin!« schnarrt er und knallt die Absätze
To order chief buzzes he and bangs the heels

zusammen.
together

Die Kunden lachen über den kleinen, komischen Mann,
The customers laugh over the small funny man

der da Soldat spielen will, aber ihr ist nicht zum
who there soldier play wants but her is not to the

Lachen zumute.
laughing at mood

Dann ist der Laden geschlossen. Fünf Viertelstunden
Then is the shop closed Five quarter hours

arbeiten sie noch eifrig miteinander, ganz mit Füttern
work they still zealously with each other completely with feeding

und Tränken und Säubern beschäftigt, beide schließlich
and quenching and cleaning occupied both finally

fast wortlos, nachdem sie auf seine Scherze, die er
almost wordless after she on his jokes which he

immer wieder versuchte, nicht eingegangen war.
always again tried not gone in was
reacted had

Frau Hete steht in der Küche, sie macht das Abendessen
Mrs Hete stands in the kitchen she makes the evening dinner

zurecht. Sie hat Bratkartoffeln in der Pfanne, richtige,
in its right place She has fried potatoes in the pan right

schöne Bratkartoffeln, mit Speck angebraten. Den Speck
beautiful fried potatoes with bacon sautéed The bacon

hat sie von einer Kundin im Austausch gegen einen
has she from a customer in the exchange against a

Harzer Roller bekommen. Sie hat sich darauf gefreut,
from the Harz roller become She has herself thereupon enjoyed

ihn mit einem so schönen Abendessen überraschen zu
him with a such beautiful evening dinner surprise to

können, denn er ißt gerne was Gutes. Die Kartoffeln
can then he eats gladly what good The potatoes
something

werden schön goldgelb.
become beautiful golden yellow

Aber plötzlich löscht sie die Gasflamme unter der
But suddenly extinguishes she the gas flame under the

Pfanne. Plötzlich kann sie auf diese Aussprache nicht
pan Suddenly can she on this pronunciation not
discussion

mehr warten. Sie geht in die Stube, lehnt sich mit
(any)more wait She goes in the room leanes herself with

dem Rücken, dunkel und massig, gegen den Ofen und
the back dark and massive against the furnace and

fragt in einem fast drohenden Tone: »Nun?«
asks in an almost threatening tone Now
Well

Er hat am Tisch gesessen, dem Abendbrottisch, den er
He has at the table sat the dinner table which he

für sie beide gedeckt hatte, vor sich hin flötend, nach
for she both covered had before himself away fluting to

seiner Gewohnheit.
his habits

Bei diesem drohenden »Nun« fährt er zusammen, er steht
at this threatening now drives he together he stands
flinches

auf und sieht zu der dunklen Gestalt hinüber.
up and looks at the dark shape over

»Ja, Hete?« sagt er. »Gibt's bald Abendessen? Ich hab
Yes Hete says he Gives it soon evening dinner I have
Is there

mächtigen Kohldampf.«
mighty coal steam
hunger

Sie möchte ihn vor Wut schlagen, diesen Mann, der
She may him for anger strike this man who
of

glaubt, sie ist bereit, einen solchen Verrat totzuschweigen!
believes she is ready a such betrayal dead-to-keep silent
to ignore

Der fühlt sich ja schon sehr sicher, dieser Herr,
THat one feels himself yes already very sure this gentleman
indeed

weil er mit ihr in einem Bett geschlafen hat! Sie ist
because he with her in one bed slept has She is

von einem ganz ungewohnten Zorn erfaßt, am liebsten
from a completely unusual anger grasped at the dearest
taken

würde sie den Kerl schütteln und schlagen, noch einmal
would she the chap shake and strike still one time
another time

und noch einmal.
and still one time
another time

Aber sie bezwingt sich und wiederholt ihr »Nun?« nur
But she restrains herself and repeats her Now only

noch drohender.
still more threatening
even

»Ach so!« sagt er. »Du meinst das mit dem Geld,
Ah like this says he You mean that with the money

Hete.« Er greift in die Tasche und zieht einen Haufen
Hete He grabs in the pocket and pulls a heap

Scheine hervor. »Da, Hete, das sind 210 Mark, und ich
notes forth There Hete those are 210 mark {money} and I

hatte 92 Mark aus der Kasse genommen.« Er lacht
had 92 mark {money} from the cash register taken He laughs

ein bißchen verlegen. »Damit ich doch auch etwas zur
a little shy There-with With that I indeed also something to the

Wirtschaft beisteuere!«
economics (household) contribute

»Und wie kommst du zu dem vielen Geld?«
And how come you to the that much money

»Heute nachmittag war das große Traberrennen in
Today afternoon was the great trotter race in

Karlshorst. Ich bin grade noch rechtzeitig gekommen, um
Karlshorst I am right still in time come for

Adebar zu setzen. Adebar, Sieg. Ich wett nämlich gerne
Adebar to set Adebar victory I bet namely gladly

auf Pferde. Ich verstehe ziemlich viel von Rennen, Hete.«
on horses I understand rather much from racing Hete

Er sagt das mit einem bei ihm ganz ungewohnten
He says that with an with him completely unusual

Stolz. »Nicht die ganzen 92, nur 50 Mark habe ich
pride Not the whole 92, only 50 mark {money} have I

gesetzt. Die Quote war ...«
set The quote was

»Und was hättest du getan, wenn das Pferd nicht
And what had you done when the horse not

gewonnen hätte?«
won would have

»Aber Adebar mußte gewinnen – da gab's gar nichts
But Adebar must win there gave it was at all nothing

anderes!«
else

»Und wenn er doch nicht gewonnen hätte?«
And when he indeed not won would have

Jetzt ist er es einmal, der sich
Now is he it once this time who himself

der Frau überlegen fühlt. Er lächelt, als er sagt: »Sieh
the woman overlayed feels He smiles as he says See
feels superior over the woman

mal, Hete, du verstehst nichts vom Rennsport, ich
once Hete you understand (are familiar with) nothing from the racing I

verstehe aber alles davon. Und wenn ich sage:
understand however everything there-from And when I say

Adebar gewinnt und riskiere sogar 50 Mark darauf ...«
Adebar wins and risk even 50 mark {money} thereupon

Sie unterbricht ihn. Sie sagt scharf: »Du hast mein Geld
She interrupts him She says sharp You have my money

riskiert! Das will ich nicht haben! Wenn du Geld
risked That want I not have When you money

brauchst, sagst du es, du sollst bei mir nicht nur für
need say you it you will with me not only for

die Kost arbeiten müssen. Aber ohne meine Erlaubnis
the cost work must But without my permission

nimmst du kein Geld aus der Kasse, verstanden?«
take you no money from the cash register understood

Bei diesem ungewohnt scharfen Ton ist er wieder völlig
At this unusually sharp tone is he again totally

unsicher geworden. Er sagt klagend (und sie weiß,
unsure become He says complaining and she knows

gleich wird er losweinen, und sie fürchtet sich schon
immediately will he start to cry and she fears herself already

vor diesen Tränen), er sagt also klagend: »Aber wie
before these tears he says thus complaining But how

redest du denn mit mir, Hete? Als ob ich nur dein
talk you then with me Hete As whether I only your

Arbeiter wäre! Natürlich nehme ich nicht wieder Geld
worker would be Of course take I not again money

aus der Kasse. Ich dachte bloß, ich würde dir eine
from the cash register I thought just I would you a

Freude machen, wenn ich so schön Geld verdiene. Wo
joy make when I so beautiful money earn Where

der Sieg doch auch ganz sicher war!«
the victory indeed also completely certain was

Sie geht gar nicht auf dieses Geschwätz ein. Das Geld
She goes at all not on this babbling in The money

war ihr ja immer Nebensache, das Wichtige war das
was her yes always side-thing the important was the
indeed not the issue main thing

enttäuschte Vertrauen. Er denkt jetzt, sie ist bloß wegen
disappointed trust He thinks now she is just because of
failed

des Geldes ärgerlich, so ein Schwachkopf! Sie sagt:
of the money annoyed such a moron She says

»Und wegen dieser Pferdewetterei hast du also einfach
And because of this horse betting have you thus simply

den Laden zugemacht?«
the shop closed

»Ja«, sagt er. »Du hättest ihn doch auch zumachen
Yes says he You had him indeed also close
it

müssen, wenn ich nicht dagewesen wäre!«
must when I not there-been would be

»Und daß du ihn zumachen wolltest, das hast du schon
And that you him close wanted that have you already
it

gewußt, als ich fortging?«
known as I went away

»Ja«, sagt er ganz dumm. Und verbessert sich rasch:
Yes says he completely dumb And corrected himself quickly

»Nein, natürlich nicht, sonst hätte ich dich um Erlaubnis
No of course not otherwise had I you for permission

gebeten. Es ist mir erst eingefallen, als ich bei dem
asked It is me first occurred as I at the

kleinen Laden von dem Buchmacher vorbeikam, in der
small shop from the bookmaker came by in the

Neuen Königstraße, weißt du. Da las ich im
new Koenigstrasse know you There read I in the

Vorbeigehen die Tips, und als ich da als Außenseiter
passing the tips and as I there as outsider

Adebar las, da habe ich mich erst entschlossen.«
Adebar read there have I myself first determined

»So!« sagt sie. Sie glaubt ihm nicht. Das hat er schon
So says she She believes him not That has he already

vorher vorgehabt, ehe er sie in die U-Bahn setzte. Ihr
before intended before he her in the subway set Her

ist eingefallen, daß er heute früh so lange mit der
is occurred that he today early so long with the

Zeitung herumgeknistert und dann lange auf einem Zettel
newspaper crackled around and then long on a note

gerechnet hat, immer noch, als schon die ersten Kunden
counted has always still as already the first customers

im Laden waren. »So!« sagte sie noch einmal. »Und du
in the shop were So said she still once And you

gehst also einfach in der Stadt spazieren, wo wir doch
go thus simply in the city walk where we indeed

ausgemacht haben, du läßt dich wegen der Gestapo
made out have you let yourself because of the gestapo
decided

möglichst nicht draußen sehen?«
as possible not outside see

»Du hast doch auch erlaubt, daß ich dich bis an die
You have indeed also allowed that I you until on the

U-Bahn bringe!«
subway bring

»Da waren wir zusammen. Und ich hatte ausdrücklich
There were we together And I had explicitly

gesagt, es sollte ein Versuch sein! Das heißt noch nicht,
said it should an attempt be That is called still not
means

daß du den halben Tag in der Stadt herumläufst. Wo
that you the half day in the city run around Where

bist du denn gewesen?«
are you then been
have

»Ach, nur in so 'nem kleinen Lokal, das ich von früher
Oh only in such a small pub that I from before

kenne. Da kommt nie einer von der Gestapo hin, da
know There comes never one from the gestapo to there

verkehren nur Buchmacher und Rennwetter.«
associate only bookmakers and race betters

»Die dich alle kennen! Die alle überall erzählen können:
Who you all know Who all everywhere tell can

Wir haben den Enno Kluge da und dort gesehen!«
We have the Enno Kluge there and there seen

»Aber die Gestapo weiß doch auch, daß ich irgendwo
But the gestapo knows indeed also that I somewhere

sein muß. Nur wo, weiß sie nicht. Das Lokal ist sehr
be must Only where knows she not The pub is very

weit ab von hier, auf dem Wedding. Und ein Bekannter
far off from here on the Wedding And an acquaintance

war nicht dort, der mich verpfeifen könnte!«
was not there who me snitch could

Er redet ganz eifrig und gutherzig; wenn man auf
He talks completely zealously and kind-hearted When one ~~on~~

ihn hört, ist er vollkommen in seinem Recht. Er versteht
him hears is he completely in his right He understands

gar nicht, wie sehr er ihr Vertrauen enttäuscht hat, was
at all not how much he her trust disappointed has what

für einen Kampf sie seinetwegen mit sich kämpft. Geld
for a fight she because of him with herself fights Money

genommen – um ihr eine Freude zu machen. Das Geschäft
taken for her a joy to make The business

geschlossen – hätte sie ja auch getan. In ein Lokal
closed had she yes also done In a pub

gegangen – war ja weit weg am Wedding. Daß sie
gone was yes far way at the Wedding That she

sich aber um ihre Liebe geängstigt hatte, davon
herself but for her love scared had there-from

verstand er gar nichts, das ging nicht in seinen Schädel
understood he at all nothing that went not in his skull

hinein.
inside

»Also, Enno«, fragt sie, »das ist alles, was du dazu
So Enno asks she that is everything what you there-to

zu sagen hast? Oder?«
to say have Or

»Ja, was soll ich denn noch sagen, Hete? Ich seh ja,
Yes what should I then still say Hete I see yes
well

du bist mächtig unzufrieden mit mir, aber ich finde
you are powerfully dissatisfied with me but I find
greatly

wirklich nicht, daß ich so viel falsch gemacht habe!« Nun
really not that I so much wrong made have Now
done

kamen sie doch, die gefürchteten Tränen. »Ach, Hete, sei
came they indeed the dreaded tears Ah Hete be

doch bloß wieder gut zu mir! Ich will dich auch gewiß
indeed just again good to me I want you also certainly

vorher nach allem fragen! Sei bloß wieder lieb zu
in advance to everything ask Be just again nice to
for

mir. So halte ich es nicht aus ...«
me So hold I it not out
stand -

Aber diesmal verfingen weder Tränen noch Bitten. Etwas
But this time entangled neither tears nor pleading Something

klang falsch darin. Es ekelte sie beinahe vor dem
sounded false therein It disgusted her almost before the

weinenden Manne.
crying man

»Das muß ich mir alles erst gut überlegen, Enno«,
That must I myself all first good consider Enno

sagte sie voll Abwehr. »Du scheinst gar nicht zu
said she full defense You seem at all not to

verstehen, wie schwer du mein Vertrauen enttäuscht hast.«
understand how heavy you my trust disappointed have
much

Und sie ging an ihm vorbei in die Küche, die Kartoffeln
And she went on him past in the kitchen the potatoes

weiterzubraten. Da hatte sie also diese Aussprache
to continue frying There had she thus this pronunciation
discussion

gehabt. Und was hatte sie gebracht? Hatte sie die
had And what had she brought Had she the
it

Verhältnisse geklärt, eine Entscheidung erleichtert?
conditions clarified a decision lightened
made easier

Nichts von alledem! Sie hatte ihr nur gezeigt, daß dieser
Nothing from all that She had her only shown that this
It

Mann gar kein Gefühl dafür hatte, wenn er schuldig
man at all no feeling therefore had when he guilty

geworden war. Daß er besinnungslos log, wenn die Lage
become was That he senseless lied when the situation

das zu erfordern schien, wobei es ihm gar nicht darauf
that to require seemed where-by it him at all not thereupon

ankam, wen er anlog.
arrived whom he lied to

Nein, solch ein Mann war nicht der richtige Mann für
No such a man was not the right man for

sie. Sie mußte mit ihm zum Schluß kommen. Freilich,
her She must with him to the end come Freely
Indeed

eines war klar, heute abend konnte sie ihn nicht
one was clear today evening could she him not
one thing

mehr auf die Straße setzen. Er wußte ja gar nicht,
(any)more on the street set He knew yes at all not
indeed

was er verbrochen hatte. Er war wie ein junger Hund,
what he broken had He was like a young dog

der ein Paar Schuhe zerbissen hat und keine Ahnung
who a few shoes to shreds bitten has and no idea

besitzt, warum sein Herr ihn eigentlich verprügelt.
possesses why his master him actually beats up

Nein, ein oder zwei Tage mußte sie ihm schon Zeit
No one or two days must she him already time

lassen, ein neues Quartier zu suchen. Wenn er dabei der
let a new quarter to search When he there-by the
- quarters

Gestapo in die Hände fällt – sie muß es darauf
gestapo in the hands falls she must it thereupon

ankommen lassen. Er läßt es ja auch darauf
arrive let He lets it yes also thereupon
indeed

ankommen – wegen einer Rennwette! Nein, sie muß
arrive because of a race bet No she must

sich von ihm frei machen, sie kann nie wieder
herself from him free make she can never again

Vertrauen zu ihm finden. Allein muß sie für sich leben,
trust to him find Alone must she for herself live

von nun an bis zu ihrem Tode! Und bei diesem
from now on until to her death And at this

Gedanken wird ihr angst.
thought becomes her fear

Aber trotz dieser Angst sagt sie nach dem Abendessen zu
But despite this fear says she after the evening dinner to

ihm: »Ich habe mir alles überlegt, Enno, wir müssen
him I have myself everything considered Enno we must

uns trennen. Du bist ein netter Mann, du bist auch ein
us separate You are a nice man you are also a

lieber Mann, aber du siehst die Welt zu sehr mit andern
sweet man but you see the world to much with other

Augen an, auf die Dauer könnten wir uns nicht
eyes on on the duration could we ourselves not
in the long term each other

vertragen.«
tolerate

Er blickt starr auf sie, die wie zur Bekräftigung ihrer
He looks rigid at her who as to the affirmation her

Worte ihm das Bett auf dem Sofa richtet. Er will erst
words him the bed on the sofa aims He wants first
makes up

seinen Ohren nicht trauen, und dann wimmert er los: »O
his ears not trust and then whimpers he loose Oh

Gott, Hete, das kannst du nicht wirklich meinen! Wo
god Hete that can you not really mean Where

wir beide uns doch so liebhaben! Das kannst du nicht
we both us indeed so love That can you not

wollen, mich auf die Straße und der Gestapo in die Arme
want me on the street and the gestapo in the arms

zu jagen!«
to chase

»Ach!« sagt sie und will sich durch die eigenen Worte
Ah says she and wants herself through the own words

beruhigen. »Das mit der Gestapo wird auch nur halb so
calm down That with the gestapo will also only half so

schlimm sein, sonst wärst du heute nicht den halben
bad be otherwise were you today not the half

Tag in der Stadt herumgelaufen!«
day in the city running around

Aber er bricht in die Knie. Wahrhaftig, er rutscht auf den
But he breaks in the knees Truly he slides on the

Knien zu ihr hin. Die Furcht hat ihn ganz
knees to her away The fear has him completely

besinnungslos gemacht. »Hete! Hete!« schreit und schluchzt
senseless made Hete Hete cries and sobs

er. »Du willst mich doch nicht töten? Du mußt mich
he You want me indeed not kill You must me

hierbehalten! Wo soll ich denn hin? Ach, Hete, hab
keep here Where should I then away go Oh Hete have

mich doch ein bißchen lieb, ich bin ja so unglücklich
me indeed a little dear I am yes indeed so unhappy

...«

Heulen und Geschrei, ein kleiner, vor Angst winselnder
Howling and crying a little for of fear whimpering

Hund!
dog

Er will ihre Beine umklammern, er faßt nach ihren
He wants her legs around clasp he grabs after her

Händen. Sie flieht vor ihm in ihr Schlafzimmer, sie
hands She flees before him in her bedroom she

riegelt sich ein. Aber die ganze Nacht hört sie ihn
locks herself in But the whole night hears she him

immer wieder gegen die Tür stoßen, die Klinke
always again against the door bump the (door) handle

probieren, wimmern und betteln ...
try whimper and beg

Sie liegt ganz still. Sie sammelt in sich alle Kraft,
She lies completely still She gathers in herself all strength

nicht nachzugeben, sich nicht weichmachen zu lassen von
not to yield herself not soften to let from

ihrem eigenen Herzen und dem Gebettel da draußen! Sie
her own heart and the beggery begging there outside She

bleibt fest bei ihrem Entschluß, nicht weiter mit ihm
remains firmly at her decision not further with him

zusammen zu leben.
together to live

Beim Frühstück sitzen sie einander mit bleichen,
At the breakfast sit they each other with pale

übernächtigen Gesichtern gegenüber. Sie sprechen kaum
overnightly sleepless faces opposite They speak hardly

ein Wort miteinander. Sie tun, als ob die
a word with each other They do as if the

Auseinandersetzung nie gewesen wäre.
confrontation never been were
had

Aber er weiß jetzt Bescheid, denkt sie, und wenn er
But he knows now information thinks she and when he

sich heute kein Zimmer sucht, morgen abend muß er
himself today no room searches tomorrow evening must he

mir doch aus dem Haus. Morgen mittag sage ich es
me indeed from the house Tomorrow afternoon say I it

ihm noch einmal. Wir müssen uns trennen!
him still once We must ourselves separate

O ja, Frau Hete Häberle ist eine ebenso mutige wie
Oh yes Mrs Hete Haberle is a likewise brave as

anständige Frau. Und daß sie ihren Entschluß dann doch
decent woman And that she her decision then indeed

nicht durchführt, daß sie den Enno doch nicht von sich
not through carries that she the Enno indeed not from herself

stößt, das liegt nicht an ihr, das liegt an Menschen, die
kicks that lies not on her that lies on people who
is not caused by is caused by

sie noch gar nicht kennt. Zum Beispiel an dem
she still at all not knows To the example on the
For by

Kommissar Escherich und dem Herrn Borkhausen.
commissioner Escherich and the Mr Borkhausen

Emil Borkhausen macht sich nützlich

Emil Borkhausen makes himself useful

Während	Enno	Kluge	und	Frau	Häberle	sich	zu	einer
While	Enno	Kluge	and	Mrs	Haberle	themselves	to	a

Lebensgemeinschaft	vereinten,	die	so	schnell	wieder
cohabitation	united	which	so	fast	again

zerbrach,	hatte	Kommissar	Escherich	schwere	Zeiten	hinter
broke	had	commissioner	Escherich	heavy	times	behind

sich.	Er	hatte	es	verschmäht,	seinem	Vorgesetzten	Prall
himself	He	had	it	spurned	his	supervisor	Prall
				decided against			

zu	verheimlichen,	daß	Enno	Kluge	seinen	Beschattern	so
to	conceal	that	Enno	Kluge	his	shadowers	so
						followers	

schnell	wieder	entronnen	und,	ohne	eine	Spur	zu
fast	again	escaped	and	without	a	trace	to

hinterlassen,	im	Meer	der	Großstadt	untergetaucht	war.
behind leave	in the	sea	of the	big city	submerged	was

Kommissar	Escherich	hatte	ergeben	all	die
Commissioner	Escherich	had	surrendered	all	the
			wearily		

Beschimpfungen	auf	sich	herabhageln	lassen,	die	infolge
insults	on	himself	hail down	let	the	because of

dieses	Geständnisses	fällig	waren:	er	war	ein	Idiot,	er	war
this	confession	due	were	he	was	an	idiot	he	was

ein	Nichtskönner,	man	würde	ihn	einlochen,	diese
a	can-nothing	one	would	him	lock in	this

Schlafmütze, die es in fast einem Jahr nicht mal
sleeping cap who it in almost a year not once
even

fertiggebracht hatte, einen blöden Postkartenschreiber zu
accomplished had a stupid postcard writer to

ermitteln!
determine
find

Und hatte er mal eine Spur, so ließ er den Kerl wieder
And had he once a trace so let he the chap again
finally

laufen. Trottel, der er war! Eigentlich hatte Kommissar
run Jerk who he was Actually had commissioner

Escherich Beihilfe zum Hochverrat geleistet, und danach
Escherich aid to the high-treason accomplished and there-after
like that

würde man auch mit ihm verfahren, wenn er nicht binnen
would one also with him proceed when he not within

heute und einer Woche diesen Enno Kluge dem
today and a week this Enno Kluge the

Obergruppenführer Prall vorführte.
over-groups-leader Prall before led

Ja, Kommissar Escherich hatte diese Beschimpfungen
Yes commissioner Escherich had these insults

ergeben angehört. Aber sie hatten eine seltsame Wirkung
surrendered listened to But they had a strange effect
wearily

auf ihn: trotzdem er genau wußte, daß dieser Enno Kluge
on him although he exactly knew that this Enno Kluge

nicht das geringste mit den Postkarten zu tun hatte, daß
not the least with the postcards to do had that

er ihm nicht einen Schritt weiter auf dem Wege zur
he him not a step further on the road to the

Feststellung des wirklichen Täters helfen konnte,
conclusion of the real perpetrator help could

trotzdem konzentrierte sich plötzlich das Interesse des
in spite of that concentrated itself suddenly the interest of the

Kommissars fast nur auf die Feststellung des kleinen,
commissary almost only on the conclusion of the small

bedeutungslosen Enno Kluge. Es war auch wirklich zu
meaningless Enno Kluge It was also really too

ärgerlich, daß diese Wanze, mit der er seinen Vorgesetzten
annoying that this bug with who he his supervisor

so schön hatte hinhalten wollen, ihm durch die Finger
so beautiful had hold up want him through the fingers

geschlüpft war. In dieser Woche war der Klabautermann
slipped was In this week was the kobold

besonders fleißig gewesen: drei Karten von ihm landeten
particularly industrious been three cards from him landed

auf dem Schreibtisch des Kommissars. Aber zum
on the desk of the commissary But at the

erstenmal, seit er diese Sache bearbeitete, interessierten
first time since he this thing worked at interested

Escherich die Karten und der Schreiber überhaupt nicht.
Escherich the cards and the writers at all not

Er vergaß sogar, auf seinem Stadtplan von Berlin die
He forgot even on his map from Berlin the

Fundstelle mit Fähnchen zu markieren.
find-spots with little flags to mark

Nein, erst wollte er diesen Enno Kluge wiederhaben, und
No first wanted he this Enno Kluge back have and

Kommissar Escherich machte wirklich ungewöhnliche
commissioner Escherich made really unusual

Anstrengungen, den Mann zu kriegen. Er fuhr sogar ins
efforts the man to get He drove even in the

Ruppinsche, zu Eva Kluge, für alle Eventualitäten mit
Ruppinsche to Eva Kluge for all contingencies with

einem Haftbefehl gegen sie und gegen ihn ausgerüstet.
an arrest warrant against her and against him equipped

Aber er sah doch bald, daß diese Frau wirklich nicht
But he saw indeed soon that this woman really not

das geringste mehr mit dem Manne zu tun hatte und
the least (any)more with the man to do had and

daß sie sehr wenig von seinem Leben im letzten Jahre
that she very little from his life in the last years

wußte.
knew

Was sie wußte, erzählte sie dem Kommissar, nicht
What she knew told she the commissioner not

besonders bereitwillig und nicht grade widerspenstig,
particularly voluntarily and not right unwilling

sondern völlig gleichgültig. Dieser Frau war es ersichtlich
but totally indifferent This woman was it evident

ganz gleichgültig, was mit dem Mann wurde, was er
completely indifferent what with the man became what he

getan hatte oder nicht getan hatte. Der Kommissar
done had or not done had The commissioner

erfuhr von ihr nur die Namen von zwei oder drei
experienced from her only the name from two or three
heard

Lokalen, in denen Enno Kluge früher verkehrt hatte, er
pubs in which Enno Kluge before associated had he
been

hörte von seiner Wettleidenschaft und erfuhr auch die
heard from his betting passion and experienced also the
heard

Adresse einer gewissen Tutti Hebekreuz, von der mal ein
address of a certain Tutti Hebekreuz from who once a

Brief in die Wohnung gekommen war. In diesem Brief war
letter in the house come was In this letter was

Enno Kluge beschuldigt worden, der Hebekreuz Geld und
Enno Kluge accused become the Hebekreuz money and

Lebensmittelkarten gestohlen zu haben. Nein, Frau Kluge
food cards stolen to have No Mrs Kluge

hatte dem Mann, als sie ihn das letzte Mal sah, weder
had the man as she him the last time saw neither

den Brief ausgehändigt noch zu ihm davon gesprochen.
the letter out-handed nor to him there-from spoken
handed over

Nur die Adresse hatte sie zufällig behalten, als
Only the address had she coincidentally kept as

Briefträgerin hatte sie für Adressen ein besonders gutes
letter-carrier had she for addresses a particularly good
female postwoman

Gedächtnis.
memory

Mit diesem Wissen ausgerüstet, war Kommissar Escherich
With this knowledge equipped was commissioner Escherich

nach Berlin zurückgekehrt. Getreu seinem Grundsatz,
to Berlin returned Faithful to his principle

Fragen zu stellen, aber keine zu beantworten, kein
questions to set but none to answer no
ask

Wissen weiterzugeben, hatte er sich gehütet, der Frau
knowledge further-to-give had he himself guarded the Mrs
to share

Kluge eine Andeutung von dem Verfahren zu machen, das
Kluge a hint from the procedure to make which

gegen sie in Berlin lief. Viel brachte er also nicht mit
against her in Berlin ran Much brought he also not along
back

nach Hause, aber es war doch ein Anfang gemacht, die
to house but it was indeed a beginning made the
home there

Spur einer Spur gewissermaßen – und er konnte dem
trace of a trace (in) certain measure and he could the
so to speak

Prall doch zeigen, daß er etwas tat, nicht nur wartete.
Prall indeed show that he something did not only waited

Darauf kam es den Herren oben allein an, daß etwas
Thereupon came it the gentlemen above alone on that something

getan wurde, mochte es auch das Falsche sein, wie ja
done became might it also the false be as yes

der ganze Fall Kluge falsch war. Aber Warten vertrugen
the whole case Kluge false was But wait tolerated

die Herren nicht.
the gentlemen not

Die Erkundigungen bei der Hebekreuz verliefen erfolglos.
The inquiries at the Hebekreuz went off unsuccessfully
passed

Sie hatte den Kluge in einem Café kennengelernt, sie
She had the Kluge in a café know-learned she
gotten to know

kannte auch seine Arbeitsstelle. Er hatte zweimal einige
knew also his place of work He had twice some

Wochen bei ihr logiert, jawohl, das war richtig, sie hatte
weeks with her lodged yes that was right she had

ihm wegen Geld und Lebensmittelkarten geschrieben.
him because of money and food cards written

Aber das hatte er bei seinem zweiten Besuch aufgeklärt,
But that had he at his second visit enlightened

die hatte ein anderer Untermieter geklaut, nicht der Enno.
that had an other subtenant clawed not the Enno
stolen

Dann war er wieder abgehauen, ohne ihr was zu
Then was he again away ran without her what something to

sagen, wohl zu irgendeinem Weib, das war so Ennos Art.
say well to some woman that was so Enno's way

Nein, sie hatte natürlich nie etwas mit ihm gehabt.
No she had of course never something with him had

Nein, sie hatte keine Ahnung, wohin er gezogen war.
No she had no idea where-to he pulled was

Aber hier in dieser Gegend war er bestimmt nicht,
But here in this area was he definitely not

sonst hätte sie längst mal von ihm gehört.
otherwise had she long once from him heard

In den beiden Kneipen war er bekannt unter dem Namen
In the both bars was he known under the name

Enno, jawohl. Er hatte sich lange nicht sehen lassen,
Enno yes He had himself long not see let

nein, aber er kam immer mal wieder. Jawohl, Herr
no but he came always once again Yes Mr

Kommissar, wir lassen uns nichts merken. Wir sind solide
commissioner we let us nothing notice We are solid

Kneipiers, bei uns verkehren nur anständige Leute, die
pubs at us associate only decent people who

Interesse für den edlen Rennsport haben. Wir werden
interest for the noble racing-sport have We will

Ihnen sofort einen Wink geben, wenn er wieder
you immediately a nudge give when he again

auftaucht. Heil Hitler, Herr Kommissar!
pops up Hail hitler Mr commissioner

Kommissar Escherich setzte zehn Leute an, die bei allen
Commissioner Escherich set ten people on who with all

Buchmachern und Kneipiers im Norden und Osten
bookmakers and pubs in the north and (the) east

Berlins Nachfrage nach Enno Kluge halten sollten. Und
of Berlin after-questions interrogations after Enno Kluge hold should And

während Escherich das Ergebnis dieser Aktion abwartete,
while Escherich the result of this action awaited

geschah ihm das zweite Merkwürdige: plötzlich schien es
happened him the second strange thing suddenly seemed it

ihm nicht mehr ganz ausgeschlossen, daß dieser
him not (any)more completely excluded impossible that this

Enno Kluge doch etwas mit den Karten zu tun hatte.
Enno Kluge indeed something with the cards to do had

Zu merkwürdige Zusammenhänge geisterten um diesen
Too strange interrelationships spirited worked for this

Burschen: die beim Arzt gefundene Karte, und dann die
lad the at the doctor found card and then the

Ehefrau, erst Nazistin, und plötzlich dieser Antrag, aus
wife first nazi woman and suddenly this application from

der Partei austreten zu dürfen, vermutlich, weil der
the (political) party step out to may probably because the

Sohn in der SS etwas getan hatte, was der Mutter
son in the ss something done had what the mother
that

nicht gefiel. Vielleicht war der Enno Kluge viel geriebener,
not pleased Perhaps was the Enno Kluge much more sly

als der Kommissar gedacht hatte, vielleicht hatte er auch
as the commissioner thought had perhaps had he also

andern Dreck am Stecken als diese Karte, aber Dreck
other filth at the stick as this card but filth
than

hatte er zu verscharren, das schien fast sicher.
had he to bury that seemed almost sure

Dies bestätigte auch der Assistent Schröder, mit dem der
This confirmed also the assistant Schroeder with whom the

Kommissar zur Auffrischung seines Gedächtnisses den
commissioner to the refresher of his memory the

ganzen Fall noch einmal langsam durchsprach. Auch der
whole case still once slowly spoke through Also the

Assistent Schröder hatte das Gefühl gehabt, mit dem
assistant Schroeder had the feeling had with the

Kluge stimmte was nicht, er verbarg etwas. Nun,
Kluge was right what not he hid something Now
something

man würde ja sehen, in dieser Sache würde bald
one would yes see in this thing would soon
well

etwas erfolgen. Der Kommissar hatte das im Gefühl,
something succeed The commissioner had that in the feeling

und in solchen Dingen täuschte ihn sein Gefühl nur
and in such things faked him his feeling only

selten.
rarely

Und dieses Mal täuschte es ihn wirklich nicht. Es geschah
And this time deceived it him really not It happened

in diesen Tagen der Bedrohung und des Ärgers, daß
in these days of the threat and of the annoyances that

dem Kommissar gemeldet wurde, ein gewisser Borkhausen
the commissioner reported became a certain Borkhausen

bitte, ihn sprechen zu dürfen.
asks him speak to may

Borkhausen? fragte sich Kommissar Escherich. Borkhausen?
Borkhausen asked himself commissioner Escherich Borkhausen

Was soll denn das für ein Borkhausen sein? Ach so, ich
What should then that for a Borkhausen be Ah so I

weiß schon, dieser kleine Spitzel, der für acht Groschen
know already this little snitch who for eight groschen

seine Mutter verraten würde.
his mother betray would

Und laut: »Soll reinkommen!« Als der Borkhausen aber
And aloud Should come in As the Borkhausen however

eintrat, sagte er zu ihm: »Wenn Sie mir nur was
in-stepped said he to him If you me only what something

über die Persickes erzählen wollen, können Sie gleich
about the Persickes tell want can you immediately

wieder kehrtmachen!«
again turn around

Der Borkhausen sah den Kommissar fest an und
The Borkhausen looked the commissioner firmly at and

schwieg. Er tat so, als ob er doch beabsichtigte, über
was silent He did so as if he indeed intended about
acted

die Persickes zu reden.
the Persickes to talk

»Na also!« sagte der Kommissar. »Warum machen Sie
Now so said the commissioner Why make you
then

nicht kehrt, Borkhausen?«
not turn Borkhausen

»Der Persicke hat doch den Radio von der Rosenthal,
The Persicke has however the radio from the Rosenthal

Herr Kommissar«, sagte er vorwurfsvoll. »Ich weiß es jetzt
Mr commissioner said he reproachfully I know it now

genau, ich habe ...«
exactly I have

»Die Rosenthal?« fragte Escherich. »Das ist doch die olle
The Rosenthal asked Escherich That is indeed the old

Jüdsche, die in der Jablonskistraße aus dem Fenster
Jewish woman who in the Jablonskistreet from the window

gesprungen ist?«
jumped is

»Das ist sie!« bestätigte Borkhausen. »Und den Radio hat
That is her confirmed Borkhausen And the radio has

er ihr einfach geklaut, das heißt, da war sie schon tot,
he her simply clawed that is called there was she already dead
stolen

aber aus der Wohnung ...«
but from the house

»Nun will ich Ihnen mal was sagen, Borkhausen«,
Now want I you once what say Borkhausen
something

erklärte Escherich. »Ich habe mich mit dem Kommissar
explained Escherich I have me with the commissioner

Rusch über den Fall besprochen. Wenn Sie damit nicht
Rusch over the case discussed When you there-with not

aufhören, gegen die Persickes zu stänkern, so fahren wir
stop against the Persickes to stir things up so drive we
will finish

hier mit Ihnen Schlitten. Wir wollen von dieser Geschichte
here with you sledges We want from this story

kein Wort mehr hören – und von Ihnen schon gar
no word (any)more hear and from you already at all

nicht! Sie sind der allerletzte, der in dieser Sache
not You are the very last who in this thing

rumstochern dürfte. Ja, Sie, Borkhausen!«
poke around might Yes you Borkhausen

»Aber er hatte den Radio doch geklaut ...« fing
But he had the radio indeed clawed caught
stolen started

Borkhausen mit jener sturen Hartnäckigkeit wieder an,
Borkhausen with that stubborn tenacity again on

die nur blinder Haß verleiht. »Wo ich es ihm doch
which only (of) blind hate loans Where I it him indeed

direkt beweisen kann ...«
directly prove can

»Jetzt nur noch raus, Borkhausen, oder ich lasse Sie
Now only still out Borkhausen or I let you

abführen, hier bei uns in den Keller!«
carry off here with us in the basement

»Dann gehe ich aufs Präsidium am Alex!« erklärte
Then go I on the praesidium at the Alex explained

Borkhausen tiefgekränkt. »Was Recht ist, muß Recht
Borkhausen deeply offended What right is must right

bleiben, und geklaut ist geklaut ...«
stay and clawed is clawed
stolen stolen

Aber Escherich war etwas anderes eingefallen, nämlich
But Escherich was something other occurred namely

ein Fall Klabautermann, der fast ständig seine Gedanken
a case kobold which almost constantly his thoughts

beschäftigte. Er hörte gar nicht mehr auf den Idioten.
employed He heard at all not (any)more on to the idiot

»Sagen Sie mal, Borkhausen«, sagte er. »Sie kennen doch
Say you once Borkhausen said he You know indeed

auch einen Haufen Leute und gehen viel in die
also a heap (of) people and go much in the

Kneipen? Kennen Sie vielleicht einen gewissen Enno
bar Know you perhaps a certain Enno

Kluge?«
Kluge

Borkhausen, der ein Geschäft witterte, sagte noch
Borkhausen who a business smelled said still

verdrossen: »Einen gewissen Enno kenne ich. Ob er
annoyed One certain Enno know I whether he

weiter Kluge heißt, soviel ist mir nicht bekannt. Ich hab
further Kluge is called so much is me not known I have

eigentlich immer gedacht, Enno wäre sein Nachname.«
actually always thought Enno would be his last name

»Kleiner, schmächtiger Mann, blaß, leise und schüchtern?«
Small skinny man pale soft and shy

»Das könnte auf meinen stimmen, Herr Kommissar.«
That could on mine point Mr commissioner

»Heller Paletot, großkarierte braune Sportmütze?«
Bright man's jacket large plaid brown sports cap

»So kenne ich ihn.«
So know I him

»Hat ewig Weibergeschichten?«
Has eternally women's stories

»Von Weibergeschichten ist mir bei meinem nichts bekannt.
Of women-stories is me at mine nothing known
adventures with women

Wo ich den gesehen habe, da verkehren keine
Where I that one seen have there associate no

Weiber.«
women

»Kleiner Pferdewetter ...«
Small horsebetter

»Stimmt, Herr Kommissar.«
True Mr commissioner

»Lokale: ›Ferner liefen‹ und ›Vor dem Start?‹«
Place Further run and Before the start

»Derselbe, Herr Kommissar. Ihr Enno Kluge, das ist mein
The same Mr commissioner Your Enno Kluge that is my

Enno!«
Enno

»Den müssen Sie mir finden, Borkhausen! Hängen Sie
That one must you me find Borkhausen Hang you

den ganzen blöden Persicke-Rummel an den Nagel, der
the whole stupid Persicke-mess on the nail that

trägt Ihnen bloß noch KZ ein! Kriegen Sie
carries you just still (a) concentration camp (konzentrationslager) in Get you

mir lieber raus, wo der Enno Kluge steckt!«
me rather out where the Enno Kluge sticks

»Aber das ist doch kein Fisch für Sie, Herr Kommissar!«
But that is indeed no fish for you Mr commissioner!

rief Borkhausen abwehrend. »Das ist doch ein ganz
called Borkhausen defensively That is indeed a completely

kleiner Pinkel! Ein reiner Nebbich ist das! Was wollen
little pee A pure Nebbich meaningless is that What want

Sie denn mit solchem Idioten, Herr Kommissar?«
you then with such (an) idiot Mr commissioner

»Das lassen Sie nur meine Sache sein, Borkhausen! Wenn
That let you only my thing be Borkhausen When

ich durch Sie den Enno Kluge kriege, sollen Sie
I through you the Enno Kluge get should you

fünfhundert Mark verdient haben!«
five hundred mark earned have
{money}

»Fünfhundert Mark, Herr Kommissar? Fünfhundert Mark
Five hundred mark Mr commissioner Five hundred mark
{money} {money}

sind zehn von meinen Ennos noch nicht wert! Da muß
are ten from my Enno's still not worth There must
even

ein Irrtum vorliegen.«
a mistake lay before
be in this

»Vielleicht liegt da sogar wirklich ein großer Irrtum vor,
Perhaps lies there even really a great mistake before

aber das geht Sie nichts an, Borkhausen. Sie kriegen Ihre
but that goes you nothing on Borkhausen You get your
matters nothing to you

fünfhundert Eier - so und so!«
five hundred eggs so and so
even so

»Na denn! Wenn Sie's sagen, Herr Kommissar, dann will
Now then When you it say Mr commissioner then want

ich mal sehen, daß ich den Enno fasse. Aber ich zeige
I once see that I the Enno grab But I show

Ihnen den Mann bloß, ich bringe ihn nicht her. Mit so
you the man just I bring him not here With such

einem rede ich ja gar nicht ...«
one speak I yes at all not

»Was habt ihr beide denn miteinander gehabt? Sonst
What have you both then with each other had Otherwise

bist du doch nicht so empfindlich, Borkhausen! Sicher
are you indeed not so sensitive Borkhausen Surely

habt ihr irgendeinen Mist zusammen vergraben. Aber ich
have you some dung together buried But I

will nicht in eure zarten Geheimnisse dringen, schwimm
want not in your gentle secrets penetrate swim

ab, Borkhausen, und stell mir den Kluge!«
off Borkhausen and set me the Kluge
present

»Ich möchte noch um einen kleinen Vorschuß gebeten
I may still for a small advance asked

haben, Herr Kommissar. Nein, um keinen Vorschuß«,
have Mr commissioner No for no advance

verbesserte er sich, »sondern um Geld für meine
corrected he himself but for money for my

Spesen.«
expenses

»Was hast du denn für Spesen, Borkhausen? Das würde
What have you then for expenses Borkhausen That would

mich doch interessieren.«
me indeed interest

»Ich muß mit der Bahn fahren, in allen möglichen
I must with the track drive in all possible

Kneipen muß ich rumstehen, hier eine Molle, da eine
bars must I stand around here a glass of beer there a

Runde ausgeben, das läuft ins Geld, Herr Kommissar!
round give out spend that runs in the money Mr commissioner

Aber, ich denke, fünfzig Mark werden genügen.«
But I think fifty mark {money} will suffice

»Ja, wenn der großmächtige Borkhausen ausgeht, da
Yes when the almighty Borkhausen goes out there

warten alle schon, daß er was ausgibt! Na, ich will dir
wait expect all already that he what out-gives Now I want you

zehn Mark geben, und nun hau wirklich ab. Glaubst du,
ten mark {money} give and now chop really off Believe you

ich habe nichts anderes zu tun, als mit dir
I have nothing else to do as than with you

rumzuquatschen?«
to blabber around

Borkhausen war tatsächlich der Ansicht, daß so ein
Borkhausen was indeed the opinion that such a

Kommissar nichts anderes zu tun hatte, als den Leuten
commissioner nothing other to do had as the people

die Würmer aus der Nase zu ziehen und andere für
the worms from the nose to pull and others for

sich arbeiten zu lassen. Aber er hütete sich wohl, das
himself work to let But he guarded himself well that

auszusprechen. Er ging nun wirklich zur Tür, wobei er
to speak out He went now really to the door where-by he

sagte: »Aber wenn ich Ihnen den Kluge schaffe, müssen
said But when I you the Kluge fetch must

Sie mir auch bei den Persickes helfen. Die Brüder haben
you me also with the Persickes help The brothers have

mich zu sehr in Rage gebracht ...«
me too much in rage brought

Mit einem Satz war Escherich hinter ihm drein, packte
With one sentence was Escherich behind him there-in packed

ihn an der Schulter und hielt ihm die Faust unter die
him on the shoulder and held him the fist under the

Nase.
nose

»Siehst du die?« schrie er wütend. »Willste mal riechen
See you that one cried he furiously Want-you once smell

an der Knospe, du dämlicher Hund? Noch ein Wort von
on the bud you stupid dog Still one word from

den Persickes, und ich schicke dich in den Bunker, und
the Persickes and I send you in the bunker and

wenn auch alle Enno Kluges von der Welt frei
when also all Enno Kluges from the world free

rumlaufen!«
walk around

Und er gab dem Überraschten einen Stoß mit dem Knie
And he gave the surprised a push with the knees

in den Hintern, daß er wie eine Kanonenkugel in den
in the back that he like a cannonball in the

Gang schoß. Er war aber grade auf eine SS-Ordonnanz
hallway shot He was but right on an ss-ordnance

abgeschossen, die ihm einen weiteren kräftigen Tritt
shot down who him a further powerful step

versetzte ...
retorted

Der Lärm, den diese zwei Abschüsse verursachten, hatte
The noise which these two firings caused had

zwei SS-Posten am Treppenpodest aufmerken lassen. Sie
two ss posts at the stair landing paying attention let They
ss guards

nahmen den noch taumelnden Borkhausen in Empfang und
took the still tumbling Borkhausen in reception and

warfen ihn die Treppe hinab, genau wie einen
threw him the stairs down exactly like a

Kartoffelsack, drunter und drüber, ganz egal, wie's
potato sack underneath and about completely equal how it

grade kam.
right came

Und als Borkhausen unten ächzend und ein wenig blutend
And as Borkhausen under groaning and a little bleeding

liegenblieb, aber nur wenig, noch ganz betäubt von
remained lying but only little still completely dazed from

dem Sturz, faßte ihn der nächste Posten beim Kragen,
the fall seized him the next post at the collar

schrie: »Willst du Schwein uns hier den schönen Fußboden
cried Want you swine us here the beautiful floor

vollsauen?«, schleppte ihn zum Ausgang und warf ihn auf
full sow dragged him to the exit and threw him on
mess up

die Straße.
the street

Der Kommissar Escherich hatte den Anfang dieses Sturzes,
The commissioner Escherich had the beginning of this fall

bis die Treppe ihn seinen Blicken entzog, mit Behagen
until the stairs him his glance withdrew with comfort
blocked

angesehen.
watched

Die Vorübergehenden auf der Prinz-Albrecht-Straße
The passers-by on the Prinz-Albrecht-straße

vermieden es ängstlich, den im Dreck liegenden
avoided it fearfully anxiously the in the filth laying

Unglücklichen zu betrachten, denn sie wußten es ja,
unhappy one to regard then they knew it yes indeed

aus welchem gefährlichen Hause er hinausgeworfen war.
from which dangerous house he thrown out was

Es war vielleicht schon ein Verbrechen, solchen
It was perhaps already a crime such

Verunglückten mitleidig anzusehen, helfen durfte man
persons who had an accident pitiful to look at help may one

ihm schon gar nicht. Der Posten aber, der mit schweren
him already at all not The post guard however who with heavy

Schritten jetzt wieder am Ausgang auftauchte, sagte:
steps now again at the exit showed up said

»Wenn du Schwein in drei Minuten noch unsere Fassade
If you swine in three minutes still our facade

schändest, denn mache ich dir Beine, und das nicht zu
desecrate then make I you legs and that not too

knapp!«
scarce

Das half. Borkhausen raffte sich auf und taumelte mit
That helped Borkhausen gathered himself up and staggered with

schweren, schmerzenden Gliedern nach Hause. Innerlich
heavy aching members (body parts) to house Internally

aber brannte er mal wieder vor hilflosem Haß und Zorn,
however burned he once again for of helpless hate and anger

und dieser Haß brannte ihn stärker, als seine
and this hate burned him stronger as than his

Verletzungen weh taten. Er war fest entschlossen, für
injuries hurt did He was firmly decided for

diesen Schurken von Kommissar keine Hand zu rühren,
this rogue from of a commissioner no hand to move

der sollte sich seinen Enno Kluge allein suchen!
that one should himself his Enno Kluge alone search

Aber am nächsten Tage, als der Zorn etwas gelinder
But at the next days as the anger somewhat lenient

geworden war und die Stimme der Vernunft wieder zu
become was and the voice of the reason again to

sprechen anfing, sagte er sich, daß er erstens vom
speak began said he himself that he first (of all) from the

Kommissar Escherich zehn Mark bekommen hatte, und
commissioner Escherich ten mark {money} become had and

für die mußte er arbeiten, sonst bekam er unweigerlich
for that must he work otherwise got he inevitably

eine Betrugsanzeige. Und zweitens war es überhaupt nicht
a report of fraud And second was it at all not

gut, es mit so hohen Herren ganz zu verderben.
good it with such high gentlemen completely to ruin

Die hatten nun mal die Macht, und wer klein war,
Those had now once the power and who small was
indeed

der mußte sich fügen. Das mit dem Rausschmiß
that one must himself suit That with the out-throwing

gestern hatte sich schließlich von selbst ergeben. Wäre er
yesterday had itself finally from self given over Were he
by itself passed

nicht gegen die Ordonnanz geprallt, wäre es ganz
not against the orderly bounced would be it completely

gelinde abgegangen. Sie sahen es wohl als einen Witz an,
mild gone off They saw it well as a joke on
finished -

und wenn Borkhausen gesehen hätte, daß man einen
and when Borkhausen seen had that one an

andern so behandelte, hätte er auch herzlich gelacht, zum
other so treated had he also heartily laughed to the

Beispiel über einen gleicherweise abgefeuerten Enno Kluge.
example over a same fired off Enno Kluge
kicked out

Ja, das war der dritte Grund, warum Borkhausen den
Yes that was the third reason why Borkhausen the

Auftrag doch lieber ausführte: er konnte damit dem
mission indeed rather elaborated he could there-with the

Enno Kluge eins auswischen, der ihm durch seine blöde
Enno Kluge one wipe out who him through his stupid

Sauferei das ganze schöne Geschäft vermasselt hatte.
binging the whole beautiful business screwed up had

So begab sich Borkhausen, wenn auch mit schmerzenden
So went himself Borkhausen when also with aching
even if

Knochen, so doch guten Willens voll, in jene beiden
bones so indeed good of will full in that both

Lokale, die auch der Kommissar Escherich aufgesucht
pubs which also the commissioner Escherich visited

hatte, und in einige weitere noch. Er fragte nicht nach
had and in some further still He asked not after

Enno bei den Wirten, er stand nur da und lümmelte
Enno at the host he stood only there and lounged

sich, er trank langsam, über eine Stunde, an einer
himself he drank slowly over an hour on a

Molle, redete auch ein bißchen von Pferden, über die
glass of beer spoke also a bit from horses over which
about

er durch das ewige Zuhören sogar etwas wußte (war
he through the eternal listening even something knew was

aber gänzlich von jeder Wettleidenschaft frei) - und ging
however completely from each betting passion free and went

dann in das nächste Lokal, um es dort genauso zu
then in the next pub for it there exactly so to

machen. Er hatte Geduld, der Borkhausen, er konnte es
make He had patience the Borkhausen he could it
do

ganze Tage so treiben, ihm kam es nicht darauf an.
whole days so drive him came it not thereupon on
do

Aber er brauchte gar nicht viel Geduld zu haben, denn
But he needed at all not much patience to have then

schon am zweiten Tag sah er den Enno im Lokal
already at the second day saw he the Enno in the pub

»Ferner liefen«. Er erlebte den Adebar-Triumph des
Further run He experienced the Adebar-triumph of the

Schmächtigen und empfand einen heftigen Neid wegen
skinny one and felt a violent envy because of

des Massels, den solch ein Idiot entwickelte. Außerdem
of the fortunes which such an idiot enveloped In addition

wunderte ihn der Fünfzigmarkschein, den Kluge dem
surprised him the fifty mark bill which Kluge the

Buchmacher gegeben hatte. Durch Arbeit war der nicht
bookmaker given had Through work was that not

erworben, das roch Borkhausen sofort. Der mußte
acquired that smelled Borkhausen immediately That one must

sich ganz hübsch gebettet haben, der kleine
himself completely handsome bedded have the little

Schleicher, der!
sneaker that one

Es ist ganz selbstverständlich, daß die Herren
It is completely self-understandably that the gentlemen
self-evidently

Borkhausen und Kluge einander nicht kannten, sie sahen
Borkhausen and Kluge each other not knew they saw
met

sich nicht einmal.
each other not once

Nicht ganz so selbstverständlich ist es, daß der
Not completely so self-understandably is it that the
self-evidently

Kneipier den Kommissar Escherich nicht anrief, trotz
pub the commissioner Escherich not addressed despite

seines festen Versprechens. Aber das war ja nun so, daß
of his firm promise But that was yes now so that

man die Gestapo fürchtete und in ständiger Angst vor
one the gestapo feared and in permanent fear before

ihr lebte; aber etwas anderes war es, ihr
her lived but something else was it her

Handlangerdienste zu tun. Nein, so weit ging es auf der
henchman services to do No so far went it on the

andern Seite auch nicht, daß Enno Kluge gewarnt wurde,
other side also not that Enno Kluge warned became

aber jedenfalls wurde er nicht verraten.
but anyhow became he not betrayed

Übrigens vergaß der Kommissar Escherich nicht diesen
By the way forgot the commissioner Escherich not this

unterlassenen Anruf. Er gab einer bestimmten Abteilung
omitted call He gave a determined department

darüber Nachricht, worauf dort über den Kneipier eine
about it message where-upon there over the pub a

Kartothekkarte angelegt wurde, auf der das Wort
cartothek card erected became on which the word

»Unzuverlässig« stand. Eines Tages, früher oder später,
Unreliable stood One day sooner or later

würde es der Kneipier schon zu spüren bekommen, was
would it the pub already to feel become what

das hieß, bei der Gestapo für unzuverlässig zu gelten.
that was called with the gestapo for unreliable to be valid
be known

Von den beiden Herren verließ Borkhausen zuerst das
From the both gentlemen left Borkhausen first the

Lokal. Er ging aber nicht weit, sondern baute sich
pub He went however not far but built himself
hid

hinter einer Litfaßsäule auf, wo er in heiterer
behind an advertising pillar up where he in more cheerful

Ruhe den Abgang des Kleinen erwartete. Borkhausen
tranquility the departure of the small one expected Borkhausen

war ein Beschatter, der sein Opfer so leicht nicht aus
was a follower who his victim so easy not from

dem Auge verlor, und dieses Opfer schon gar nicht. Er
the eye lost and this victim already at all not He

brachte es sogar fertig, sich auf der U-Bahn in den
brought it even ready himself on the subway in the
managed it even

gleichen Wagen mit ihm zu quetschen, und obwohl
(the) same carriage with him to squeeze and although

Borkhausen lang war, sah ihn Enno Kluge nicht.
Borkhausen tall was saw him Enno Kluge not

Enno Kluge dachte nur an seinen Triumph mit Adebar, an
Enno Kluge thought only on his triumph with Adebar on
of of

das Geld, das endlich wieder einmal reichlich in seiner
the money that finally again once richly in his

Tasche knisterte, und dann dachte er an Hete, bei der
pocket crackled and then thought he on Hete at whom
of

er es doch sehr gut hatte. Mit Liebe und Rührung
he it indeed very good had With love and emotion

dachte er an die gute, ältliche Zerfließende, aber er
thought he on the good elderly deliquescent but he

dachte nicht daran, daß er sie vor ein paar Stunden
thought not there-on that he her before a few hours
of it a few hours earlier

belogen und bestohlen hatte.
lied to and robbed had

Freilich, als er dann vor dem Laden ankam und sah,
Freely as he then before the shop arrived and saw
Indeed

der Rolladen war hochgezogen, und sie wirkte schon
the roller shutter was uplifted and she worked already

wieder im Geschäft, und sie hatte ihm sein Weglaufen
again in the business and she had him his away-walking
running away

bestimmt übelgenommen, da sank seine gute Stimmung
definitely resented there sank his good mood

wieder. Aber mit dem Fatalismus, mit dem sich Leute
again But with the fatalism with which himself people

seines Schlages auch in das Widrigste fügen, betrat er
of his beat also in the most adverse suit entered he
sort to

den Laden und ging seiner Abreibung entgegen. Daß er
the shop and went his abrasion towards That he
beating

aber, mit solchen Gedanken beschäftigt, nicht grade sehr
however with such thoughts occupied not right very

genau darauf achtete, wer ihm auf den Fersen saß,
exactly thereupon paid attention who him on the heels sat

das kann niemanden wundernehmen.
that can no one take wonder
surprise

Der Borkhausen hatte den Kluge im Laden verschwinden
The Borkhausen had the Kluge in the shop disappear

sehen. Er stand etwas entfernt in einem Torweg, denn
see He stood somewhat removed in a gateway then

er nahm an, Kluge wolle dort etwas kaufen und werde
he took on Kluge wanted there something buy and will
assumed

gleich wieder herauskommen. Aber die Kunden gingen
immediately again come out But the customers went

und kamen, gingen und kamen, und Borkhausen wurde
and came went and came and Borkhausen became

schon ganz nervös. Wenn er Kluges Herauskommen
already completely nervous When he Kluge's coming out

übersehen hatte - er hatte die fünfhundert Eier schon
overlooked had he had the five hundred eggs already

ganz sicher in seiner Tasche gefühlt, diesen Abend
completely sure in his pocket felt this evening

noch.
still

Nun ging laut der Rolladen herunter, und jetzt war es
Now went loud the roller shutter down and now was it

sicher: der Enno hatte sich irgendwie verdrückt. Vielleicht
sure the Enno had himself somehow stowed away Perhaps

hatte er doch Witterung von seinem Beschatter gehabt,
had he indeed scent from his shadower follower had

war unter irgendeinem Vorwand durch den Laden in das
was under some pretext through the shop in the

Haus gegangen und durch die Haustür wieder heraus.
house gone and through the house door again out

Borkhausen verfluchte sich ob seiner Dummheit, nicht
Borkhausen cursed himself whether his stupidity not

auch die Haustür im Auge behalten zu haben. Immer
also the house door in the eye keep to have Always

hatte er nur auf die Ladentür geglotzt, Kamel, das er
had he only on the store door gawked camel that he

war!
was

Nun, es gab ja die Möglichkeit, Enno morgen oder
Now it gave yes the possibility Enno tomorrow or

übermorgen wieder in dem Lokal zu treffen. Jetzt, wo
day after tomorrow again in the pub to meet Now where

er durch Adebar so einen Reibach gemacht hatte,
he through Adebar such a big winnings made had

würde sein Wettfimmel ihm schon keine Ruhe lassen. Er
would his betting mania him already no rest let He

würde jeden Tag kommen und solange wetten, bis das
would every day come and so long bet until the

Geld alle war. Ein Außenseiter wie Adebar lief nicht
money all finished was An outsider like Adebar ran not

alle Wochen, und wenn er lief, hatte man nicht auf ihn
all weeks and when he ran had one not on him

gesetzt. Der Enno würde sein Geld schon rasch loswerden.
set betted The Enno would his money already quickly get rid of loose

Der Borkhausen schob auf seinem Heimweg noch nahe an
The Borkhausen pushed on his way home still close on

dem kleinen Tierladen vorbei. Da sah er plötzlich durch
the small animal store past There saw he suddenly through

die Schaufensterscheibe (nur die Ladentür war durch den

the shop window only the store door was through the

by

Rolladen versperrt), daß ein einsames Licht im Laden

roller shutter blocked that a lonely light in the shop

brannte, und wie er nun die Nase an der Scheibe platt

burned and as he now the nose on the disc flat

window pane

drückte und über die Aquarien durch die Vogelkäfige

squeezed and over the aquariums through the bird cages

linste, da sah er, daß noch zwei Gestalten im Laden

peeked there saw he that still two shapes in the shop

wirkten: ein aufgegangener Pudding von einer Alten im

worked a risen pudding of an old person in the

gefährlichsten Alter, wie er gleich richtig schätzte, und

most dangerous age as he immediately correctly estimated and

dazu sein Freund Enno. Enno in Hemdsärmeln und einer

there-to his friend Enno Enno in shirt sleeves and a

blauen Schürze, der fleißig Futternäpfe füllte, Wasser

blue apron who industriously food bowls filled water

eingoß, einen Scotch putzte.

poured in a scotch cleaned

(dog)

Was für einen Dusel solch ein Idiot wie der Enno doch

What for a dumb luck such an idiot as the Enno indeed

hatte! Was die Weiber an dem nur sahen? Er, der

had What the women on that one only saw He the

in

Borkhausen, saß fest mit der Otti und fünf Blagen, und
Borkhausen sat stuck with the Otti and five brats and

so ein oller Knacker, der kam daher und setzte sich
so an old cracker who came there-from and set himself

gleich in eine ganze Tierhandlung, komplett mit Frau,
immediately in a whole pet shop complete with woman

Fischen und Vögeln.
fish and birds

Verächtlich spuckte Borkhausen aus. Was für eine
Contemptuously spat Borkhausen out What for a

saublöde Welt das war, die dem Borkhausen alles
sow-stupid world that was which the Borkhausen everything

Gute vorenthielt, um es einem solchen Idioten in den
good withheld for it a such idiot in the

Schoß zu werfen!
lap to throw

Aber je länger Borkhausen guckte, um so klarer wurde
But the longer Borkhausen looked for so clearer became

ihm, daß um das Paar da drinnen kein Liebeszauber
him that for the pair there inside no love spell

blühte. Sondern sie redeten kaum miteinander, sie sahen
bloomed Instead they talked hardly with each other they looked

sich fast nie an, und es war sehr möglich, daß der
each other almost never at and it was very possible that the

kleine Enno Kluge nichts darstellte als einen Arbeiter, der
little Enno Kluge nothing represented as a worker who

die Frau da drinnen beim Aufräumen des Ladens
the woman there inside at the cleaning up of the store

unterstützte. Dann mußte er in absehbarer Zeit aus dem
supported Then must he in foreseeable time from the

Haus herauskommen.
house come out

Borkhausen zog sich also von neuem auf seinen
Borkhausen pulled himself thus from new on his
again

Beobachtungsposten im Torweg zurück. Da der
observation post in the gateway back There the
Since

Rolladen geschlossen war, würde Kluge aus der Haustür
roller shutter closed was would Kluge from the house door

kommen, und so behielt Borkhausen die im Auge.
come and so kept Borkhausen that one in the eye

Aber das Licht im Laden war erloschen, und Kluge war
But the light in the shop was extinguished and Kluge was

noch immer nicht gekommen. Da entschloß sich
still always not come There decided himself

Borkhausen, viel zu wagen. Auf die Gefahr hin, den Enno
Borkhausen much to dare On the danger away the Enno

im Treppenhaus zu treffen, schlich er sich in das
in the stairwell to meet sneaked he himself in the

Haus.
house

Borkhausen notierte zuerst den Namen »H. Häberle« in
Borkhausen noted first the name H. Häberle in

seinem Hirn und schlich dann auf den Hof hinaus. Und
his brain and sneaked then on the court out And

siehe, er hatte Glück, sie brannten schon Licht, obwohl
see he had luck they burned already light although

es kaum dämmerig geworden war, und an einem
it hardly dim become was and on a

schiefhängenden Store vorbeiblickend konnte Borkhausen
lopsided hanging net curtain looking past could Borkhausen
curtain

die Stube bestens übersehen. Was er da aber sah, das
the room the best overlook What he there however saw that

überraschte ihn derart, daß er fast einen Schreck
surprised him in such a way that he almost a fright

bekam.
got

Denn da kniete sein Freund Enno auf der Erde, kniend
Then there kneeled his friend Enno on the ground kneeling

rutschte er hinter der dicken Frau her, die mit ängstlich
slid he behind the thick woman away who with fearfully
anxiously

angezogenen Röcken Schritt für Schritt vor ihm
pulled up skirts step for step for him

zurückwich. Ennochen aber hatte die Ärmchen erhoben,
backed away Little Enno however had the little arms lifted

er schien zu weinen und Klagelaute auszustoßen.
he seemed to cry and lamentations to emit

Ihr lieben Leute! dachte Borkhausen und trat auf seinem
You dear people thought borkhausen and stepped on his

Beobachtungsposten vor Entzücken von einem Bein auf
observation post before rapture from a leg on

das andere, ihr lieben Leute, wenn ihr euch so Appetit
the other you dear people when you you so apetite

auf die Nacht macht, dann proste Mahlzeit, dann seid ihr
on the night make then cheers meal then are you

ja verdammt ulkige Kruken! Da will ich gerne hier die
yes damned funny pitchers There want I gladly here the

halbe Nacht stehen und euch zukieken.
half night stand and you peep at

Aber da schlug die Tür hinter der Alten zu, und der
But there struck the door behind the old one to and the

Enno stand an der Tür, bewegte die Klinke auf und
Enno stood at the door moved the (door) handle up and

ab und schien weiter zu flennen und zu beschwören.
down and seemed further to blubber and to swear

Vielleicht war's nicht nur so 'ne kleine Vorfeier für
Perhaps was it not only such a little pre-celebration for

die Nacht, dachte Borkhausen. Vielleicht haben sie
the night thought Borkhausen Perhaps have they

sich gestritten, oder Enno hat was von ihr haben
themselves argued or Enno has what from her have

wollen, was sie ihm nicht gibt, oder sie will überhaupt
want what she him not gives or she wants at all

von dem verliebten alten Gockel nichts wissen ... Was
from the in love old rooster nothing know What

geht es mich an? Jedenfalls bleibt er hier zur Nacht,
goes it me on Anyhow remains he here for the night

wozu wäre ihm sonst auf dem Sofa ein so schönes
to which would be him otherwise on the sofa a such beautiful

weißes Bettchen zurechtgemacht?
white bed trimmed

Der Enno Kluge stand grade vor dem Bettchen.
The Enno Kluge stood right before the bed

Borkhausen konnte das Gesicht seines ehemaligen Kumpels
Borkhausen could the face of his former mates

ganz deutlich sehen. Es war zum Verwundern, wie es
completely clearly see It was to the astonishment how it

jetzt ausschaute. Eben noch Weinen und Wehklagen, und
now looked Just still crying and wailing and

nun grinste der Mann, sah zur Tür, grinste wieder ...
now grinned the man looked at the door grinned again

Der hat der Alten also nur ein Theater vorgespielt. Na,
That one has the old one thus only a theater played before Now

denn also, mein Junge, viel Glück! Ich fürchte nur, der
then thus my young much luck I fear only the

Escherich spuckt dir in deine Suppe!
Escherich spit you in your soup

Der Kluge hatte sich eine Zigarette angesteckt. Nun ging
The Kluge had himself a cigarette lit Now went

er direkt auf das Fenster zu, durch das Borkhausen
he directly on the window to through which Borkhausen

spähte. Der fuhr erschrocken zur Seite - das
spied That one drove frightened to the side the

Verdunklungsrouleau sauste herunter, und Borkhausen
blackout roll (curtain) zoomed down and Borkhausen

konnte ruhig seinen Beobachtungsposten für diese Nacht
could calm his observation post for this night

aufgeben. Große Aufregungen waren nicht mehr zu
give up Great excitements were not (any)more to

erwarten, wenigstens würde er davon nichts mehr zu
expect at least would he there-from nothing (any)more to

sehen bekommen. Der Enno aber war ihm für diese
see become The Enno however was him for this

Nacht sicher ...
night sure

Eigentlich war mit dem Kommissar Escherich vereinbart
Actually was with the commissioner Escherich agreed

worden, daß Borkhausen ihn sofort nach der
become that Borkhausen him immediately after the

Entdeckung Enno Kluges anrufen sollte, einerlei ob Tag
discovery (of) Enno Kluge call should be it either day

oder Nacht. Aber wie Borkhausen da in der Nacht
or night But as Borkhausen there in the night

immer weiter vom Königstor fortging, wurde ihm
always further from the King's gate went away became him

stets zweifelhafter, ob ein sofortiger Anruf wirklich
all the time dubious whether an immediate call really

das Richtige war, das für Borkhausens Nutzen. Ihm war
the right was that for Borkhausen use Him was

eingefallen, daß es in dieser Sache doch zwei Parteien
fallen in that it in this thing indeed two parties

gab, daß er also eigentlich von beiden Nutzen ziehen
gave that he thus actually from both use pull

konnte.
could

Das Geld von Escherich war ihm sicher, warum sollte er
The money from Escherich was him sure why should he

nicht versuchen, auch aus Enno Kluge ein bißchen Geld
not try also from Enno Kluge a little money

zu machen? Da hatte dieser Bursche einen
to make There had this lad a

Fünfzigmarkschein in der Hand gehabt, den er durch den
fifty mark bill in the hand had which he through the

Sieg Adebars auf über zweihundert Mark vermehrt hatte
victory of Adebar on over two hundred mark {money} increased had

– nun, warum sollte nicht er, Borkhausen, auch dieses
now why should not he Borkhausen also this

Geld haben? Dem Escherich geschah kein Schaden
money have The Escherich happened no harm

dadurch, der bekam seinen Enno trotzdem, und Enno
there-through that one got his Enno in spite of it and Enno
through that

geschah auch kein Schade, denn die auf der Gestapo
happened also no harm since the ones on the gestapo

nahmen ihm doch das Geld ab. Also?
took him indeed the money away So

Und dann war da diese dicke Frau, hinter der Enno
And then was there this fat woman behind whom Enno

so komisch auf den Knien gerutscht war. Die hatte
so comically on the knees slipped was That one had

sicher Geld, vielleicht sogar eine ganze Menge. Das
surely money perhaps even a whole mass The

Geschäft sah gut aus, hatte noch viel Ware, und an
business saw good out had still much goods and on

Kunden schien es ihr auch nicht zu fehlen. Nein, diese
customers seemed it her also not to lack No this

Flennerei und Rutscherei Kluges sah nicht grade danach
flender and slippery of Kluge saw not right there-after

aus, daß die beiden schon in allen Dingen einig waren,
out that they both already in all things agreed were

das nicht, zugegeben, aber wer liefert denn grade einen
that not admitted but who supplies then right a

Liebhaber, und sei es auch ein abgewiesener, der Gestapo
lover and be it also a rejected the gestapo

aus? Die Tatsache, daß die Alte den Enno trotz der
out The fact that the old one the Enno despite the

Abweisung noch bei sich duldete, daß sie ihm ein
rejection still with herself tolerated that she him a

Nachtlager auf dem Sofa bereitet hatte, bewies, daß ihr
night camp on the sofa prepared had proved that her
night lodging

noch was an Enno lag. Und lag ihr noch was an dem
still what on Enno lay And lay her still what on the

alten Graukopf, so würde sie auch zahlen, vielleicht nicht
old greyhead so would she also count perhaps not

viel, aber doch etwas. Und dieses Etwas wollte
much but indeed something And this something wanted

Borkhausen sich keinesfalls entgehen lassen.
Borkhausen himself not at all escape let

Wenn Borkhausen so weit mit seinen Gedanken gekommen
When Borkhausen so far with his thoughts come

war – und er kam auf diesem Heimweg und in der
was and he came on this way home and in the

Nacht neben seiner Otti liegend noch mehrfach so weit
night beside his Otti lying still multiple times so far

–, so faßte ihn immer ein leichter Schreck, denn dann
so seized him always an easier fright then then

fiel ihm ein, daß er ein ziemlich gefährliches Spiel
fell him in that he a rather dangerous play

vorhatte. Dieser Escherich war bestimmt kein Mann, der
intended This Escherich was definitely no man who

Eigenmächtigkeiten duldete, alle diese Herren bei der
idiosyncrasies tolerated all these gentlemen at the

Gestapo waren nicht so, und es war die einfachste Sache
gestapo were not so and it was the easiest thing

von der Welt für ihn, einen Mann ins KZ zu
from the world for him a man in the concentration camp to
(konzentrationslager)

schicken. Vor dem KZ aber hatte Borkhausen
send For the concentration camp however had Borkhausen
(konzentrationslager)

eine gewaltige Angst.
a violent fear
terrible

Immerhin war er so weit von all den Verbrechergedanken
After all was he so far from all the criminal thoughts

und ihrer Moral angesteckt, daß er sich sagte, ein Ding,
and her moral on-stuck that he himself said one thing
infected

das zu drehen war, müsse auch gedreht werden, das
that to turn was must also turned become that

gehörte sich nun einmal so. Und dieses Ding ließ sich
belonged to itself now once so And this thing let itself

unzweifelhaft drehen. Borkhausen würde die ganze Sache
undoubtedly turn Borkhausen would the whole thing

erst noch einmal beschlafen, und wenn es dann Morgen
first still once sleep over and when it then morning

war, würde er wissen, ob er gleich zu Escherich
was would he know whether he immediately to Escherich

ging oder erst bei Kluge vorschaute. Jetzt wollte er
went or first at Kluge previewed Now wanted he

schlafen ...
sleep

Aber er schlief nicht ein, sondern überlegte, daß einer in
But he slept not in but considered that one in

dieser Sache zu wenig war. Er, Borkhausen, mußte ein
this thing too little was He Borkhausen must a

wenig Beweglichkeit haben. Er mußte zum Beispiel rasch
little agility have He must to the for example quickly

zu Escherich, und solange war der Enno Kluge ohne
to Escherich and for so long was the Enno Kluge without

Bewachung. Oder wenn er die Dicke in die Zange nahm,
guarding Or when he the fat one in the pliers took

lief unterdes der Enno womöglich fort. Nein, einer war zu
ran under-that meanwhile the Enno possibly away No one was too

wenig. Aber es gab keinen zweiten, dem er vertrauen
little But it gave no second which he trust

konnte, und außerdem würde dieser zweite seinen Anteil
could and in addition would this second one his part

an dem Geschäft verlangen. Und für Teilen war
on the business desire And for sharing was

Borkhausen gar nicht.
Borkhausen at all not

Schließlich fiel Borkhausen ein, daß unter seinen fünf
Finally fell Borkhausen in that under his five

Gören doch auch ein Sohn von dreizehn Jahren war, unter
brats indeed also a son of thirteen years was under

Umständen sogar sein Sohn. Er hatte immer das Gefühl
circumstances even his son He had always the feeling

gehabt, daß dieser Bengel mit dem piekfeinen Namen
had that this kid with the posh name

Kuno-Dieter vielleicht doch von ihm sein könne, trotzdem
Kuno-Dieter perhaps indeed from him be could although

die Otti stets behauptet hatte, er sei von einem
the Otti all the time claimed had he be from a

Grafen, einem Großgrundbesitzer aus Pommern. Aber Otti
count a large landowner from Pomerania But Otti

war immer eine Angeberin gewesen, wie schon der
was always a show-off been as already the
had

Vorname des Jungen – nach seinem angeblichen Vater –
first name of the boy after his alleged father

bewies.
proved

Mit einem schweren Seufzer entschloß Borkhausen sich,
With a heavy sigh decided Borkhausen himself

den Jungen als Reserveaufpasser mitzunehmen. Das würde
the boy as reserve watcher to take along That would

nicht mehr als ein bißchen Krach mit der Otti und
not (any)more as a bit of noise with of the Otti and

ein paar Mark für den Jungen kosten. Dann fingen
a few mark {money} for the boy cost Then caught started

Borkhausens Gedanken von neuem an, über alledem zu
Borkhausen thoughts from new again on - over all that to

kreisen, wurden langsam undeutlicher, und schließlich war
circle became slowly more indistinct and finally was

er doch eingeschlafen.
he indeed slept in (asleep fallen)

Hübsche kleine Erpressung

Pretty little blackmail

Es war bereits berichtet worden, daß Frau Hete Häberle
It was already reported become that Mrs Hete Haberle

und Enno Kluge an diesem Morgen fast ohne Worte
and Enno Kluge on this morning almost without words

miteinander frühstückten und im Laden arbeiteten, beide
with each other breakfasted and in the shop worked both

blaß von einer fast durchwachten Nacht und stark mit
pale from an almost through-wakened night and strongly with
sleepless

ihren Gedanken beschäftigt. Frau Häberle dachte daran,
their thoughts occupied Mrs Haberle thought there-on
reflected on the fact

daß Enno morgen unbedingt aus dem Hause müsse, Enno,
that Enno tomorrow absolutely from the house must Enno

daß er sich keinesfalls fortschicken lassen würde.
that he himself not at all send away let would

In diese Stille trat als erster Kunde ein langer Mann
In this quiet stepped as first customer a tall man

und sagte zu Frau Häberle: »Hörense mal, Sie haben da
and said to Mrs Haberle Hear you once You have there

so ein paar Wellensittiche im Fenster. Was soll denn
so a few budgies in the window What should then

ein Paar von denen kosten? Es müßte aber ein Pärchen
a pair from those cost It must however a little couple

sein, ich bin immer für Pärchen gewesen ...« Und
be I am always for little couples been And
have

Borkhausen fuhr herum, in gespieltem Erstaunen, in
Borkhausen drove around in played astonishment in
walked

absichtlich schlecht gespieltem Erstaunen rief er den
intentionally bad played astonishment called he the

Kluge an, der sich eben sachte in die Hinterstube des
Kluge on who himself just softly in the back room of the

Ladens verdrücken wollte: »Aber das bist du doch, Enno!
store press away wanted But that are you indeed Enno
stalk away

Nanu, ich rede, ich kieke, ich denke, das kann doch
Well now I speak I look I think that can indeed
(dialect)

nicht der Enno sein, was soll denn der Enno in so
not the Enno be what should then the Enno in such

'nem kleinen Tierzoo? Und nun bist du es doch, Kumpel!
a small animal zoo And now are you it indeed comrade

Na, was machste denn noch so, Kumpel?«
Now what do you then still so buddy

Enno war, die Klinke in der Hand, wie gebannt auf
Enno was the (door) handle in the hand as captured on

seinem Platz stehengeblieben, gleich unfähig, fortzulaufen
his place stand-remained immediately unable to run away
halted

und zu antworten.
and to answer

Frau Hete aber starrte den langen Mann, der so
Mrs Hete however stared the tall man who so

freundlich auf Enno einredete, mit großen Augen an, ihre
friendly on Enno talked in with large eyes at her
coaxed

Lippen fingen an zu zittern und die Knie wurden ihr
lips caught on to tremble and the knees became her
started

weich. Da war sie also doch, die Gefahr, alles war
soft There was she also indeed the danger everything was
it

also nicht gelogen, was Enno erzählt hatte von seiner
thus not lied what Enno told had from his

Bedrängnis durch die Gestapo. Denn, daß dieser Mann mit
distress through the gestapo Then that this man with

dem ebenso feigen wie brutalen Gesicht ein Spitzel der
the likewise cowardly as brutal face a snitch of the

Gestapo war, daran zweifelte sie keinen Augenblick.
gestapo was there-on doubted she no moment
not a

Aber als nun diese Gefahr wirklich geworden war, da
But as now this danger real become was there

zitterte nur der Körper von Frau Hete. Ihr Geist war
trembled only the body from Mrs Hete Her spirit was

ruhig, und dieser Geist sagte ihr: Jetzt, in dieser Gefahr,
calm and this spirit told her Now in this danger

kannst du den Enno unmöglich im Stich lassen, er mag
can you the Enno impossibly in the sting let he may
abandon

sein wie er will.
be how he wants
is

Und Frau Hete sagte zu diesem Mann mit dem
And Mrs Hete said to this man with the

stechenden Blick, der immer wieder abirrte, sie sagte zu
piercing glance which always again strayed she said to

diesem Mann, der wie ein richtiger Achtgroschenjunge
this man who like a true eight groschenjunge

aussah: »Vielleicht trinken Sie eine Tasse Kaffee mit uns,
looked Perhaps drink you a cup coffee with us

Herr – wie ist doch Ihr Name?«
Mr how is indeed your name

»Borkhausen, Emil Borkhausen«,
Borkhausen Emil Borkhausen

stellte der Spitzel sich vor. »Bin ein alter Freund von
set the snitch himself before Am an old friend from
presented the snitch himself

dem Enno, Sportsfreund. Was sagen Sie nun, Frau
the Enno sports-friend What say you now Mrs

Häberle, zu dem großartigen Coup, den er gestern auf
Haberle to the great coup which he yesterday on

Adebar gelandet hat? Wir haben uns in der
Adebar landed has We have us in the
each other

Sportkneipe getroffen – hat er es Ihnen nicht gesagt?«
sports pub hit has he it you not said
met

Frau Hete warf einen raschen Blick auf Enno. Da stand
Mrs Hete threw a quick glance at Enno There stood

er noch immer, die Hand auf der Klinke, genau wie
he still always the hand on the (door) handle exactly as

ihn die vertrauliche Ansprache Borkhausens überrascht
him the confidential speech Borkhausen surprised

hatte. Ein Bild hilfloser Angst. Nein, er hatte ihr nichts
had A picture (of) helpless fear No he had her nothing

von diesem Treffen mit dem alten Bekannten gesagt, er
from this meeting with the old acquaintance said he

hatte sogar behauptet, er hätte niemanden Bekanntes
had even claimed he had no one familiar

gesehen. Er hatte sie also wieder mal belogen – und sehr
seen He had her thus again once lied to and much

zu seinem eigenen Schaden hatte er das getan, denn nun
to his own harm had he that done then now

war ja ganz klar, wie dieser Spitzel seine Zuflucht
was yes completely clear how this snitch his refuge
indeed

bei ihr gefunden hatte. Hätte er gestern abend schon
at her found had Had he yesterday evening already

etwas von diesem Bekannten gesagt, so hätte man ihn
something from this acquaintance said so had one him

noch fortschaffen können ...
still away fetch can
manage to get away

Aber dies war nicht der Augenblick, mit Enno Kluge zu
But this was not the moment with Enno Kluge to

hadern oder ihm seine Lügen vorzuwerfen. Dies war der
ponder or him his lies accuse This was the

Augenblick, zu handeln. Und so sagte sie denn noch
moment to deal And so said she then still

einmal: »Also trinken wir eine Tasse Kaffee, Herr
once Also drink we a cup (of) coffee Mr

Borkhausen. Jetzt kommt noch nicht so viel Kundschaft,
Borkhausen Now come still not so many customers

Enno, du paßt auf den Laden auf. Ich werde zuerst
Enno you suits on the shop on I will first
take care of

einmal mit deinem Freund reden ...«
once with your friend talk

Jetzt war Frau Hete auch über das Zittern des Körpers
Now was Mrs Hete also over the trembling of the body

hinaus. Sondern sie dachte nur daran, wie es damals
out But she thought only there-on how it at that time
cured

mit ihrem Walter gegangen war, und diese Erinnerungen
with her Walter gone was and these memories

gaben ihr Kraft. Sie wußte, diesen Leuten gegenüber
gave her strength She knew these people opposite

half kein Zittern, Klagen, Anrufen des Mitleids, sie
helped no trembling complaining calling of the pity they

hatten kein Herz, diese Henkerslieferanten von Hitler und
had no heart this hangman suppliers from hitler and

Himmler. Sondern wenn eines half, so war es
himmler On the contrary when one (thing) helped so was it

Mut, Nichtfeigesein, Nieangsthaben. Die glaubten, alle
courage not-cowardly-be no-fear-have They believed all

Deutschen seien feige, wie es jetzt der Enno war; aber
Germans are cowardly like it now the Enno was but

sie war es nicht, Frau Hete, verwitwete Häberle, war es
she was it not Mrs Hete widowed Haberle was it

nicht.
not

Sie erreichte durch ihr ruhiges Auftreten auch, daß die
She achieved through her calm performance also that the

beiden Männer sich ihr widerspruchslos fügten. Im
both men themselves to her without contradiction fitted obeyed In the

Abgehen zur Stube sagte sie noch: »Und keine
down going to the room said she still And no

Dummheiten, Enno! Kein sinnloses Fortlaufen! Denke daran,
stupidities Enno No senseless running away Think there-on

dein Mantel hängt in der Stube, und Geld wirst du auch
your coat hangs in the room and money will you also

kaum in der Tasche haben.«
hardly in the pocket have

»Sie sind 'ne kluge Frau«, sagte Borkhausen, indem er
You are a smart woman said Borkhausen while he

sich an den Tisch niedersetzte und zusah, wie sie ihm
himself at the table set down and watched how she him

eine Kaffeetasse hinstellte. »Und energisch sind Sie auch,
a coffee cup put down And energetical are you also

hätte ich gar nicht gedacht, wie ich Sie gestern abend
had I at all not thought as I you yesterday evening

zum erstenmal sah.«
for the first time saw

Ihre Blicke begegneten sich.
Their looks met each other

»Na ja«, setzte Borkhausen dann schnell hinzu, »eigentlich
Now yes set Borkhausen then quickly there-to actually

waren Sie gestern abend auch energisch, wie er da auf
were you yesterday evening also energetical as he there on

den Knien vor Ihnen rumrutschte, und Sie schlossen ihm
the knees before you slid around and you closed him

die Tür vor der Nase ab. Sie werden sie ja wohl
the door before the nose off You become her yes well
it indeed

über Nacht nicht wieder aufgeschlossen haben - oder?«
over night not again up-locked have or
unlocked

Ein wenig Rot war bei dieser schamlosen Anspielung in
A little red was at this shameless allusion in

Frau Hetes Wangen gestiegen, die beschämende, die
Mrs Hete's cheeks risen the shameful the

ekelhafte Szene von gestern abend hatte also sogar einen
disgusting scene from yesterday evening had thus even a

Zeugen gehabt, und solch widerlichen dazu! Aber sie
witness had and such (a) disgusting (one) there-to But she
at that

faßte sich rasch und sagte: »Ich nehme an, Sie sind
seized herself quickly and said I take on you are
gathered assume

auch ein kluger Mann, Herr Borkhausen, wir wollen doch
also a smart man Mr Borkhausen we want indeed

jetzt gar nicht von Nebensachen reden, sondern nur
now at all not from side affairs talk but only

vom Geschäft. Ich nehme an, es kann ein Geschäft
from the business I take on it can a business
assume

werden?«
become

»Vielleicht, vielleicht sicher ...« beeilte sich Borkhausen
Perhaps perhaps sure hurried himself Borkhausen

zu beteuern, unwillkürlich eingeschüchtert von dem Tempo,
to affirm involuntarily intimidated from the tempo
by speed

das diese Frau vorlegte.
that this woman submitted
presented

»Sie wollen also«, fuhr Frau Hete fort, »ein Paar
You want so drove Mrs Hete away a few
continued -

Wellensittiche kaufen. Ich nehme an, um sie dann fliegen
budgies buy I take on for they then fly
assume

zu lassen. Denn wenn sie weiter im Käfig bleiben,
to let Since when they further in the cage stay

haben die Sittiche doch nichts davon ...«
have the parakeets indeed nothing there-from

Borkhausen kratzte sich den Kopf. »Frau Häberle«, sagte
Borkhausen scratched himself the head Mrs Häberle said

er dann, »das mit den Sittichen, das wird mir zu
he then that with the parakeets that becomes me to

kompliziert. Ich bin bloß ein einfacher Mensch,
complicated I am just a simple human

wahrscheinlich sind Sie viel schlauer als ich. Hoffentlich
probably are you much smarter than me Hopefully

legen Sie mich nicht rein.«
put you me not in
trick -

»Und Sie mich nicht!«
And you me not

»Keine Ahnung! Ich will ganz offen mit Ihnen reden,
No idea I want completely open with you talk

nichts von Sittichen und so. Ich sage Ihnen alles, wie
nothing from parakeets and so I say you everything as

es ist, die ganze Wahrheit. Ich habe nämlich von der
it is the whole truth I have namely from the

Gestapo den Auftrag, von dem Kommissar Escherich habe
gestapo the mission from the commissioner Escherich have

ich ihn, wenn der Ihnen ein Begriff ist?« Frau Hete
I him when that one you a term is Mrs Hete
it known

schüttelte den Kopf. »Also ich hab den Auftrag, zu
shook the head So I have the mission to

ermitteln, wo der Enno steckt. Weiter nichts. Warum und
fulfil where the Enno sticks Further nothing Why and

wieso, davon habe ich keine Ahnung. Ich will Ihnen was
how so there-from have I no idea I want you what

sagen, Frau Häberle, ich bin ein ganz einfacher,
say Mrs Haberle I am a completely simple

offener Mensch ...«
open human

Er neigte sich zu ihr hinüber; sie sah ihm in die
He bowed himself to her over she saw him in the

Augen, die stechend waren. Sein Blick irrte ab, der
eyes which stinging were His glance wandered off the

Blick des einfachen, offenen Menschen.
glance of the simple open human

»Ich habe mich eigentlich über den Auftrag gewundert,
I have myself actually over the mission wondered

Frau Häberle, das will ich Ihnen ehrlich sagen. Denn wir
Mrs Haberle that want I you honest say Then we

beide wissen doch, was der Enno für ein Mensch ist,
both know indeed what the Enno for a human is

nämlich ein Garnichts, nur mit ein bißchen Rennwetten
namely a nothing at all only with a bit race-betting

und Weibergeschichten im Kopf. Und nach diesem Enno
and women-stories in the head And after this Enno
adventures with women

jagt jetzt die Gestapo, und sogar noch die Politische
chases now the gestapo and even still the political

Abteilung, wo alles Hochverrat und Kohlrübe ab
department where everything high-treason and cabbage beet off
head removed

wird. Ich versteh das nicht – verstehen Sie das?« Er
becomes I understand that not understand you that He

sah sie erwartungsvoll an. Wieder begegneten sich
looked she expectantly at Again encountered each other

ihre Blicke, und wieder geschah es wie vorhin: er konnte
their looks and again happened it as before he could

sie nicht ansehen.
her not look at

»Erzählen Sie ruhig weiter, Herr Borkhausen«,
Tell you calm further Mr Borkhausen

fuhr sie fort. »Ich hör zu ...«
drove she away I hear to
she continued am listening

»Kluge Frau!« nickte Borkhausen. »Verdammt kluge Frau
Smart woman nodded Borkhausen Damned smart woman

und energisch. Das gestern abend mit der Knierutscherei
and energetical That yesterday evening with the kneeling

...«

»Wir wollten nur vom Geschäft reden, Herr Borkhausen!«
We want only from the business talk Mr Borkhausen
will deal

»Na gewiß doch! Ich bin nämlich ein braver, richtig
Now certainly indeed I am namely a good right

offener deutscher Mensch, und da werden Sie sich
open German human and there will you yourself
man

vielleicht wundern, daß ich bei der Gestapo bin. Das
perhaps wonder that I at the gestapo am That

denken Sie vielleicht. Nee, Frau Häberle, ich bin nicht bei
think you perhaps No Mrs Haberle I am not at

der Gestapo, ich arbeite nur manchmal für sie.
the gestapo I work only sometimes for them

Der Mensch will leben, nicht wahr, und ich habe fünf
The human wants to live not true and I have five
Man

Gören zu Haus, der Älteste grade erst dreizehn. Alle muß
brats at house the oldest right first thirteen All must
at home

ich sie ernähren ...«
I them nourish

»Das Geschäft, Herr Borkhausen!«
The deal Mr Borkhausen

»Nee, Frau Häberle, ich bin nicht bei der Gestapo, ich
No Mrs Haberle I am not with the gestapo I

bin ein ehrlicher Mensch. Und wie ich das hörte, daß sie
am an honest human And as I that heard that they
man

meinen Freund Enno suchen und sogar hohe Belohnungen
my friend Enno search and even high rewards

auf ihn aussetzen, und ich kenne doch den Enno von
on him out-set and I know indeed the Enno from
put up

früher und bin sein richtiger Freund, wenn wir uns auch
before and am his true friend when we us also
good

mal gestritten haben da habe ich also gedacht, Frau
once argued have there have I thus thought Mrs

Häberle: Kieke da, den Enno suchen sie! Den kleinen
Haberle Lookee there the Enno search they The small

Garnichts. Wenn ich ihn nur fände, hab ich gedacht,
nothing at all When I him only would find have I thought

verstehen Sie, Frau Häberle, dann könnte ich ihm
understand you Mrs Haberle then could I him

vielleicht einen Wink geben, daß er abhaut, solange es
perhaps a nudge give that he departs as long (as) it

noch Zeit ist. Und ich hab zu dem Kommissar Escherich
still time is And I have to the commissioner Escherich

gesagt: ›Wegen dem Enno machen Sie sich man keine
said Cause of the Enno make you yourself once (mal) no

Mühe, den schaff ich Ihnen, weil er nämlich ein alter
trouble that one fetch I you because he namely an old

Freund von mir ist.‹ Und da habe ich denn den Auftrag
friend from me is And there have I then the mission

gekriegt, Frau Häberle, und der Enno wirtschaftet im
received Mrs Haberle and the Enno housekeeps in the

Laden, und es ist alles eigentlich in bester Butter ...«
shop and it is everything actually in most best butter

Eine Weile schwiegen beide, Borkhausen abwartend, Frau
A while remained silent both Borkhausen awaiting Mrs

Häberle nachdenklich.
Haberle thoughtful

Dann sagte sie: »Die Gestapo hat also noch keine
Then said she The gestapo has thus still no

Nachricht von Ihnen bekommen?«
message from them become

»I wo, mit denen habe ich es doch nicht eilig, mir das
I where with those have I it indeed not hurried me the
No way

ganze Geschäft zu vermasseln!« Er verbesserte sich: »Erst
whole business to screw up He corrected himself First

wollte ich meinem alten Freund Enno doch mal einen
wanted I my old friend Enno indeed once a

Wink geben ...«
nudge give

Und wieder schwiegen sie. Und wieder fragte Frau Hete
And again remained silent they And again asked Mrs Hete

schließlich: »Und was hat Ihnen denn die Gestapo für
finally And what has you then the gestapo for

eine Belohnung versprochen?«
a reward promised

»Tausend Mark! Ist 'ne Masse Geld für so einen
Thousand mark Is a mass (of) money for such a
{money}

Garnichts, gebe ich zu, Frau Häberle, ich war selbst
nothing at all give I to Mrs Haberle I was myself
I admit

ganz ganz verblüfft. Aber der Kommissar Escherich
completely completely perplexed But the commissioner Escherich

hat zu mir gesagt: ›Bringen Sie mir mal den Kluge, und
has to me said Bring you me once the Kluge and

ich zahle Ihnen tausend Mark.‹ Das hat der Escherich
I pay you (a) thousand mark That has the Escherich

gesagt. Und hundert Mark Spesen hat er mir auch
said And hundred mark expenses has he me also
{money}

bewilligt, die habe ich schon gekriegt, die kämen zu
approved those have I already received those would come to

den tausend Mark Belohnung noch dazu.«
the thousand mark reward still there-to
{money} added to it

Sie saßen lange nachdenklich da.
They sat long thoughtful there

Dann fing Frau Hete wieder an: »Ich habe das vorhin
Then caught Mrs Hete again on I have that a while ago
started -

mit den Wellensittichen nicht ohne Absicht gesagt, Herr
with the budgies not without intention said Mr

Borkhausen. Denn wenn ich Ihnen tausend Mark zahle
Borkhausen Then when I you (a) thousand mark pay
{money}

...«

»Zweitausend Mark, Frau Häberle, unter Freunden immer
Two thousand mark Mrs Haberle under friends always
{money}

zweitausend Mark. Und dann kämen noch die hundert
two thousand mark And then would come still the hundred
{money}

Mark Spesen dazu ...«
mark expenses there-to
{money}

»Nun also, selbst wenn ich Ihnen das zahlen würde, und
Now thus even when I you that pay would and

Sie wissen doch, der Herr Kluge hat kein Geld, und mich
you know indeed the Mr Kluge has no money and me

bindet an ihn nichts ...«
binds to him nothing

»Na, Frau Häberle, na! Sie, 'ne hochanständige Frau! Sie
Now Mrs Haberle now You a highly decent woman You

werden doch Ihren Freund, der auf den Knien zu Ihnen
will however your friend who on the knees to you

gerutscht ist, nicht um so 'n bißchen Geld der Gestapo
slided is not for such a bit of money the gestapo

ausliefern? Wo ich Ihnen extra gesagt habe, es ist
deliver Where I you extra said have it is

alles da, Hochverrat und Kohlrübe ab? Das werden
everything there high-treason and cabbage beet off That will
head removed

Sie doch nicht tun, Frau Häberle!«
you indeed not do Mrs Häberle

Sie hätte ihm ja sagen können, daß er, der schlichte,
She had him indeed say can that he the plain
could tell

ehrliche deutsche Mann, grade das zu tun im Begriff
honest German man right that to do in the understood
about to

war, was sie als hochanständige Frau keinesfalls tun
was what she as highly decent woman not at all do

durfte, nämlich den Freund verkaufen. Aber sie wußte es
might namely the friend sell But she knew it

ja, derartige Bemerkungen hatten keinen Zweck, für so
yes such remarks had no purpose for so
indeed

was besaßen diese Herren keinen Sinn.
what possessed these gentlemen no mind

Und so sagte sie denn: »Ja, also wenn ich selbst die
And so said she then Yes so when I (my)self the

zweitausendeinhundert zahlen würde, wer garantiert mir
two thousand one hundred pay would who guarantees me

denn dafür, daß die Wellensittiche nicht doch im Käfig
then therefore that the budgies not indeed in the cage

bleiben?« Sie entschloß sich, da sie sah, wie er schon
stay She decided herself there she saw how he already
since

wieder den Kopf verwirrt kratzte, auch ganz schamlos
again the head confused scratched also completely shameless

zu werden: »Also, wer garantiert mir dafür, daß Sie
to become Also who guarantees me therefore that you

nicht meine zweitausendeinhundert nehmen und gehen dann
not my two thousand one hundred take and go then

doch zu dem Escherich und nehmen auch noch seine
still to the Escherich and take also still his
after all

tausend?«
thousand

»Aber ich garantiere Ihnen dafür, Frau Häberle! Ich gebe
But I guarantee you therefore of it Mrs. Haberle I give

Ihnen mein Wort darauf; ich bin ein einfacher, offener
you my word thereupon I am a simple open

Mensch, und wenn ich was verspreche, dann halte ich
human and when I what something promise then keep I

das auch. Sie haben's ja gesehen, ich bin gleich zu
that also You have it yes seen I am immediately to

dem Enno gelaufen und habe ihn gewarnt, auf die Gefahr
the Enno ran and have him warned on the danger

hin, daß er aus dem Laden einen Flitzer macht. Und
away that he from the shop a speedster makes And

dann ist das ganze Geschäft doch Essig.«
then is the whole business indeed vinegar

Frau Hete sah ihn mit einem schwachen Lächeln an.
Mrs Hete looked him with a weak smiling at

»Das ist ja alles schön und gut, Herr Borkhausen«,
That is yes indeed everything beautiful and good Mr Borkhausen

sagte sie dann. »Aber grade weil Sie ein so guter
said she then But right because you a such good

Freund von dem Enno sind, werden Sie verstehen, daß
friend from the Enno are will you understand that

ich jede Sicherheit für ihn haben muß. Wenn ich das
I each security for him have must When I the

Geld überhaupt auftreiben kann.«
money at all drive up can
get together

Borkhausen machte eine beschwichtigende Bewegung, die
Borkhausen made a soothing movement that

sagen sollte, daß es daran bei einer Frau, wie sie war,
say should that it there-on at a woman like she was

nie fehlen könnte.
never lack could

»Nein, Herr Borkhausen«, fuhr Frau Hete fort, denn sie
No Mr Borkhausen drove Mrs Hete away then she
continued Mrs Hete

sah ja, für Ironie war er nicht empfänglich, sie mußte
saw well for irony was he not receptive she must

schon ganz offen mit ihm reden, »wer steht mir denn
already completely open with him talk who stands me then

dafür, daß Sie mein Geld jetzt nicht nehmen ...«
therefore that you my money now not take

Borkhausen wurde ganz aufgeregt bei dem Gedanken,
Borkhausen became completely excited at the thoughts

er könne die schwindelnde, die nie gesehene Summe von
he could the dizzying the never seen sum from

zweitausend Mark jetzt gleich bekommen ...
two thousand mark now immediately become
{money} get

»... und vor der Tür steht ein Gestapoagent und nimmt
and before the door stands a gestapo agent and takes

den Enno fest? Da muß ich schon andere Garantien von
the Enno firmly There must I already other guarantees from

Ihnen haben!«
you have

»Es steht aber keiner vor der Tür, das schwöre ich
It stands however none before the door that swear I
There

Ihnen, Frau Häberle! Ich bin doch ein ehrlicher Mensch,
you Mrs Haberle I am indeed an honest human

wozu soll ich Sie denn belügen?! Ich komme direkt
where-for should I you then lie to I come directly

von Haus, da können Sie auch meine Otti danach
from house there can you also my Otti afterwards

fragen!«
ask

Sie unterbrach den Aufgeregten: »Also überlegen Sie mal,
She interrupted the excited one Also consider you once

was für eine Garantie Sie mir sonst noch geben können
what for a guarantee you me otherwise still give can

– außer Ihrem Wort?«
except your word

»Aber da gibt's doch gar keine! Das ist doch so
But there gives it indeed at all none That is indeed such
will there be

'n Geschäft, das beruht ganz allein auf Vertrauen. Und
a business that is based completely alone on trust And

Vertrauen werden Sie doch zu mir haben, Frau Häberle,
trust will you indeed to me have Mrs Haberle

jetzt, wo ich so offen mit Ihnen gesprochen habe?«
now where I so open with you spoken have

»Ja, das Vertrauen ...« antwortete Frau Häberle
Yes the trust answered Mrs Haberle

gedankenlos, und dann versanken sie beide in ein langes
thoughtless and then sank they both in a long

Schweigen, er einfach abwartend, was sie wohl beschließen
silence he simply awaiting what she well decide

würde, sie sich den Kopf zergrübelnd, wie sie wenigstens
would she herself the head musing how she at least

ein Minimum von Sicherheit erreichen könnte.
a minimum from security reach could
acquire

Im Laden wirtschaftete unterdes der Enno Kluge. Er
In the shop economized under-that the Enno Kluge He
meanwhile

bediente die nun schon reichlicher strömende Kundschaft
served the now already more richly streaming customers
more abundant flowing

rasch und nicht ungeschickt, sogar zu Witzchen verstieg er
quickly and not awkward even to joke moved he

sich schon wieder. Der erste Schreck, den er bei
himself already again the first fright the he at

Borkhausens Anblick empfunden, war schon wieder
Borkhausen sight perceived was already again

verflogen. Die Hete saß in der Stube und sprach mit
flown away The Hete sat in the room and spoke with

Borkhausen, sie würde die Sache schon in Ordnung
Borkhausen she would the thing already in order

bringen. Aber daß sie die Sache in Ordnung brachte, das
bring But that she the thing in order brought the

bewies, daß es ihr gar nicht ernst gewesen war mit der
proved that it her at all not serious been was with the

Drohung, ihn fortzuschicken. So war er nur erleichtert
threat him to send away So was he only lightened
more relaxed

jetzt, und darum reichte es auch schon wieder zu
now and therefore reached it also already again to
was enough

Witzchen!
joke

Hinten in der Stube brach Frau Häberle das lange
In the back in the room broke Mrs Haberle the long

Schweigen. Sie sagte entschlossen: »Also, Herr Borkhausen,
silence she said decided So Mr Borkhausen

ich habe mir das so überlegt. Ich will das Geschäft
I have myself that so considered I want the business

unter folgenden Bedingungen mit Ihnen abschließen ...«
under (the) following conditions with you lock off
conclude

»Ja ...? Sagen Sie doch!« drängte gierig Borkhausen. Er
Yes Say you then pushed greedily Borkhausen He

sah seinen Lohn jetzt schon nahe.
saw his reward now already close

»Ich gebe Ihnen zweitausend Mark, aber ich gebe sie
I give you two thousand mark but I give you
{money}

Ihnen nicht hier. Ich gebe sie Ihnen in München.«
them not here I give you them in Munich

»In München?« Er glotzte dämlich. »Ich komme doch nie
In Munich He gawked stupidly I come indeed never

nach München! Was soll ich denn in München?«
to munich What should I then in Munich

»Wir gehen«, fuhr sie fort, »jetzt zusammen auf das
We go drove she away now together on the

Postamt, und ich zahle eine Postanweisung auf zweitausend
post office and I pay a postal order on two thousand

Mark an Sie ein: Hauptpostlagernd München. Und dann
mark to you in Main post office Munich And then
{money}

bringe ich Sie auf die Bahn, und Sie fahren mit dem
bring I you on the track and you drive with the
to the station

nächsten Zug nach München und holen sich dort das
next train to Munich and get yourself there the

Geld. Auf dem Anhalter-Bahnhof werde ich Ihnen
money On the Hitchhiker Station will I you
(former railway terminus in Berlin)

noch zweihundert Mark für die Reise geben außer der
still two hundred mark for the journey give outside of the
{money}

Fahrkarte ...«
ticket

»Nee!« rief Borkhausen erbittert. »So was mache ich
No called Borkhausen embittered So what do I
bitter

nicht! Auf so was lasse ich mich nicht ein! Nachher
not On so what let I myself not in After
With

fahre ich runter nach München, und Sie haben sich
drive I down to munich and you have yourself

Ihre Anweisung von der Post zurückgeholt!«
your instruction from the mail retrieved

»Ich werde Ihnen bei der Abfahrt die Einzahlungsquittung
I will you at the departure the deposit receipt

geben, dann kann ich das nicht tun.«
give then can I that not do

»Und München?« rief er wieder. »Wozu denn München?
And Munich called he again Where-to then Munich

Wir sind doch ehrliche Menschen! Warum denn nicht hier,
We are indeed honest people Why then not here

gleich jetzt hier im Laden, und es hat geschnappt!
immediately now here in the shop and it has snapped

Nach München und zurück, da brauche ich doch
To Munich and back there need I indeed

mindestens zwei Tage und eine Nacht, und unterdes ist
at least two days and a night and under-that is
meanwhile

der Enno hier natürlich getürmt!«
the Enno here of course towered
skedaddled

»Aber, Herr Borkhausen, das hatten wir doch abgemacht,
But Mr Borkhausen that had we indeed agreed

deswegen gebe ich Ihnen doch das Geld! Der
because of that give I you indeed the money The

Wellensittich sollte doch nicht in seinem Käfig bleiben. Ich
budgie should indeed not in his cage stay I

meine, der Enno soll sich doch verstecken können,
mean the Enno should himself indeed hide be able

dafür zahle ich Ihnen doch die zweitausend Mark!«
therefore pay I you indeed the two thousand mark

Mürrisch sagte Borkhausen, der darauf nichts Rechtes zu
Grumpily said Borkhausen who thereupon nothing true to

entgegnen hatte: »Und hundert Mark Spesen kriege ich
counter had And hundred mark expenses get I
{money}

auch noch!«
also still

»Die kriegen Sie auch noch. In bar. Auf dem Anhalter.«
That get you also still In cash On the Hitchhiker (station)

Aber auch diese Zusage konnte Borkhausens Stimmung
But also this commitment could Borkhausen's mood

nicht verbessern. Er blieb mürrisch. »München, ich hab
not improve He remained grumpy Munich I have

noch nie so 'n Quatsch gehört! Es wäre alles so
still never such a nonsense heard It would be everything so

schön einfach gewesen – und nun München!
beautifully simple been and now Munich

Ausgerechnet München! Warum sagen Sie nicht gleich
Of all places Munich Why say you not immediately

London – da kann ich ja dann nach dem Kriege
London there can I yes then after the war

hinfahren! Und alles vermasselt! Es ginge so schön
to go And everything screwed up It went so beautifully

einfach, aber nee, es muß kompliziert sein! Und warum?
simple but no it must complicated be And why

Weil Sie kein Vertrauen zu Ihren Mitmenschen haben,
Because you no trust to your fellow human have

weil Sie ein mißtrauischer Mensch sind, Frau Häberle!
because you a mistrustful human are Mrs Haberle

Ich bin so ehrlich zu Ihnen gewesen ...«
I am so honest to you been have

»Und ich bin ehrlich zu Ihnen! So mache ich dies
And I am honest to you So make I this

Geschäft und anders nicht!«
business and different not

»Na denn!« sagte er. »Denn kann ich ja gehen.« Er
Now then said he Then can I yes indeed go He

stand auf, nahm seine Schiebermütze. Aber er ging nicht.
stood up took his beanie But he went not

»München kommt für mich gar nicht in Frage ...«
Munich comes for me at all not in question

»Es wird eine ganz interessante kleine Reise für Sie
It will a completely interesting little journey for you

sein«, redete ihm Frau Häberle zu. »Die Fahrt ist hübsch,
be spoke him Mrs Haberle to The ride is pretty

und in München soll es noch sehr gut zu essen und zu
and in Munich should it still very good to eat and to

trinken geben. Sehr viel stärkeres Bier als hier bei uns,
drink give Very much stronger beer as here with us

Herr Borkhausen!«
Mr Borkhausen

»Ich mach mir nichts aus Trinken«, sagte er wieder, aber
I make me nothing from drink said he again but

nicht so sehr mürrisch wie gedankenvoll.
not so very grumpily as thoughtful

Frau Hete sah ihm an, daß er seinen Kopf zergrübelte
Mrs Hete saw him on that he his head dimpled

nach einem Ausweg, wie er das Geld nehmen und den
to a way out how he the money take and the

Enno trotzdem ausliefern könnte. Sie prüfte nochmals ihren
Enno in spite of it deliver could She tried again her
tested

Vorschlag. Er schien ihr gut. Er schaffte den
suggestion He seemed her good He acquired the
It It {anschaffen; to acquire}

Borkhausen für mindestens zwei Tage aus dem Wege, und
Borkhausen for at least two days out (of) the way and

wenn das Haus wirklich nicht unter Bewachung stand
when the house really not under guarding stood

(wovon sie sich schnell genug überzeugen würde), so
where-from she herself fast enough convince would so

war das Zeit genug, den Enno unterdes fortzuschaffen.
was that time enough the Enno under-that to move away
there meanwhile

»Na ja«, sagte Borkhausen schließlich und sah sie an.
Now yes said Borkhausen finally and saw her on
looked her in the face

»Sie tun's nicht anders, Frau Häberle?«
You do it not different Mrs Haberle

»Nein«, sagte Frau Hete. »So sind meine Bedingungen,
No said Mrs Hete So are my conditions

von denen gehe ich nicht ab.«
from which go I not off

»Dann muß ich's wohl tun«, sagte Borkhausen. »Ich kann
Then must I it well do said Borkhausen I can

doch nicht einfach die zweitausend Eier in den Wind
indeed not simply the two thousand eggs in the wind

schlagen.«
beat

Das hatte er mehr zu sich, zu seiner eigenen
That had he more to himself to his own

Rechtfertigung vor sich selbst gesagt.
justification before himself himself said

»Dann werde ich also nach München fahren. Und Sie
Then will I thus to Munich drive And you

gehen jetzt gleich mit mir aufs Postamt.«
go now immediately with me on the post office
to the

»Gleich«, sagte Frau Häberle gedankenvoll. Nun, da er
Right away said Mrs Haberle thoughtfully Now there he

doch zugesagt hatte, war sie noch immer nicht zufrieden.
indeed promised had was she still always not satisfied

Sie war ganz überzeugt, er plante eine neue
She was completely convinced he planted a new

Gemeinheit. Sie mußte rauskriegen, welche ...
meanness She must get out which

»Ja, wir gehen gleich«, sagte sie noch einmal. »Das
Yes we go right away said she still once That

heißt: erst muß ich mich ein bißchen zurechtmachen und
is called first must I myself a little right make and
make fashionable

den Laden schließen.«
the shop close

Er sagte rasch: »Wozu wollen Sie denn den Laden
He said quickly Where-to want you then the shop

zumachen, Frau Häberle? Der Enno ist doch hier!«
close Mrs Haberle The Enno is indeed here

»Der Enno geht mit uns«, sagte sie.
The enno goes with us said she

»Wozu denn das nu wieder? Der Enno hat doch mit
Where-to then that now again The Enno has indeed with

dem ganzen Geschäft nichts zu tun!«
the whole business nothing to do

»Weil ich es so haben will. Es könnte sonst nämlich
Because I it so have want It could otherwise namely

sein«, setzte sie hinzu, »daß der Enno gerade in dem
be set she there-to that the Enno just in the

Augenblick verhaftet wird, wenn ich das Geld an Sie
moment arrested becomes when I the money to you

einzahle. Solche Versehen können vorkommen, Herr
pay in Such mistakes can (be) prevented Mr

Borkhausen.«
Borkhausen

»Aber wer soll ihn denn verhaften?«
But who should him then arrest

»Na, zum Beispiel der Spitzel vor der Tür ...«
Now to the for example the snitch before the door

»Ist ja gar kein Spitzel vor der Tür!«
Is yes at all no snitch before the door

Sie lächelte.
She smiled

»Sie können sich überzeugen, Frau Häberle. Gehen Sie
You can yourself convince Mrs Haberle Go you

doch rum, sehen Sie sich alle Leute an. Ich habe
indeed around look you yourself all people at I have

keinen Spitzel vor der Tür! Ich bin ein ehrlicher Mensch
no snitch before the door I am an honest human

...«

Sie sagte beharrlich: »Ich will den Enno bei mir haben.
She said persistent I want the Enno with me have

Es ist schon sicherer.«
It is already safer

»Sie sind hartmäulig wie ein oller Maulesel!« rief er
You are hard-packed as an old (one) mule called he
(alter)

wütend. »Na also schön, soll der Enno auch mitgehn.
furious Now thus beautiful should the Enno also go along

Aber nun machen Sie auch ein bißchen fix!«
But now make you also a little haste

»So große Eile haben wir nicht«, sagte sie. »Der
Such great haste have we not said she The

Münchner Zug geht erst um zwölf herum. Wir haben
of München train goes first around twelve around We have
only at

alle Zeit. Und nun entschuldigen Sie mich für eine
all time And now apologize you me for a
forgive

Viertelstunde, ich möchte mich ein bißchen
quarter of an hour I may myself a little

zurechtmachen.« Sie sah ihn, wie er da am Tisch saß,
right make She saw him how he there at the table sat
clean up

immer das Auge aufmerksam auf die Glasscheibe gerichtet,
always the eye attentive on the glass pane directed

durch die er den Laden beobachten konnte, prüfend an.
through which he the shop observe could examining on

»Und eine Bitte noch, Herr Borkhausen: Reden Sie jetzt
And one demand still Mr Borkhausen Talk you now

nicht mit dem Enno, er hat reichlich im Laden zu tun,
not with the Enno he has richly lots in the shop to do

und überhaupt ...«
and at all

»Was ich mit dem Idioten wohl reden soll!« sagte
What I with the idiot well talk should said

Borkhausen ärgerlich. »Mit so 'nem Quatschkopf rede ich
Borkhausen annoyed With such a gobshite speech I

doch überhaupt kein Wort!«
indeed at all no word

Aber er setzte sich gehorsam anders, so daß er jetzt
But he set himself obediently different so that he now

ihre Stubentür und das Hoffenster vor Augen hatte.
her room door and the court window before eyes had

Ennos Austreibung

Enno's expulsion

Zwei	Stunden	später	war	alles	ausgestanden.	Der
Two	hours	later	was	everything	stood out endured	The

Münchner	Schnellzug	war	mit	Borkhausen	in	einem
of München	fast train express	was	with	Borkhausen	in	a

Abteil	zweiter	Klasse	aus	der	Halle	des
compartment	of second	class	from	the	hall	of the

Anhalter-Bahnhofs	gerollt,	mit	einem	lächerlich
Hitchhiker Station (former Berlin station)	rolled	with	a	ridiculous

angeberischen,	geschwollenen	Borkhausen,	der	zum	ersten
bragging	swollen	Borkhausen	who	for the	first

Male	in	seinem	Leben	ein	Abteil	zweiter	Klasse
time	in	his	life	a	compartment	of second	class

benutzte.	Ja,	Frau	Häberle,	die	auch	großzügig	sein
used	Yes	Mrs	Haberle	who	also	generous	be

konnte,	hatte	diesem	kleinen	Spitzel	auf	seine	Bitte	hin
could	had	this	small	snitch	on	his	ask	away

im	Zuge	noch	eine	Zuschlagskarte	Zweiter	gelöst,	um
in the	train	still	a	surcharge card	of second	solved	for

ihn	bei	guter	Laune	zu	halten,	oder	auch,	weil	sie
him	at	good	mood	to	keep	or	also	because	she

selbst froh war, diesen Kerl für mindestens zwei Tage
herself happy was this chap for at least two days

los zu sein.
loose to be

Nun, als sich die andern Reisebegleiter langsam durch
Now as themselves the other travel companions slowly through

die Sperre drängten, sagte sie leise zu Enno: »Warte
the barrier pressed said she softly to Enno Wait

einmal, Enno, wir setzen uns einen Augenblick da in den
once Enno we set us a moment there in the

Wartesaal und überlegen, was nun zu tun ist.«
waiting room and consider what now to do is

Sie setzten sich so, daß sie die Eingangstür im Auge
She set herself so that she the entrance door in the eye

hatten. Der Wartesaal war nur mäßig besetzt, nach
had The waiting room was only moderately occupied after

ihnen kam eine lange Zeit keiner mehr herein.
them came a long time no one (any)more in

Frau Hete fragte: »Hast du darauf geachtet, Enno, was
Mrs Hete asked Have you thereupon guarded Enno what

ich dir gesagt habe? Glaubst du, daß wir beobachtet
I you said have Believe you that we observed

worden sind?«
become are

Und Enno Kluge mit seinem gewohnten Leichtsinn, kaum
And Enno Kluge with his habitual carelessness hardly

war die dringendste Gefahr vorüber: »I wo! Beobachtet?
was the most urgent danger past I where Observed
had No way

Glaubst du, jemand läßt sich von so 'nem Idioten, wie
Believe you someone lets himself from such an idiot as

es Borkhausen ist, schicken? So blau! So dußlig ist
it Borkhausen is send So blue So silly is

keiner!«
none

Sie hatte es auf der Zunge, ihm zu sagen, daß sie
She had it on the tongue him to say that she

diesen Borkhausen mit seiner argwöhnischen Gerissenheit
this Borkhausen with his suspicious cunning

für erheblich intelligenter hielt als den kleinen, feigen,
for considerably more intelligent held as the small cowardly

leichtsinnigen Mann an ihrer Seite. Aber sie sagte es
reckless man on her side But she said it

nicht. Sie hatte es sich heute früh beim Umkleiden
not She had it herself today early at the changing

zugeschworen, daß es mit allen Vorwürfen vorbei sein
sworn to that it with all accusations past be

sollte. Ihre Aufgabe war nur noch, diesen Enno Kluge in
should Her task was only still this Enno Kluge in

Sicherheit zu bringen. War diese Aufgabe erfüllt, wollte sie
security to bring Was this task filled wanted she

ihn nie wiedersehen.
him never see again

Er sagte aus dem immer wieder gleichen Gedanken
He said from the always again same thoughts

heraus, der ihn seit einer Stunde quälte, er sagte voll
out which him since an hour tormented he said full

Neid: »Wenn ich du wäre, ich hätte diesem Kerl nie
(of) envy If I you would be I had this chap never

zweitausendeinhundert Mark bezahlt. Und dann noch
two thousand one hundred mark {money} paid And then still

zweihundertfünfzig Mark Reisespesen. Und dann noch
two hundred and fifty mark {money} travel expenses And then still

Fahrkarte und Zuschlagkarte. Du hast dem Kerl über
ticket and surcharge card You have the chap over

zweitausendfünfhundert gegeben, so 'nem Schwein! Ich
two thousand five hundred given such a swine I

hätt's nie getan!«
it would have never done

Sie fragte: »Und was wäre aus dir geworden, wenn
She asked And what would be from you become when

ich's nicht getan hätte?«
I it not done would have

»Hättest du mir zweitausendfünfhundert gegeben, du
Would have you me two thousand five hundred given you

hättest sehen sollen, wie fein ich das Ding gedreht hätte!
had see should how fine I the thing turned had

Das kannst du glauben, der Borkhausen wäre auch mit
That can you believe the Borkhausen would be also with

fünfhundert zufrieden gewesen!«
fivehundred satisfied been

»Tausend hat ihm ja schon die Gestapo versprochen!«
Thousand has him yes already the gestapo promised

»Tausend – da muß ich doch lachen! Als wenn die auf
Thousand there must I indeed laughing As when those on

der Gestapo mit den Tausendern nur so schmissen! Und
the gestapo with the thousands only so threw And

dann noch an so einen kleinen Spitzel, wie es der
then still on such a small snitch as it the

Borkhausen ist! Dem brauchen sie doch nur zu befehlen
Borkhausen is That one need they indeed only to order

– und er muß tun, was sie wollen, für fünf Mark
and he must do what they want for five mark {money}

Tagegeld! Tausend, zweitausendfünfhundert – der hat
daily allowance Thousand two thousand five hundred that one has

dich aber bildschön gerupft, Hete!«
you but beautifully plucked Hete

Er lachte spöttisch.
He laughed mocking

Seine Undankbarkeit verletzte sie. Aber sie hatte keine
His ingratitude injured her But she had no

Lust, sich mit ihm auf Erörterungen einzulassen. Sie
desire herself with him on discussions to let inside She

sagte nur etwas scharf: »Ich will davon nicht mehr
said only something sharp I want there-from not (any)more

reden! Verstehst du, ich will nicht!« Sie sah ihn so
talk Understand you I want not She looked him so

lange fest an, bis seine blassen Augen sich senkten.
long firmly at until his pale eyes themselves lowered

»Wir wollen jetzt lieber überlegen, was wir nun mit dir
We want now rather consider what we now with you

tun.«
do

»Ach, das hat doch noch Zeit«, sagte er. »Vor
Oh that has indeed still time said he Before

übermorgen kann er nicht zurück sein. Wir gehen jetzt
day after tomorrow can he not back be We go now

zum Geschäft zurück, bis übermorgen fällt uns schon
to the shop back until day after tomorrow falls us already

was ein.«
what in

»Ich weiß nicht, ich möchte dich nicht wieder ins
I know not I may you not again in the

Geschäft mitnehmen, oder höchstens, um deine Sachen zu
shop take along or at most for your things to

packen. Ich bin so unruhig – vielleicht sind wir doch
get I am so restless perhaps are we indeed

bespitzelt worden?«
spied on become

»Aber ich sage dir, wir sind's nicht! Ich versteh mehr
But I say you we are it not I understand more
haven't been (spied on)

von so was als du! Und der Borkhausen kann sich
from so what as you And the Borkhausen can himself
from something like that than

auch nie einen Spitzel halten, der hat ja nie Geld!«
also never a snitch keep that one has yes never money
pay

»Aber die Gestapo kann ihm einen stellen!«
But the gestapo can him one stellen

»Und der Spitzel von der Gestapo sieht zu, wie der
And the snitch from the gestapo sees to how the

Borkhausen nach München, fährt und ich ihn zur Bahn
Borkhausen to Munich drives and I him to the track
goes

bringe! So blau, Hete!«
bring So blue Hete
naive

Sie mußte zugeben, daß er mit diesem Einwand recht
She must admit that he with this objection right

hatte. Aber ihre Unruhe blieb. Sie fragte: »Ist dir das
had But her unrest remained She asked Is you that
was

nicht aufgefallen mit den Zigaretten?«
not noticed with the cigarettes

Er erinnerte sich nicht mehr. Sie mußte es ihm erst
He remembered himself not (any)more She must it him first

erzählen, wie der Borkhausen, sie waren kaum aus dem
tell how the Borkhausen they were hardly from the

Haus, überall nach Zigaretten herumsuchte, er mußte
house everywhere after cigarettes sought around he must
looked for

durchaus welche haben. Er hatte auch Hete und Enno
throughout which have He had also Hete and Enno
at all some

deswegen angeschnorrt. Aber die hatten auch keine,
because of that scrounged But those had also none

Enno hatte in der Nacht alle aufgeraucht. Borkhausen war
Enno had in the night all smoked out Borkhausen was

aber dabei geblieben, er müsse welche haben, er hielte
but there-by remained he must which have he held
some

das nicht aus, er sei es gewohnt, eine am Morgen zu
that not out he be it used (to) one at the morning to

stoßen. Er hatte sich rasch von Hete zwanzig Mark
bump He had himself quickly from Hete twenty mark
smoke {money}

»geborgt« und einen älteren Jungen angerufen, der mit
borrowed and an older boy called who with

viel Geschrei auf der Straße herumspielte.
much shouting on the street played around

»Du, hör mal, Ede, weeßte hier nich wen, bei den du
You hear once Ede knowed here not whom at whom you

Zigaretten krichst? Aber Tabakkarte hab ick keene.«
cigarettes gets But tobacco card have I none

»Valleicht weeß ick eenen. Ha'm Se denn Jeld?«
Maybe know I one Have you then money

Es war ein sehr blonder, blauäugiger Junge in der Tracht
It was a very blond blue-eyed boy in the costume

des Jungvolks gewesen, mit dem Borkhausen da
of the jungvolks been with whom Borkhausen there

gesprochen hatte, ein echtes, helles Berliner Gewächs.
spoken had a real bright from Berlin growth

»Na, jeb'n Se ma den Zwanzijer her, ick wer hol'n ...«
Now give you but the twenty away I will fetch

»Und det Wiederkomm vajess'n! Nee, ick jeh mit dir.
And that come again vajess'n No I go with you

Augenblick mal, Frau Häberle!«
Moment once Mrs Häberle

Damit waren die beiden in einem Hause verschwunden.
There-with were they both in a house disappeared

Nach einer Weile war dann Borkhausen allein
After a while was then Borkhausen alone

zurückgekommen und hatte Frau Hete die zwanzig Mark
come back and had Mrs Hete the twenty mark {money}

ohne alle Aufforderung zurückgegeben.
without all request given back

»Die hatten keine. Der Rotzjunge hat mich natürlich bloß
They had none The snotty boy has me of course just

um die zwanzig Mark beschummeln wollen. Ich hab ihm
for the twenty mark {money} cheat want I have him

aber eine geschallert, der liegt noch auf dem Hof!«
however one sounded beating give that one lies still on the yard

Sie waren weitergegangen, zur Post, zum Reisebüro.
They were had walked on to the mail to the travel agency

»Na, und was findest du da Komisches bei, Hete? Der
Now and what find you there funny at Hete The

Borkhausen ist da wie ich: Wenn es den roochert, der
Borkhausen is there as I When it the smokes that one

ist imstande und quatscht 'nen General auf der Straße an
is able and blabs a general on the street up

und bittet ihn um die Kippe!«
and asks him for the tilt

»Aber er hat hinterher nicht ein Wort mehr von
But he has after not a word (any)more from

Zigaretten gesagt, trotzdem er keine gekriegt hat! Ich
cigarettes said although he none received has I

finde das komisch. Ob er doch was mit dem Jungen
find that comical Whether he indeed what with the boy

vorgehabt hat?«
intended has

»Was soll er denn mit dem Jungen vorgehabt haben,
What should he then with the boy intended have

Hete? Dem hat er eine geschallert, das wird schon
Hete That one has he one sounded that will already
beating given

stimmen.«
sound
be alright

»Ob der Bengel vielleicht unser Aufpasser ist?«
If the kid perhaps our watchdog is

Einen Augenblick stutzte selbst Enno Kluge. Aber dann
One moment stopped short himself Enno Kluge But then

sagte er mit seinem gewohnten Leichtsinn: »Was du dir
said he with his habitual carelessness What you yourself

alles wieder einbildest! Deine Sorgen möchte ich
everything again imagine Your worries may I

wirklich haben!«
really have

Sie schwieg. Aber die Unruhe saß weiter in ihr, und so
She was silent But the unrest sat further in her and so

bestand sie auch darauf, daß sie jetzt nur kurz in den
insisted she also thereupon that she now only short in the

Laden gingen, um seine Sachen zu holen. Dann wollte sie
shop went for his things to get Then wanted she

ihn mit aller erdenklichen Vorsicht bei einer Freundin
him with all imaginable attention with a (female) friend

unterbringen.
accommodate

Ihm paßte das gar nicht. Er fühlte: Sie wollte sich von
Him suited that at all not He felt she wanted himself from

ihm lösen. Und er wollte nicht gehen. Bei ihr war
him loosen get rid of And he wanted not go At her was

Sicherheit und gutes Essen und nicht mehr Arbeit, als
security and good food and not more work as than

ihm behagte. Und Liebe und Wärme und Trösten. Und
him pleased And love and warmth and console And

dann: Sie war so ein gutes Wollschaf, der Borkhausen
then She was such a good wool sheep the Borkhausen

hatte sie eben um zweitausendfünfhundert geschoren, nun
had her just for two thousand five hundred shaved now

war er dran!
was he there-on

»Deine Freundin!« sagte er unzufrieden. »Was ist denn das
Your girlfriend said he dissatisfied What is then that

für eine Frau? Ich gehe nicht gern bei fremde Leute.«
for a woman I go not gladly at strange people
strangers

Hete hätte ihm sagen können, daß diese Freundin eine
Hete had him say can that this (female) friend an

alte Mitarbeiterin ihres Mannes war, daß sie jetzt noch in
old employee of her man was that she now still in

aller Stille weiterwirkte, und daß jeder Verfolgte bei ihr
all quiet continued to operate and that each pursued one at her

Zuflucht fand. Aber sie mißtraute jetzt Enno, ein paarmal
refuge found But she distrusted now Enno a few times

hatte sie ihn schon feige gesehen, er mußte nicht
had she him already cowardly seen he must not

zuviel wissen.
too much know

»Meine Freundin?« sagte sie darum. »Das ist eine Frau
My girlfriend said she therefore That is a woman

wie ich. In meinen Jahren. Vielleicht ein paar Jahre
like I In my years Perhaps a few years

jünger.«
younger

»Und was tut sie? Wovon lebt sie?« forschte er weiter.
And what does she Where-from lives she inquired he further

»Weiß ich nicht genau, ist wohl irgendwo Sekretärin.
Know I not exactly is well somewhere secretary

Übrigens ist sie unverheiratet.«
By the way is she unmarried

»In deinen Jahren, wenn sie das ist, dann wird's aber
In your years when she that is then becomes it but however

langsam Zeit«, sagte er spöttisch.
slowly time said he mocking

Sie zuckte zusammen, antwortete aber nicht.
She flinched together answered but however not

»Nee, Hete«, sagte er und gab seiner Stimme einen
No Hete said he and gave his voice a

zärtlichen Ton. »Was soll ich denn bei deiner Freundin?
tender tone What should I then at your (female) friend

Wir beide allein, das ist doch das Schönste. Laß mich
We both alone that is indeed the most beautiful Let me

bei dir bleiben - der Borkhausen kommt ja erst
with you stay the Borkhausen comes yes indeed first

übermorgen - wenigstens bis übermorgen!«
day after tomorrow at least until day after tomorrow

»Nein, Enno!« sagte sie. »Ich möchte jetzt, daß du das
No Enno said she I may now that you that
want

tust, was ich dir sage. Ich gehe allein in die Wohnung
do what I you say I go alone in the house

und packe. Du kannst unterdessen in einer Wirtschaft
and pack You can under this in a pub
(meanwhile)

warten. Dann fahren wir gemeinsam zu meiner Freundin.«
wait Then go we together to my girlfriend

Er hatte noch viele Widerworte, aber schließlich fügte er
He had still many counter-words but finally suited he
objections

sich. Er fügte sich, als sie - nicht ohne Berechnung -
himself He suited himself as she not without calculation

sagte: »Du wirst auch Geld brauchen. Ich lege dir Geld
said You will also money need I lie you money

obenauf in deinen Koffer, genug, daß du für die erste
over-up in your suitcase enough that you for the first
on top

Zeit aus der Not bist.«
time from the need are

Die Aussicht, bald Geld in seinem Koffer zu finden (und
The view soon money in his suitcase to find and

sie konnte ihm doch unmöglich weniger geben, als sie
she could him indeed impossible less give as she

dem Borkhausen gegeben hatte!), diese Aussicht lockte ihn,
the Borkhausen given had This view lured him

bestimmte ihn. Blieb er bis übermorgen bei ihr, gab
decided him Remained he until day after tomorrow at her gave

es erst übermorgen Geld. Er aber wollte sofort
it first day after tomorrow money He but however wanted immediately

wissen, wieviel sie ihm zugedacht hatte.
know how much she him intended had

Sie sah mit Kummer, was ihn zum Einlenken bestimmte.
She saw with sorrow what him to the giving in decided

Er sorgte selbst dafür, daß der letzte Rest von Achtung
He provided himself therefore that the last rest of caution

und Liebe in ihr zerstört wurde. Aber sie fand sich
and love in her destroyed became But she found herself

darein ohne Murren. Sie wußte es längst aus ihrem
therein without grumble She knew it long from her

Leben, daß man für alles bezahlen mußte, und für das
life that one for everything pay must and for the

meiste mehr, als es wert war. Die Hauptsache blieb, daß
most more as it worth was The main thing remained that

er ihr jetzt den Willen tat.
he her now the will did

Als Frau Hete Häberle sich ihrer Wohnung näherte, sah
As Mrs Hete Haberle herself her house approached saw

sie wieder den blonden, blauäugigen Jungen von vorhin
she again the blonde blue-eyed boy from a while ago

mit einer Rotte anderer auf der Straße toben. Sie
with a batch (of) others on the street rage She

schreckte zusammen. Dann winkte sie ihn zu sich heran:
scared together Then waved she him to herself near

»Was machst du denn hier immer noch?« fragte sie.
What do you then here always still asked she

»Mußt du denn ausgerechnet hier rumtoben?«
Must you then of all places here romp around

»Ick wohn hier doch!« sagte er. »Wo soll ick denn
I live here then said he Where should I then

sonst toben?«
otherwise romp

Sie spähte nach den Spuren von einem Schlag in seinem
She spied after the traces from a strike in his

Gesicht, aber sie konnte nichts sehen. Sichtlich hatte der
face but she could nothing see Visibly had the

Bengel sie nicht wiedererkannt, bei seinem Gespräch mit
kid her not recognized at his conversation with

Borkhausen hatte er sie wohl gar nicht beachtet. Das
Borkhausen had he her well at all not regarded That

würde gegen Spitzelei sprechen.
would against snitching speak

»Hier wohnst du?« fragte sie. »Ich hab dich doch noch
Here live you asked she I have you indeed still

nie hier auf der Straße gesehen.«
never here on the street seen

»Kann ick for Ihre Oogen?!« fragte er frech. Er pfiff
Can I for your eyes asked he fresh cheeky He whistled

durchdringend den Ludenpfiff auf einem Finger. Er schrie
penetrating the load whistle on a finger He cried

an dem Hause hoch: »Mutta, kiek mal aus't Fenster! Da
to the house high Mother look once out the window There

is 'ne Frau, die will nich gloob'n, dette schielst! Mutta,
is a woman who wants not believe that (you) squint Mother

schiel ihr mal watt!«
cross-eye her once something

Lachend lief Frau Hete in ihren Laden, jetzt auch völlig
Laughing ran Mrs Hete in her shop now also totally

überzeugt, daß sie, was diesen Jungen anlangte, Gespenster
convinced that she what this boy concerned ghosts

gesehen hatte.
seen had

Aber beim Packen wurde sie wieder ernst. Ihr kamen
But at the packing became she again serious Her came

Bedenken, ob sie auch recht daran tat, den Enno zu
doubts whether she also right there-on did the Enno to

ihrer Freundin Anna Schönlein zu bringen. Gewiß, die
her (female) friend Anna Schönlein to bring Certainly the

Änne riskierte alle Tage ihr Leben für jeden Unbekannten,
Anne risked all days her life for every unknown

dem sie Obdach gewährte. Aber der Frau Hete war es,
who she shelter granted But the Mrs Hete was it

als schmuggle sie der Änne doch mit Enno Kluge ein
as smuggle she the Anne indeed with Enno Kluge a

rechtes Kuckucksei ein. Zwar schien der Enno wirklich ein
true cuckoo egg in Indeed seemed the Enno really a

politischer, kein gewöhnlicher Verbrecher, das hatte jetzt
political no ordinary criminal that had now

sogar der Borkhausen bestätigt, aber ...
even the Borkhausen confirms but

Er war so leichtsinnig, nicht so sehr aus Unbedachtheit,
He was so reckless not so much out imprudence

sondern aus einer völligen Gleichgültigkeit gegen das
but from a complete indifference against the

Schicksal seiner Mitmenschen heraus. Es kam ihm gar
fate of his fellow human out It came him at all

nicht darauf an, was mit ihnen geschah. Er dachte
not thereupon on what with them happened He thought

immer nur an sich, und er war imstande, jeden Tag
always only on himself and he was able every day

zweimal zu ihr, zur Hete, zu laufen, unter dem Vorgeben,
twice to her to the Hete to run under the pretend

er sehne sich nach ihr, und zog so alle Gefahr auf
he long himself to her and pulled so all danger on

Ännes Kopf. Sie, die Hete, hatte Autorität über ihn, die
Anne's head She the Hete had authority over him the

Änne aber nicht.
Anne however not

Mit einem schweren Seufzer tut Frau Hete Häberle
With a heavy sigh does Mrs Hete Haberle

dreihundert Mark in einen Umschlag, den sie oben in
three hundred mark {money} in an envelope which she above in

den Koffer legt. Heute hat sie mehr Geld ausgegeben,
the suitcases lays Today has she more money spent

als sie in zwei Jahren gespart hat. Aber sie wird noch
as she in two years saved has But she becomes still

ein weiteres Opfer bringen, sie wird dem Enno für jeden
an additional sacrifice bring she will the Enno for every

Tag, an dem er die Wohnung der Freundin überhaupt
day on which he the house of the (female) friend at all

nicht verläßt, hundert Mark versprechen. Er ist ja
not leaves hundred mark {money} promise He is yes

leider so, daß sie ihm einen solchen Vorschlag machen
unfortunately so that she him a such suggestion make

kann. Er wird nicht gekränkt sein, er wird höchstens im
can He will not hurt be he will at most in the

ersten Augenblick ein bißchen gekränkt tun. Aber das wird
first moment a bit hurt do But that will

ihn wohl im Hause halten, er ist auf Geld gierig.
him well in the house hold he is on money greedy

Mit dem Koffer in der Hand verläßt Frau Hete das Haus.
With the suitcase in the hand leaves Mrs Hete the house

Der blonde Junge spielt nicht mehr auf der Straße,
The blonde young plays not (any)more on the street

vielleicht ist er jetzt bei seiner schielenden Mutter. Sie
perhaps is he now at his cross-eyed mother She

geht zu der Kneipe am Alexanderplatz, wo sie den
goes to the pub at the Alexanderplatz where she the

Enno treffen wird.
Enno meet will

Emil Borkhausen und sein Sohn

Emil Borkhausen and his son

Ja, Borkhausen hatte sich sehr wohl gefühlt in diesem
Yes Borkhausen had himself very well felt in this

vornehmen D-Zug im noblen Zweiter-Klasse-Abteil mit
take in front d-train in the noble second class compartment with
take apart

Offizieren und Generalen und Damen, die so wunderschön
officers and general and ladies who so wondrously

rochen. Es störte ihn gar nicht, daß er weder elegant
smoked it bothered him at all not that he neither elegant

noch wohlriechend war und daß seine Mitreisenden keine
nor fragrant was and that his with-travellers no
fellow passengers

freundlichen Blicke auf ihn warfen, Borkhausen war es
friendly looks on him threw Borkhausen was it

gewohnt, unfreundlich angesehen zu werden. Kaum je in
used unfriendly looked at to become Hardly yet in

seinem jämmerlichen Leben hatte ein Mitmensch einen
his pathetic life had a fellow human being a

freundlichen Blick für ihn übrig gehabt.
friendly glance for him left had

Borkhausen genoß sein kurzes Glück mit vollen Zügen,
Borkhausen enjoyed his short fortune with full pulls
completely

denn kurz war es nur. Es mußte nicht bis München
then short was it only It must not until Munich

währen, dieses Glück, nicht einmal bis Leipzig, wie er
endure this fortune not once even until Leipzig as he

zuerst gefürchtet hatte, sondern nur bis Lichterfelde, denn
first been afraid of had but only until Lichterfelde then

dieser Zug hielt noch einmal in Lichterfelde. Das war der
this train held still once in Lichterfelde That was the

Fehler in Frau Hetes Berechnung gewesen. Man mußte,
error in Mrs Hete's calculation been One must

hatte man Geld in München zu bekommen, nicht gleich
had one money in Munich to become not immediately

dorthin fahren. Man konnte es später tun, wenn man die
there-to drive One could it later do when one the

dringendsten Geschäfte in der Stadt Berlin erledigt hatte.
most urgent business deals in the city Berlin finished had

Und das dringendste Geschäft war jetzt, den Enno dem
And the most urgent business was now the Enno the

Escherich zu melden und fünfhundert Mark zu kassieren.
Escherich to report and fivehundred mark {money} to cash

Übrigens brauchte man vielleicht überhaupt nicht nach
By the way needed one perhaps at all not to

München zu fahren, man brauchte der Post nur zu
Munich to drive one needed the mail only to

schreiben, daß sie das Geld hierher nach Berlin zur
write that she the money hereto to Berlin to the

Auszahlung senden sollte. Jedenfalls kam eine sofortige
payout send should Anyhow came an instant

Reise nach München nicht in Frage.
journey to Munich not in question

Also stieg – nicht ohne leises Bedauern – Emil
Thus mounted not without slight pity Emil

Borkhausen in Lichterfelde aus. Er hatte noch eine kleine,
Borkhausen in Lichterfelde out He had still a little

lebhafte Debatte mit dem Fahrdienstleiter, der nicht
lively debate with the dispatcher who not

einsehen wollte, daß man sich im Zuge zwischen
in-see wanted that one himself in the train between

Anhalter Bahnhof und Lichterfelde noch einmal eine
Anhalter railway station and Lichterfelde still once a

Reise nach München anders überlegen kann. Überhaupt
journey to Munich differently consider decide can At all

kam diesem Manne der ganze Borkhausen höchst
came this man the whole Borkhausen highest

verdächtig vor.
suspicious before

Borkhausen aber blieb unerschütterlich:
Borkhausen however remained unperturbable

»Rufen Sie nur auf der Gestapo an, Kommissar Escherich,
Call you only on the gestapo on commissioner Escherich

und Sie werden sehen, wer recht hat, Herr
and you will see who right has Mr

Stationsvorsteher! Aber die Läuse, die Sie sich dann in
station manager But the lice which you yourself then in

den Pelz gesetzt haben! Ich bin nämlich dienstlich!«
the fur set have I am namely on duty

Schließlich ließ ihm der Rotmützige achselzuckend sein
Finally let him the red cap shrugging his

Fahrgeld zurückzahlen, ihm war es egal. Möglich war
fare repay him was it equal Possible was

alles heute, möglich war es schon, daß solche
everything today possible was it already that such

fragwürdigen Gestalten im Auftrage der Gestapo
questionable figures in the assignment of the gestapo

herumliefen. Um so schlimmer!
ran around For so (much) worse

Emil Borkhausen aber machte sich auf die Suche
Emil Borkhausen buthowever made set himself on the search

nach seinem Sohn.
to his son

Aber vor der Tierhandlung von Hete Häberle fand er ihn
But before the pet shop from Hete Haberle found he him

nicht, obwohl das Geschäft geöffnet war und Kunden aus
not although the business opened was and customers out

und ein gingen. Hinter einer Anschlagsäule verborgen,
and in went Behind a poster column concealed

überlegte Borkhausen, immer die Augen auf die Ladentür
considered borkhausen always the eyes on the store door

gerichtet, was geschehen sein konnte. Hatte Kuno-Dieter
directed what happened be could Had Kuno-Dieter

einfach aus Langeweile seinen Posten verlassen? Oder war
simply from boredom his post left Or was

Enno weggegangen – vielleicht wieder nach »Ferner
Enno away gone perhaps again to further

liefen«? Oder war der kleine Mann ganz fortgezogen,
walk Or was the little man completely moved away

und die Frau wirkte nun allein im Laden?
and the woman worked now alone in the shop

Emil Borkhausen erwog es grade bei sich, ob er
Emil Borkhausen considered it right at himself whether he

noch einmal ganz schamlos vor die überlistete Häberle
still once completely shameless before the duped Haberle

treten und Auskünfte von ihr verlangen sollte, als ein
step and information from her desire should as a

vielleicht neunjähriger Bengel ihn anquatschte: »Hörense
perhaps nine year old kid him chatted up Hear you

ma! Sind Sie der Vata von den Kuno?«
but Are you the father from the Kuno

»Bin ich! Was ist denn?«
Am I What is it then

»'ne Mark sollnse mir jeb'n!«
A mark {money} shall you me give

»Wozu soll ich dir denn 'ne Mark geben?«
Where-to should I you then a mark {money} give

»Det ich Sie sare, wat ick weeß!«
That I you say wat I know

Borkhausen tat einen raschen Griff nach dem Jungen.
Borkhausen did a quick grab after the boy

»Erst Ware, dann Geld!« sagte er.
First goods then money said he

Aber der Junge war schneller als er, er war ihm unter
But the boy was faster as he he was him under

dem Arm durchgeschlüpft und rief: »Na, denn nich!
the arm slipped through and called Now then not

Behalten Se man Ihre Mark!« Und er gesellte sich
Keep you but your mark And he joined himself

wieder zu seinen Spielgefährten, die auf der Fahrbahn
again to his playmates who on the roadway

direkt vor dem Laden tobten.
directly before the shop played around

Dorthin konnte Borkhausen ihm nicht folgen, er wollte
There-to could Borkhausen him not follow he wanted

sich doch lieber nicht sehen lassen. Er rief und pfiff
himself indeed rather not see let He called and whistled

nach dem Jungen, den er zugleich mit seiner eigenen,
to the boy who he at the same time with his own

hier so unangebrachten Sparsamkeit verfluchte. Aber der
here so inappropriate thrift cursed But the

Junge ließ sich nicht so leicht listen und locken; erst
boy let himself not so easy trick and lure first

eine gute Viertelstunde später tauchte er wieder bei
a good quarter of an hour later ducked he again at

Borkhausen auf, stellte sich vorsichtig in einiger
Borkhausen up set himself carefully in some

Entfernung von dem zornigen Mann auf und verkündete
distance from the angry man up and announced

frech: »Jetzt kost det zwee Märker!«
fresh Now cost that two marks
cheekily

Borkhausen hätte sich den Bengel wiederum lieber
Borkhausen had himself the kid again rather

gegriffen und nach Noten durchgeprügelt, aber was sollte
grasped and to notes beaten through but what should

er tun? Er war in seiner Hand, denn er konnte ihm
he do He was in his hand then he could him

nicht nachlaufen. »Ick wer dir 'ne Mark jeb'n«, sagte er
not to run after I will you a mark give said he
{money}

finster.
dark

»Nee! Zwee Mark!«
No Two mark

»Jut, du sollst zwee Mark haben!«
Good you will two mark have
(Gut) (zwei) {money}

Borkhausen nahm einen Packen Scheine aus der Tasche,
Borkhausen took a pack bills from the pocket

fand einen Zweimärker, stopfte die andern Scheine zurück
found a two-marker stuffed the other shines back

und hielt dem Jungen das Geld hin.
and held the boy the money forth

Der schüttelte den Kopf. »Ihnen kenn ick doch!« sagte
That one shook the head You know I then said

er. »Wenn ick det Jeld nehme, langen Se nach mir. Nee,
he If I that money take long you after me No
grab

legen Se's da uff't Pflaster!«
put you it there on the ground

Finster, ohne ein Wort, tat Borkhausen, was der Junge
Dark without a word did Borkhausen what the boy

ihn geheißen. »Na?« sagte er dann, richtete sich
him been commanded Now said he then rose himself

wieder auf und trat einen Schritt zurück.
again up and stepped a step back

Der Junge pirschte sich langsam an den Schein heran,
The boy stalked himself slowly on the note near

stets wachsam das Auge auf den Mann geheftet. Als
all the time watchful the eye on the man stapled As

er sich nach dem Gelde bückte, konnte Borkhausen kaum
he himself to the money bent could Borkhausen hardly

der Versuchung widerstehen, sich dieses kleine Aas zu
the temptation resist himself this little carrion to

langen und abzuwackeln. Er hätte ihn fassen können, aber
long and to shake off He had him take be able but
grab to beat

er widerstand dieser Versuchung, vielleicht bekam er dann
he resisted this temptation perhaps got he then

überhaupt keine Auskunft, und der Bengel würde so
at all no message and the kid would so

schreien, daß die ganze Straße zusammenlief.
shout that the whole street ran together

»Na?« fragte er noch einmal und diesmal drohend.
Now asked he still once and this time menacing

Der Junge antwortete: »Ich könnte ja jetzt ooch 'n Aas
The boy answered I could yes now also a carrion

sind und nochma Jeld von Sie valangen und nochma und
be and again money from you desire and again and
(verlangen)

immer wieda. Aba ick bin nich so. Ick weeß jut, Sie
always again But I am not so I know good you

wollten mir ebent wieda uff de Pelle, aba ick, ick bin
wanted me just now again off the skin but I I am

nich so 'n Aas!« Dann, nachdem er seine moralische
not so a carrion Then after he his moral

Überlegenheit über Borkhausen so gebührend ans Licht
superiority over Borkhausen so duly to the light

gestellt hatte, sagte er rasch: »Se soll'n in Ihre Wohnung
set had said he quickly You should in your house

uff Bescheid von Kuno'n warten!« Und der Junge war
for information from Kuno wait And the boy was

weg.
gone

Die guten zwei Stunden, die Borkhausen in seiner
The good two hours which Borkhausen in his

Kellerwohnung auf den Bescheid von Kuno warten mußte,
basement apartment on the information from Kuno wait must

verminderten seinen Zorn nicht, nein, sie vermehrten ihn
reduced his anger not no they increased him

noch. Die Gören plärrten, Otti war im Wege, sie sparte
still The brats whined Otti was in the road she spared

nicht mit spitzen Bemerkungen über solche faulen
not with sharp remarks over such rotten

Schweine, die den ganzen Tag rumsitzen, nischt tun wie
pigs who the whole day sit around nuthin' do as
nichts

Zigaretten qualmen und der Frau alle Arbeit lassen.
cigarettes smoke and the woman all work leave (for)

Er hätte einen Zehn- oder Fünfzigmarkschein hervorziehen
He had a ten or fifty mark bill pull out

und dadurch Ottis Stinklaune in das schönste
and there-through Otti's stinky mood in the most beautiful
through that

Mützenwetter verwandeln können, aber er wollte nicht. Er
cap weather transform been able but he wanted not He

wollte nicht schon wieder Geld verschenken, eben erst
wanted not already again money give away just first

hatte er zwei Mark für eine dußlige Nachricht
had he two mark for a stupid message
{money}

verschenkt, auf die er auch von allein hätte kommen
given away on which he also from alone had come
by himself

können. Eine Wut erfüllte ihn auf den Kuno-Dieter, der
been able An anger filled him on the Kuno-Dieter who

ihm solch ein kleines Aas auf den Hals geschickt, der
him such a little carrion on the neck sent who

sicher was verbockt hatte! Der Kuno-Dieter sollte,
surely something screwed up had The Kuno-Dieter should

dazu war Borkhausen fest entschlossen, nun die Keile
there-to was Borkhausen firmly decided now the wedges

beziehen, um die der Kleine sich gedrückt hatte.
draw for which the little (one) himself pressed had
get avoided

Dann klopfte es gegen die Tür, und statt des erwarteten
Then knocked it against the door and instead of the expected

Boten von Kuno-Dieter stand dort eine Zivilfigur, der
messenger from Kuno-Dieter stood there a civil figure who

man den ehemaligen Feldwebel noch deutlich genug
one the former sergeant-at-arms still clearly enough

ansah.
on-saw
could see in

»Sind Sie der Borkhausen?«
Are you the Borkhausen

»Ja, was ist denn?«
Yes what is it then

»Sie sollen zum Kommissar Escherich kommen. Machen Sie
You should to the commissioner Escherich come Make you

sich fertig, ich bring Sie.«
yourself ready I bring you

»Ich kann jetzt nicht«, widersprach Borkhausen, »ich wart
I can now not against-spoke Borkhausen I wait
countered

auf einen Boten. Sagen Sie dem Kommissar, ich hab den
on a messenger Say you the commissioner I have the

Fisch gefangen.«
fish caught

»Ich soll Sie mitnehmen zum Kommissar«, sagte der
I should you take along to the commissioner said the

ehemalige Feldwebel halsstarrig.
former sergeant-at-arms stiff-necked

»Nicht jetzt! Ich laß mir mein Geschäft nicht vermasseln!
Not now I let me my business not screw up

Nicht von euch Brüdern!« Borkhausen war zornig, aber er
Not from you brothers Borkhausen was angry but he

bezwang sich. »Sagen Sie dem Herrn Kommissar, ich
defeated himself Say you the gentleman commissioner I
held in

hätt den Vogel, und ich käme heute noch bei ihm
had the bird and I would come today still by him

vorbei!«
over

»Also machen Sie jetzt keine langen Geschichten und
Also make you now no long stories and

kommen Sie mit!« wiederholte stur der andere.
come you along repeated stubbornly the other

»Das haben Sie wohl auswendig gelernt, was anderes
That have you well by heart learned what else

können Sie wohl nicht pfeifen wie das ›Kommen Sie
can you well not whistle as that Come you

mit!‹?« schrie Borkhausen. »Du kannst wohl nicht kapieren,
along cried Borkhausen You can well not understand

was ich dir sage? Ewig ›Kommense mit‹! Das kannst du
what I you say Eternally Come you along That can you

wohl nicht begreifen, daß ich dir sage, ich warte hier auf
well not comprehend that I you say I wait here on
for

Bescheid, ich muß hier sitzen, sonst geht der Hase mir
information I must here sit otherwise goes the hare me

aus der Schlinge? Das ist wohl zu hoch für dich?« Er
from the snare That is well too high for you He

sah sein Gegenüber ein wenig atemlos an. Dann setzte er
saw his opposite a little breathless on Then set he

mürrisch hinzu: »Den Hasen soll ich nämlich für den
grumpily there-to The hare should I namely for the

Kommissar fangen, verstehen Sie?«
commissioner catch understand you

Der ehemalige Feldwebel sagte ungerührt: »Von all dem
The former sergeant-at-arms said untouched Of all that

weiß ich nichts. Der Kommissar hat zu mir gesagt:
know I nothing The commissioner has to me said

Fritsche, hol den Borkhausen. Also kommense schon!«
Fritsche get the Borkhausen So come already

»Nee!« sagte Borkhausen. »Du bist mir zu dämlich. Ich
No said Borkhausen You are me too stupid I

bleibe – oder willst du mich verhaften?« Er sah es dem
remain or want you me arrest He saw it the

andern an der Nase an, daß er das nicht konnte. »Also
other on the nose on that he that not could So

hau schon ab!« rief er und schlug dem die Tür vor
chop already off called he and struck that one the door before

der Nase zu.
the nose to shut

Drei Minuten darauf sah er den alten Feldwebel über
Three minutes thereupon saw he the old sergeant-at-arms over

den Hof abtrümmern, der hatte es sich anders
the court chipping that one had it himself different

überlegt, das »Kommense mit«!
considered that Come you along

Und sobald der Mann durch die Toreinfahrt des
And as soon as the man through the gateway of the

Vorderhauses verschwunden war, überkam Borkhausen Angst
front house disappeared was overcame Borkhausen fear

wegen der Folgen, die sein freches Auftreten vor
because of the consequences that his cheeky performance before

dem Sendboten des allmächtigen Kommissars haben
the messenger of the almighty commissary have

konnte. Nur der Zorn über diesen Kuno-Dieter hatte ihn
could Only the anger over this Kuno-Dieter had him

dazu gebracht. Es war eine Unverschämtheit, den Vater
there-to brought It was an impudence the father

Stunden um Stunden sitzenzulassen, womöglich bis in die
hours for after hours sitting to let possibly until in the

Nacht hinein. Überall gab es Bengels, an jeder
night inside Everywhere gave it rascals on each

Straßenecke gab es jemand, den man mit einer Botschaft
street corner gave it someone who one with a message

schicken konnte! Aber er würde es dem Kuno schon
send could But he would it the Kuno already

zeigen, was er von seinem Benehmen hielt, er sollte
show what he from his behavior held he should
thought

sich solche Witzchen nicht ungestraft erlauben.
himself such jokes not unpunished permit
leave

Borkhausen schwelgte ordentlich in Phantasien, wie er den
Borkhausen reveled properly in fantasies how he the

Burschen vermöbeln wollte. Er sah sich beim Prügeln
lad lambast wanted He saw himself at the beating

dieses kindlichen Körpers, und ein Lächeln lag auf seinem
of this childly body and a smile lay on his

Gesicht, aber es war kein Lächeln abklingender Wut ... Er
face but it was no smile of subsiding anger He

hörte ihn schreien, und er legte ihm die eine Hand auf
heard him shout and he put him the a hand on

den schreienden Mund, während die andere weiterschlug,
the screaming mouth while the other continued

so lange weiterschlug, bis der ganze Junge zitterte und
so long continued until the whole boy trembled and

sein Mund nur noch wimmerte ...
his mouth only still whimpered

Borkhausen wurde es nicht müde, sich diese Bilder
Borkhausen became it not tired himself this images

immer wieder vorzustellen. Dabei streckte er sich auf
always again to imagine There-by stretched he himself on

seinem Sofa und stöhnte wollüstig.
his sofa and groaned voluptuous

Beinah kam ihm der Junge, endlich der Sendbote
Almost came him the boy finally the message

Kuno-Dieters, störend, der jetzt klopfte. »Was ist?« fragte
of Kuno-Dieter disturbing who now knocked What is it asked

er kurz.
he curtly

»Ich soll Sie zu Kuno bringen.«
I should you to Kuno bring

Diesmal war es ein großer Junge von vierzehn oder
This time was it a bigger boy from fourteen or

fünfzehn Jahren in der HJ-Bluse.
fifteen years in the HJ-shirt (hitler jugend)

»Aber erst geben Sie mir mal fünf Mark.«
But first give you me once five mark

»Fünf Mark!« grollte Borkhausen und wagte sich diesem
Five mark rumbled Borkhausen and dared himself this

großen Bengel im braunen Hemd doch nicht offen zu
large kid in the brown shirt indeed not openly to

widersetzen. »Fünf Mark! Ihr Jungens könnt ja fein mit
oppose Five mark {money} You boys could yes fine with

meinem Gelde rumschmeißen!« Er suchte zwischen den
my money toss around He searched between the

Scheinen.
(bank)notes

Der große HJ-Junge sah gespannt auf den Packen Geld
The great HJ boy saw anxiously on the pack (of) money

in der Hand des andern. »Ich hab Fahrgeld
in the hand of the other I have traveling money

ausgegeben«, sagte er. »Und dann, was denken Sie, was
spent said he And then what think you what

ich für Zeit versäumt habe, ganz aus dem Westen bis
I for time missed have completely from the west up to

hier?«
here

»Und deine Zeit kostet viel Geld, was?« Borkhausen hatte
And your time costs much money what Borkhausen had

den richtigen Schein immer noch nicht gefunden. »Und
the right (bank)note always still not found And

Westen, das sagst du so, Westen kann nie stimmen! Was
west that say you so west can never be right What

bei dir wohl Westen ist? Vielleicht meinst du Stadtmitte,
with you well west is Perhaps mean you city center

das könnte noch eher passen!«
that could still rather suit

»Na, wenn die Ansbacher nicht im Westen ist ...«
Now when the Ansbach not in the west is

Zu spät sah der Junge, daß er sich verplappert hatte.
Too late saw the boy that he himself blabbered had

Borkhausen hatte die Scheine schon weggesteckt! »Danke!«
Borkhausen had the note already tucked away Thank you

lachte er spöttisch. »Du brauchst deine teure Zeit nicht
laughed he mocking You need your expensive time not

weiter zu versäumen. Ich find jetzt schon allein. Am
further to miss I find now already alone At the

besten fahre ich wohl mit der Untergrundbahn zum
best drive I well with the subway to the

Viktoria-Luise-Platz, was?«
Viktoria Luise square what

»Das machen Sie nicht mit mir! So was werden Sie nicht
That do you not with me So what will you not

mit mir machen!« sagte der HJ-Bengel und trat mit
with me do said the HJ brat and stepped with

geballten Fäusten auf den Mann zu. Seine dunklen Augen
clenched fists on the man to His dark eyes

leuchteten vor Zorn. »Ich habe Fahrgeld ausgegeben, ich
shone before anger I have fare spent I

habe ...«
have

»Du hast deine kostbare Zeit versäumt, weiß schon!«
You have your costly time wasted know already

lachte Borkhausen. »Hau ab, mein Sohn, Doofheit hat
laughed Borkhausen Chop off my son stupidity has

immer Geld gekostet!« Plötzlich faßte ihn wieder die Wut.
always money cost Suddenly seized him again the anger

»Was stehst du hier noch rum in meiner Stube? Willst
What stand you here still around in my room Want

du mich in meiner eigenen Stube vertrimmen? Mach, daß
you me in my own room trim down Make that
beat up

du jetzt rauskommst, oder ich laß dich dein eigenes
you now get out or I let you your own

Geschrei hören!«
shouting hear

Er drängelte roh den erzürnten Jungen aus dem Zimmer,
He jostled raw the enraged boy from the room

schlug die Tür vor seiner Nase zu. Und den ganzen
struck the door before his nose to And the whole
shut

Weg, bis sie aus der Untergrundbahn am
way until they out the subway at the

Viktoria-Luise-Platz stiegen, hatte er abwechselnd spöttische
Viktoria Luise square climbed had he alternating mocking

und zornige Bemerkungen für diesen Bengel, der nicht
and angry one remarks for this kid who not

von seiner Seite wich, der aber – obwohl blaß vor
from his side retreated who however although pale for of

Zorn – doch nicht mehr mit einem einzigen Wort auf
anger indeed not (any)more with a single word on

alle seine Anzapfungen einging.
all his taps jeers entered

Oben auf dem Viktoria-Luise-Platz, aus dem Schacht der
Over on the Viktoria Luise square out of the shaft tunnel of the

U-Bahn kommend, setzte sich der Junge plötzlich in Trab
subway coming set himself the boy suddenly in trot

und war dem Manne weit voraus. Borkhausen mußte sich
and was the man far in front Borkhausen must himself

entschließen, ihm so rasch, wie es nur ging, nachzueilen:
decide him so quickly as it only went after to haste (to chase)

allzulange wollte er die beiden Bengels nicht miteinander
too long wanted he the both rascals not with each other

reden lassen. Er war sich nicht ganz sicher, für wen
talk let He was himself not completely sure for whom

sich Kuno-Dieter entscheiden würde, für seinen Vater oder
himself Kuno-Dieter decide would for his father or

für diese Sautöle.
for these sour oils

Sie standen wirklich vor einem Haus der Ansbacher.
They stood really before a house of the Ansbach

Der HJ-Junge redete eifrig auf Kuno-Dieter ein, der mit
The HJ boy spoke zealously on Kuno-Dieter in who with

gesenktem Kopf ihn anhörte. Als Borkhausen herankam,
lowered head him listened to As Borkhausen approached

zog sich der Bote zehn Schritte zurück und ließ
pulled himself the messenger ten steps back and let

die beiden allein miteinander reden.
them both alone with each other talk

»Was denkst du dir eigentlich, Kuno-Dieter?« fing
What think you yourself actually Kuno-Dieter caught
started

Borkhausen zornig an. »Daß du mir ewig solche Kerle
Borkhausen angrily on That you me eternally such guys
-

auf den Hals schickst, unverschämte Burschen, die
on the neck send outrageous lads who

vorneweg ihr Geld fordern?«
up front their money demand

»Ohne Jeld tut keener wat, Vata«, antwortete Kuno-Dieter
Without money does no one what dad answered Kuno-Dieter
(Geld) (keiner) (was)

gleichmütig. »Det weeßte ja selbst. Und ick will ooch
indifferently That know you yes self And I want also
(weisste) yourself (ich) (auch)

wissen, wat ick bei dem Jeschäft vadiene, ick hab
know wat I at the affair earn I have
(Geschäft) (verdiene)

Fahrjeld ausjejem ...«
traveling money spent
(Fahrgeld) (ausgegeben)

»Immer dieselbe Tour, daß euch aber gar nischt anderes
Always the same trip that you but at all nuthin' else
(nichts)

einfällt! Nee, Kuno-Dieter, jetzt sagste deinem Vater erst
comes to mind No Kuno-Dieter now tell your father first

mal ordentlich, was hier eigentlich los ist in der
once properly what here actually loose is in the

Ansbacher, und denn wirste ja sehn, wat dein Vata für
Ansbach and then will you yes see wat your dad for

dich tut. Dein Vata ist gar nicht so, nur Drängeln,
you does Your dad is at all not so only jostle

Drängeln verträgt dein Vater nicht!«
jostle tolerates your father not

»Nee, Vata«, sagte Kuno-Dieter wieder. »Ick hab Angst, du
No dad said Kuno-Dieter again I have fear you

vajißt et nachher mit dem Bezahln – det Jeld natürlich.
forget it after with the pay that money of course
(vergesst)

Maulschellen wirste schon zum Bezahln haben. Du hast
Muzzle clamps will you already to the pay have You have
Slaps

schon 'ne Masse Jeld in diese Sache bekommen und
already a mass of money in this thing become and

wirst wohl noch mehr dabei erben, denk ick. Ick stehe
will well still (any)more there-by inherit think I I stand

hier nu schon den janzen Tag for dir rum, ohne Essen,
here now already the whole day for you around without food

da will ick ooch ma Jeld sehn. Ick habe jedacht, fufzig
there want I also but money see I have anyone fifty

Mark ...«
mark {money}

»Fünfzig Mark!« Es verschlug Borkhausen fast die Luft,
Fifty mark It hit away took away Borkhausen almost the air

als er diese unverschämte Forderung hörte. »Ick wer dir
as he this outrageous demand heard I will you

sagen, wat ick dir jeb'n werde. Ick wer dir fünf Mark
say what I you give will I will you five mark {money}

jeb'n, jenau die fünf Mark, die der Lulatsch da haben
give exactly the five mark {money} which the dipshit there have

wollte, und darüber wirste dir jefälligst noch freun! Ick
wanted and about it will you yourself kindly still please I

bin nicht so, aba ...«
am not so but

»Nee, Vata«, sagte Kuno-Dieter und sah aus seinen blauen
No dad said Kuno-Dieter and saw from his blue

Augen Borkhausen trotzig an. »Da vadienst 'ne Stange
eyes Borkhausen defiantly on There earn you a pole

Jold	bei	det	Jeschäft,	ich	mach	nich	die	janze	Arbeet
money	at	that	affair	I	make	not	the	whole	work

und	lasse	mir	mit	fünf	Mark	abspeisen,	so	blau,	denn
and	let	me	with	five	mark	fob off	so	blue	then
					{money}				

sar	ick	dir	eben	jar	nischt!«
say	I	you	just	at all	nothing
					(nichts)

»Wat	willste	mir	denn	noch	jroß	erzähln!«	lachte
What	want-you	me	then	still	big	tell	laughed
					(gross)		

Borkhausen	spöttisch.	»Daß	der	Kleene	in	dem	Haus	da
Borkhausen	mocking	That	the	little one	in	the	house	there
				(Kleine)				

drin	steckt,	det	weeß	ick	nu	ooch	so.	Und	det	andre
there in	sticks	that	know	I	now	also	so	And	that	other

wer	ick	schon	alleene	rauskriegen.	Nee,	jeh	man	jetzt
will	I	already	alone	get out	No	go	one	now
				find out		(geh)		

nach	Hause	und	laß	dir	von	Mutter	wat	zu	essen	jeb'n!
to	house	and	let	you	from	mother	wat	to	eat	give

Für	janz	dumm	läßt	sich	dein	Vata	doch	nich	vakoofen!
For	totally	stupid	lets	himself	your	dad	indeed	not	sell

Ihr	beiden	Helden!«
You	both	heroes

»Denn jeh ick da ruff«, sagte Kuno-Dieter entschlossen,
Then go I there up said Kuno-Dieter decided

»und sare dem Kleenen, det de uff ihn paßt. Denn
and say the little one that of on him suits Then
(sage) (Kleinen)

vapfeif ick dir, Vata!«
betray I you dad
(verpfeif) (ich)

»Du verdammter Rotzjunge, du!« schrie Borkhausen und
You damned snotty boy you cried Borkhausen and

schlug nach dem Sohne.
struck after the son

Aber der lief schon, lief in den Nebeneingang des
But that one ran already ran in the side entrance of the

Hauses hinein. Borkhausen lief ihm nach, folgte ihm über
house inside Borkhausen ran him after followed him over

den Hof, und auf der untersten Treppe des
the court and on the lowest stairs of the

Hinterhauses holte er ihn ein. Er schlug ihn zu
back part of the house hauled he him in He struck him to
took over

Boden und fing dann an, auf den Liegenden, mit den
(the) ground and caught then on on the laying one with the
started -

Füßen Stoßenden einzuprügeln. Es war beinahe so, wie er
feet bumping to beat in It was almost so as he

es sich vorher auf dem Sofa ausgemalt hatte, nur
it himself before on the sofa drawn out pictured had only

Kuno-Dieter schrie nicht, sondern wehrte sich mit
Kuno-Dieter cried not but resisted himself with

verbissener Wut. Das steigerte Borkhausens Zorn noch. Mit
dogged anger That increased Borkhausen anger still With

voller Überlegung schlug er dem Jungen ins Gesicht und
full consideration struck he the boy in the face and

trat mit den Füßen nach seinem Bauch. »Dir Aas will
stepped with the feet after his belly You carrion want

ick det schon weisen!« keuchte er, und ein roter Nebel
I that already show coughed he and a red fog

schwamm vor seinen Augen.
swam before his eyes

Plötzlich fühlte er, wie ihn was von hinten packte,
Suddenly felt he how him something from in the back grabbed

jemand hielt seinen Arm fest. Etwas riß an dem
someone held his arm firm Something ripped on the

einen, etwas an dem andern Bein. Er sah sich hastig
one something on the other leg He saw himself hastily

um; es war dieser Hitler-Junge, es war eine ganze Rotte
around it was this hitler boy it was a whole batch

Bengels, Halbstarke, vier oder fünf Burschen, die sich
(of) rascals half strong four or five lads who themselves

da auf ihn gestürzt hatten. Er mußte von Kuno-Dieter
there on him rushed had He must from Kuno-Dieter

ablassen, er mußte sich dieser Bengels erwehren, von
let go he must himself these rascals defend (against) from

denen er jeden einzelnen mit einer Hand hätte
which he every single one with one hand had

niederschlagen können, die aber in ihrer Gesamtheit ihm
knock down been able who however in their entirety him

höchst gefährlich werden konnten.
most high dangerous become could
most

»Ihr verdammte, feige Bande!« schrie er und versuchte,
You damned cowardly gang cried he and tried

den Jungen, der ihm auf dem Rücken hing, durch
the boy who him on the back hung through

Rammen gegen die Wand loszuwerden. Aber sie rissen
ramming against the wall get rid of But they tore

ihm die Beine unter dem Leib weg. Sie brachten ihn zu
him the legs under the body away They brought him to

Fall.
fall

»Kuno!« keuchte er. »Hilf deinem Vater! Die feige Bande
Kuno coughed he Help your father The cowardly band
gasped

...«

Aber Kuno half seinem Vater nicht. Jetzt hatte er sich
But Kuno helped his father not Now had he himself

aufgerappelt, und er war es, der den ersten Schlag in
raised and he was it who the first strike in

Borkhausens Gesicht führte.
Borkhausen's face led

Ein murrendes Brummen, fast ein tiefes Stöhnen kam aus
A grumbling humming almost a deep stoaning came from

der Brust des Mannes. Dann rollte er sich mit den
the breast of the man Then rolled he himself with the

Bengels auf dem Boden, immer bestrebt, die an ihm
rascals on the ground always anxious the on him

Hängenden gegen Stufen und Wände zu stoßen, sie zu
hanging against steps and walls to bump them to

quetschen, um wieder auf die Beine zu kommen.
squeeze for again on the legs to come

Jetzt war nur noch das atemlose Stöhnen der Kämpfenden
Now was only still the breathless stoaning of the fighters

zu hören, das Geräusch von Schlägen, das Scharren der
to hear the sound of beatings the scraping of the

Füße ... Wortlos, in wildester Erbitterung kämpften sie.
feet Wordless in wildest bitterness struggled they

Eine alte Dame, die die Treppe hinabkam, blieb vor
An old lady who the stairs came down remained for of

Entsetzen stehen, als sie den wilden Kampf zu ihren
fright stand as she the wild fight at their

Füßen sah. Sie klammerte sich an das Geländer, sie rief
feet saw She clung herself on the railing she called

hilflos: »Aber! Aber nein ...! In unserm guten Haus!«
helplessly But But no In our good house

Ihr veilchenfarbener Umhang wallte. Dann entschloß sie
Her violet cape waved Then decided she

sich und stieß einen wilden Entsetzensschrei aus.
herself and uttered a wild cry of horror out

Die Jungen rissen sich von Borkhausen los und
The boys tore themselves from Borkhausen loose and

verschwanden. Der Mann setzte sich auf und starrte die
disappeared The man set himself up and stared the

alte Dame wild an.
old lady wildly on

»So 'ne Bande!« keuchte er. »Wollen 'nen ollen Mann
Such a gang gasped he Want an old man

versohlen, und der eigene Junge dabei!«
spank and the own boy at it

Auf den Schrei der alten Dame hatten sich ein paar
On the cry of the old lady had themselves a few

Türen geöffnet, ein paar Nachbarn kamen ängstlich hervor
doors opened a few neighbors came fearfully anxiously forth

und flüsterten miteinander, auf den sitzenden Mann
and whispered with each other at the sitting man

blickend.
looking

»Die haben sich geprügelt!« piepste die alte
They have each other punched peeped the old

Veilchenfarbene. »Die haben sich in unserm guten Haus
violet painted They have each other in our good house

geprügelt!«
punched

Borkhausen besann sich. Wenn Enno Kluge jetzt hier
Borkhausen re-thought himself When Enno Kluge now here

wohnte, so war es höchste Zeit für ihn, zu verschwinden.
lived so was it highest time for him to disappear

Jeden Augenblick konnte auch er auftauchen, neugierig zu
Every moment could also he duck up appear curious to

sehen, was dieser Trubel bedeutete.
see what this hustle and bustle meant

»Hab nur meinen Jungen ein bißchen abgewackelt«,
Have only my boy a little shaken off

erklärte er grinsend den ihn schweigend anstarrenden
explained he grinning the him in silence staring at

Mietern. »Hat nichts zu sagen. Alles in Ordnung.
tenants Has nothing to say Everything in order

Alles in bester Butter.«
Everything in most best butter

Er stand auf und ging über den Hinterhof, durch den
He stood up and went over the backyard through the

»Garten«, wieder auf die Straße, wobei er an seinen
garden again on the street where-by he on his

Kleidern herumstrich und den Schlips neu band. Von den
clothes stroke around and the slips again bound From the

Bengels war natürlich keine Spur mehr zu sehen. Na,
rascals was of course no trace (any)more to see Now

warte, der Kuno-Dieter sollte ihn heute abend
wait the Kuno-Dieter should him today evening

kennenlernen! Gegen seinen eigenen Vater zu kämpfen, als
get to know Against his own father to fight as

erster ihm ins Gesicht zu schlagen! Keine Otti in der
first him in the face to strike No Otti in the

Welt sollte sich schützend vor ihn stellen können! Nee,
world should herself protectively before him places can No

die konnte auch noch eine Wucht beziehen für dieses
that one could also still a force draw for this
get

verdammte Kuckucksei, das sie ihm da ins Nest gelegt
damned cuckoo egg that she him there in the nest laid

hatte!
had

Während Borkhausen das Haus unter Bewachung hält,
While borkhausen the house under guarding holds

steigt sein Zorn gegen diesen Kuno-Dieter immer mehr. Er
rises his anger against this Kuno-Dieter always more He

wird aber fast besinnungslos, als er entdeckt, daß die
becomes however almost senseless as he discovers that the

Bengels ihm beim Kampf das ganze Paket Scheine aus
rascals him at the fight the whole package (of) bills from

der Tasche gestohlen haben. Nur ein paar einzelne Mark
the pocket stolen have Only a few single marks {money}

in der Westentasche sind ihm geblieben. So ein Sauvolk,
in the vest pocket are have him remained Such a sow-folk

solche verdammte Zucht. Am liebsten stürzte er auf der
such damned breed At the dearest crashed he on the

Stelle los, sie zu finden, Gulasch aus ihnen zu machen,
spot loose them to find goulash from them to make

sich sein Geld wiederzuholen!
himself his money again-to-get get back

Und er stürzt auch schon los.
And he rushed also already loose

Als er sich besinnt: er kann doch nicht weg! Er muß
As he himself rethinks he can indeed not away He must

hier stehenbleiben, sonst laufen ihm die fünfhundert
here stand remain otherwise run him the fivehundred

Mark auch noch fort! Es ist ja klar: nie kriegt er
mark {money} also still away It is yes clear never gets he

sein Geld von diesen Bengels wieder, da will er sehen,
his money from these rascals again there wants he see

daß er wenigstens die fünfhundert rettet!
that he at least the fivehundred rescues

Er geht, völlig verwüstet von ätzendem Zorn, in ein
He goes totally devastated from caustic biting away anger in a

kleines Café und telefoniert von dort mit dem
little coffee shop and phones from there with the

Kommissar Escherich. Dann geht er auf seinen
commissioner Escherich Then goes he on his

Beobachtungsposten zurück und wartet ungeduldig auf das
observation post back and waits impatiently on the

Kommen von Escherich. Ach, wie triste ihm ist! Alle diese
coming of Escherich Ah how dreary him it is All this

Mühe, die er sich gegeben hat – und immer ist
trouble which he himself given has and always is

alles gegen ihn! Andern gelingt, was sie nur anfassen,
everything against him Others succeeds what they only touch

solch kleines Biest wie der Enno kriegt 'ne Frau mit
such (a) little beast as the Enno gets a woman with

viel Geld, einen schönen Laden, so ein Garnichts setzt
much money a beautiful shop so a nothing at all set
bet

nur auf ein Pferd, und schon gewinnt er - aber er! Er
only on a horse and already wins he but he He

kann tun, was er will: alles mißlingt ihm. Was für 'ne
can do what he wants everything fails him What for a

Mühe hat er sich mit dieser Häberle gegeben, hat sich
trouble has he himself with this Haberle given has himself

gefreut, ein bißchen Geld in der Tasche zu haben -
enjoyed a bit money in the pocket to have

schon ist es wieder weg! Das Armband damals von der
already is it again way The bracelet at that time from the

Rosenthal - weg! Der schöne Einbruch, eine ganze
Rosenthal away The beautiful burglary a whole

Handlung mit Wäsche - weg! Was er auch anfaßt,
deal with wash away What he also takes on
clothing begins

alles geht ihm schief.
everything goes him crooked

Bin ein Schieflieger, das bin ich! sagt er voll Bitternis
Am an crooked-layer that am I says he full (of) bitterness
cursed person

zu sich selbst. Na, wenn der Kommissar wenigstens die
to himself himself Now when the commissioner at least the

fünfhundert Eier mitbringt! Und den Kuno schlage ich
fivehundred eggs brings along And the Kuno beat I

einfach tot! Den zwiebele ich so lange, den laß
simply dead That one onion I so long that one let
to death beat

ich hungern, bis er krepiert! Das vergeß ich ihm nie!
I starve until he dies That forget I him never

Borkhausen hat am Telefon dem Kommissar gesagt, er
Borkhausen has at the phone the commissioner said he

solle das Geld gleich mitbringen.
should the money immediately bring along

»Will mal sehen!« hat der Kommissar geantwortet.
Want once see has the commissioner answered
We will

Was das nun wieder heißen soll? Will der mich auch
What that now again mean should Wants that one me also

anscheißen ...? So was gibt's doch gar nicht!
shit on So what gives it indeed at all not
will there be

Nein, an dieser ganzen Sache interessiert ihn nur das
No on this whole thing interested him only the

Geld. Sobald er das Geld hat, wird er abhauen, aus
money As soon as he the money has will he chop off from

dem Enno mag werden, was da will! Der interessiert ihn
the Enno may become what there wants That interested him

nicht mehr! Und vielleicht fährt er dann wirklich nach
not (any)more And perhaps drives he then really to
goes

München. Er hat hier alles so über! Er mag einfach
Munich He has here everything so over He may simply

nicht mehr. Kuno, der ihm in die Fresse haut und ihm
not (any)more Kuno who him in the mug chops and him

Geld klaut - so was hat's noch nie gegeben, der eigene
money steals so what had it still never given the own

Sohn!
son

Nein, die Häberle hat recht: er wird nach München
No the Haberle has right he will to Munich
is

fahren. Wenn Escherich das Geld bringt, sonst kann er
drive When Escherich the money brings otherwise can he

die Fahrkarte nicht kaufen. Aber ein Kommissar, der nicht
the ticket not buy But a commissioner who not

Wort hält, so was kann doch einfach nicht sein! Oder?
(his) word keeps so what can indeed simply not be Or

Besuch bei Fräulein Anna Schönlein

Visit to Miss Anna Schonlein

Die telefonische Nachricht Borkhausens, er habe den Enno
The telephone message (of) Borkhausen he have the Enno

Kluge im Berliner Westen aufgestöbert, hatte den
Kluge in the Berlin West tracked down had the

Kommissar Escherich in arge Verlegenheit gestürzt.
commissioner Escherich in severe embarrassment precipitated

Unwillkürlich hatte er geantwortet: »Ja, ich komme. Komme
Involuntarily had he answered Yes I come Come

sofort!« Er hatte sich schon zum Fortgehen
right away He had himself already to the away go

fertiggemacht, und dann waren ihm doch wieder Bedenken
ready made and then were him indeed again doubts

gekommen.
come

Jawohl, nun hatte er ihn also, den so sehnlich
Yes now had he him thus the so ardently

Erwünschten, den seit Tagen Gejagten. Da hatte er ihn,
desired (one) the since days hunted (one) There had he him

er brauchte nur die Hand auf ihn zu legen, und er hatte
he needed only the hand on him to lay and he had

ihn fest, den Burschen. Während des angestrengten,
him caught the lad During of the strained

ungeduldigen Recherchierens hatte er immer nur an den
impatient researching had he always only on the

Augenblick gedacht, daß er ihn fassen mußte; mit Gewalt
moment thought that he him take must with force

hatte er jeden Gedanken an das, was mit dem Gefaßten
had he every thought on that what with the caught one

zu tun sei, verjagt.
to do be chased away

Aber nun war es soweit. Nur erhob sich diese Frage:
But now was it so far Only raised itself this question

Was sollte er denn eigentlich mit dem Enno anfangen? Er
What should he then actually with the Enno begin He

wußte es doch, jetzt wußte er es wieder ganz klar:
knew it indeed now knew he it again completely clear

der Enno Kluge war der Kartenschreiber nicht, wußte es
the Enno Kluge was the card writer not (he) knew it

mit aller Klarheit. Während des Suchens hatte er sich
with all clarity During of the search had he himself

das vernebeln können, er hatte sogar mit dem Assistenten
that obfuscate been able he had even with the assistant

Schröder davon geschwatzt, daß der Kluge bestimmt
Schroeder there-from chatted that the Kluge definitely

noch was anderes auf dem Kerbholz hatte.
still something else on the carve-wood had
done wrong

Ja, eben was anderes, aber nicht dieses, nicht er
Yes just something else but not this not he

hatte die Karten geschrieben! Nie! Nahm er ihn fest,
had the cards written never took he him firmly

brachte er ihn hierher in die Prinz-Albrecht-Straße, so
brought he him hereto in the Prinz-Albrecht-Straße so

würde nichts den Obergruppenführer abhalten können, den
would nothing the Over-groups-leader off-hold been able the
prevent

Kluge selbst zu vernehmen, und daß dann alles
Kluge himself to hear and that then everything
interrogate

herauskam, nämlich gar nichts von den Karten, aber viel
came out namely at all nothing from the cards but much

von einer abgelisteten Protokollunterschrift, das war klar!
from a delisted signature of the minutes that was clear

Nein, es war unmöglich, den Kluge hierherzubringen!
No it was impossible the Kluge bring here

Aber ebenso unmöglich war es, den Kluge weiter draußen
But likewise impossible was it the Kluge further outside

zu lassen, selbst unter ständiger Bewachung, nie würde
to let even under permanent guarding never would
leave

Prall das zugeben. Er würde sich auch nicht mehr
Prall that allow He would himself also not (any)more

lange vertrösten lassen, selbst wenn Escherich ihm
long put off let himself when Escherich him

vorläufig die Auffindung Kluges verschwieg. Ein paarmal
for now the finding of Kluge concealed A few times

hatte er schon recht kräftig angedeutet, daß er diesen
had he already right powerfully indicated that he this

ganzen Fall Klabautermann in andere Hände legen würde,
whole case Kobold in other hands put would

in etwas schlauere! Und so konnte der Kommissar sich
in something smarter And so could the commissioner himself

nicht blamieren lassen - außerdem hing er an dem Fall,
not disgrace let in addition hung he on the case

er war ihm wichtig geworden.
he was him important become
it

Escherich sitzt an seinem Schreibtisch und starrt vor
Escherich sits on his desk and stares before

sich hin, er zerbeißt den geliebten sandfarbenen
himself away he bites the beloved sand-colored

Schnurrbart. Eine verdammte Sackgasse, sagt er bei sich.
moustache A damned bag-alley says he by himself
dead end

Eine verdammte Sackgasse, in die ich mich da
A damned bag-alleydead end in which I myself there

bugsiert habe! Was ich auch tue, ist falsch, und wenn ich
juggled have What I also do is false and when I
Whatever I

nichts tue, ist es erst recht falsch! Elende Sackgasse!
nothing do is it first right false Wretched bag-alley
even really wrong dead end

Er sitzt da und grübelt. Die Zeit vergeht, und
He sits there and ponders The time passes and

Kommissar Escherich sitzt immer noch da und grübelt.
commissioner Escherich sits always still there and ponders

Der Borkhausen - zur Hölle mit diesem Borkhausen! Er
The borkhausen to the hell with this Borkhausen He

soll da nur stehen und auf das Haus passen! Er hat
should there only stand and on the house fit He has
keep an eye

Zeit genug dazu! Und wenn ihm der Enno unterdes
time enough there-to And when him the Enno under-that
meanwhile

durch die Lappen geht, so wird er ihm die Eingeweide
through the rag goes so will he him the intestines

stückweise aus dem Leibe reißen! Fünfhundert Mark und
piecemeal from the body tear Fivehundred mark and
{money}

gleich mitbringen! Der ganze Enno, hundert Ennos sind
immediately bring along The whole Enno hundred Enno's are

keine fünfhundert Mark wert! In die Fresse wird er dem
no fivehundred mark worth In the mug will he the
{money}

Borkhausen schlagen, so ein dämlicher Hund! Was geht
Borkhausen hit so a stupid dog What goes

ihn der Kluge an, er braucht den Kartenschreiber!
him the Kluge on he needs the card writer

Aber dann, während er da still sitzt und immer
But then while he there quietly sits and always

weitergrübelt, wird Kommissar Escherich doch vielleicht
mulls on becomes commissioner Escherich indeed perhaps

anderer Ansicht im Falle Borkhausen. Jedenfalls steht er
other opinion in the case Borkhausen Anyhow stands he

auf und geht zur Kasse. Er läßt sich dort
up and goes to the cash register He lets himself there

fünfhundert Mark geben («wird später abgerechnet») und
fivehundred mark {money} give will be later settled and

kehrt in sein Zimmer zurück. Er hat im Dienstwagen in
turns in his room back He has in the service car in

die Ansbacher fahren wollen, auch zwei von seinen
the Ansbach (district) drive want also two from his

Leuten mitnehmen - aber das bestellt er jetzt um, er
people take along but that orders he now around he

braucht weder Wagen noch Leute.
needs neither car nor people

Vielleicht ist Escherich nicht nur, was diesen Borkhausen
Perhaps is Escherich not only what this Borkhausen

angeht, anderer Ansicht geworden, vielleicht ist ihm auch
concerns other opinion become perhaps is him also

etwas zum Fall Enno Kluge eingefallen. Jedenfalls nimmt
something to the case Enno Kluge fallen in Anyhow takes

er jetzt seinen Dienstrevolver, die Kanone, aus der
he now his service revolver the canon from the

Hosentasche und steckt dafür eine leichte Pistole ein,
pocket and sticks therefore instead a light pistol in

die aus einer kürzlich durchgeführten Beschlagnahme
which from a recently through-led implemented seizure

stammt. Er hat es schon versucht, das kleine Ding liegt
originates He has it already tried the little thing lies

ausgezeichnet in der Hand und schießt gut.
excellent in the hand and shoots good

Nun also, gehen wir. Auf der Schwelle seines Zimmers
Now thus go we On the threshold of his room

bleibt der Kommissar stehen, dreht sich noch einmal
remains the commissioner stand turns himself still once

um. Etwas Merkwürdiges geschieht: er macht, ohne es
around Something strange happens he makes without it

zu wollen, eine grüßende, eine abschiednehmende
to want a greeting a farewell

Bewegung zu diesem Zimmer. Lebe wohl ... Ein dunkles
movement to this room Live well A dark

Gefühl, eine Ahnung, deren er sich doch beinah
feeling an idea for which he himself indeed almost

schämt, daß Kommissar Escherich dieses Zimmer nicht so
is ashamed that commissioner Escherich this room not so

wiedersehen wird, wie er es jetzt verläßt. Bisher war er
see again will as he it now leaves Until-here was he
Until now

ein Beamter, der Menschen jagt, wie ein anderer
a civil servant who people chases as an other
chases people

Briefmarken verkauft, ordentlich, fleißig, nach den
stamps sold properly industrious after the
following

Vorschriften.
regulations

Wenn er heute aber oder erst morgen früh in dies
When he today however or first tomorrow early in this
only

Zimmer zurückkehrt, wird er vielleicht nicht mehr
room returns will he perhaps not (any)more

derselbe Beamte sein. Er wird sich etwas vorzuwerfen
the same official be He will himself something in front-to-throw
to blame

haben, etwas, das nicht zu vergessen ist. Etwas, das
have something that not to forget is Something that

vielleicht nur er weiß, aber um so schlimmer: er weiß es,
perhaps only he knows but for so worse he knows it

und nie kann er sich freisprechen.
and never can he himself free-speak
acquit

So grüßt Escherich sein Zimmer und geht und schämt
So greets Escherich his room and goes and is ashamed

sich halb des Abschiedsgrußes. Wir werden ja sehen,
himself half of the farewell We will yes see
well

sagt er beruhigend zu sich. Es kann alles noch
says he soothing to himself It can everything still

ganz anders kommen. Erst muß ich mal mit dem
completely different come First must I once with the
happen

Kluge reden ...
Kluge talk

Auch er benutzt die U-Bahn, und es wird schon Abend,
Also he uses the subway and it becomes already evening

als er in die Ansbacher Straße kommt.
when he in the Ansbach street comes
arrives

»Sie können einen aber auch fein warten lassen!« knurrt
You can one but also fine wait let growls
however

Borkhausen wütend bei seinem Anblick. »Ganzen Tag noch
Borkhausen furiously at his sight (The) entire day still

nischt gegessen! Haben Sie mein Geld mitgebracht, Herr
nuthin' eaten Have you my money brought along Mr
nichts

Kommissar?«
commissioner

»Halt die Klappe!« knurrt der Kommissar, was Borkhausen
Hold the flap growls the commissioner what Borkhausen
Shut

ganz richtig für eine Bejahung nimmt. Sein Herz fängt
completely right for an affirmative takes His heart catches
starts

wieder an, leichter zu schlagen: Geld in Aussicht!
again on easier to strike Money in view

»Wo wohnt der denn hier, der Kluge?« wird er
Where lives that one then here the Kluge becomes he

vom Kommissar gefragt.
from the commissioner asked

»Weiß ich doch nicht!« sagt Borkhausen sofort
Know I indeed not says Borkhausen immediately

gekränkt, um etwaigen Vorwürfen zuvorzukommen. »Ich
hurt for any accusations before-to-come I
to anticipate

kann doch nicht hier ins Haus gehen und nach ihm
can indeed not here in the house go and after him

fragen, wo er mich von früher her kennt! Nee, aber er
ask where he me from before away knows No but he

wird wohl im Gartenhaus wohnen, das werden Sie schon
will well in the garden shed live that will you already

selber rauskriegen, Herr Kommissar. Ich habe meine Arbeit
self get out Mr commissioner I have my work

gemacht, ich möchte jetzt mein Geld.«
made I may now my money
done can have

Escherich beachtet das gar nicht, er fragt Borkhausen,
Escherich regarded that at all not he asks Borkhausen

wieso der Enno jetzt hier im Westen wohnt, wie er ihm
how so the Enno now here in the west lives how he him

auf die Spur gekommen ist?
on the trace come is

Borkhausen muß das ausführlich berichten, der Kommissar
Borkhausen must that extensively report the commissioner

macht sich Notizen über Frau Hete Häberle, die
makes himself notes about woman Hete Haberle the

Tierhandlung, die abendliche Knieszene: diesmal schreibt
pet shop the evening knee scene this time writes

der Kommissar alles auf. Natürlich ist der Bericht, den
the commissioner everything up Of course is the report which

Borkhausen macht, nicht ganz vollständig, das kann man
Borkhausen makes not totally complete that can one

aber auch nicht verlangen. Niemand kann von einem
however also not desire Nobody can from a

Manne verlangen, daß er seinen eigenen Reinfall gesteht.
man desire that he his own there-in-fall confesses
failure

Denn wenn Borkhausen berichtet, wie er zu dem Geld
Then when borkhausen reported how he to the money

der Häberle gekommen ist, müßte er auch berichten, wie
of the Haberle come is must he also report how

es wegkam. Er müßte wohl auch von den zweitausend
it came away He must well also from the two thousand

Eiern erzählen, die jetzt für ihn nach München rollen.
eggs tell which now for him to Munich roll
Marks

Nee, aber das kann keiner von ihm verlangen!
No but that can none from him desire

Wäre Escherich ein bißchen besser in Form gewesen, so
Would be Escherich a little better in form been so

wären ihm einige Ungereimtheiten in dem Bericht seines
were him some inconsistencies in the message of his

Spitzels aufgefallen. Aber Escherich ist innerlich immer
snitch noticed But Escherich is internally always

noch stark mit andern Dingen beschäftigt, am liebsten
still strongly with other things occupied at the dearest

schickte er diesen Borkhausen fort.
sent he this Borkhausen away

Aber er braucht ihn noch eine Weile, und so sagt er
But he needs him still a while and so says he

denn zu ihm: »Warten Sie hier!« und geht ins Haus.
then to him Wait you here and goes in the house

Doch er geht nicht gleich in das Gartengebäude,
Indeed he goes not immediately in the garden building

sondern begibt sich in die Portierloge des Vorderhauses
but gives himself in the porter lodge of the front house
moves

und zieht dort Erkundigungen ein. Dann erst betritt er,
and pulls there inquiries in Then first enters he
asks for

begleitet von dem Portier, das Gartenhaus und beginnt
accompanied from the porter the garden shed and begins

langsam die Treppe bis in den vierten Stock
slowly the stairs until in the fourth floor

hinaufzusteigen.
to climb up

Daß der Enno Kluge hier im Haus ist, hat der Portier
That the Enno Kluge here in the house is has the porter

ihm nicht bestätigen können. Der Portier ist nur für die
him not confirm been able The porter is only for the

Herrschaften im Vorderhaus da, nicht für die Leute im
gentlemen in the front building there not for the people in the

Gartengebäude. Aber er kennt natürlich alle, die dort
garden building But he knows of course all who there

wohnen, schon weil er die Lebensmittelkarten zu
live already because he the food cards to

verteilen hat. Manche kennt er gut, manche kennt er
distribute has Many knows he well many knows he

weniger gut. Da ist zum Beispiel das Fräulein Anna
less well There is for the example the miss Anna

Schönlein im vierten Stock, der ist das ohne weiteres
Schönlein in the fourth floor that one is the without additional

zuzutrauen, daß sie solchen Mann aufnimmt. Die hat
to entrust that she such a man takes up That one has

der Portier sowieso auf dem Strich, ewig übernachtet
the porter anyway on the brush eternally over-nights
stays over

alles mögliche Gesindel bei der, und der Postsekretär in
all possible riffraff at that one and the post secretary in

der dritten Etage darunter behauptet ja steif und fest,
the third floor under it claimed yes stiff and firmly

sie höre nachts auch ausländische Sender ab. Nur
she hear at night also foreign (radio) channels off Only

konnte es der Sekretär noch nicht beschwören, aber er
could it the secretary still not swear but he

wollte fleißig weiterhorchen. Ja, der Portier hatte
wanted industriously continue listen Yes the porter had

wegen dieser Schönlein schon mal mit dem Blockwalter
because of this Schönlein already once with the block manager

sprechen wollen, aber ebensogut sagte er es jetzt dem
speak want but just as well said he it now the

Herrn Kommissar. Der sollte es zuerst ruhig bei der
gentleman commissioner That one should it first calm at the

Schönlein versuchen, und erst wenn sich herausstellte, dort
Schönlein try and first when itself turned out there

war der Mann wirklich nicht, könnte man auf den andern
was the man really not could one on the other

Etagen nachfragen. Aber im allgemeinen wohnten nur
floors after-ask ask But in the general lived only

anständige Leute auch hier hinten im Gartenhaus.
decent people also here in the back in the garden shed

»Hier ist es!« flüsterte der Portier.
Here is it whispered the porter

»Bleiben Sie hier stehen, damit man Sie durchs
Remain you here stand there-with so one you through the

Guckloch sieht«, flüsterte der Kommissar zurück.
peephole sees whispered the commissioner back

»Sagen Sie irgendwas, warum Sie kommen, wegen des
Say you anything why you come because of of the

Schweinefutters für die NSV oder wegen dem WHW.«
pig feed for the NSV or because of the WHW

»Ist gemacht!« sagt der Portier und klingelt.
Is done says the porter and rings

Eine Weile erfolgt gar nichts, der Portier klingelt ein
A while happens at all nothing the porter rings a

zweites und ein drittes Mal. Aber in der Wohnung bleibt
second and a (a) third time But in the house remains

alles still.
everything quiet

»Nicht zu Hause?« flüstert der Kommissar.
Not at home whispers the commissioner

»Ich weiß doch nicht!« sagt der Portier. »Ich habe die
I know indeed not says the porter I have the

Schönlein heute noch nicht auf der Straße gesehen.«
Schönlein today still not on the street seen

Und er klingelt ein viertes Mal.
And he rings a fourth once

Ganz plötzlich öffnet sich die Tür, die beiden haben
Completely suddenly opens itself the door the both have

kein Geräusch aus der Wohnung gehört. Eine lange dürre
no sound from the house heard A tall dried out

Frau steht vor ihnen. Sie hat ausgebeutelte, verfärbte
woman stands before them She has bagged discolored

Trainingshosen an, und oben trägt sie einen
training pants on and above carries she a

kanariengelben Pullover mit roten Knöpfen. Sie hat ein
canary yellow sweater with red buttons She has a

scharfliniges mageres Gesicht, das rotfleckig ist, rotfleckig,
sharp lean face which red spotted is red spotted

wie es so oft die Gesichter der Tuberkulösen sind. Auch
as it so often the faces of the tuberculous are Also

ihre Augen glänzen wie im Fieber.
her eyes shine as in the fever

»Was ist?« fragt sie kurz und verrät keinerlei Erschrecken,
What is it asks she curtly and betrays none at all scare

als der Kommissar sich so dicht in die Tür stellt, daß
as the commissioner himself so close in the door puts that

sie nicht geschlossen werden kann.
she not closed become can

»Ich möchte gerne mal ein paar Worte mit Ihnen
I may gladly once a few words with you

sprechen, Fräulein Schönlein. Ich bin der Kommissar
speak miss Schönlein I am the commissioner

Escherich von der Geheimen Staatspolizei.«
Escherich from the secret state police

Wieder nichts von Erschrecken; die Frau sieht ihn nur
Again nothing from scare the woman sees him only

immer weiter mit ihren glänzenden Augen an. Dann sagt
always further with her shining eyes on Then says

sie rasch: »Kommen Sie!« und geht ihm voran in die
she quickly Come you and goes him in front in the

Wohnung.
house

»Sie bleiben hier an der Tür«, flüstert der Kommissar
You stay here at the door whispers the commissioner

dem Portier zu. »Und wenn jemand raus oder rein will,
the porter to And when someone out or in wants

rufen Sie mich!«
call you me

Es ist ein etwas liederliches, verstaubtes Zimmer, in das
It is a somewhat messy dusty room in which

der Kommissar geführt wird. Uralte Plüschmöbel mit
the commissioner led becomes Ancient plush furniture with

Säulen und Kugeln aus Großvaters Zeiten. Vorhänge aus
columns and balls from grandfather's times Curtains from

Samt. Eine Staffelei, auf der das Bild eines vollbärtigen
velvet An easel on which the picture of a full bearded

Mannes steht, ein vergrößertes koloriertes Foto. In der
man stands an enlarged colored photo In the

Luft hängt Zigarettenrauch, ein paar Stummel liegen im
air hangs cigarette smoke a few stubs lie in the

Aschenbecher.
ashtray

»Was ist?« fragt Fräulein Schönlein wieder.
What is it asks miss Schönlein again

Sie ist am Tisch stehen geblieben, hat den Kommissar
She is at the table stand remained has the commissioner

nicht zum Sitzen aufgefordert.
not to the sit asked

Aber der Kommissar setzt sich doch, er zieht eine
But the commissioner sets himself indeed he pulls a

Schachtel mit Zigaretten aus der Tasche und deutet dabei
box with cigarettes from the pocket and points there-by
shows

auf das Bild. »Wer ist denn das?« fragt er.
on the picture Who is then that asks he

»Mein Vater«, sagt die Frau. Und fragt noch einmal: »Was
My father says the woman And asks still once What

ist?«
is it

»Ich wollte Sie verschiedenes fragen, Fräulein Schönlein«,
I wanted you various (things) ask miss Schonlein

sagt der Kommissar und hält ihr die Zigaretten hin.
says the commissioner and holds her the cigarettes away

»Aber setzen Sie sich doch und nehmen Sie sich eine
But set you yourself indeed and take she yourself a

Zigarette!«
cigarette

Die Frau sagt rasch: »Ich rauche nie!«
The woman says quickly I smoke never

»Eins, zwei, drei, vier«, zählt Escherich die Stummel im
One two three four counts Escherich the stub in the

Aschenbecher. »Und Tabakrauch im Zimmer. Sie haben
ashtray And tobacco smoke in the room You have

Besuch, Fräulein Schönlein?«
visitors miss Schonlein

Sie sah ihn ohne Schrecken und ohne Angst an. »Ich
She looked him without fright and without fear at I

gebe nie zu, daß ich rauche«, sagt sie dann, »weil mir
give never to that I smoke says she then because me
admit -

der Arzt nämlich das Rauchen wegen meiner Lungen
the doctor namely the smoking because of my lungs

verboten hat.«
forbidden has

»Sie haben also keinen Besuch?«
You have thus no visitors

»Ich habe also keinen Besuch.«
I have thus no visitors

»Ich werde mir mal rasch Ihre Wohnung ansehen«,
I will myself once quickly your house look at

erklärt der Kommissar und steht auf. »Nein, bitte,
explained the commissioner and stands up No please

bemühen Sie sich nicht. Ich finde meinen Weg schon.«
trouble you yourself not I find my way already

Er ging schnell durch die beiden andern, mit Sofas,
He went fast through the both other with sofas

Vertikos, Schränken, Sesseln und Säulen überfüllten
verticos the shelves armchairs and columns crowded

Zimmer. Einmal blieb er stehen und lauschte, das
rooms Once remained he stand and listened the

Gesicht einem Schrank zugewendet, er lächelte dabei.
face a closet turned to he smiled there-by

Dann kehrte er zu Fräulein Schönlein zurück. Sie stand
Then turned he to miss Schönlein back She stood

noch, wie er sie verlassen, am Tisch.
still as he her left at the table

»Mir ist gemeldet worden«, sagte er, sich wieder
Me is reported been said he himself again

hinsetzend, »daß Sie viel Besuch empfangen, Besuch, der
sitting down that you much visitors receive visitors who

meist über ein paar Nächte bei Ihnen bleibt, der aber
mostly over a few nights at you stay who however

nie gemeldet wird. Sie kennen die Bestimmungen über
never reported become You know the provisions about
rules

die Meldepflicht?«
the reporting requirements

»Bei meinen Besuchen handelt es sich fast nur um
By my visits deals it itself almost only about

Neffen und Nichten, die nie mehr als höchstens zwei
nephews and nieces who never (any)more as at most two

Nächte bei mir bleiben. Ich glaube, die Meldepflicht
nights at me stay I believe the obligation to report

beginnt erst mit der vierten Übernachtung.«
begins first with the fourth overnight

»Sie müssen eine sehr große Familie haben, Fräulein
You must a very great family have miss

Schönlein«, sagte der Kommissar gedankenvoll, »fast jede
Schonlein said the commissioner thoughtful nearly each

Nacht kampieren ein, zwei, manchmal auch drei Personen
night camp one two sometimes also three people

bei Ihnen.«
at you

»Das ist maßlos übertrieben. Übrigens habe ich
That is measureless exaggerated By the way have I

tatsächlich eine sehr große Familie. Sechs Geschwister, alle
indeed a very great family Six siblings all

kinderreich verheiratet.«
rich in children married

»Und so würdige alte Herren und Damen unter Ihren
And so worthy old gentlemen and ladies under your

Neffen und Nichten!«
nephews and nieces

»Ihre Eltern besuchen mich natürlich auch dann und
Their parents visit me of course also then and

wann.«
when

»Eine sehr große, reiselustige Familie ... Übrigens, was
A very great travel enthusiast family By the way what

ich noch fragen wollte: Wo haben Sie Ihren Radioapparat
I still ask wanted Where have you your radio

zu stehen, Fräulein Schönlein? Ich habe eben keinen
to stand miss Schonlein I have just none

gesehen.«
seen

Sie preßte die Lippen fest zusammen. »Ich besitze keinen
She pressed the lips firmly together I own no

Radioapparat.«
radio

»Sicher!« sagte der Kommissar. »Sicher. Genau, wie Sie
Sure said the commissioner For sure Exactly as you

nie zugeben werden, daß Sie Zigaretten rauchen. Aber
never admit will that you cigarettes smoke But

Radiomusik ist der Lunge nicht schädlich.«
radio music is the lungs not harmful

»Aber der politischen Gesinnung«, antwortete sie ein wenig
But the political attitude answered she a little
way of thinking

spöttisch. »Nein, ich besitze keinen Radioapparat. Wenn
mocking No I own no radio When

Musik aus meiner Wohnung gehört worden ist, so handelt
music from my house heard become is so deals

es sich dabei um ein Koffergrammophon, das dort in
it itself there-by for a suitcase gramophone that there in

Ihrem Rücken auf dem Regal steht.«
your back on the shelf stands

»Und das in fremden Sprachen spricht«, ergänzte der
And that in foreign languages speaks supplemented the

Kommissar.
commissioner

»Ich habe viele ausländische Tanzplatten. Ich halte es für
I have many foreign dance disks I hold it for

kein Verbrechen, sie auch jetzt im Kriege meinen
no crime them also now in the war my

Besuchern gelegentlich vorzuspielen.«
visitors occasionally to play for

»Ihren Neffen und Nichten? Nein, das wäre wirklich kein
Your nephews and nieces No that would be really no

Verbrechen.«
crime

Er stand auf, die Hände in den Taschen. Plötzlich sprach
He stood up the hands in the pockets Suddenly spoke

er nicht mehr spöttisch, er sagte brutal: »Was meinen
he not (any)more mocking he said brutally What mean think

Sie, was wird, wenn ich Sie jetzt hops nehme,
you what will (happen) when I you now hops take arrest just like that

Fräulein Schönlein, und einen kleinen heimlichen Posten
miss Schönlein and a small secret post
guard

hier in Ihrer Wohnung placiere? Der würde dann Ihre
here in your house place That one would then your

Besucher in Empfang nehmen und sich die Papiere Ihrer
visitors in reception take and himself the papers of your

Neffen und Nichten genauer ansehen. Vielleicht bringt
nephews and nieces more exactly look at Perhaps brings

einer der Besucher sogar einen Radioapparat mit! Was
one of the visitors even a radio along What

meinen Sie?«
mean you
think

»Ich meine«, sagte Fräulein Schönlein unerschrocken, »daß
I mean said miss Schönlein undaunted that
think

Sie von vornherein die Absicht hatten, mich festzunehmen.
you from in advance the intention had me to detain

Also ist es ganz gleichgültig, was ich sage. Gehen wir!
Thus is it completely indifferent what I say Go we

Ich darf nur wohl schnell ein Kleid statt dieser
I may only well quickly a dress instead of these

Trainingshose anziehen?«
training pants pull on

»Einen Augenblick noch, Fräulein Schönlein!« rief der
One moment still miss Schonlein called the

Kommissar ihr nach.
commissioner her after

Sie blieb stehen und wandte sich, die Hand auf der
She remained stand and turned herself the hand on the

Klinke, nach dem Mann um.
(door) handle to the man around

»Einen Augenblick noch! Es ist natürlich vollkommen
One moment still It is of course completely

richtig, wenn Sie den Herrn in Ihrem Kleiderschrank
right when you the gentleman in your closet

noch vor unserm Fortgehen befreien. Schon vorhin, als
still before our away go free Already a while ago as

ich durch Ihr Schlafzimmer ging, schien er mir stark
I through your bedroom went seemed he me strongly

unter Luftmangel zu leiden. Auch ist wahrscheinlich viel
under air shortage to suffer Also is probably much

Mottenpulver in dem Schrank ...«
moth powder in the closet

Jetzt waren die roten Flecke aus ihrem Gesicht
Now were the red spots from her face

verschwunden, weiß wie ein Laken starrte sie ihn an.
disappeared white as a sheet stared she him at

Er schüttelte den Kopf. »Kinder! Kinder!« sagte er mit
He shook the head Children Children said he with

spöttischer Mißbilligung. »Wie leicht ihr es uns doch
mocking disapproval How easy you it us indeed

macht! Und ihr wollt Verschwörer sein? Ihr wollt was
make And you want conspirator be You want something

gegen diesen Staat ausrichten mit euren kindischen
against this country do with your childish

Mätzchen? Ihr schadet allein euch!«
antics You hurt alone you

Sie starrte ihn noch immer an. Ihr Mund war fest
She stared him still always at Her mouth was firmly

geschlossen, die Augen glänzten fieberisch, die Hand lag
closed the eyes shone feverishly the hand lay

noch immer auf der Klinke.
still always on the (door) handle

»Nun, Sie haben Glück, Fräulein Schönlein«, fuhr der
Now you have luck miss Schonlein drove continued the

Kommissar immer in dem Ton leichter, verächtlicher
commissioner always in the tone of light disdainful

Überlegenheit fort, »insofern, als Sie mir heute ganz
superiority away inasmuch as you me today completely

uninteressant sind. Ich interessiere mich heute nur für
uninteresting are I interest me today only for

diesen Herrn in Ihrem Kleiderschrank. Es kann sein,
this gentleman in your closet It can be

wenn ich mir auf meinem Büro Ihren Fall genauer
when I myself on my office your case more exactly

überlege, daß ich mich dann verpflichtet fühle, der
consider that I myself then obliged feel the

zuständigen Stelle über Sie eine Meldung zu machen. Es
responsible spot over you a report to make It

kann sein, sage ich, ich weiß es noch nicht. Vielleicht
can be say I I know it still not Perhaps

scheint mir dann Ihr Fall zu unbeträchtlich – besonders
seems me then your case to inconsiderable particularly

im Hinblick auf Ihr Lungenleiden ...«
in the view on your lung disease

Plötzlich brach es aus ihr hervor: »Ich will keine Gnade
Suddenly broke it from her forth I want no mercy

von euch! Ich hasse euer Mitleid! Mein Fall ist nicht
from you I hate your compassion My case is not

unbeträchtlich! Jawohl, ich habe regelmäßig politisch
inconsiderable Yes I have regularly politically

Verfolgten Unterkunft gewährt! Ich habe ausländische
pursued accommodation granted I have foreign

Sender abgehört! So, nun wissen Sie es! Nun können
(radio) channels listened to So now know you it Now can

Sie mich nicht mehr schonen – trotz meiner Lunge!«
you me not (any)more spare despite my lungs

»Mädchen!« sagte er spöttisch und sah die seltsam
Girls said he mocking and saw the strangely

altjüngferliche Gestalt in der Trainingshose und dem
old young shape in the training pants and the

gelben, rotknöpfigen Pullover fast mitleidig an. »Bei Ihnen
yellow red button sweater almost pitiful at With you

ist es ja nicht nur die Lunge, bei Ihnen sind es auch
is it yes not only the lungs with you are it also

die Nerven! Eine halbe Stunde Verhör bei uns, und
the nerves A half hour interrogation with us and

Sie würden staunen, was für ein schreiender, jammervoller
you would amaze what for a screaming miserable

Dreckhaufen Ihr Leib ist! Es ist sehr unangenehm, wenn
dirt pile your body is It is very unpleasant when

man das an sich entdeckt, diese Kränkung des
one that on himself discovers this insult of the

Selbstgefühls verwinden manche nie, bammeln sich
self-confidence get over many never bammeln themselves

hinterher auf.«
after up

Er sah sie noch einmal an, nickte nachdenklich. Er sagte
He looked her still once at nodded thoughtful He said

verächtlich: »Und so was nennt sich Verschwörer!«
contemptuously And so what calls herself conspirator

Sie zuckte zusammen, wie von einer Peitsche getroffen,
She shrugged together as from a whip hit

aber sie antwortete mit keinem Wort.
but she answered with no word

»Doch wir vergessen über unserer netten Unterhaltung
But we forget about our nice conversation

ganz Ihren Besucher im Kleiderschrank«, fuhr er dann
completely your visitor in the closet drove he then

fort. »Kommen Sie, Fräulein Schönlein! Wenn wir ihn nicht
away Come you miss Schonlein When we him not

bald erlösen, ist er hinüber.«
soon redeem is he over

Er war wirklich nahe am Ersticken, der Enno Kluge, als
He was really close at the suffocate the Enno Kluge as

ihn Escherich aus dem Schrank zog. Der Kommissar legte
him Escherich from the closet pulled The commissioner put

das Männlein auf eine Chaiselongue und bewegte ein
the little men on a chaise longue and moved a

paarmal seine Arme auf und ab, um bessere Luft in seine
few times his arms on and off for better air in his

Lungen zu bringen.
lungs to bring

»Und nun«, sagte er und sah zu der Frau hin, die
And well said he and looked at the woman away who

wortlos im Zimmer stand, »und nun, Fräulein Schönlein,
wordless in the room stood and now miss Schonlein

lassen Sie mich am besten eine Viertelstunde mit dem
let you me at the best a quarter of an hour with the

Herrn Kluge allein. Sie setzen sich wohl in die Küche,
gentleman Kluge alone You set yourself well in the kitchen

die ist zum Lauschen am ungeeignetsten.«
that one is for the listening at the most inappropriate

»Ich lausche nie!«
I listen never

»Nein, wie Sie nie Zigaretten rauchen und nur Neffen
No like you never cigarettes smoke and only nephews

und Nichten mit Schallplattenmusik erfreuen! Nein, besser,
and nieces with record music delight No better

Sie setzen sich in die Küche. Ich werde Sie rufen,
you set yourself in the kitchen I will you call

wenn ich Sie brauche!«
when I you need

Er nickte ihr noch einmal zu und überzeugte sich
He nodded her still once to and convinced himself

davon, daß sie wirklich in die Küche gegangen war.
there-from that she really in the kitchen gone was

Dann wendete er sich zu Herrn Kluge, der jetzt auf
Then turned he himself to Mr Kluge who now on

dem Sofa saß und mit seinen farblosen Augen angstvoll
the sofa sat and with his colorless eyes fearfully

auf den Kommissar starrte. Schon fingen die Tränen an,
at the commissioner stared Already caught the tears on
started -

über sein Gesicht zu rollen.
over his face to roll

»Nu, nu, Herr Kluge«, sagte der Kommissar beruhigend.
Now now Mr Kluge said the commissioner soothing

»So sehr freuen Sie sich über das Wiedersehen mit dem
So very enjoy you yourself over the see again with the

ollen Kommissar Escherich? Sie haben sich also nach
old commissioner Escherich You have yourself thus to

mir gesehnt? Die Wahrheit zu sagen, ich habe mich auch
me longed The truth to say I have myself also

nach Ihnen gesehnt und bin glücklich, Sie wiedergefunden
to you longed and am happy you found back

zu haben. Nun soll uns so bald nichts wieder trennen,
to have Now should us so soon nothing again separate

lieber Herr Kluge!«
dear Mr Kluge

Die Tränen Ennos rannen stromweise. Er schluchzte hastig:
The tears of Enno ran in a current He sobbed hastily

»Ach, Herr Kommissar, Sie haben mir doch fest
Oh Mr commissioner you have me indeed firmly

versprochen, mich freizulassen!«
promised me to release

»Habe ich Sie denn nicht freigelassen?« fragte der
Have I you then not released asked the

Kommissar erstaunt. »Aber das schließt doch nicht aus,
commissioner astonished But that closes indeed not out
excludes -

daß ich Sie immer mal wieder festnehme, wenn ich mich
that I you always once again firm-take when I myself
arrest

nach Ihnen sehne. Vielleicht habe ich ein neues Protokoll
after you long Perhaps have I a new protocol
report

zu unterschreiben, was, Herr Kluge? Sie als mein guter
to under-write what Mr Kluge You as my good
sign

Freund werden mir doch so einen kleinen Gefallen nicht
friend become me indeed so a small pleasure not

abschlagen, was?«
knock off what
refuse

Enno erzitterte unter dem Blick dieser mitleidlos auf ihn
Enno trembled under the look of this merciless at him

gerichteten höhnischen Augen. Er wußte, diese Augen
directed mocking eyes He knew these eyes

würden alles aus ihm herausziehen, alles würde er
would everything from him pull out everything would he

gleich ausquatschen, und dann war er verloren, für
immediately babble out and then was he lost for

immer und ewig, so oder so ...
always and eternally so or so

Escherich und Kluge gehen spazieren

Escherich and Kluge go (for a) walk

Es	war	schon	ganz	dunkel,	als	Kommissar	Escherich
it	was	already	completely	dark	as	commissioner	Escherich

mit	Enno	Kluge	das	Gartenhaus	in	der	Ansbacher	Straße
with	Enno	Kluge	the	garden shed	in	the	Ansbach	street

verließ.	Nein,	trotz	der	Lunge	hatte	sich	der	Kommissar
left	No	despite	the	lungs	had	himself	the	commissioner

nicht	entschließen	können,	den	Fall	von	Fräulein	Anna
not	decide	can	the	case	of	miss	Anna
	been able to decide						

Schönlein	als	unbeträchtlich	anzusehen.	Diese	alte	Jungfer
Schönlein	as	inconsiderable	to look at	This	old	maiden

schien	ja	ganz	wahllos	jeden	Verbrecher	bei	sich
seemed	yes	completely	choice-less	every	criminal	at	herself
			randomly				

aufzunehmen,	ohne	auch	nur	seine	Geschichte	zu	kennen.
to take up	without	also	only	his	story	to	know
to register		even					

Den	Enno	Kluge	zum	Beispiel	hatte	sie	nicht	einmal	nach
The	Enno	Kluge	to the	example	had	she	not	once	after
			for						for

seinem	Namen	gefragt,	sie	hatte	ihn	versteckt,	bloß	weil
his	name	asked	she	had	him	hidden	just	because

eine	Freundin	ihn	angeschleppt	hatte.
a	(female) friend	him	dragged in	had

Auch diese Frau Häberle würde man sich näher
Also this woman Haberle would one himself closer

ansehen. Es war ein Jammer mit diesem Volk! Jetzt, wo
look at It was a misery with this people Now where

der größte Krieg für seine glückliche Zukunft geführt
the greatest war for his happy future led

wurde, selbst jetzt noch war es widerspenstig. Überall,
became even now still was it unwilling Everywhere

wo man hinroch, stank es. Kommissar Escherich war
where one smelled stank it Commissioner Escherich was

fest davon überzeugt, daß er in beinah jedem deutschen
firmly there-from convinced that he in almost each German

Haus solch einen Wust von Heimlichkeiten und Lüge
house such a wilderness of secrets and lies

finden würde. Fast keiner, der ein reines Gewissen hatte
find would Almost no one who a pure conscious had

– von den Parteigenossen natürlich abgesehen. Übrigens
from the party comrades of course aside By the way

würde er sich schön hüten, bei Parteigenossen solche
would he himself beautifully care for at party comrades such
avoid

Untersuchung wie eben die bei der Schönlein
research as just that one at the Schönlein

durchzuführen.
to perform

Nun, er hatte jedenfalls den Portier als Wache in die
Now he had anyhow the porter as guard in the

Wohnung gesetzt. Der schien ein ganz verläßlicher
house set That one seemed a completely more reliable

Bursche zu sein, übrigens auch Parteimitglied; man mußte
lad to be by the way also party member one must

mal sehen, daß er irgendeinen kleinen gutbezahlten Posten
once see that he some small well paid post

bekam. Das machte solche Leute munter und schärfte
got That made such people lively and sharpened
(giddy up)

ihnen Blick und Gehör. Belohnen und Bestrafen, das war
them glance and hearing Reward and punish that was
the sight

die beste Art zu regieren.
the best way to govern

Der Kommissar mit seinem Enno Kluge am Arm geht auf
The commissioner with his Enno Kluge at the arm goes on

die Säule zu, hinter der Borkhausen steckt. Borkhausen
the column to behind which Borkhausen sticks Borkhausen

will seinen ehemaligen Kumpel jetzt gar nicht so gern
wants his former comrade now at all not so gladly

sehen; er geht, seinem Anblick zu entgehen, rund um
see he goes his sight to escape round around

die Säule. Aber der Kommissar, der kehrtgemacht hat,
the column But the commissioner who turned around has

erwischt ihn doch, und Emil und Enno stehen einander
caught him indeed and Emil and Enno stand each other

gegenüber.
opposite

»'n Abend, Enno!« sagt Borkhausen und streckt die Hand
n evening Enno says Borkhausen and stretches the hand
reaches

aus.
from

Aber Kluge nimmt sie nicht. Ein bißchen Empörung regt
But Kluge takes her not A bit (of) indignation moves
it

sich jetzt selbst in diesem jämmerlichen Geschöpf. Er haßt
itself now even in this pathetic creature He hates

diesen Borkhausen, der ihn zu einem Einbruch überredete,
this Borkhausen who him to a burglary persuaded

wo es nur Schläge gab, der heute früh Tausende
where it only blows gave who today early thousands
which only resulted in a beating

erpreßte und der ihn nun doch verraten hat.
extorted and who him now indeed betrayed has

»Herr Kommissar«, sagt Kluge eifrig, »hat Ihnen der
Mr commissioner says Kluge zealously has you the

Borkhausen nicht gesagt, daß er heute früh von meiner
Borkhausen not said that he today early from my

Freundin, der Frau Häberle, zweitausendfünfhundert
(female) friend the woman Haberle two thousand five hundred

Mark erpreßt hat? Er wollte mich dafür laufenlassen,
mark extorted has He wanted me therefore let run
{money}

und nun hat er ...«
and now has he

Der Kommissar hat den Borkhausen nur aufgesucht, um
The commissioner has the Borkhausen only visited for

ihm sein Geld zu geben und ihn nach Haus zu schicken.
him his money to give and him to house to send

Aber jetzt läßt er das Geldpäckchen in seiner Tasche
But now lets he the money pack in his pocket

wieder los und hört erheitert, wie Borkhausen grob
again loose go and hears amused how Borkhausen rough

antwortet: »Und habe ich dich nicht laufenlassen, Enno?
answers And have I you not let run Enno

Wenn du Ochse dich gleich wieder fangen läßt, dafür
When you ox you immediately again catch let therefore

kann ich nichts. Ich habe mein Versprechen gehalten.«
can I nothing I have my promise kept

Der Kommissar sagt: »Na, darüber unterhalten wir uns
The commissioner says Now there-about converse we ourselves

noch mal, Borkhausen. Jetzt machen Sie, daß Sie nach
still once Borkhausen Now make you that you to

Haus kommen.«
house come

»Aber vorher will ich mein Geld, Herr Kommissar«,
But before want I my money Mr commissioner

verlangt Borkhausen. »Sie haben mir fest fünfhundert Eier
requires Borkhausen You have me firmly fivehundred eggs

versprochen, wenn ich Ihnen Enno liefere. Da haben Sie
promised when I you Enno deliver There have you

ihn am Arm, und nun spucken Sie auch aus!«
him at the arm and now spit you also out

»Zweimal werden Sie in der gleichen Sache nicht bezahlt,
Twice become you in the (the) same thing not paid

Borkhausen!« weist der Kommissar ihn ab. »Wenn Sie
Borkhausen points rejects the commissioner him off - If you

schon zweitausendfünfhundert bekommen haben!«
already two thousand five hundred become have

»Aber ich habe das Geld doch noch gar nicht!«
But I have the money indeed still at all not

protestiert der schon wieder enttäuschte Borkhausen fast
protested the already again disappointed Borkhausen almost

schreiend. »Sie hat's doch postlagernd nach München
crying She had it indeed poste restante to Munich

geschickt, damit ich ihnen hier aus dem Wege bin!«
sent there-with I them here out the way am

»Kluge Frau!« lobt der Kommissar. »Oder war das Ihr
Smart woman praises the commissioner Or was that your

Einfall, Herr Kluge?«
idea Mr Kluge

»Er lügt ja schon wieder!« schreit Enno erbittert. »Nur
He lies yes already again cries Enno embittered Only
bitter

zweitausend sind nach München gesandt. Fünfhundert, und
two thousand are to Munich sent Fivehundred and

mehr als fünfhundert, hat er bar gekriegt. Sehen Sie nur
more as fivehundred has he cash received See you only

in seinen Taschen nach, Herr Kommissar!«
in his pockets after Mr commissioner!

»Die sind mir doch geklaut worden! Eine Rotte
Those are me indeed clawed become A batch
stolen

Halbstarker hat mich überfallen und hat mir das ganze
half-strong has me ambushed and has me the whole
youth

Geld geklaut! Sie können mich von oben bis unten
money clawed You can me from above until under
stolen

nachsehen, Herr Kommissar, ich habe nur noch ein paar
check after Mr commissioner I have only still a few

Mark bei mir, die ich zufällig in der Weste hatte!«
mark at me which I coincidentally in the vest had
{money}

»Ihnen kann man kein Geld anvertrauen, Borkhausen«,
You can one no money entrust Borkhausen

sagt der Kommissar kopfschüttelnd. »Sie können nicht mit
says the commissioner head shaking You can not with

Geld umgehen. Sich von Halbstarken beklauen lassen, ein
money around-go deal Yourself from half-strong youth steal from let a

großer Mann!«
big man

Borkhausen fängt wieder an zu betteln, zu verlangen, zu
Borkhausen catches starts again on to beg to require to

überreden, aber der Kommissar befiehlt - sie sind jetzt
persuade but the commissioner commands you are now

schon am Viktoria-Luise-Platz: »Sie machen jetzt, daß Sie
already at the Viktoria-Luise square You make now that you

nach Hause kommen, Borkhausen!«
to house come Borkhausen

»Herr Kommissar, Sie haben mir fest versprochen ...«
Mr commissioner you have me firmly promised

»Und wenn Sie jetzt nicht sofort in die U-Bahn
And when you now not immediately in the subway

verschwinden, übergebe ich Sie da dem Schupo!
disappear hand over I you there the bobby (schutz polizei)

Der kann Sie gleich mal wegen Erpressung
That one can you immediately once because of blackmail

festnehmen.«
detain

Damit geht der Kommissar auf den Schupo zu,
There-with goes the commissioner on(to) the bobby (schutz polizei) towards

und Borkhausen, der zornige Borkhausen, dieser
and Borkhausen the angry Borkhausen this

Möchtegern-Verbrecher, dem immer direkt vor dem Siege
would-be criminal who always directly before the victory

der Gewinn entrissen wird, macht, daß er vom
the profit ripped away becomes makes that he from the

Viktoria-Luise-Platz verschwindet. (Warte nur, Kuno-Dieter,
Viktoria-Luise square disappears Wait only Kuno-Dieter

wenn ich nach Hause komme!)
when I to house come

Der Kommissar spricht wirklich den Schupo an, er
The commissioner speaks really the bobby (schutz polizei) to he

weist sich aus und gibt ihm den Auftrag, das Fräulein
points himself out and gives him the mission the miss

Anna Schönlein festzunehmen und erst mal auf der Wache
Anna Schönlein to detain and first once on the guard

festzuhalten, wegen: »Na, sagen wir erst einmal, wegen
fast to hold because of Now say we first once because of

Abhörens feindlicher Sender. Keine Vernehmungen, bitte
hearing enemy (radio) channels No interrogations ask

ich mir aus. Es kommt morgen einer von uns und holt
I from me out It comes tomorrow one from us and gets

sich das Frauenzimmer. 'n Abend, Herr Wachtmeister!«
himself the woman a evening Mr guard-master
sergeant

»Heil Hitler, Herr Kommissar!«
Hail hitler Mr commissioner!

»Ja«, sagt der Kommissar, auf der Motzstraße in der
Yes says the commissioner on the Motzstrasse in the

Richtung auf den Nollendorfplatz weitergehend. »Was
direction on the Nollendorfplatz further going What

machen wir nun? Ich habe Hunger, es ist meine
make we now I have hunger it is my
do am hungry

Essenszeit. Wissen Sie was, ich lade Sie zum Abendessen
dinnertime Know you what I invite you to the evening dinner

ein. Sie werden es ja nicht so furchtbar eilig haben,
in You will it yes not so terribly hurriedly have

zu uns auf die Gestapo zu kommen. Ich fürchte, das
to us on the gestapo to come I fear the

Essen läßt bei uns zu wünschen übrig, und die Leute
food leaves at us to wish over and the people
everything to desire

sind so vergeßlich, manchmal bringen sie zwei, drei Tage
are so forgetful sometimes bring they two three days

gar nichts. Nicht mal Wasser. Schlecht organisiert. Tja,
at all nothing Not once even water Bad organized Well

was meinen Sie, Herr Kluge?«
what mean you Mr Kluge

Mit solchem und ähnlichem Geschwätz hat der Kommissar
With such and similar chatter has the commissioner

den völlig verwirrten Kluge in eine kleine Weinstube
the totally confused Kluge in a little wine bar

gezogen, wo er bekannt zu sein scheint. Der Kommissar
pulled where he known to be seems The commissioner

ißt üppig, es gibt nicht nur ausgezeichnetes reichliches
eats lush it gives there is not only excellent abundant

Essen mit Wein und Schnäpschen, es gibt auch
food with wine and schnapps it gives there are also

Bohnenkaffee, Kuchen und Zigaretten. Dabei erklärt
bean coffee cake and cigarettes There-by explains

Escherich ganz schamlos: »Denken Sie bloß nicht, daß
Escherich completely shameless Think you just not that

ich das bezahle, Kluge! Das geht alles auf
I that pay Kluge That goes everything on

Borkhausensche Rechnung. Das bezahle ich nämlich von
Borkhausen's bill That pay I namely from

dem Geld, das er eigentlich hätte kriegen sollen. Ist doch
the money that he actually had get should Is indeed

hübsch, daß Sie sich den Wanst von der Belohnung
handsome that you yourself the tummy from the reward

vollschlagen, die für Ihre Ergreifung ausgesetzt ist.
fill up which for your seizure exposed is
arrest

Ausgleichende Gerechtigkeit ...«
Balancing justice

Der Kommissar redet und redet, aber vielleicht ist er
The commissioner talks and talks but perhaps is he

nicht ganz so überlegen, wie er tut. Er hat wenig
not completely so considerate as he does He has little

gegessen, dafür rasch und viel getrunken. Vielleicht sitzt
eaten therefore quickly and much drunk Perhaps sits
instead

eine Unruhe in ihm, der ganze Mann ist von einer bei
an unrest in him the whole man is from one with

ihm ungewohnten Nervosität. Mal spielt er mit Brotkugeln,
him unusual nervousness Once plays he with bread balls
buns

und dann faßt er ganz plötzlich rasch nach der
and then grabs he completely suddenly quickly after the

Gesäßtasche, in der die leichte Pistole sitzt, wobei er
back pocket in which the light pistol sits where-by he

einen raschen Blick auf Kluge wirft.
a quick glance on Kluge throws

Der Enno sitzt ziemlich teilnahmslos dabei. Er hat
The Enno sits rather without taking part there-by He has

tüchtig gegessen, aber kaum getrunken. Er ist immer
thoroughly eaten but hardly drunk He is always

noch völlig verwirrt, er weiß nicht, was er aus dem
still totally confused he knows not what he from the

Kommissar machen soll. Ist er nun verhaftet, oder ist er
commissioner make should Is he now arrested or is he

es nicht? Enno kapiert nichts.
it not Enno understands nothing

Das erklärt ihm gerade der Escherich. »Da sitzen Sie,
That explains him just the Escherich There sit you

Herr Kluge«, sagt er, »und wundern sich über mich. Ich
Mr Kluge says he and wonder yourself about me I

habe natürlich geschwindelt, mein Hunger war gar nicht
have of course swindled my hunger was at all not

so groß, ich will nur die Zeit totschlagen bis nach zehn
so large I want only the time dead-beat to kill until after ten

Uhr. Wir müssen nämlich einen kleinen Spaziergang
hour o'clock We must namely a small walk

machen, und da wird sich ja zeigen, was ich mit Ihnen
make and there will itself yes show what I with you

anfangen soll. Ja – das – wird – sich da – zeigen ...«
start should yes that will itself there show

Der Kommissar hat immer leiser, nachdenklicher und
The commissioner has always quieter more thoughtful and

langsamer gesprochen, und Enno Kluge wirft einen
slower spoken and Enno Kluge throws a

argwöhnischen Blick auf ihn. Irgendeine neue Teufelei
suspicious glance at him Some new devilry

steckt sicher hinter dem kleinen Spaziergang um zehn
sticks sure behind the small walk around ten
at

Uhr nachts. Aber welche? Und wie kann er ihr
hour at night But which And how can he her
o'clock it

entgehen? Der Escherich paßt auf wie der Teufel, nicht
escape The Escherich guards on like the devil not
pays attention

einmal auf die Toilette darf Kluge allein.
once on the toilet may Kluge alone
even

Der Kommissar fährt fort: »Die Sache ist die, daß ich
The commissioner drives forth The thing is this one that I
goes

meinen Mann erst nach zehn Uhr erreiche. Er wohnt
my man first after ten hour reach He lives
o'clock

draußen in Schlachtensee, verstehen Sie, Herr Kluge? Das
outside in Schlachtensee understand you Mr Kluge That

ist das, was ich einen kleinen Spaziergang nenne.«
is that what I a small walk name
call

»Und was habe ich damit zu tun? Kenne ich den
And what have I there-with to do Know I the

Mann? Ich kenne doch keinen Menschen in Schlachtensee!
man I know indeed no people in Schlachtensee

Ich habe immer um den Friedrichshain rum gewohnt

I have always around the Friedrichshain around used

...«

»Ich denke, daß Sie ihn vielleicht doch kennen. Ich

I think that you him perhaps indeed know I

möchte, daß Sie ihn sich einmal ansehen.«

would like that you him yourself once look at

»Und wenn ich ihn angesehen habe, und es hat sich

And when I him watched have and it has itself

herausgestellt, daß ich ihn nicht kenne, was dann? Was

out-laid that I him not know what then What
shown

wird dann mit mir?«

becomes then with me
of

Der Kommissar macht eine gleichgültige Bewegung: »Das

The commissioner makes an indifferent movement That

wird sich dann schon zeigen. Ich denke mir, Sie werden

will itself then already show I think myself you will

den Mann kennen.«

the man know

Beide schweigen. Dann fragt Enno Kluge: »Hat das wieder

Both kept silent Then asks Enno Kluge Has that again

mit dieser verdammten Postkartengeschichte zu tun? Ich

with this cursed postcard history to do I

wollte, ich hätte dieses Protokoll nie unterschrieben. Ich
wanted I had this protocol never signed I
report

hätte Ihnen den Gefallen nicht tun sollen, Herr
had you the pleasure not do should Mr

Kommissar.«
commissioner

»Wirklich? Ich glaube beinah, Sie haben recht, für Sie wie
Really I believe almost you have right for you as
are

für mich wäre es besser gewesen, Sie hätten nicht
for me would be it better been you had not

unterschrieben, Herr Kluge!« Er starrt sein Gegenüber so
signed Mr Kluge He stares his opposite so

düster an, daß Enno Kluge einen neuen Schreck bekommt.
bleakly on that Enno Kluge a new fright gets

Der Kommissar bemerkt es. »Nu, nu«, sagt er beruhigend,
The commissioner notices it Now nu says he soothing

»wir werden ja sehen. Ich denke, wir trinken noch
we will indeed see I think we drink still

einen Schnaps und fahren dann los. Ich möchte gern
a schnapps and drive then loose I may gladly
go away

noch den letzten Zug in die Stadt zurück bekommen.«
still the last train in the city back get

Kluge starrt ihn entsetzt an. »Und ich?« fragt er mit
Kluge stares him appalled on And me asks he with

zitternden Lippen. »Soll ich – da – draußen – bleiben?«
trembling lips Should I there outside stay

»Sie?« Der Kommissar lacht. »Sie werden natürlich mit
You The commissioner laughs You will of course with

mir fahren, Herr Kluge! Was starren Sie mich denn so
me drive Mr Kluge What stare you me then so

entsetzt an? Ich habe doch nichts gesagt, das Sie so
appalled on I have indeed nothing said that you so

erschrecken könnte. Natürlich werden wir beide zusammen
scare could Of course will we both together

in die Stadt zurückfahren. Da kommt der Kellner mit
in the city go back There comes the waiter with

unserm Schnaps. Ober, warten Sie einen Augenblick, wir
our schnapps Waiter wait you a moment we

geben Ihnen die Gläser gleich zum Umtauschen.«
give you the glasses immediately to the exchange

Wenig später waren sie auf dem Weg zum Bahnhof
Little later were they on the way to the railway station

Zoo. Sie fuhren mit der S-Bahn, und als sie in
zoo They drove with the s-bahn and as they in

Schlachtensee ausstiegen, war die Nacht so dunkel, daß
schlachtensee got out was the night so dark that

sie im ersten Augenblick ratlos auf dem Bahnhofsplatz
they in the first moment at a loss on the station square

standen. Wegen der Verdunklung sah man nirgends ein
stood Because of the blackout saw one nowhere a

Licht.
light

»In dieser Finsternis finden wir nie den Weg«, sagte
In this darkness find we never the way said

Kluge angstvoll. »Herr Kommissar, bitte, lassen Sie uns
Kluge fearfully Mr commissioner please let you us

zurückfahren! Bitte! Ich will lieber die Nacht bei Ihnen
go back Please I want rather the night at you

auf der Gestapo sitzen, als ...«
on the gestapo sit than

»Reden Sie keinen Unsinn, Kluge!« unterbrach ihn der
Talk you no nonsense Kluge Interrupted him the

Kommissar grob und zog den Arm des Schmächtigen
commissioner roughly and pulled the arm of the lanky one

fest durch den seinen. »Glauben Sie, ich fahre hier die
firmly through the his Believe you I drive here the

halbe Nacht mit Ihnen spazieren, um eine Viertelstunde
half night with you to walk for a quarter of an hour

vor dem Ziel umzukehren?« Etwas sanfter
before the target to turn back Somewhat more gentle

fuhr er fort: »Ich kann jetzt schon ganz gut sehen.
drove he away I can now already completely well see
continued he

Wir müssen den Nebenweg da nehmen, da kommen wir
We must the byway there take there come we

am schnellsten zum See ...«
at the fastest to the lake

Schweigend gingen sie los, beide vorsichtig mit den
In silence went they loose both carefully with the
started they to walk

Füßen nach unsichtbaren Hindernissen tastend.
feet after invisible obstacles groping

Als sie ein Stück Weg gegangen waren, schien die Luft
As they a piece (of) way gone were seemed the air

vor ihnen heller zu werden.
before them clear to become

»Sehen Sie, Kluge«, sagte der Kommissar, »ich wußte
See you Kluge said the commissioner I knew
Look

doch, ich kann mich auf meinen Ortssinn verlassen. Da
indeed I can myself on my sense of place leave There

haben wir schon den See!«
have we already the lake

Kluge schwieg, und schweigend gingen sie weiter.
Kluge was silent and in silence went they further

Es war eine ganz windstille Nacht, alles war ruhig.
It was a completely windless night everything was calm

Kein Mensch begegnete ihnen. Das glatte Wasser des
No human met them The smoothness water of the

Sees, das sie eher ahnten als sahen, schien eine graue
lake that they rather sensed than saw seemed a gray

Helle auszudünsten, als gäbe es den schwächsten Schein
brightness to exhale as gave it the weakest shine

des am Tage aufgefangenen Lichts zurück. Der
of the at the days retrieved light back The

Kommissar räusperte sich, als wollte er sprechen, und
commissioner cleared throat himself as wanted he speak and
cleared his throat

schwieg weiter.
was silent further

Plötzlich hielt Enno Kluge an. Mit einem Ruck befreite er
Suddenly held Enno Kluge on With a jerk released he
stopped Enno Kluge

seinen Arm aus dem seines Begleiters. Er rief fast
his arm from that of his companion He called almost

schreiend: »Jetzt gehe ich keinen Schritt mehr! Wenn Sie
crying Now go I no step (any)more When you

mir was tun wollen, können Sie es ebensogut hier wie
me what do want can you it just as well here as

eine Viertelstunde weiter tun! Kein Mensch kann mir zu
a quarter of an hour further do No human can me to

Hilfe kommen! Es muß Mitternacht sein!«
help come It must midnight be

Wie um diese Worte zu bestätigen, fing eine Uhr
As for these words to confirm caught an hour
clock

plötzlich zu schlagen an. Der Klang kam überraschend nah
suddenly to strike on The sound came surprisingly near

und stark durch die dunkle Nacht. Unwillkürlich zählten
and strong through the dark night Involuntarily counted

die Männer mit.
the men along

»Elf!« sagte dann der Kommissar. »Elf Uhr. Es ist noch
Eleven said then the commissioner Eleven hour It is still
o'clock

eine Stunde bis Mitternacht. Kommen Sie, Kluge, wir
an hour until midnight Come you Kluge we

haben nur noch fünf Minuten zu gehen.«
have only still five minutes to go

Und wieder faßte er nach dem Arm des andern.
And again grabbed he after the arm of the other

Aber Kluge riß sich mit überraschender Kraft los:
But Kluge ripped himself with surprising strength loose

»Ich hab gesagt, ich geh keinen Schritt weiter, und ich
I have said I go no step further and I

geh keinen Schritt weiter!«
go no step further

Seine Stimme überschlug sich vor Angst, so schrie er.
His voice rolled over itself for fear so cried he
cracked

Aufgeschreckt flog ein Wasservogel im Schilf hoch und
Startled flew a waterfowl in the reed high and

strich schwerfällig ab.
stroke heavily off
took clumsily

»Schreien Sie doch nicht so!« sagte der Kommissar
Scream you indeed not so said the commissioner

ärgerlich, »Sie machen ja den ganzen See rebellisch!«
annoyed You make yes the whole lake rebellious

Dann besann er sich: »Also schön, ruhen Sie sich
Then re-thought he himself Also beautiful rest you yourself
fine

einen Augenblick aus. Sie werden schon Vernunft
a moment out You will already reason

annehmen. Wollen wir uns hier hinsetzen?«
take on Want we ourselves here sit down

Und wieder faßte er nach Kluges Arm.
And again grabbed he after Kluges arm

Enno schlug nach der fassenden Hand. »Ich lasse mich
Enno struck after the grasping hand I let myself

nicht mehr von Ihnen anfassen! Tun Sie mit mir, was
not (any)more from you touch Do you with me what

Sie wollen, aber fassen Sie mich nicht an!«
you want but grab you me not on

Der Kommissar sagte scharf: »Das ist nicht der Ton, in
The commissioner said sharply That is not the tone in

dem man mit mir spricht, Kluge! Was bist du denn? Ein
which one with me speaks Kluge What are you then A

feiger, kleiner, dreckiger Hund!«
cowardly little dirty dog

Auch den Kommissar begannen seine Nerven zu verlassen.
Also the commissioner began his nerves to leave

»Und Sie?« schrie wieder Kluge. »Und was sind Sie? Ein
And you cried again Kluge And what are you A

Mörder sind Sie, ein gemeiner Meuchelmörder!«
murderer are you a common assassin

Er erschrak selbst über das, was er da gesagt hatte.
He was frightened himself over that what he there said had

Er murmelte: »Ach, entschuldigen Sie, Herr Kommissar, ich
He murmured Oh apologize you Mr commissioner I
forgive me

habe das nicht so gemeint ...«
have that not so meant

»Das sind die Nerven«, sagte der Kommissar. »Sie müßten
That are the nerves said the commissioner You must

ein anderes Leben führen, Kluge, dies Leben halten Ihre
an other life lead Kluge this life hold your

Nerven nicht aus. Also setzen wir uns dort auf den
nerves not out Thus set we us there on the

Bootssteg. Haben Sie keine Bange, ich faß Sie nicht
boat dock Have you no fear I grab you not

wieder an, wenn Sie solche Angst vor mir haben.«
again on when you such fear for me have

Sie gingen auf den Bootssteg zu. Das Holz knarrte, als
They went on(to) the boat dock to The wood creaked as

sie ihn betraten. »Noch ein paar Schritte«, ermunterte
they it entered Still a few steps encouraged

Escherich. »Am besten setzen wir uns auf die Spitze. Ich
Escherich At the best set we us at the tip I

sitze gern auf so 'nem Dings, nur Wasser um mich ...«
sit gladly on so a thing only water around me

Aber wieder weigerte sich Kluge. Er, der eben noch
But again refused himself Kluge He who just still

einen Anflug von entschlossenem Mut gezeigt hatte,
an approach of determined courage shown had

fing plötzlich zu wimmern an: »Ich gehe nicht weiter!
caught suddenly to whimper on I go not further

Oh, haben Sie doch Erbarmen mit mir, Herr Kommissar!
Oh have you indeed pity with me Mr commissioner

Ersäufen Sie mich nicht! Ich kann nicht schwimmen, ich
Drown you me not can not swim I

sage es Ihnen gleich! Ich habe immer solche Angst vor
say it you immediately I have always such fear for

dem Wasser gehabt! Ich will Ihnen jedes Protokoll
the water had I want you each protocol report

unterschreiben! Hilfe! Hilfe! Hil...«
under-write sign Help Help Hel...

Der Kommissar hatte den kleinen Kerl gepackt und trug
The commissioner had the small chap taken and carried

den Zappelnden an das Ende des Stegs. Das Gesicht
the fidgeting to the end of the dock the face

Ennos hatte er fest gegen seine Brust gedrückt, so fest,
enno's had he firmly against his breast put so firmly

daß Kluge nicht weiterschreien konnte. So trug er ihn
that kluge not continue shouting could so carried he him

bis zum Ende des Stegs und hielt ihn dort nahe über
until to the end of the stegs and held him there close over

das Wasser.
the water

»Wenn du noch einmal schreist, du Hund, werde ich dich
If you still once cry you dog will I you

hineinwerfen!«
throw in

Ein tiefes Schluchzen entrang sich Ennos Kehle. »Ich
A deep sobbing wrang out itself (from) Enno's throat I

werde nicht schreien«, sagte er flüsternd. »Ach, ich bin
will not scream said he whispering Oh I am

ja doch hin, werfen Sie mich doch rein! Ich halte das
yes indeed gone throw you me indeed there-in I hold that

nicht mehr aus ...«
not (any)more out

Der Kommissar setzte ihn auf den Steg und nahm neben
The commissioner set him on the dock and took beside
sat beside

ihm Platz.
him place
sat beside

»So«, sagte er. »Und nachdem du nun gesehen hast, daß
So said he And after you now seen have that

ich dich in den See werfen kann und tu's doch nicht,
I you in the lake throw can and do it indeed not

wirst du wohl begreifen, daß ich kein Mörder bin,
will you well comprehend that I no murderer am

Kluge?«
Kluge

Kluge murmelte etwas Unverständliches. Seine Zähne
Kluge murmured something incomprehensible His teeth

schlugen laut gegeneinander.
struck loud against each other

»So, und nun höre zu. Ich hab dir was zu sagen.
So and now hear to I have you something to say

Das mit dem Mann, den du hier in Schlachtensee
That with the man which you here in Schlachtensee

erkennen sollst, das ist natürlich Schwindel.«
recognize will that is of course nonense

»Aber warum?«
But why

»Warte ab. Und ich weiß auch, daß du mit dem
Wait off And I know also that you with the

Postkartenschreiber nichts zu tun hast; ich habe geglaubt,
postcard writer nothing to do have I have believed

es wäre mit dem Protokoll gut, daß ich wenigstens für
it would be with the protocol report good that I at least for

meine Vorgesetzten eine Spur hätte, bis ich den richtigen
my supervisor a trace had until I the true

Täter gefaßt habe. Aber es war nicht gut. Sie wollen
offender taken have But it was not good They want

dich jetzt haben, Kluge, die hohen Herren von der SS,
you now have Kluge the high gentlemen from the SS

und sie wollen dich vornehmen auf ihre Weise. Sie
and they want you take in front take apart on their manner They

glauben an das Protokoll, sie halten dich für den
believe on the protocol report they hold you for the

Schreiber oder doch für seinen Verteiler. Und sie werden
writer or indeed for his distributer And you will

das schon aus dir rausquetschen, sie werden alles, was
that already from you squeeze out you will everything what

sie wollen, mit ihren Verhören aus dir rausquetschen,
they want with their interrogations from you squeeze out

sie werden dich auspressen wie eine Zitrone, und dann
you will yourself squeeze like a lemon and then

werden sie dich totschlagen oder vor den
will they you beat to death or before the

Volksgerichtshof bringen, und das läuft auf dasselbe hinaus,
people's court bring and that runs on the same away-out

nur daß die Quälerei noch ein paar Wochen länger
only that the torment still a few weeks longer

dauert.«
lasts

Der Kommissar machte eine Pause, und der völlig
The commissioner made a pause and the totally

verängstigte Enno schmiegte sich jetzt zitternd an den,
scared Enno snuggled himself now trembling on the one

den er eben noch »Mörder« genannt, als suche er Hilfe
who he just still murderer called as search he help

bei ihm.
with him

»Sie wissen, ich bin's nicht gewesen!« stotterte er. »Heilig
You know I am it not been stuttered he Holy

wahr! Sie können mich nicht zu denen hinbringen, ich
true You can me not to them to-bring bring I

halte das nicht aus, ich schreie ...«
hold that not out I cry

»Gewiß wirst du schreien«, bestätigte der Kommissar
Certainly will you scream confirmed the commissioner

gleichmütig. »Natürlich tust du das. Aber das kümmert
indifferently Of course do you that But that care about

die nicht, das macht denen nur Spaß. Weißt du, Kluge,
they not that makes them only fun Know you Kluge

die werden dich auf einen Schemel setzen und einen
those will you on a stool set and a

ganz scharfen Scheinwerfer direkt vor deinem Gesicht
completely sharp headlights directly before your face

aufstellen, und du mußt immer in das Licht starren und
put up and you must always in the light stare and

wirst vor Hitze und Helle vergehen. Und dabei werden
will for heat and bright go away / wither And there-by will

sie dich fragen, Stunden um Stunden werden sie dich
they you question hours around / after hours will they you

befragen, einer wird den andern ablösen, aber dich wird
question one will the other relieve but you will

keiner ablösen, du magst noch so müde sein. Und wenn
none relieve you will still so tired be And when

du vor Erschöpfung umfällst, so werden sie dich mit
you before exhaustion fall over so will they you with

Fußtritten und Peitschenhieben hochjagen, und sie werden
kicks and whiplashes chase up and they will

dir Salzwasser zu trinken geben, und wenn das alles
you saltwater to drink give and when that everything

nichts mehr hilft, werden sie dir jeden Gelenkknochen
nothing (any)more helps will they you every joint bones

an den Fingern einzeln ausdrehen. Sie werden Säure auf
on the fingers alone unscrew They will acid on

deine Füße gießen ...«
your feet pour

»Hören Sie auf, ach, bitte, hören Sie doch auf, ich kann
Hear you up oh please hear she indeed up I can
Stop indeed you stop

das nicht anhören ...«
that not listen to

»Du wirst es nicht nur anhören, du wirst es aushalten
You will it not only listen to you will it bear

müssen, Kluge, einen Tag, zwei, drei, fünf Tage – immer,
must Kluge one day two three five days always
have to

Tag und Nacht, und dabei werden sie dich hungern
day and night and there-by will they you starve

lassen, daß dein Magen zusammenschrumpft wie eine
let that your stomach shrinks like a

Bohne, daß du vor Schmerzen innen und außen
bean that you for pain inside and outside

umzukommen meinst. Aber du wirst nicht umkommen; so
to perish think But you will not perish So

leicht lassen die einen, den sie mal in ihren Fängen
light let they one who they once in their talons
easy

haben, nicht los. Sondern sie werden dich ...«
have not loose But they will you

»Nein, nein, nein«, schrie der kleine Enno und hielt sich
No no no cried the little Enno and held himself

die Ohren zu. »Ich will nichts mehr hören! Kein Wort
the ears closed I want nothing (any)more hear No word

mehr! Dann lieber gleich tot!«
(any)more Then rather immediately dead

»Ja, das denke ich auch«, bestätigte der Kommissar. »Dann
Yes that think I also confirmed the commissioner Then

lieber gleich tot!«
rather immediately dead

Eine Zeitlang herrschte tiefstes Schweigen zwischen beiden.
A while ruled deepest silence between both
prevailed

Dann sagte der kleine Enno Kluge plötzlich
Then said the little Enno Kluge suddenly

zusammenschauernd: »Aber ins Wasser gehe ich nicht ...«
shuddering But in the water go I not

»Nein, nein«, sagte der Kommissar gütig zuredend. »Das
No no said the commissioner kindly to-talking That
coaxing

sollen Sie auch nicht, Kluge. Sehen Sie, ich habe Ihnen
should you also not Kluge See you I have (for) you

hier was anderes mitgebracht, sehen Sie nur, so 'ne
here something different brought along see you only such a

hübsche kleine Pistole. Die brauchen Sie nur gegen die
pretty little pistol That one need you only against the

Stirn zu drücken, haben Sie keine Angst, ich werde
forehead to press have you no fear I will

Ihnen die Hand halten, daß sie nicht zittert, und dann
you the hand hold that she not trembles and then
it

machen Sie den Finger nur ein klein bißchen krumm ...
make you the finger only a small bit bent

Sie werden keinen Schmerz spüren, plötzlich sind Sie weg
You will no pain feel suddenly are you away

von all diesen Quälereien und Verfolgungen und haben
from all these torments and prosecutions and have

endlich mal Ruhe und Frieden ...«
finally once rest and peace

»Und die Freiheit«, sagte der kleine Enno Kluge
And the freedom said the little Enno Kluge

nachdenklich. »Das ist genauso, Herr Kommissar, wie Sie
thoughtfully That is exactly Mr commissioner as you

mich damals mit dem Protokoll überredet haben, auch
me at that time with the protocol persuaded have also
report

damals haben Sie mir die Freiheit versprochen. Ob's
at that time have you me the freedom promised Whether it

diesmal wahr sein wird? Was meinst du?«
this time true be will What mean you
think

»Aber natürlich, Kluge. Das ist die einzige wirkliche
But of course Kluge That is the only real

Freiheit, die für uns Menschen in Frage kommt. Da
freedom which for us people in question comes There

kann ich dich nicht wieder einfangen und von neuem
can I you not again capture and of new
again

ängstigen und quälen. Keiner kann das mehr. Du wirst
scare and hurt No one can that (any)more You will

uns alle auslachen ...«
us all laugh at

»Und was wird hinterher kommen, hinter der Ruhe und
And what will after come behind the rest and

Freiheit? Wird's da noch was geben, hinterher? Was
freedom Will it there still something give after What
have

glaubst du?«
believe you

»Ich glaub nicht, daß noch was hinterher kommt, kein
I believe not that still something after comes no

Strafgericht und keine Hölle. Nur Ruhe und Freiheit wird's
criminal court and no hell Only rest and freedom will it

da geben.«
there give
have

»Und wozu hab ich denn gelebt? Warum habe ich dann
And where-to for what have I then lived Why have I then

hier so viel aushalten müssen? Ich hab doch nichts
here so much bear must I have indeed nothing

getan, keinem Menschen habe ich zur Freude gelebt,
done no people have I to the joy lived

nie habe ich jemanden wirklich gern gehabt.«
never have I someone really gladly had

»Tja«, meinte der Kommissar, »ein großer Held bist du
Well thought the commissioner a great hero are have you

nicht gewesen, Kluge. Und irgendwie nützlich hast du
not been Kluge And somehow useful have you

dich wohl auch nicht gemacht. Aber warum willst du
yourself well also not made But why want you

jetzt darüber nachdenken? Jetzt ist es unter allen
now about it ponder Now is it under all

Umständen zu spät, ob du das nun tust, was ich dir
circumstances too late whether you that now do what I you

vorschlage, oder ob du mit mir zur Gestapo gehst.
propose or whether you with me to the gestapo go

Ich sage dir, Kluge, in der ersten halben Stunde schon
I say you Kluge in the first half hour already

wirst du auf den Knien um eine Kugel bitten. Aber es
will you on the knees for a bullet ask But it

wird viele, viele halbe Stunden dauern, bis sie dich aus
will many many half hours last until they you from

deinem Leben zum Tode gequält haben ...«
your life to the death tormented have

»Nein, nein«, sagte Enno Kluge. »Zu denen gehe ich
No no said Enno Kluge To them go I

nicht. Gib mir mal die Pistole in die Hand – ist es so
not Give me once the pistol in the hand is it so

richtig, wie ich sie halte?«
right as I her hold
it

»Ja ...«
Yes

»Und wo soll ich sie ansetzen? Da an die Schläfe?«
And where should I her attach There on the temple
put against

»Ja ...«
Yes

»Und nun den Finger hier an den Hahn legen. Ich will's
And now the finger here on the cock lay I will it

vorsichtig tun, jetzt will ich noch nicht ... Ich möchte
carefully do now want I still not I may

noch ein bißchen mit dir reden ...«
still a bit with you talk

»Du brauchst keine Angst zu haben, die Pistole ist noch
You need no fear to have the pistol is still

gesichert ...«
secured

»Weißt du auch, Escherich, daß du der letzte Mensch
Know you also Escherich that you the last human

bist, mit dem ich spreche? Danach wird's nur noch Ruhe
are with whom I speak Afterwards will it only still rest

geben, nie wieder werde ich mit einem Menschen
give never again will I with a person

sprechen können.«
speak can

Er schauderte zusammen.
He shivered together

»Als ich eben die Pistole an die Schläfe gesetzt hatte,
As I just the pistol on the temple set had

ging so eine Kälte von ihr aus. So eisig muß die Ruhe
went so a coldness from her out So icy must the rest

und die Freiheit sein, die mich nachher erwarten.«
and the freedom be which me after expect

Er beugte sich nahe zum Kommissar und flüsterte:
He bowed himself close to the commissioner and whispered

»Willst du mir eins fest versprechen, Escherich?«
Want you me one (thing) firmly promise Escherich

»Ja. Was ist denn?«
Yes What is it then

»Aber du mußt dein Versprechen auch halten!«
But you must your promise also hold

»Das tu ich schon, wenn ich's kann.«
That do I already when I it can

»Laß mich nicht ins Wasser rutschen, wenn ich tot bin,
Let me not in the water slide when I dead am

versprich mir das. Vor dem Wasser habe ich Angst. Laß
promise me that For the water have I fear let

mich hier oben liegen, auf dem trockenen Steg.«
me here above lie on the dry dock

»Natürlich. Das verspreche ich dir!«
Of course That promise I you

»Schön, gib mir die Hand darauf, Escherich.«
Beautiful give me the hand thereupon Escherich

»Hier!«
Here

»Und du wirst mich nicht betrügen, Escherich? Siehst du,
And you will me not cheat Escherich See you

ich bin nur ein kleines, elendes Aas. Es macht nicht
I am only a little miserable carrion It makes not

viel aus, ob man mich betrügt oder nicht. Aber du
much out whether one me cheats or not But you

wirst es nicht tun?«
will it not do

»Ich werde es bestimmt nicht tun, Kluge!«
I will it definitely not do Kluge

»Gib mir noch mal die Pistole, Escherich – ist sie jetzt
Give me still once the pistol Escherich is she now

entsichert?«
unlocked

»Nein, noch nicht, erst wenn du's sagst.«
No still not first when you it say

»Habe ich sie so richtig angesetzt, ja? Jetzt fühle ich die
Have I her so right set on put yes Now feel I the

Kälte vom Lauf kaum noch, ich bin ebenso kalt wie
coldness from the barrel hardly still I am likewise cold as

der Lauf. Weißt du, daß ich eine Frau und Kinder habe?«
the barrel Know you that I a wife and children have

»Ich habe sogar mit deiner Frau gesprochen, Kluge.«
I have even with your wife spoken Kluge

»Oh!« Der Kleine war so interessiert, daß er die Pistole
Oh The little (one) was so interested that he the pistol

rasch wieder absetzte. »Ist sie hier in Berlin? Ich würde
quickly again put away Is she here in Berlin I would

sie gern noch einmal sprechen.«
her gladly still once speak

»Nein, sie ist nicht in Berlin«, antwortete der Kommissar
No she is not in Berlin answered the commissioner

und verfluchte sich, weil er seinem Grundsatz, nie
and cursed himself because he his principle never

eine Mitteilung zu geben, untreu geworden war. Gleich
a notice to give unfaithful become was Immediately
share

hatte man die Folgen! »Sie ist immer noch im
had one the consequences She is always still in the

Ruppinschen bei ihren Verwandten. Und es ist schon
Ruppinsch at her relatives And it is already

besser, du sprichst nicht mit ihr, Kluge.«
better you speak not with her Kluge

»Sie ist nicht gut auf mich zu sprechen?«
She is not good on me to speak
about

»Nein, gar nicht, sie ist nur böse auf dich zu
No at all not she is only angry on you to
about

sprechen.«
speak

»Schade«, sagte der Kleine. »Schade. Eigentlich ist es
Pity said the little (one) Pity Actually is it

komisch, Escherich. Ich bin doch ein reiner Garnichts, den
comical Escherich I am indeed a pure nothing at all who

niemand lieben kann. Aber hassen, hassen tun mich viele.«
nobody love can But hate hate do me many

»Ich weiß nicht, ob das Haß ist bei deiner Frau, ich
I know not whether it hate is with your wife I

glaube, sie will nur Ruhe vor dir haben. Du störst sie
believe she want only rest for from you have You disturb her

...«

»Die Pistole ist doch noch gesichert, Kommissar?«
The pistol is indeed still secured commissioner

»Ja«, antwortete der Kommissar verwundert, daß Kluge, der
Yes answered the commissioner surprised that Kuge who

die letzte Viertelstunde ganz ruhig geworden war,
the last quarter of an hour completely calm become was

plötzlich wieder so aufgeregt fragte. »Ja, die ist noch
suddenly again so excited asked Yes it is still

immer gesichert ... Was zum Teufel?«
always secured What to the devil

Die Pistole zündete mit ihrem Mündungsfeuer so nahe an
The pistol lit with her muzzle flash so close on

seinen Augen vorbei, daß er ächzend auf den Steg
his eyes past that he groaning on the little bridge

zurückfiel; immer im Gefühl, geblendet zu sein, preßte er
fell back always in the feeling dazzled to be pressed he

die Hände vor die Augen.
the hands before the eyes

Der Kluge flüsterte an seinem Ohr: »Ich wußte es, sie
The Kluge whispered on his ear I knew it she
by

war nicht gesichert! Wieder einmal wolltest du mich
was not secured Again once wanted you me

betrügen! Und jetzt bist du in meiner Hand, jetzt kann
cheat And now are you in my hand now can

ich dir deine Ruhe und Freiheit geben ...« Er hielt den
I you your rest and freedom give He held the

Pistolenlauf gegen die Stirn des Stöhnenden, er kicherte:
pistol barrel against the forehead of the moaning (one) he giggled

»Fühlst du, wie kalt das ist? Das ist die Ruhe und der
Feel you how cold that is That is the rest and the

Frieden, das ist das Eis, in dem wir begraben sein
peace that is the ice in which we buried be

werden, immer und immer ...«
will always and always

Der Kommissar richtete sich ächzend auf. »Hast du das
The commissioner arranged himself groaning up Have you that

mit Absicht getan, Kluge?« fragte er streng und riß die
with intention done Kluge asked he strictly and ripped the

wundbrennenden Lider hoch von den schmerzenden Augen.
chafing eyelids high from the aching eyes

Ihm war, als sähe er den andern neben sich wie
Him was as would see he the other one beside himself as

einen schwärzeren Klumpen in all dem Nachtdunkel.
a blacker lump in all the night dark

»Ja, mit Absicht«, kicherte der Kleine.
Yes with intention giggled the little (one)

»Das war ein Mordversuch!« sagte der Kommissar.
That was an attempted murder said the commissioner

»Aber du hast doch gesagt, die Waffe ist gesichert!«
But you have indeed said the weapon is secured

Jetzt war dem Kommissar ganz gewiß, daß seinen
Now was the commissioner completely certain that his

Augen nichts geschehen war.
eyes nothing happened was

»Ich werde dich ins Wasser schmeißen, du Lump! Das
I will you in the water throw you lump That

ist dann nur Notwehr!« Und er packte den Kleinen bei
is then only self-defense And he grabbed the little (one) at

der Schulter.
the shoulder

»Nein, nein, bitte nicht! Bitte das nicht! Ich werde das
No no please not Please that not I will that

andere auch bestimmt tun! Nur nicht ins Wasser! Du
other also definitely do Only not in the water You

hast es mir heilig versprochen ...«
have it me holy promised

Der Kommissar hatte ihn bei der Schulter gepackt.
The commissioner had him at the shoulder grabbed

»Ach was! Jetzt keine Winseleien mehr! Du hast doch
Oh what Now no whining (any)more You have indeed

nie die Courage dazu! Ins Wasser ...!«
never the courage there-to In the water

Zwei Schüsse fielen rasch hintereinander. Der Kommissar
Two shots fell quickly behind each other The commissioner

fühlte, wie der Mann zwischen seinen Fäusten
felt how the man between his fists

zusammenfiel, er sackte in sich, unaufhaltsam. Einen
coincided he sagged in himself unstoppable One

Augenblick machte Escherich eine Bewegung, als er den
moment made Escherich a movement as he the

Toten über den Stegrand ins Wasser rutschen sah. Seine
dead over the dock edge in the water slide saw His

Hände wollten ihn noch halten.
hands wanted it still hold

Und achselzuckend sah der Kommissar zu, wie der
And shrugging saw the commissioner to how the

schwere Körper ins Wasser klatschte und sofort
heavy body in the water clapped and immediately

verschwand.
disappeared

Besser so! sagte er sich und befeuchtete die
Better so said he (to) himself and moistened the

trockenen Lippen. Weniger Verdachtsmaterial.
dry lips Less suspected material

Einen Augenblick stand er noch, zweifelnd, ob er die
One moment stood he still doubting whether he the

auf dem Steg liegende Pistole ins Wasser stoßen sollte
on the dock lying pistol in the water bump should

oder nicht. Dann ließ er sie liegen. Er ging langsam
or not Then let he her lie He went slowly

vom Bootssteg, den Uferhang hinan, nach dem
from the boat dock the bank upon to the

Bahnhof zu.
railway station towards

Der Bahnhof war geschlossen, der letzte Zug
The railway station was closed the last train

abgefahren. Der Kommissar schickte sich gleichmütig
departed The commissioner sent himself indifferent

an, den weiten Weg nach Berlin unter seine Füße zu
on(wards) the far road to Berlin under his feet to

nehmen.
take

Eben fing die Uhr wieder an zu schlagen.
Just caught the hour again on to strike
clock

Mitternacht, dachte der Kommissar. Er hat's geschafft.
Midnight thought the commissioner He had it managed

Mitternacht. Bin neugierig, wie ihm sein Friede gefallen
Midnight Am curious how him his peace pleasure

wird, wirklich neugierig. Ob er sich wieder betrogen
will really curious Whether he himself again betrayed

vorkommt? Aas, kleines, winselndes Aas!
occurs Carrion little whimpering carrion
thinks